Tim Parks

A SEASON WITH VERONA

Travels around Italy
in search of illusion,
national character
and...*goals*!

VINTAGE

Published by Vintage 2003

2 4 6 8 10 9 7 5 3 1

First published in Great Britain in 2002 by
Secker & Warburg

Vintage
Random House, 20 Vauxhall Bridge Road,
London SW1V 2SA

Random House Australia (Pty) Limited
20 Alfred Street, Milsons Point, Sydney
New South Wales 2061, Australia

Random House New Zealand Limited
18 Poland Road, Glenfield,
Auckland 10, New Zealand

Random House (Pty) Limited
Endulini, 5A Jubilee Road, Parktown 2193,
South Africa

The Random House Group Limited Reg. No. 954009
www.randomhouse.co.uk

A CIP catalogue record for this book
is available from the British Library

ISBN 0 099 42267 0

Papers used by Random House are natural, recyclable products made from wood grown in sustainable forests. The manufacturing processes conform to the environmental regulations of the country of origin

Printed and bound in Great Britain by
Cox & Wyman Limited, Reading, Berkshire

A SEASON WITH VERONA

Tim Parks studied at Cambridge and Harvard. He lives near Verona with his wife and three children. His novel *Europa* was shortlisted for the Booker Prize.

This book is dedicated to the boys
who travel on the Zanzibar bus

Infame, i nomi non si scrivono!
1°FEBBRAIO/=\87

(Worm, you mustn't write their names!)

In line with this sensible precept, all names
of fans have been altered.

Contents

Acknowledgments

Many thanks to Hellas Verona football club for their generosity and help, and in particular to Saverio Guette for his exemplary kindness. Alvise Lunardi, Matteo Fontana, Eugenio Ciuccietti and Massimo Bocchiola all gave invaluable advice and input, for which I am immensely grateful. Other thanks must go to Penn, Pam, Dany, Paruca, McDan, la Maestrina, Camelot, Cris and all the Più-mati, the world's oddest fan club. Last but not least, I must not forget actor and radio commentator Roberto Puliero, whose extraordinary voice first drew me to the Bentegodi stadium.

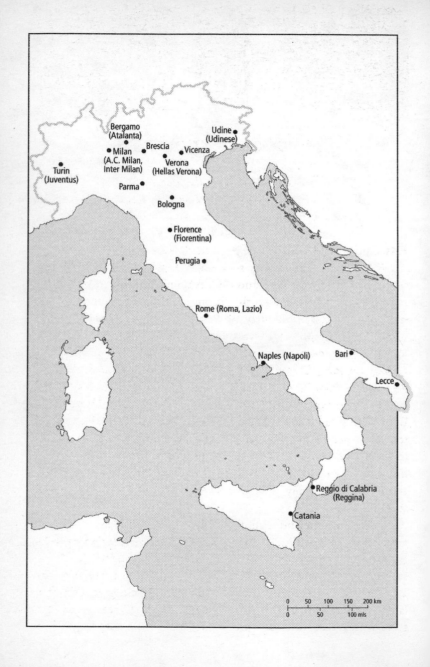

Bergamo
(Atalanta)

Udine
(Udinese)

Brescia

Vicenza

Milan
(A.C. Milan,
Inter Milan)

Verona
(Hellas Verona)

Turin
(Juventus)

Parma

Bologna

Florence
(Fiorentina)

Perugia

Rome (Roma, Lazio)

Naples (Napoli)

Bari

Lecce

Reggio di Calabria
(Reggina)

Catania

0   50   100   150   200 km

0   50   100 mls

Facci Sognare

Proud to be among the worst . . .
McDan, Verona, Veneto

FACCI SOGNARE, says the banner. Make us dream! Please!

We're in the Bentegodi stadium, Verona. My son and I are sitting on the edge of the famous Curva Sud. The South End. Ten minutes ago, hurrying with the throng up the stairs, our path was suddenly blocked. Somebody thrust a plastic stick across the steps. Tightly wrapped around it was a blue and yellow flag. I agreed to a 'donation' of a thousand lire. So now the whole *curva* is a rising tide of flags, of shiny blue and yellow plastic, mass-produced, fiercely waved, and from beneath that flutter comes the slow loud swell of ten thousand voices chanting: 'Haaaayllas. Haaaayllas. Haaaayllas!' Because the team's official name is Hellas Verona. At the bottom of the curve, draped over the parapet where the terraces look down on the goal, a huge and beautiful banner proclaims 19/=\03, indicating the date when the club was formed and the little ladder, symbol of the Scaligeri family, ancient masters of Verona. The fans know their history.

Hellas – Homeland. Fan, from fanatic, from the Latin *fanaticus*, which means a worshipper at a temple. 'CIAO CAMPO!' somebody has written in spray-paint on the concrete of the tunnel that leads us out into the stadium – Hello Pitch! – and then beside this, in English, since everything is more solemn when written in a foreign language: I LOVE YOU. As if it were the place rather than the team or the game that was important, this temple, the Bentegodi stadium. Certainly when you push out of that tunnel after a choking switchback of dusty stairs and corridors, when you emerge into the sunshine or the floodlights, the head lifts and the heart expands quite marvellously. The sense of occasion, with the crowd now ranged in slanted tiers and the pitch hugely green beneath you, is enormous.

The football stadium is one of the few really large constructions that turns its wrong side out. The oval bowl excludes the world, reserves its mysteries for initiates. The TV cannot violate it, cannot even begin to catch it. It's a place of collective obsession, of exaltation. Even a grumpy misanthrope like myself can feel the lift of communal delirium. Even I am chanting, Haaaayllas, Haaaayllas, Haaaayllas, waving my plastic flag. It's the first home game of the season. Verona face the daunting Udinese, already well advanced in the UEFA cup. Please don't lose. A chant starts up. '*Verona, Verona segna per noi!*' Verona, score for us. It spreads round the *curva*. '*Verona Verona, vinci per noi!*' Win for us. It's a liturgy. *Hellas Verona, facci sognare!* Make us dream.

But not all dreams are happy, and even fewer untroubled. My own season actually began two weeks ago. For years I have been a regular at the Bentegodi, but this season, for the first time, I have decided to go to all the away games too. And to write about them. Partly, the writing is an excuse. How can I explain to my wife that I am going to be away every other Sunday for nine months if I'm not writing about it? If I'm not making money. It's such a mad indulgence: to watch Verona play in Rome, in Naples, in Lecce and Reggio Calabria. 'It'll be a travel book,' I insist. 'At last I'll write a real travel book.' I can't wait to see those games. I can't believe I'm going to do this.

But at the same time, I want to get my mind around it too. I want to think and think long about the way people, the way Italians, Veronese, relate to football, the way they, we, dream this dream, at once so intense and so utterly, it seems, unimportant. And the way the dream intersects with ordinary life, private and public. For years now I've had the suspicion that there is something emblematically modern about the football crowd. They are truly fanatical, in the Curva Sud, but simultaneously ironic, even comic. A sticky film of self-parody clings to every gesture of fandom. We cannot take ourselves entirely seriously. Or perhaps this *is* the serious thing, this mixture of delirium and irony, this indulgence in strong emotions without being burned up by them. When the Haaaayllas chant ends everybody claps in self-congratulation and lots of them burst out laughing. *Forza Hellas!* We know we're ridiculous.

But to go back a step; the first game being away from home, the season began, for me, one evening towards the end of September, when I stopped the car outside Bar Zanzibar, rendezvous of the notorious Brigate Gialloblù, the Yellow-Blue Brigades, the hardcore. In the cluttered window a handwritten announcement said that the coach trip to Bari would cost a hundred thousand lire return. Thirty pounds. Bari is about five hundred and fifty miles away and since the game is at three in the afternoon, fans are invited to meet for departure outside the Zanzibar at midnight the evening before. It's a baptism of fire.

I push through the doors, produce my hundred thousand, ask for a ticket. The pair behind the bar are middle-aged, man and wife, straightforward and gruff, bent over the sink. They are clearly surprised not to know a face. Everybody here knows everybody else by name, by nickname, big boys and old men vigorously slapping down cards on chequered tablecloths and shouting at each other. You'll never understand whether they're arguing or not. They're arguing without being angry. Or they're angry without arguing. In any event the bar booms with noise. The TV has been turned up to deal with it. I have to repeat myself: I want to go to Bari!

And now the couple are surprised again that they can't place my accent. Why would I support Verona if I wasn't Veronese? Verona are not Juventus.

I'm handed no more than a torn-off scrap of grubby paper with the biro scribble *BARI, PAGATO*, on it. Paid. Nothing is rung up on the till. But now a full sheet of A4 is produced and smoothed out on a copy of a magazine that shows celebrities bare-breasted on their yachts. At the top, somewhat laboriously, her hands damp from a sink full of glasses, the woman writes: BARI. BUS. And she asks my name. 'Tim.' At once I know I should have said Tino. 'Like the phone company,' I explain. 'TIM – Telefonia Italia Mobile.' She shakes her grey hair and writes. *1. Tim. Pagato*. Five days before departure I am actually the first fan to sign up.

And as it happens, I'm the first to sign up for what is, in absolute terms, the very first game of the Italian season. Most league games in Italy are played Sunday afternoon, but for the sake of pay TV each week one game is moved forward to Saturday at three, another to Saturday evening, and one is shifted back to Sunday evening. The evening games, at peak viewing hours, involve the big teams: Juventus, AC Milan, Inter Milan, Lazio, Rome. One of those five will win the championship. Nobody doubts it. The Saturday afternoon games are strictly for the '*provinciali*', the also-rans, us.

So I am the first person to sign up for what is perceived to be the least-important fixture of the weekend. What can Bari and Verona ever do but try to keep their miserable heads above the dark waters of the relegation zone? Serie A and the company of the elite will always be a luxury for the likes of us. Serie B is always there with open arms ready to draw us into the abyss of provincial anonymity. And immediately, even before the innumerable refereeing aberrations that will doubtless mar the season at our expense, this decision to move the match forward to Saturday afternoon becomes the occasion for that most common of Italian emotions, small-town resentment. My son, Michele, is furious. He wants to come with me to the game – what an adventure to travel through the night to Bari! – but he can't, because Saturday is a regular school-day: eight until one, six days a week. 'This would never have happened if we were Juventus.' He shakes his head bitterly. '*Bastardi!*' Every small town footballing dream is dreamed despite the *bastardi*, against the *bastardi*; every victory is achieved in the teeth of the *bastardi*. Apart from the referees, we have no idea who they are.

In any event, it's late September now and everybody is desperate to see a game again. Everybody is yearning for that stupid excitement of waiting for a goal, for or against, trembling on the edge of our seats, on the edge of euphoria or disappointment. The season has been delayed a month so as not to clash with the Olympic Games, with that intolerable mix of noble sentiments and growth hormones.

Needless to say, this is a television-driven decision. Nobody who goes to the stadium would ever dream of missing a game for a long jump competition, or the prurient pantomime of synchronised swimming. What tedium! I swear to God I have not watched a single event of the Olympic Games on TV, not one, and would not travel a single mile to watch them live. How could any of that grim athleticism and loathsome armchair nationalism compare with what is at stake when Verona play Inter, when the familiar players stream out on to the pitch and come to salute the *curva* and your heart is in your mouth at the thought that the five reserves they have on the bench are worth more than our whole twenty-five-strong squad put together.

'*Cazzo di Olimpiadi*,' someone has written on The Wall, the club's internet 'guestbook'. Fucking Olympics. I couldn't agree more. 'And then the *bastardi* go and put the first game on Saturday,' Michele says. Saturday! He has two hours of Latin, he complains, and I at least twenty-two, there and back, on the coach. Or do I? When I drive by the Zanzibar at ten to midnight Friday evening, the place is closed and the street empty.

There is a general belief that away from the busy downtown, the suburbs of our modern cities Europe-wide are all the same. It's not true. So fine at creating a generous and thriving muddle around the noble monuments of their ancient centres, or again a charming languor in the skewed piazzas of their knotty hillside villages, the Italians ran out of imagination when it came to modern suburbs. In the modern suburbs they have achieved the last word in desolation and dull conservatism.

So the *periferie* of Verona have neither the blowy luxuriance of the English garden suburb, nor the gritty romanticism of the spectacularly depressed area. Here block after six-storey block of featureless flats string amorphously either side of wide, straight, featureless roads. In inevitable reaction, the late-night drivers hurtle at junctions which are often just large empty asphalt spaces with not much indication as to how you're supposed to behave when you get to them. And if the original plan was at least sensible, maintenance is desultory. The coarse grass on the verges is cut only when it reaches knee height. There are no pavements on the side-streets, only expensive cars.

Perhaps, it occurs to me, locking up the old Citroën, perhaps since it was built round the stadium, the whole purpose of this suburb was to design a place of such spiritual emptiness as to more or less oblige everybody to go to the game on Sundays. In which case they could hardly have done it better. To show the full extent of their imagination, or as a clue to their undeclared brief, they called the suburb Stadio. Why not? Giving up on the Zanzibar I walk, disconcerted, back to the main square outside the Bentegodi, and find that there is just one bar open.

Or half-open. It already has its iron grille pulled down a little, to threaten closing time. I slip under and ask for a beer. The only two customers are kissing, not passionately perhaps, but certainly determinedly. In any event they are not thinking about Bari– Verona. And at this point – you don't need a glass, do you? the barman asks – I suddenly see myself travelling down to the southern seaport on my own. Yes, I will be the only passenger on an empty coach. I will stand alone on the hostile terraces, the only supporter of *la squadra gialloblù*. The cameras putting together the evening's highlights will focus on me for one split second. I'm shrieking with anger as the referee refuses to grant us a penalty.

But it's impossible to support a football team on your own. Can we imagine a fan on his own? It would be like being the only worshipper of a god, the only speaker of a language. You'd be incomprehensible to everyone. Fandom, like family, is a destiny you do together. At ten past midnight a slim figure ducks under the grille and orders a beer. He's thirtyish, shy, sad, broken-nosed, and he has a blue-and-yellow scarf round his neck. 'Bari?' I ask. 'Bari,' he confirms. It's begun.

The troops gather on the corner of the square. It's twelve forty-five. The bar has closed, but everybody has supplies of beer or spirits. They're carrying them in those little pinky, yellowy backpacks Italian children use to take their books to school. The night is cloudy. The summer is suddenly over. After two months without rain, it has started to drizzle. Football weather. We stand under a concrete portico, waiting for the coach. There are about twenty youngish boys, three or four girls and a dozen men. One boy seems to suffer from a mild case of phocomelia. With his short arms he arranges his yellow–blue cap crosswise on his head, glad to be part of the group.

'*Dio boia!*' the boy next to me suddenly shouts. 'Executioner God', it means, a strictly local blasphemy. For some reason Italians find the expression particularly foul, perhaps because of the way the *boia* is pronounced. You begin with an explosive 'b', popping your lips as if you were a big fish, then you swallow the 'oi' in a long, slow adenoidal sound, lingering on a sort of 'y' deep in the tonsils, before snapping the word shut with an axe-blow, 'a!!' '*Dio bboiyyya!*' he repeats, apropos of nothing. Then he starts shaking his head. '*Abbiamo fatto una figura di merda. Dio boia!*' He tips up his beer can. The beer dribbles down his chin. 'Covered ourselves in shit,' he protests. 'We covered ourselves in shit.'

Nobody is talking about football. Nobody is interested in discussing the team, at least half of whom are new this year, some of them the merest kids. Nobody is reflecting on the fact that we have lost Cesare Prandelli, the brilliant coach who got us back into Serie A and then took us up to ninth place last season, the coach who brought us victories against Juventus and Lazio. Nobody mentions that the hated owner of Hellas F.C., Giambattista Pastorello, has put the club up for sale, a disastrous move because it now turns out that nobody wants to buy it. Nobody mentions the fact that the official sponsor, Marsilli Salumi, suddenly withdrew its support two weeks ago, announcing that it was pointless attaching the image of its excellent sausages to a team that sold all its best players as soon as anybody waved any money at them, a team that was thus sure to be back in Serie B by the end of this season.

For me all these developments are fascinating. I've spent half my summer reading about them. Every day the *Arena*, the local paper, has at least a half-page dedicated to the city's football team. Every single day, summer and winter alike. Often it's a whole page. After a game it's three pages. I have read oceans of accusations, denials, rumours. That space has to be filled. I have sworn to myself that I will understand the mechanics of football finance before the year is out. I want to know if the dream element distorts the figures, if investments are made in football that no one would dream of making in any other business. Or if it's as merciless as Marsilli's meat-packing. Are we really destined for Serie B even before the season starts? Has Pastorello given up on us? Is he a genius or a fool, well-meaning or a shark? And is it or is it not ominous, given the recent disastrous performance of Nasdaq, that we are the first Serie A football team to be sponsored by an internet company, the hitherto unheard-of Net Business? Suddenly I want to know what is *really* happening. I want to know who really possesses the team: the supporters, the players or the businessmen? I want to know if we're going to get thrashed down in Bari, or whether we can give the bastards some kind of a game. Who is the new striker we've just bought?

But this is not what the fans are discussing. Or not these fans. 'It was a fucking disgrace! *Dio boia!*' the man leaning on the wall beside me suddenly says, speaking very loudly. He is tall and thin, one eye wild and the other immobile, glass perhaps, and he has a can of beer in every pocket of his big jacket, inside and out. 'We covered ourselves in shit. *Dio boia.* In shit! The boss says: "OK *ragazzi*, explain yourselves! Go on explain." We were all there. And nobody answered. Nobody answered, *Dio boia!* Everybody with his eyes on the floor. On the floor, *Dio can!* I was the only one who said anything, *Dio boia, Dio can.* The only one, what's wrong with us!'

Dio can! Dog God. For best effect the expression is inserted before or after *Dio boia. Dio bon*, a milder blasphemy, can be used as a soft option when winding up or winding down. And *Dio porco* is another possibility, though it tends to stand on its own. *Dio porco* is the only one of the three that can be safely reversed: *Porco Dio.* The divine can be substantive or attribute. But already, as you can see, the variations are numerous. No need to run through them now: they will be heard often enough in the course of the night ahead.

I have ended up with the real *brigate*, that's the truth of the matter. It's Gianni who finally explains the situation. Gianni is the shy, broken-nosed figure who arrived in the bar almost half an hour before anyone else. 'If you buy your ticket at the Zanzibar, you're in with the real *brigate*.'

I tell him that I've bought various tickets in the past from the Zanzibar, to go to Bergamo, or Brescia, or Venice, and the crowd were a fairly mixed lot. But he points out that when the venue is only an hour or two away, there will be at least ten coaches and the hardcore are diluted by all kinds of 'normal people'.

That's obvious. In the same way, in the Bentegodi on Sundays, the hardcore are there at the heart of it all, they provide all the energy for the chants, all the humour and the violence, there would be no real excitement without them. But they're held back and watered down by the vast crowd at the fringes. It's a big, complex, self-correcting community, the Curva Sud, looked at as a whole.

But tonight we have only the nuts. Gianni uses the word *pazzi*, the mad, as if he suspects that I need warning. 'Only one coach is going from the Zanzibar,' he says. 'Who but a *pazzo* would travel five hundred and fifty miles to watch Verona away? They almost always lose away.' Then he gives me a searching look from soft eyes. Am I a *pazzo*?

'I planned to bring a couple of friends from England,' I lie, 'and my son. But the friends chickened out, *bastardi*, and my son has school on Saturday.'

'*Bastardi*,' Gianni says, 'putting our game first.'

'*Bastardi*,' I agree.

'*BUTEI!*' a voice roars.

A tall and very handsome young man has appeared, waving a sheet of paper. It's the paper that begins 'BARI, BUS. 1. Tim.'

'*BUTEI!*'

This is the local strictly Veronese word for *bambini*, small *bambini*. The supporters always call themselves *butei*. Little kids. *I butei gialloblù*. When one fan calls the others, he shouts: '*Butei!*' When someone joins the discussion on The Wall, he writes '*Butei!*' It's understood, then, that they're infantile, or that they're playing at being infantile. The word is affectionate and ironic. And they always speak to each other in the fiercest local dialect. Which excludes everybody who wasn't born within a thirty-mile radius of the town. However much you can learn Italian, you can never learn the dialect. You may understand it, but you'll never speak it. Now the handsome man is going to take the roll and my foreignness will be exposed. Quite honestly, I hadn't thought about this as a problem before now.

'Get your cash out, *Dio boia*,' the handsome fellow is saying. 'Why did nobody pay in advance, *Dio can? Che figura di merda!*'

'I paid,' I announce.

We're in the streetlight under the portico.

'Tim,' I tell him.

'Teem,' he says.

He stares at me. 'Yes, you've paid.' He doesn't know what to say. Who the hell am I? But then our voices are drowned by a huge shout.

'*CHI NOI SIAMO?*' Who are we?

Everybody picks it up. It's deafening. *Chi noi siamo?* The *Chi* and the *noi* are sharp and staccato. The *siamo* falls away rapidly.

'*GLIELO DICIAMO?*' Shall we tell them?

Again the solo voice is picked up by the group. *Chi noi siamo* is repeated. Then a huge chorus.

'*BRIGATE, BRIGATE GIALLOBLÙ!*'

The words are shouted with fists in the air, the 'ga' of *brigate* is given all the stress in a fierce yell. And from the chant they move straight into a song: '*Siamo l'armata del Verona!*' We're Verona's army. And all at once they're a group, a single entity. Every time they get together for an away game, this is the first chant. This is the moment when they stop being separate people hanging around in twos and threes, and become the Brigades. 'Every place we go,' someone suddenly shouts, 'people always ask us *CHI NOI SIAMO?*' Who are we? Shall we tell them? It's a declaration of identity, a rallying to Hellas, to the homeland. And I'm a bit out of it. They would never understand how I come to be here. I don't really understand myself. But at least I've paid, *Dio bon*.

There follows an hour, under the portico, with the drizzle sifting down, of trying to get people to pay and trying to establish who is coming and who isn't. Sadly, the girls aren't coming. And then trying to establish who is going to beg to come without paying. Notably the wildest, the best supplied with beer. The leader with the sheet of paper insistently repeats the expression *figura di merda*, and even *brigate di merda*, though this doesn't seem to have anything to do with the *figura di merda* that Glass-eye is going on and on about quite obsessively. 'The boss says, OK explain yourselves, and did anyone have the courage to speak up, *Dio boia*? I was the only one, *Dio can*.'

Apparently there has been some encounter between the representatives of authority and the *brigate* over some unpleasant incident or other. Or at least that appears to be the gist. Perhaps I've misunderstood. 'We can say we made a mistake without covering ourselves in shit, can't we, *Dio boia*?' Glass-eye insists. '*Porco Dio*, can we or can we not? We're not the only ones to fuck up,' he starts to scream. He doesn't seem to need anybody in particular to speak to. 'Some self-respect, *Dio boia*,' he shrieks. Since I'm really not used to these things, it takes me a good half an hour to appreciate that he is coked out of his mind.

The leader is now on his *telefonino*. 'Get out your phones, *butei*,' he orders. It seems there are people whose names are on the list but who haven't turned up. It's a disgrace! A *figura di merda*. It's happening too often. People have no sense of responsibility. They book and they don't come. The word *merda* is pronounced frequently and rhythmically, taking all the stress from the words around it. The 'r' rolls hard into the 'd'. The *Dio boia*s abound. There's an incantatory outrage to almost everything that is said. You can feel it in your blood. We're warming up.

Everybody pulls out a *telefonino*. I am the only one who hasn't brought a *telefonino*. They are phoning people at one-thirty in the morning. '*Cretino!* Get your butt along here. No, now, *Dio boia*, or you're a dead man.'

'*Assenza giustificata*,' someone shouts. 'The Fish' it seems is on the night shift. Funnily enough '*assenza giustificata*' is exactly the formula Head of Faculty uses at the university where I teach when somebody doesn't turn up for one of our tedious committee meetings: 'absence justified'. 'The Fish' is working night shift but wants to be kept informed about the group's antics through the small hours. He has his *telefonino* beside his machine. Am I going to get any sleep?

Then a squadron of about a dozen Vespas comes racing round the broad road that circles the stadium. They're in formation occupying the entire street. Ignoring the danger of the big junction they go flying past us. At once someone is livid.

'It's Fosso, *Dio bon*. It's Fosso!'

'*Fosso*' means ditch. They all have nicknames. *Bastardo*. Fosso! 'Your name's on this list, *Dio boia!*' Somebody runs after the Vespas waving his hands. '*Merda!*' The Vespas disappear. Everybody is disgusted. '*Una figura del cazzo.*' A fucking disgrace.

One or two more people appear, though whether because phoned or because experience tells them that the coach will be spectacularly late, I've no idea. After all, they won't be coming from very far. Almost everybody hails from the apartment blocks that circle the city.

'The coach!' someone screams. 'The coach, *butei!*'

A blue bus has appeared.

'They've given us white headrests, *Dio bon*,' our leader shouts. 'White headrests, *Dio boia*. For the *brigate*. We're kings, *Dio can!*'

My heart sinks. This is no luxury vehicle. It's one of the old blue buses they use to bring kids to school and workers to town from outlying villages. We must be renting from the local government. Who else would rent a vehicle to the Brigate Gialloblù? I've travelled on these buses. I know them of old. Stiff upright seats, no radio, no TV, no toilet, no suspension, no speed. And in fact the vehicle idles up to the corner at an incredibly slow pace. But then, we do still have thirteen hours before kick-off. The two drivers climb out: a wiry, waxy-faced kid who looks no more than eighteen and a man about my own age, moustached, wry, taciturn, ready for the worst. With reason. Even as we bundle on, the insults begin.

'*Autista di merda!*' (Shithead driver.)

'*Autista del cazzo!*' (Fucking driver.)

'*Autista cornuto!*' (Your wife's having if off with someone else.)

'*Autista frocio!*' (Queer.)

Then a steady chant: '*Allerta, autista, la figlia è stata aperta*' (watch out driver, your daughter's been fucked).

As we settle in our seats there are about five minutes of this, five minutes of the most violent abuse. Clearly it's something that has to be got through. The drivers don't appear to notice. The drivers are the authorities in our midst, impotent, abused, spat-on. They will never answer back, but they will never take instructions from us as far as the driving is concerned. Thank God for that.

Our leader climbs on to the bus to make an announcement, though now it appears that he himself is going to go down to Bari by car. '*Butei*, you can do anything you want, OK? Coke, grass, booze. Anything. Have a good time, *butei*. Do what you like. But you're going to leave this fucking coach as you fucking well find it. OK? Anyone who damages this coach answers to me, in person. To me! And the headrests stay white OK. White headrests, *butei*!'

'*Gialloblù. Gialloblù. Gialloblùùùùù!!!*' The boys are singing and clapping. It's the triumphal march from *Aida*. The bus is rocking. The youngest kids have chosen the seats at the back. 'Lights off, *autista di merda! Dio boia.*' 'Turn the lights back on, *autista del cazzo.*' 'Turn the red light on, *cornuto autista.*' 'The nightlight, not the main light.' 'What the fuck have you turned the nightlight on for, *autista di merda*?'

The coach finally pulls away. 'Drive straight, driver. *Dio boia.*' 'What d'you turn for driver?' 'Your daughter fucks niggers, driver, she takes it up the ass from niggers.' 'From gypsies, *Dio can!*' The drivers are completely unperturbed. They have done this before of course. Perhaps it's a joke. Meantime, nobody, I reflect, trying to make myself comfortable, absolutely nobody has mentioned Verona's last-minute purchase of the eighteen-year-old striker Alberto Gilardino, already in the national under-twenty-one team. Nobody has mentioned the game, Bari–Verona, the first game of a season starting almost a month late, the first game of, as the papers always say, *il campionato più bello del mondo*, the best championship in the world. Try to sleep, Tim, I decide. Try to sleep.

Forget sleep. I'm sitting in the middle of the coach on the left.

The seats are *rigidissimi*. The big dark window is hard and icy. Originally, I had planned to bring such luxuries as a change of clothes, some washing kit, etc., but at the last minute I saw the folly of this and left them in the car. All I have is my sweatshirt, with hood fortunately, a couple of hundred thousand lire in my pocket, and a two litre bottle of . . . water. I'm fully aware that if I took such an obscene thing along with a group of Manchester United supporters, I would probably by lynched. But Italy is a different place. About an hour into the trip, the bloke in front of me who is taking swigs from a bottle of Amaro Montenegro, a sour after-dinner spirit, politely asks if he can drink from my water bottle. 'Go ahead.' Then the guys behind me, who are smoking dope, also ask if they can drink from my water bottle. 'Go ahead.' Water is respectable in Italy.

But what is mostly being drunk is beer, the majority stewing slowly and in the end quite modestly, one can a little while after another among innumerable cigarettes. Just a couple of guys have bottles of fancy liqueurs, the kind of things advertised on the TV with glamorous women in evening undress.

After insulting the driver and then singing, mainly in praise of deviant behaviour ('we go everywhere, we fight everywhere, barricades, charges, urban warfare, we're not afraid of the police') – after perhaps an hour of this, most people are ready to settle down and sleep. But three or four are high on coke, and these guys are not going to calm down. There's something demonic about them. Quite deliberately, they are not going to let anyone sleep.

The kid two rows up from me on the right is a good-looking twenty-year-old in dark glasses, with a neatly trimmed, even dapper beard, an expensive haircut, a dapper jacket. He's a million miles from the image of the soccer hooligan. But his head is swaying, he has a wild grin on strangely red, very full lips. '*Bomba!*' he suddenly shouts. 'Stop driver, *Dio boia*, there's a bomb on the coach.'

For reasons I can't understand everybody finds this hilarious. The kids at the back are laughing uncontrollably. Gianni is smiling. Then the boy begins to repeat rhythmically. '*C'è una bomba! C'è una bomba!*' There's a bomb. There's a bomb. Every time he says *bomba*, he puts all the stress on the *om* until the phrase has become madly rhythmical. And he begins a thousand variations. '*Sul pullman c'è una bomba. Nelle mutande c'è una bomba.*' There's a bomb on the bus. There's a bomb in my pants. He goes on and on. Others join in. Needless to say the chant is punctuated with endless *Dio boia*s. The kid jumps up and begins to run wildly up and down the aisle between the seats, hands flailing, chanting rhythmically: '*C'è una bomba, Dio boia.*'

'Who's got some dope?' he demands. I wonder how much he can see in the dark coach with his sunglasses on. He asks me for dope, then drinks from my water bottle. 'Dope, I want dope.' In the other hand he has a bottle of the treacly almond liqueur Amaretto di Saronno. He runs up and down, pulling faces, jumping like a dog in a cage. '*Sulla strada c'è una bomba!* Drive straight, *autista di merda*. Your daughter's a *bomba*. Your wife fucks like a *bomba*. With a black who's a *bomba*.' It goes on for hours.

He's called Fondo. A *fondo* is the bottom of something and *senza fondo* means bottomless. Could it be some reference to his drinking? But you never know how someone got their nickname. Nicknames are not like the crass things you hear about English supporters, Paraffin Pete, Jimmy-fivebellies. They go way back, even to infancy, and they are cryptic and secretive. Someone is called Peru, somebody Rete, goal, or net. There's Penna, feather, and II morto, the dead man. And when these people do at last die, the little poster that appears to announce that death on the walls of the neighbourhood will give the baptismal name, and then in brackets beneath, '*detto Locomotiva*', otherwise known as The Train.

Fondo hangs upside-down from the luggage rack, he takes his sweater off, then his T-shirt, then puts his jacket back on together with his Verona cap and his expensive sunglasses. Swaying from side to side, he pours beer all over himself. His face gleams. 'In the can there's a *bomba*. Drive straight driver, *Dio boia! autista di merda!*'

The others started by applauding, but now they're getting bored. The four or five older men want to sleep. I in particular really want to sleep. On the other hand, this is a group who have invested all their collective identity in the idea that they are incorrigible. So how can they correct each other?

Again, Fondo hangs upside-down on the racks, feet on one side of the aisle, hands on the other. This time he arranges himself so that his face, upside-down, is almost touching mine. 'Who the fuck are you?' he demands. 'I've never seen you.' I pull off his *gialloblù* cap and throw it to the boy sitting opposite me, a sensible kid who is pulling one thick sandwich after another from his backpack. He throws it to somebody further up the aisle. Fondo runs off waving his arms cartoon fashion. 'My cap, *Dio boia!* In my cap there's a *bomba.*' It's three in the morning.

Then somebody else, somebody older, is standing in the aisle, looking down towards the back; in a loud voice he shouts: 'So what about the Jew. What about him, *butei*. What do you make of the Jew? *Bastardo!*'

This man is small and squat, with thick glasses, and he's wearing a T-shirt that says: 'I'm proud to be one of the five thousand guilty ones.' A date beneath the writing allows me to work out that this must be a reference to a notorious away game with Cesena some years ago. Verona would be staying up in Serie A if they won, going down if they drew or lost. Five thousand went down to support them. Verona lost. There was havoc.

But now he's talking about something that interests me. What about Marsiglia, *butei*? What do we think about the Jew? I can see I shall have to open a long parenthesis.

In the Italian national consciousness, so far as such a thing exists, the north-east of Italy, and Verona in particular, is stigmatised as irretrievably racist. It is also considered bigoted, workaholic, uncultured, crude and gross. So while British or German tourists explore the *piazze* and *palazzi* of the Veneto, in a daze of admiration, imagining themselves, at last, in one of the few places in the world that has managed to preserve the centuries-old elegance of an impeccable Renaissance humanism, the rest of the country has written off this part of the peninsula as a national disgrace, a pocket of the most loathsome and backward right-wing dogmatism.

The historical reasons for this assessment are many, from the area's long relationship with the Austro-Hungarian empire, to its vigorous support for the die-hard Fascist government in Salò and, more recently, the formation of the separatist and xenophobic Lega Nord. But it's also true that the criticism has much to do with the traditional Italian rivalry between cities and regions. If you can find a stick to beat a neighbour with, use it. And what bigger stick can there be to beat someone with in these pious times than the accusation of bigotry and racist intolerance? Wield it with glee.

In any event, one never senses, travelling the rest of Italy, any desire that Verona should be anything but bigoted, nor anywhere but in the dock, and the easy target for complacent criticism. 'When Rome asks us for something special on the region,' an executive of national public radio in Venice once told me, 'they only want news that reinforces that stereotype. For example, they sent us out on *ferragosto* (August bank-holiday) and we were supposed to interview Veronese who were working through the holiday or, even better, making their immigrant labourers work. We couldn't find anybody. Or we're supposed to run a survey on racism; we have to interview a Moroccan who's been beaten up. And we just can't find one.'

Well, thank God for that. But the fact is that recently someone has been making a great deal of fuss about being beaten up in Verona, yes, right in the centre of ancient and beautiful Verona. And this is what the bespectacled man standing in the aisle of the bus at three in the morning, as the Brigate Gialloblù head south towards the Adriatic, wants the drunken boys to talk about: the case of the Jewish South American religious-instruction teacher Luìs Ignacio Marsiglia.

The bus is travelling on the night of Friday 29 September. Some eleven days before, on the evening of the 18th, Luìs Marsiglia, forty-three years old, balding and thickly bearded, walked into Casualty at the city's main hospital and declared that he had been attacked by three young men wearing motorcycle helmets who banged his head against the wall shouting, 'Dirty Jew get out of here', and 'Long live Haider.' They beat him about the legs with sticks, performed a sort of ritual laceration of his forearms, with some ugly sharp instrument, then would doubtless have gone on to kill him, if they hadn't feared they were about to be discovered and run off.

The case hit the national headlines. Rightly so. Everybody

was deeply shocked, most of all the Veronese. Neighbours ran to Marsiglia's apartment with consolatory gifts of olive oil and Parma ham and bottles of Valpolicella. The declarations of solidarity were endless and genuine. Verona is actually a very ordinary place.

But then a typically Italian dynamic sets in. The national press sent its reporters north and began to present Verona as hopelessly Fascist and racist. The minister for internal affairs made an announcement in parliament stating that the attack was clearly the work of dangerous neo-Nazi elements, many of them close to the infamous Brigate Gialloblù. '*I ragazzi gialloblù, Dio boia,*' shouts the bespectacled man standing right beside me in the aisle of the bus. 'Have we ever hit a Jew? Would we recognise a Jew if we saw one?' Actually he looks rather Jewish himself.

The case was then raised by left-wing Italian members in the European Parliament with the suggestion that moves be made against the Lega Nord. The big national papers, who mostly support the centre-left government, began to suggest that there was some kind of complicity between Verona's eternally centre-right local authorities and this sort of xenophobic violence. The mayor had done nothing to stop it, they said. 'The right will lead us back to fascism and beatings in the street.' Here it has to be said that 2001 will be an election year and all opinion polls are suggesting that the incumbent government is going to lose. So this story of Nazis beating Jews in the bigoted right-wing Veneto is clearly worth exploiting. The police began their interviews.

But many of us who live in Verona were not so much shocked as amazed. Nobody denies that there is a certain level of resentment towards immigrants here. My wife rings up a few people who have advertised rooms in the papers and asks them if they have a place for an American friend who is visiting the city for a month. 'Is he black or white?' they ask. The *ragazzi gialloblù* themselves never forget to make their monkey grunts when a black from an opposing team touches the ball at Bentegodi. One says opposing team because Verona have never had a black player. Or rather, they once signed such a player, but he only played twenty minutes all season and that was in an away game.

Anyway, we know all this. It's unpleasant. But the idea that a man somatically indistinguishable from your average Italian should be beaten up because Jewish, and in the centre of town, an affluent pedestrian haven for culture-tourists and well-dressed locals strutting up and down for their evening *passeggiata*, this is unthinkable. There must be something more to it.

There is. As well as talking about the way he was attacked, Marsiglia informs the police that for some days now he has been receiving offensive and threatening mail. A large photograph in every Italian paper shows the teacher, gloomy but determined, holding a large sheet of paper on which, in a collage of letters cut from a variety of newspapers, somebody has written:

> Marsiglia *ebreo di Merda*
> Long Live Christ the King.

But the paper also says something else.

Finally out of the Maffei.

The Maffei? It is here that the story starts to get complicated and to intersect in all kinds of ways with so many areas of Italian public life, and, very strangely, with the Brigate Gialloblù.

The Maffei is a Liceo classico: a school for fourteen- to eighteen-year-olds where Latin and Greek are among the main subjects. What's more it is *the* elite state school for the would-be best-educated of Verona's middle classes.

'How can they say that he was beaten up to have him chucked out of the Maffei,' the squat bespectacled figure in the aisle is protesting. He has a pleasantly piggy, if permanently sweaty face. His name it turns out is Albe, short for *albergo* (hotel). This is not because he works in a hotel but because, as I discovered, he comes from San Martino Buon Albergo, which is to say St Martin Good Hotel.

'As if we would wear crash helmets to beat someone up,' Albe goes on. 'A likely story. Who has ever seen the *brigate* in crash helmets? They would get in your way. As if he would have been able to walk to hospital if we'd beaten him up!'

'Haaaayllas, Haaaayllas, Haaaayllas!' the boys begin to chant. They're well away. They don't give a toss. But I'm fascinated.

Day by day the papers have been producing more and more facts surrounding the case. Born in Uruguay to Italian parents, Marsiglia, a practising Catholic, studied theology in Montevideo and continued his studies in Verona, where some years ago he applied for a position as a teacher of religious instruction.

But there was a problem. Marsiglia wasn't able to present his degree certificate. The crucial piece of paper had been lost, it seemed, in a fire at Montevideo university. But he promised to acquire some kind of copy within the year, and one morning in the office of the appropriate Monsignor he broke down in tears saying he desperately needed the work to support himself and his sick wife. A position was vacant at the elite Maffei and Marsiglia got it.

So the man from Uruguay penetrated the exclusive classrooms of the Maffei, where Verona's brightest and best soon learned that although he was of the Catholic faith and selected by the *Curia*, he was of the Jewish race and not at all interested in teaching the tenets of religious faith. He liked, instead, to talk about the Holocaust and how it should never be allowed to happen again. Fair enough. Many students took to him. He was popular. Politically engaged youngsters visited his apartment at the weekends. But others were not so happy. Some parents wrote to protest that the teacher's classes were more about politics than religious instruction.

The headmaster had words with Marsiglia. He wanted to understand what was going on. The *Curia* asked if he could please find a copy of his degree certificate. Mid-September, just before the new school year, when he was still unable to produce the copy, they told him that as part of a general policy of moving teachers from school to school he would not be at the Maffei the next year but would be given work in other schools.

Though his salary would be unaffected, Marsiglia encouraged the students of the Maffei to protest on his behalf. Then came the assault, the three Nazis in their motorcycle helmets with their boots and sticks. The teacher was afraid for his life, he announced to excited journalists, but absolutely determined to stay. Eagerly, the national papers now attacked the bigoted well-to-do Veronese who could not bear an enlightened teacher. There must be a connection, they decided, between these conservative Catholic parents and the neo-Nazi attackers who were close to . . . the unspeakable Brigate Gialloblù.

'Us, *Dio boia!* Next it'll turn out we run the Mafia.'

The police seized papers from the houses of a number of affluent Veronese families. Marsiglia was given a twenty-four-hour police escort. Members of left-wing student movements slept outside his flat to defend him against potential attack. Two largescale marches protesting against racism were organised in Piazza Bra, Verona's huge central square. Twenty youngsters were taken to hospital after a right-wing group tried to join the march, apparently in a gesture of solidarity. They weren't welcome. Each side blamed the other. Marsiglia wrote a letter to the *Manifesto*, the paper of the far left, announcing: 'Verona is falling into the dark night of the Italian Republic. You must reawaken people's consciences. The church is even worse than my aggressors.'

'This bastard Jew', Albe is saying, in the dark coach at three-thirty in the morning, a bottle of *limoncello* in his hand, 'is covering our city with shit.' *Limoncello* is a powerful and fearfully sweet liqueur. 'He's pissing on us, *Dio boia*.'

The kids are still chanting '*Alè Verona, alè!*' and sucking on their beer cans between songs. They ask Albe if he can sing the song about the Juventus supporters killed at Heysel. They want to learn it. Albe, it turns out, is one of those who have a talent for inventing songs. But right now he's not interested. 'Covering our city with shit!' he insists. The familiar tone of outrage is welling. 'Have you read the papers? The whole fucking country is calling us racists. Filthy southerners.' (*Limoncello*, by the way, is very much a Neapolitan drink.) 'If we wanted to beat people up we could have killed half a dozen black whores before even getting on the bus.'

Albe is right. Actually, he has a rather merry face, a glint in his eyes, the tone of someone who might be joking. He knows it's ridiculous to complain about racism and then talk about filthy southerners. He's not stupid. And it's true that the area between the station and the stadium is thickly patrolled by black prostitutes. If there were violent gangs roaming around they would have no end of soft targets. The Brigate Gialloblù, on the other hand, have shown no interest at all in attacking anybody. All they have done is sing things about guerrilla warfare and urban combat ('*Come ogni fine settimana, guerriglia urbana, guerriglia urbana*' – every weekend, urban terrorism), and now they want to sing about the Juve fans who died at Heysel. 'There were thirty thousand when they left, thirty-three didn't come back . . . Blood on the terraces . . . Honour to Liverpool . . . Champions of Heysel. *Juve di merda.*'

When the singing has died down, I ask Albe: 'But do you really believe Marsiglia was beaten up?'

Like everybody else when I speak to them, Albe looks at me as if I were from another planet, only with more suspicion.

'What do you mean?' He takes a swig of *limoncello*.

'Well, he had a few scratches on his arms and some bruising on his knees. He says he threw the tracksuit top with the blood on it in a waste-bin, but it hasn't been found. He said he was attacked right near his house, but then walked almost a kilometre to call an ambulance from a public call-box. The guy just didn't want to be fired from school,' I protest. 'He set it up.'

Actually, I'm not quite sure I believe this version, but that's certainly one possibility I'd be looking at if I were the police. I remember reading in a detective story that people who want to fake an assault on themselves almost always hack at their forearms. Apparently it's one of the few forms of self-wounding that most of us can contemplate. Marsiglia's wounds were on his forearms.

'Who are you?' Albe asks.

I explain that I'm an English fan of Verona. Strictly a home-game fan. This trip is just an aberration. 'The season has started so late and I need to see some football.'

'If you're working for Papalia,' he tells me, 'I promise you we'll kill you. We'll chop you in bits.'

Now I've heard the name Papalia, in fact I've heard it a great deal, but just for the moment, I can't place the name.

'*Per carità*!' I laugh. One of the things about the *ragazzi gialloblù*, I'm telling myself, unlike supporters of, say, Juventus or Manchester United, is that it would be unimaginable for someone from outside Verona to infiltrate them. Their community is so genuinely tight-knit, so radically local and such a well-defined linguistic island, that the idea of masquerading as one of them is unthinkable. You can't even be suspected.

Albe seems to appreciate this. He smiles. 'We're doing our own research,' he says. 'We'll find out who did it.'

'You?'

'If it's who they say it was, we'll know sooner than they will.'

'In the Maffei there's a *bomba*,' Fondo starts to chant. 'The Jew is a *bomba*. At Heysel there was a *bomba*.'

His sunglasses have lost one of their lenses. Exposed in the coach nightlight, the one dark-rimmed eye is fearfully red. '*Dio boia una bomba, dio boia dio can una bomba, dio boia dio can dio boia dio can dio boia dio can dio boia dio can.*' It goes on and on and on. '*Dio boia dio can dio boia dio can.*' Some of the kids are giggling uncontrollably. Suddenly, the bus swings into a service station.

One of my concerns before the trip was that I would wake up in the middle of the night, needing a pee, as I invariably do, and that I wouldn't be able to go. The whole coach would be asleep and the teens and twenties with their wonderfully elastic bladders would sleep the night through while I sat there in my miserable mid-forties with my legs pressed together.

How ingenuous! No sooner were we on the *autostrada* than we were stopping for a pee. '*Autista di merda*, I've got to piss! Stop this fucking bus. I'm going to piss on the floor, *cornuto autista di merda*, if you don't stop this bus.'

Never have I crossed the Po valley so slowly. Never have I had a chance to see how absolutely identical are the many so-called *autogrill*, the service stations, down the Adriatic coast. The coach stops yet again. The boys stumble through the bottles and cans now littering the floor. Most of them get no further than the first oleander. They pee. Some of them are peeing under the coach. I get out myself but only for fresh air, I've hardly drunk anything. A sirocco is blowing, warm, damp and unpleasant. To one side are the steep hills, the olives, the vines, to the other the rocks, then the sea. 'Back in the coach, *Dio boia! Autista di merda*, we'll never get to Bari.' On board again, the air is stale, the floor sticky. Somebody kicks a few bottles and other assorted trash out on to the tarmac and we're off.

The night drags on. Towards five the talking has finally ended, but as the bus brakes or changes lanes the cans shift uneasily up and down the aisle. It's a constant slow clatter. Amazingly, the boy opposite me, who has drunk little, said less, but eaten a considerable number of sandwiches from the seemingly unlimited supply in his backpack, is fast asleep with his head directly against the hard windowpane. How can he do that?

Somewhere in the coach a phone rings. Fish, on the nightshift, has to be kept informed. We're beyond Ancona. I can see the faintly luminous expanse of the Adriatic to my left. Somebody else is whispering to his girlfriend. Since I didn't hear his phone ring, I figure he must have called her. It's funny to think what my wife would say if I called her at five in the morning.

Unable to sleep, I try to focus on the racist question. The boys indulge in racist chants, they define their group by its exclusion of all outsiders, it's a declared if sometimes pantomime hatred of all surrounding cities, teams and regions. '*Vicentino infame, per te ci sono le lame,*' someone writes when a Vicenza fan dares to send a message to the Hellas Wall. 'Vicentino disgrace, for you the mace.' This might just be fun, I reflect, but then someone else wrote: 'If Pastorello buys a black, we'll kill him. I'll shred my season ticket. We'll have nothing to do with negroes. *Hellas contro tutti!*' Somebody's been reading *Mein Kampf.*

And yet they're furious when the press accuses them of a racist attack, of actually *doing* something. At once they are convinced that such accusations are part of an agenda to smear themselves and their city. And it might even affect the team's results! If Verona becomes a national pariah (but Verona is already a national pariah!) referees will do anything to make sure they don't get very far. Already Verona's goals are shown less on TV sports programmes than those of any other team. Even the local newspaper has pointed out the fact. 'Did you see', somebody writes to The Wall, 'they showed everybody's goals but ours.' *Bastardi!* When the *brigate* get really angry, I conclude, it's with the journalists and politicians. Blacks, Jews and even the odd Vicenza fan are quite forgotten.

But if it often seems that the *brigate* are vocally racist mainly in order to prolong a quarrel with the pieties-that-be, the press are hardly more consistent. They are fervently anti-racist, of course, but they don't seem to have any desire that a racist attack should not have taken place. What would they rave about otherwise? If the Marsiglia incident had happened in Rome, they might have stopped a moment to wonder. But in Verona, it must be Nazi violence. Verona is unlivable.

Still, to anybody reading between the lines, I reflect, mulling things over on the coach in the hour before dawn, to anyone weighing up the details that have emerged over the last week, it is now pretty clear that there is something not quite right with the R.I. teacher's story. The Jewish community in Verona have declared that they have no knowledge of Marsiglia. They didn't know he was there, or that he was Jewish. Explaining his presence in the street where he was attacked, Marsiglia says he was going to see a friend, unnamed, whose address he couldn't quite remember. The hospital report on the wounds the man suffered has not been made public. Marsiglia has found a lawyer to sue all those who doubt that he is telling the truth. In a dramatic press conference, he declares, 'Do I have to show you my wounds?' as if he were Christ speaking to Thomas. But Christ did at least then show his wounds and that was that.

Also Marsiglia misses no chance to insist that the church bureaucracy which is taking him away from the Maffei is *more* guilty than his aggressors. Removing him from his post they *legitimised* the Nazi attack. In his most recent announcement he has declared that since they won't reinstate him at school, he is abjuring the faith. He is giving up on Christianity. He will have nothing to do with

Catholicism. The move is applauded by *Il Manifesto*, which speaks rather of the teacher having suffered the trauma of having his family massacred in the camps. Marsiglia was born in 1956. He is younger than I am.

Then at last I remember who Papalia is: Guido Papalia is Verona's chief prosecuting magistrate, the man leading the investigation into the assault against Marsiglia. And he also led the investigation, I remember reading, that brought about the interminable trial, still going on, of forty so-called Nazi skins, charged with having stirred up racial hatred and accused in particular of 'studying similar groups in England' in order to 'borrow their methods'. Does Albe imagine I am some kind of English policeman come to verify that the methods the *brigate* used were indeed borrowed from the home of all hooliganism? Surely not. But now I am a little concerned. I came to watch the football.

The *brigate*, I reflect, are not a savoury bunch, but in so far as they define themselves by being against somebody, it is the liberal press they are against, the perennial p.c. of contemporary society. That's why I feel a certain sympathy with them. Every public statement is so predictably pious, the stadium offers the only place where you can stand up and yell something excitingly foul. In any event, it's clear that the two antagonists are actually in complicity with each other. The *brigate* chant their racist chants and then are outraged by the hypocrisy of the press. The press are delighted to have such an easy target.

Albe has sat down beside me now. 'Want some Montenegro?' He's switched to Montenegro now, a bitter liqueur. 'I'll swap it for a swig of water.' 'Sure.' Then, to try him out, I say, 'You know there was a black in the *curva* for the friendly against Inter.' This was in early September. 'Really?' He doesn't seem overly surprised. 'In the *curva*, OK at the edge, where I hang out, but still in the *curva*.' Albe sighs. 'Well, he must have balls.' 'Nobody touched him,' I said. 'They wouldn't,' Albe tells me. As if to say, Why on earth would anybody touch him? 'Sooner or later there are bound to be blacks at the stadium,' I insist. 'It's happened everywhere else.' 'For sure,' Albe agrees, with apparent equanimity. 'Meantime they pour shit on us of course.' Merely because they begin grunting like monkeys every time a black touches the ball.

'*Dio boia*, I need paper,' a voice cries. 'Paper, *Dio bon*.'

It's Glass-eye; we're at a service station again. I must have slept a few minutes. He needs a shit. There's no paper.

'Has anybody got some paper? *Porco dio*, I'm going to shit myself.'

I hand over my tissues. Water and tissues seem to be my special gifts to the *ragazzi gialloblù*. I feel like a helpful, unobtrusive parent on a rather deviant Sunday school outing.

To stretch my legs I go into the station, grab a coffee at the bar, pick up another bottle of water and head back to the coach. Only a few are left inside. In the seat in front of me the only other man feasibly in his forties is chatting quietly to Albe. Disturbingly, his nickname appears to be Cain.

'It's all very well', he's saying, 'talking about blood on the terraces, but tomorrow's another day, and Monday another and Tuesday another. And then the time will come when I'll have to pack it in, it's inevitable, I'll be too old, won't I? They only have to wait. They don't have to fight us. So I said, if you like, let's sort it out between us. We can meet under the railway bridge and have it out. No weapons, I said. I know I can take a beating from him, the same way he could take one from me. I'm not afraid.'

It's a moment or two before I appreciate why this speech seems so strange. They are the first words I have heard for six or seven hours that have not been constantly punctuated by the words *Dio boia*. Is there a struggle under way, I wonder, for control of the Curva Sud? And what do I care if there is? Nothing. But on this trip the violence, when finally it happens, has nothing to do with rival fans, or journalists, or blacks or Jews . . .

Most of the boys are back on the coach, freshly supplied with beer and cigarettes and *limoncello* and whisky and Amaro Montenegro and, in one or two cases I notice, water. But Glass-eye is not back. The driver remarks that despite setting out with ample time, we should now get a move on. 'He must be shitting a football, *Dio boia*,' someone says. '*Una bomba*,' Fondo begins. 'He's shitting

27

a *bomba*.' Then someone says they saw him come out of the loo ages ago.

Everybody is getting seriously irritated by the delay when we catch the sound of approaching yells: 'Drive, driver, *Dio boia!* Drive! Move!' Glass-eye comes racing across the dark car park with another figure, one of the maddest, a tall, dark, deeply flushed young man in a long black coat. He seems to be called Pista, which is what a cyclist or skier or runner shouts when someone is in his way: *Pista!* Clear off, I'm coming through. Now he screams, 'Drive, *Dio boia*.'

The two explode on to the bus. The young driver is one of those who become calmer and slower the more others are excited. In no hurry at all he reaches down and turns the key, waits for the engine to steady.

Glass-eye is wild. Pista is shrieking, a bottle in his hand. 'Get out of the station. *Porco Dio!*'

Just as the driver pulls away, with exemplary caution, because to our left a German coach is just spilling its pensioners out on to the tarmac, I suddenly become aware of the lorry. A big articulated truck is roaring towards us across the two hundred yards of parking space and link road. It's accelerating, flashing its headlights. It's going far too fast for the car park. And as our coach pulls away, the truck lurches in front of us, brakes violently, shudders, stops. Our driver likewise hits the brake. The whole floor seems to shift as scores of cans and bottles slide forward. Then we're stopped, blocked.

Everybody is on their feet. '*Bastardo! Dio boia!*' Operating the door himself, Glass-eye and the wildest lads all rush out to confront the trucker who has effectively trapped us in our parking bay. The older contingent and soberer kids stay put. The phocomelia case hesitates on the steps. Albe is shouting for everybody to get back in the coach. Outside I can see the bewildered German folk huddling round the luggage bay of their luxury vehicle. To a man they seem old enough to have been here fifty-five years ago.

Somebody throws a can. Perhaps two. I can't see. Something rattles off the trailer. 'What's happened?' I ask Cain. We've both kept our seats. He seems unimpressed, shrugs his shoulders. Then in a move worthy of Hollywood the truck driver abruptly reverses, jack-knifing his vehicle toward the neon lights of the petrol station. Throwing the cab round, he hits the accelerator and seems to want to mow down the kids waving their arms at his windscreen, shouting obscenities, throwing cans.

Judging by how fast the truck moves, it must be unloaded. The kids jump aside, but the truck driver again throws his vehicle into a violent manoeuvre, twisting sharply to the right, so that for one moment I was sure someone must have been caught in the closing angle between cab and trailer. Frankly, I have never seen a truck behave like this, yet what struck me was how predictable it seemed, how exactly like the drama we have all seen in films. Perhaps my relative security in the coach seat reinforces the feeling.

Then the *brigate* are all piling back on board, breathless. 'Drive, *autista di merrrrda*! Drive!' This time the boy doesn't hang around. He stands on the accelerator. The Germans scatter. *Alè Verona alè!* We get past the petrol station, but now the truck has managed to turn round again and is chasing us. Why is it so much faster than we are? It pulls up along our left side, so that it's only inches from our window, trying to force us off the slip road. Despite insults, the driver keeps his nerve and a moment later both vehicles burst out on to the *autostrada* together.

Fortunately, the road is empty. It's the last half-hour before dawn. The truck drops back and hangs threateningly on our tail, less than two yards behind. Pista opens one of the small upper slide windows and throws a bottle, but I can see it's only plastic. Then he finds a glass bottle. 'Stop!' Cain shouts. No, he doesn't even have to shout. His voice is loud, but calm. 'Not the glass,' he says. 'We don't throw glass.' Surprisingly, certain rules exist and are obeyed. Pista stands there with the bottle half out of the window, we're already travelling at sixty odd, then he pulls it back in.

'On the truck there's a *bomba*,' Fondo is chanting, delighted with developments. 'The truck is a *bomba*. We've got to defuse a *bomba*.'

'Attacked me,' I swear, Glass-eye is insisting. 'Christ, don't we have the right to exist? I was minding my own business. Don't we have the right to walk across a service station?'

Nobody's convinced.

'What happened?' I ask Cain.

'Five minutes and the police will be here,' he says.

In the event, it was more like two minutes.

With just a short burst of its sirens a police car overtakes and pulls us over. The truck stops behind. Glass-eye and Pista are fighting to get out and confront the driver, but the others now drag them back from the door and trap them in the middle of the coach, where I am, while a man with a completely shaved and glistening scalp gets out of the coach with a couple of others to deal with the situation.

The facts, or at least some kind of story, drift back from seat to seat. Glass-eye got into a fight with the truck driver. The truck driver sent him flying against a promotional display covered with a big sheet of glass beside the petrol station. The display shattered. The petrol station want damages. The truck driver claims it was he who was first insulted, then assaulted. 'It's a lie, *Dio boia*, a lie!' Glass-eye wants to get out there and give his version to the police. He kicks and pushes and shrieks that it's a basic human liberty to be able to speak for yourself.

But the interesting thing, as Glass-eye thrashes madly about and, outside, the supporter with shaved scalp talks to the police, is the protective way the others are embracing him and trying to quiet him down. There's a real affection being expressed, not just a pragmatic response to the fear of escalation. They are looking after their drugged friend. They are holding him still, keeping him away from the kind of violence their songs all celebrate. If he speaks to the police now he will doubtless be banned from attending football games for at least a season.

The police tell us we'll have to go to the police station. Apparently there's one at the next exit beside the toll booths. Everybody is furious. We're going to miss the game. They'll take us in the station and spend hours looking at all our ID cards and deliberately make us miss the game. What story can we tell them? Everyone must agree on the same story. Glass-eye and Pista were attacked by three truck drivers swinging spanners. 'Exaggerate. If we all tell the same story what can they do?' 'Clear up the beer cans. Stick the cans in bags under the seats. They'll have a dog, dope out of the window, *Dio boia*. Coke out of the window.'

The shaven-headed guy seems to be called Forza. He has a fine, strong bright face, with thick, well-moulded lips and gleaming eyes. You can see at once that he could be violent, or he could be witty, he could be terrifying or he could be well-spoken and polite. At the police station, after a brief parley with Cain, he tells us to behave and gets out with the extremely sober drivers. While they talk to the police, Glass-eye again mills his arms and screams and tries to force his way down the aisle. He wants to show the bastards. His friends cling on to him, embrace him. Someone even has a hand round his neck, stroking his hair. The bus stinks of sweat and beer and cigarettes.

Day is dawning. Are we going to miss the game? I had promised myself I would see every game Verona played this season and now I am about to miss the first. The truck driver has arrived too now. He is thickset, squat and glowering, evidently a southerner, wearing his trucker's cap. There are two very smart policemen and an attractive young woman officer. The driver is remonstrating, shouting. I can't hear what's being said, but Forza certainly looks extremely civilised beside him, almost, despite the skinhead image, a gentleman. Finally, he climbs back on the bus.

'They'll let us go to the game if we pay damages. Three hundred thousand lire. Ten thousand each.'

It's about three pounds a head. Nothing.

Glass-eye refuses to pay. 'It's against my human rights, *Dio boia*. I haven't done anything wrong. I won't pay.'

For the first time I get involved. 'We're fucking well paying,' I tell him. I'm furious. 'I'm not missing the first game for ten fucking thousand lire.'

Despite my strangeness and doubtless English accent – I can't say *Dio boia*, it would sound ridiculous in my mouth – everybody agrees. 'Pay, *Dio boia*.' Someone is already whipping round a hat. *Hellas for ever*, the badge says, upside-down. But not everybody has the cash, or is ready to come out with it. 'I'll pay twice,' I offer, 'if necessary. Let's pay and go.' Sitting down, I realise that, quite unintentionally, I've established my credentials. I want to see the game. I am not a policeman.

The Stadio San Nicola sits like a huge flying saucer in the vast area of barren scrub to the north of the industrial port of Bari. Saint Nicholas is the patron saint of Bari and his bones are laid in the thousand-year-old Basilica San Nicola in the centre of the city. But the Brigate Gialloblù will not be allowed to pray to those sacred bones, nor will they see the fine twelfth-century Romanesque cathedral, or climb the ramparts of the remarkable Norman castle rebuilt by Frederick II. The Brigate Gialloblù will not be able to visit the old town centre, or even penetrate the grim suburbs for a pizza. For the last three hundred kilometres, from Pescara to Bari, we've been under strict police escort.

In fact it's all the *brigate* can now do to get out of their bus and relieve themselves. Again and again the driver indicates that he wants to enter a service station. Again and again the police cars back and front hit their sirens and flash their lights. Finally the driver turns in anyway and immediately we are confronted by more police. They have surrounded the bus. One has a machine gun.

'It's a basic human right, *Dio boia*,' Glass-eye is screaming. 'In my bladder there's a *bomba!*' Fondo yells. Barely out of the door, he starts pissing where he stands. Then he tries to cadge a cigarette off a watching Frenchman. Glass-eye meantime is yelling at the police. 'Are we doing anything wrong?' He's put his Verona cap on. Italian champions 1985, it says. The year of the miracle. Verona won the *scudetto*. 'Have we done anything wrong, *Dio boia*. Have we?'

A few kids make a break for it, slip between the police, and dash to the service station with the police chasing after. I follow, desperate for another coffee. And as I do so, I can't help realising that the mechanism is exactly the same as with the Marsiglia case. The *brigate* engage in deviant, provocative behaviour, but without really doing much. Then they're furious when the police behave as if they really were going to get engaged in urban warfare.

'Why do you hate us, *Dio boia*, what have we done?' The sentiment is genuine. In the service station everybody picks up their stuff and pays like perfectly reasonable citizens. Back in the coach, Forza announces that we will have to alter the song that runs '*Della questura non abbiam' paura*' – of the police we're not afraid. We'll have to add the line: 'Since we've always got ten thousand lire to pay.' Everybody cheers.

But has everybody got the thirty thousand lire to pay for the admission ticket to the game? As the stadium finally comes into view, a certain hush comes over the group. San Nicola is impressive. It's the temple of today's opposition. The *brigate*, like all fans, are knowledgeable about stadiums and respect them. Built for the 1990 World Cup, inevitably the object of years of investigation for illegal financing and kickbacks, San Nicola is special in that it is broken up into huge cement segments with gaps between them, like a great fist unclenching, or some fantastic space vehicle landed in the wilderness and opening up for the first contact between indigenous and alien life.

Southerners and northerners.

'*Meridionali di merda*,' someone is shouting out of a window at a group of kids by the road. '*Terroni figli di puttana*.' The liturgy of standard insults begins as soon as we leave the *autostrada*, though since the stadium is so isolated, so utterly split off from any community or urban fabric, and since we've arrived more than an hour and a half before the game, there is almost no one around to insult. '*Terroni Terroni!*' the kids chant. For '*terrone*' my dictionary just gives 'Southern Italian (derogatory).' But the idea is of someone close to the earth, *terra*, someone crude and uncultivated. Unlike us cultured northerners, that is. The comedy of this is that about half Verona's team are southern Italians. And the fans are aware of that comedy. Most of them have southern friends themselves.

The area round the stadium is little more than scorched earth. A vast car park is made of thin strips of decaying asphalt on a bed of desert sand. Immediately out of the coach, we're funnelled between lines of police toward a tiny prefab kiosk, laughably makeshift beside the huge stadium to one side and the vast empty landscape to the other. Behind thick Perspex, a man is ready to sell us tickets at thirty thousand lire. Everybody thinks this is outrageously expensive.

'Pay and go in,' we're told. An official with a radio has come to speak to us.

'We don't have enough,' Forza protests. 'We had to spend it paying damages for something we didn't even break.'

'Don't imagine you can get in free. Anybody who doesn't have the money will have to stay on the bus.'

'Driver,' Fondo starts shouting. 'Driver, take me to the *puttane*. I don't want to see the game, I want a prostitute. Take me to a prostitute, *Dio boia, autista di merda*.'

There's a fierce wind, something I hadn't expected, a gale almost, fresh and sharp from the sea, whipping up dust and litter. We're surrounded by policemen and officials with radios and truncheons and riot helmets. Cain and Albe are confabulating. Would it be possible to break for it and run under the Bari *curva* with the big banner they've brought?

'Bari is a serious *curva*,' Cain says. He shakes his head. 'If the other coaches had arrived at the same time we might have managed. But we never agree on anything.'

So only now do I realise that another group is coming in two other coaches; except that they were leaving at three in the morning, and they were not from the Zanzibar. 'They'll be late, *Dio bon*,' Albe says. 'They're always late.' 'We're not in a hurry to pay,' Glass-eye tells a policeman. 'We're not in a hurry to go in the ground. It's early. We want something to eat.'

We are told in no uncertain terms to go in now, immediately, or miss the game. We'll be taken to hospital to check alcohol levels. 'You're not going in the ground for a start,' Glass-eye is told. 'You're drunk. Nor you,' the official turns to Fondo.

'The carabiniere is a *bomba*,' Fondo begins. 'In the stadium there's a *bomba*. *Autista di merda*. Drive us to the *puttane*. I want a *puttana*.'

He's taken his T-shirt off and his torso is surprisingly handsome and tanned. Then he starts to run around as if looking for a place to break out of the police cordon. Immediately they block him. He runs back and throws himself against the glass of the kiosk, hands outspread. Then he tries to climb over it, gets a foot on the base of the window. The police pin him down. His minders rush to look after him, to pull him away from trouble. 'Can't you see, he's just a bit excited, *Dio bon*. Don't worry, we'll look after him.' And they shout in outrage, 'What's he done? Leave him alone, *Dio boia*.'

I'm getting used to the exercise now. It's a false confrontation. They're going to arrive at the point where there is shouting and insult and outrage and then they're going to do exactly what they're told. And in a way it *is* outrageous that we've come all the way to Bari and we can't even go to the seaside, or look at the town or have a pizza. Five hundred and fifty miles and we won't see anything, maybe not even the game. But if you want to be a deviant group and shout racist slogans, if you want the honour of a cage then in the end you have to accept it. And in the end after a show of severity the authorities also are going to back down and compromise, as they always do in Italy: Fondo, Glass-eye and Pista are all let in free, having no doubt spent far more than thirty thousand on booze and dope.

Through the turnstiles we're severely frisked, then we're let loose to walk fifty metres between what must once have been flowerbeds, planted perhaps for the third-place final between England and Italy, back in 1990. Now they are just arid stretches of soil and stones.

Forza is disgusted. 'See the south,' he speaks to me for the first time. At once I recognise the voice of the northern Italian explaining to the foreigner that he will never be able to understand the perversity of the south. 'Look at it. This is the south. They frisk you, then they let you walk across an area where you could fill your pockets with stones, *Dio boia*. With big stones, *Dio can*. The size of your fist.'

He's right. We could all pick up handfuls of stones. But perhaps what really makes the *brigate* uneasy is the way this carelessness exposes how tame they are. At least today. Because nobody picks up anything. Nobody's interested in trouble. Only, as we break out into the vast and empty stadium, Pista, Glass-eye and a couple of the younger kids start up the most amazing chorus of foul insults.

The stadium is huge and as ugly within as it is impressive

without. The terraces are too steep. You're afraid you might fall down the high steps. The wind is fierce through the big gaps between the separate segments. It swirls and hums round the stadium in sudden eddies, lifting the litter scattered everywhere. There's litter on the terraces. They haven't been cleaned. Even the pitch is strewn with litter, plastic bags and torn newspapers, lifted and tossed by the wind. Properly drunk, you might easily mistake the place for the second circle of Dante's hell where those who gave themselves over to passion were forever blown about against their will, shrieking and clapping their hands and cursing the power of God.

Clapping his hands, bare-breasted despite the growing chill, Pista begins to curse into the wind and the echoey stadium.

'*Africani, Dio boia!*'

'*Animali, Dio can!*'

'*Albanesi, Dio boia!*'

'*Criminali, Dio can!*'

'*Kurdi, Dio boia!*'

'*Terroni, Dio porco!*'

'*Contrabandisti!*' (Smugglers.)

'*Zingari!*' (Gypsies.)

'*Froci!*' (Queers.)

'*Bestie!*' (Beasts.)

'*Tua madre lo prende in culo!*' (Your mother takes it up the ass.)

'*Tuo padre è cornuto!*' (Your father's a cuckold.)

'*Scafisti di merda!*' (The *scafisti* are those who run the big rubber motorboats that daily bring illegal immigrants from Albania, a group notorious for the ruthlessness with which they will throw children into the sea when being chased by the coastguards.)

'*Tua madre è una puttana, scopa con tutti!*' (Your mother's a whore and fucks everyone.)

'*Le nostre tasse pagano per voi!*' (Our taxes pay for you.)

'*Non esistete senza di noi.*' (You wouldn't exist without us: that is, without the rich taxpaying north.)

Etc.

Glass-eye joins in. It goes on and on as the rest of us spread out over the small segment allotted to us. Then finally there's a moment of wild comedy, a moment that unmasks the mad theatre of it all. They've been at it a good twenty minutes, Pista and Glass-eye, leaning over the parapet, shrieking insult after insult at the sparse huddles of Bari fans all around, when a particularly strong gust of wind carries off Glass-eye's cap, his Verona-Champions-of-Italy-1985 cap. It soars up in the air, sails beautifully across the high fence at the side of the segment, crosses the gap between segments and lands gently on an empty section of terraces defended by a line of policemen who have evidently been positioned to prevent any Bari fans from running up to the fence and throwing things at us.

'I've lost my hat, give me my hat back!' Then rather surprisingly Glass-eye adds, '*Per favore*, please!' And then: '*Dio boia*, give me back my hat!'

The police won't budge. They have their blue riot helmets and gas canisters. There must be at least three hundred police to about forty-five of us.

'My hat, *Dio boia*, my old hat.' It wouldn't be easy to get hold of a genuine 1985 Verona champions of Italy hat. 'I was ten years old, *Dio can!*' Verona are not likely to be champions again. Faced with such a grievous loss, Glass-eye suddenly seems to be acting like the most normal of people. '*Ragazzi*,' he shouts to the Bari fans beyond the police. '*Abbiate pietà!*' Have mercy. His voice is hoarse with yelling. 'Please, can you get me my old hat!'

The Bari fans all have red-and-white scarves. A couple of youngsters move up to the police line, but the police turn them back. The wind is howling. The litter is shifting back and forth and the hat twitches and rolls on the terraces. The Verona fans begin to shriek at the police: 'He only wants his fucking hat. What's wrong with you? Aren't you human. Animals! Our taxes pay for you.'

The stand-off drags on for about five minutes. The police are impassive. Their orders are to keep the opposing fans apart at all costs. They look at the Veronese as if they came from another planet, some of them occasionally grinning at each other, the way

37

one grins at the antics of monkeys at the zoo. Then at last two brave Bari fans rush through the police line and make a dash to the hat. A few policemen follow, but half-heartedly. They're not going to get rough with the locals. The fans pounce on the hat. '*Hellas*,' it says: '*Campioni d'Italia 1985*', the year my son was born.

My first thought then was that the Bari boys were going to make off with the hat, as a punishment for all the insults they'd been hearing. Perhaps they would burn it, and chant *Verona Verona, vaffanculo*, staple cry of opposing fans. But in the event the tallest boy comes up to the fence, perhaps three yards from Glass-eye, and, waiting for a lull in the wind, concentrating so as to make sure the hat will go over the high fence and then across the frightening gap in the cement floor, he tosses the precious thing into the air and it comes spinning down on our side.

Immediately, the Verona fans are roaring approval. 'Ba-ri! Ba-ri!' they applaud. The Bari fans behind the police strike up a cry of '*Lecce Lecce vaffanculo*', Lecce being their nearest and so most-hated rivals. Taking the prompt, the *brigate* join in. '*Lecce Lecce vaffanculo*.' In the silence that follows, Glass-eye yells, 'OK, enough of that, insults in the other direction,' and, turning away from the fans to the left, who recovered his hat, he and Pista walk to the other side of the enclosure and start to insult the fans on the right:

'*Albanesi, Dio boia!*'

'*Criminali, Dio can!*'

'*Terroni, Dio porco!*'

So, a situation has been created where the simple gesture of recovering a hat takes on huge significance in the teeth of concentration camp conditions. That Bari boy will go home proud to have faced the police and picked up that Verona Campioni d'Italia cap. How could he have experienced emotions like that if he'd watched the game on TV?

Meanwhile, thanks to the cage we're in and the cordon of police around us, the *brigate* can enjoy an orgy of community spirit. Nobody has to decide how far they're going to go, because it's impossible to go anywhere. Nobody need criticise the excesses of the others, because excesses can only get so far. When the other two coachloads arrive half an hour before the game, the terrace mills with boys embracing. There are even a few girls. One can only hope the players will show the same group spirit.

Let's compare players and fans.

Sleepless and wild, the *brigate* travelled through the night in the most uncomfortable conditions. The team no doubt came down yesterday by plane and spent the night in a four-star hotel.

Smoking to a man, eating poorly, drinking heavily, the *brigate* are not in the best physical condition. The team work out hours every day under the guidance of experts and the care of specialised medical staff.

The *brigate* all hail from inside an area of about fifty square kilometres. They speak a highly specific regional dialect. The team includes a Dane, a Serb, a Croatian, a Romanian, a Brasilian and then a dozen boys from all over the *bel paese*. Our captain, the much beloved Leo Colucci, is himself from Bari. One hopes they can all communicate in standard Italian.

The *brigate* have known each other as long as they have known anyone. Most probably they have been friends since nursery school. They care deeply about Hellas Verona. Gilardino, our new striker, arrived in Verona on Thursday morning and has had only one training session with the team. The goalkeeper is new this year. The two wingbacks are new. Two members of the midfield are new and one attacker. They don't give a damn about Hellas Verona, except in so far as their own prospects are furthered or damaged by the team's performance.

So what relation can there possibly be between the hundred and fifty bleary beery boys around me and the eleven individual careerists now trotting out on to the field? The answer is simple: the fans must communicate to the players the one hugely positive thing they have, a sense of unity. The Brigate Gialloblù can give Colucci & Co. what no television camera ever can, an immediate vocal response to whatever they do, a response of admiration, or of scorn, but above all of encouragement, a sense of urgency. And this surely is the agony of the football business manager: that in the end the game does need these wild boys to make it work. A huge injection of excitement, of spilt libido and perverted civic pride, is absolutely necessary.

From the moment the team step out on to the field, a transformation takes place in the *brigate*. The individual insults stop. The boys are now solid as a well-trained chorus line. They give their voices generously, unceasingly. They do a job, a job that is actually admired by conservative members of society, sports commentators, marketing men and the like. Despite being hopelessly outnumbered and sometimes quite overwhelmed by surrounding voices, they are nevertheless compact and reliable. They obey a well-established hierarchy, responding immediately to cues from their leaders. They never flag, they never disobey. In short, from now until half-time they will not stop clapping and singing and chanting. It's exhausting. It's heroic.

'*Con il mare negli occhi e il sole nel cuore, Bari ti giuriamo eterno amore.*' So says the main banner the Bari fans have opened out right across the lower parapet of their *curva*: With the sea in our eyes and the sun in our hearts, Bari we swear our eternal love. The south, I reflect, watching the boys work out on the pitch before the game, does tend to be a little more sentimental than the north.

Their other main banner reads: 'We honour the colours of our city.' There's a fantastic medieval solemnity about it. On Verona's website, The Wall, in the endless debate over the selling and buying of players this summer, somebody responded to the idea of boycotting the stadium with the line: 'The *brigate* honour the colours *gialloblù*, not the players, not the trainer, not the owner, only the colours.' On the coach the boys sang: 'Players and trainers come and go, but we are for ever, for ever, *brigate, brigate gialloblù.*' What delirium! What security in the close ties of an undying community! And from this chant they go straight into their corruption of the song of the glorious Bersaglieri, perhaps Italy's only crack military regiment: '*Aprite le porte, che passano, che passano, aprite le porte, che passano i gialloblù!*' Open the doors, the yellow-blues are passing through. And this when we all know that most probably they won't be passing through at all. The chances are that we will be going under today. Bari have a good record at home. It's not easy to start the season with an away game against a direct relegation rival. Bari are fielding the same team they had last year, with the same manager. They will be solid and determined.

'Open the doors, the yellow-blues are coming through!' Sober and drunk alike, the *brigate* sing with all their might. Am I myself so fanatic? I've often wondered about the way I switch back and forth from 'we' to 'they' when I talk about Verona. I've often wondered over the years how badly the team would have to play for me to stop going to watch. It almost happened last season. There was a moment when I gave up, when I lost faith. It was a game that, had it finished as it was at half-time, would have meant the end for me.

This was immediately after Christmas. Halfway through the season, Verona were second to bottom. We had come up to Serie A three years before, promptly gone back down again, come up once more after two seasons in the miserable and violent Serie B, and now it looked as though we were going right back down again. The opposition that particular Sunday was Parma, a classy side, winners of the penultimate Cup Winners' Cup, participants in the Champions' League. They had international stars like Crespo, Thuram, Cannavaro, Benarrivo, Amoroso.

To keep hopes alive, Verona needed a result at all costs and started out with great determination, scoring after only three minutes. Parma didn't even look perturbed. Rightly so. It wasn't long before they had equalised and by half-time they were ahead three—one. 'This is it,' I told my son. 'We're going down. I can't bear it. I can't watch it.' It wasn't just the result, it was the extent to which the team were outclassed, the ease with which Parma were dismissing us. If football were purely an aesthetic experience, I should have been able to enjoy this, to admire it, but I couldn't. I couldn't enjoy the absolutely splendid way Crespo & Co. were destroying us. I have invested too much emotion in this team, I thought. And I thought: with the excuse of being with my son, of coming to the stadium with my son, I have embarked, over a period of some years now, in supporting a second-rate provincial side, to wit Hellas Verona F.C., something I am no doubt doing to satisfy all kinds of infantile dreams which hardly bear investigation.

And now the side is letting me down. The boys are making a fool of me. Hellas Verona football club is not my destiny, I decided, not in the way it is for these people around me, these people who grew up speaking the local dialect, who cannot imagine a different life. I can tear myself away from this, I thought. I can say 'they' not 'we'. I can and must detach myself.

Before the half-time break was over I had formally and finally decided to become less interested, to forget next year's season ticket, to call it a day. It's a reaction I often have with Italy in general. This is not necessarily my destiny, I will tell myself, when something goes seriously wrong, something particularly and miserably Italian, some tussle with Bourbonic bureaucracy, or the nth wildcat strike on the Milan metro. You could leave this place, Tim, I announce. I say these things out loud sometimes. You are merely resident here. You could go tomorrow if you wanted to. Tomorrow! How many times have I told myself that?

'We're not getting a season ticket next year,' I told Michele. 'This is it. It's over. I can't face another season in Serie B.'

My son was gloomy, watching his feet as he scuffed up the glossy match programme in disgust.

'We can fly to Old Trafford twice a year,' I said. 'Why not? I was born in Manchester,' I insisted. 'I saw my first games at Old Trafford. It's perfectly acceptable for me to support United.'

'But I was born here,' he said. He ground the programme hard into the cement. 'And the team stinks.'

Everybody around us on the terraces agreed that we were going down. There was resignation in the air. Why weren't they angrier? I wondered. Why weren't they furious? We were going down, the pessimist know-all who always sits in front of us was explaining resignedly, because the owner Pastorello was no more than a businessman. The man had no passion for the team. He wouldn't spend money on it. He was tight. He didn't have Verona in his blood. He didn't suffer when Verona lost. What had he done when we started losing? What had he done? He had found a player on loan again. On loan! A player, what's more, from *the only team that was below us*, Cagliari. Could you believe that, a player *not even Cagliari* wanted to put on the field. His name was Morfeo. 'We're second from bottom and he gets hold of a player not even the bottom team will field! What can Morfeo do? It's incredible,' the pessimist said, but without anger. 'What has he done in the first half? Nothing. Because he can't do anything. We're going down,' he said. 'Next week Milan away. We're finished.'

The team had left the field to whistles. They returned to the kind of cheers and chants that are shouted against the grain through gritted teeth. Duty chants. We have to support you, we're going to support you, but you don't fucking-well deserve it. Then another chant began, to the tune of a clock chiming the hour: '*Pas-to-rel-lo vaf-fan-cu-lo.*' 'Morfeo's useless,' the guy in front kept saying. 'He's too small; he's too slight. He tries to do everything himself. Not even Cagliari would play him. What did we get Morfeo for?'

Within five minutes Morfeo had scored. Then he set up the equaliser from a beautifully placed free kick. Ten minutes from time, the big Thuram fumbled in the box and we had the winner. In injury time Morfeo struck a bouncing ball from thirty yards and hit the bar. We left the stadium euphoric. We had destroyed Parma. They had been routed, humiliated. Humiliated! What a wonderful word that is when you're not on the receiving end. The emotion was uncontrollable. We killed them! People were on the edge of tears. My son was shaking his head, endlessly repeating, 'We did it, we did it, we did it. *Siamo grandi. Siamo grandissimi!* Great. Truly great.' Sitting in the car, taking hold of the wheel, I found my hands and wrists were trembling.

'Unrestrained joy and deep depression always and only occur in one and the same person,' wrote Schopenhauer, 'since each provokes the other and both are the result of a great vivacity of spirit.' Less flatteringly he goes on: 'Behind any experience of excessive grief or extravagant jubilation, there is always an error of thinking and a false belief.'

In error or not, true or false, I was hooked again. That game did it to me. I was hooked on the team, I was hooked on my son's response to the team, his home team. And above all I was hooked on the amazing Morfeo. Why had Cagliari let us have him? He was a miracle. And from that day until the end of the season, indeed until today's game with Bari, Hellas Verona had not lost a single league match. Fifteen games without defeat. In Italy's Serie A, that's an amazing achievement. In the growing excitement as we climbed up and up the table, this book was born. A book, for me, has always been a form of defence, I think, against excessive joy, excessive pain, a nosing about a false belief, or something that I would prefer, more positively, to call an illusion. Standing on the terraces in Bari, I tell myself, get ready for it, Tim.

Get ready for what? Nothing. Morfeo is no longer with us. Bar our great Dane in defence, the stars of last season are gone. They are sitting on the benches of Inter, Fiorentina, Parma. Our veteran central defender, Apolloni, is injured. The new trainer, Attilio Perotti, has never coached a Serie A side before. And he's in his fifties. There's a bland, too-amiable look about the man. He wears glasses. His chin is weak. He talks about needing time. Time! In the event, he fields a team of humdrum runabouts, busy and dull. A line of four in defence, moving jerkily up and down like a faulty windscreen wiper. A mill of six in midfield, furious and uninspired. And nobody in attack, since, having only bought a centre-forward the day before yesterday, they haven't even stuck him on the pitch. He won't know the other guys' names yet. Needless to say absolutely nothing happens. On either side.

The players run around in the litter. Or rather they fall over in the litter. They are constantly falling over. The referee constantly blows his whistle. Two people go up to head the ball, foul. Someone lifts his leg, foul. Slide-tackle, foul. A total of fifty-nine fouls, tomorrow's *Gazzetta dello Sport* will note in its canonical list of statistics. This game is being stopped every ninety-one seconds, for God's sake. And this is typical of the new-style Italian referee, a great show of authority and severity and very little effort to distinguish between the real foul and the fake fall. The ball strikes Laursen, our Dane, on the elbow, handball. Their goalkeeper stumbles at a corner, foul.

But I should have expected as much. Before the game Captain Leo Colucci, speaking in the local paper, referred to Bari as '*cattivo*'.

It's an impossible word to translate. The dictionary gives 'bad', 'wicked', 'evil'. But Colucci doesn't mean it in a pejorative sense. For he adds, 'We've got to become more "*cattivi*" ourselves.' He means hard, tough, smart, fouling when fouling is necessary, falling over whenever the ref will give a foul. To investigate how '*cattivo*' comes to be used in a positive sense in the particular context of football would be to open up the whole conundrum: is it more important that my team play well, or that they don't lose? An impossible question. I'm not even going to ask myself: would you mind them losing if only the game was watchable. Of course I'd mind. Meantime, Colucci has a personal investment in *cattiveria*. He is our one '*scontrista*' – the midfield player who determinedly confronts the others, an Ince figure. But then I loved Ince. I love Colucci. I love his spirit. I'll watch Colucci, I decide. It's something I always do when the game is dull. I choose a single player and follow him, try to see what he's up to.

But if only they'd clear the litter, damn it! This is something I find it hard to believe. There are a good two hundred policemen at the game. There was a pre-match parade of junior teams. There are officials and groundsmen galore, and with all these people they haven't cleared the litter, for the first game of the season, televised nationwide! At least we could look at a nice green pitch.

The game is dull, dull, dull! Not a single incident to describe. This is a game when absolutely nothing is going to happen, I realise. Until what does happen is that quite suddenly I need a shit. It's infuriating. I need a shit immediately. You travel twelve hours in a coach, your body behaving admirably, you eat and drink judiciously, you congratulate yourself on not feeling that bad despite not having slept all night, you console yourself that if Verona are not doing anything interesting, then neither are Bari, who still, after thirty minutes, haven't had a single shot on goal, or even remotely around the goal. And just when you're thinking, I can even enjoy the litter in a way, the way it flutters and mills around, suddenly you need a shit. At once. '*Terroni di merda*,' the *brigate* are shouting. *Terroni shitheads*.

I'm standing just beside the knot of the chorus. Not among

them. This is what writers do perhaps. They're drawn to the energy of groups, then they stand just to one side of them. They never know if they're saying 'we' or 'they'. It's an illness.

But now my bowels force me to cross that short space. 'Where's the bog?' 'Don't know.' 'Where's the loo?' 'No idea.' I have to walk right through the core of the group and ask a policeman. He looks at me suspiciously. 'Underground,' he says. 'There's another flight of stairs when you get to the ground.' As I head off down the stairs he starts to follow me. '*Per la Madonna*,' I tell him. 'I just need a shit.' Convinced, he retreats.

Then I'm halfway down, tackling one huge deserted flight after another, the whole thing open to the desert scrub to the east whence a ferocious wind is clutching at my clothes, when a great roar comes from inside the stadium. Oh no! It can't be!

Rushing over to the side of the flight I see the first advantage of a stadium designed in segments. Through the gap between one section and the next, through pillars and beams, I have a low view of the field. Verona have a free kick on the edge of the box. The Bari players are protesting furiously. The ref forces them back. Italiano is going to take it. Vincenzo Italiano is our free-kick specialist. Another southerner. Amazing we haven't sold him. Two minutes fussing over the barrier, while I'm pressing my knees together. Hurry up! Italiano takes his long run up, the shot goes over the bar. And I rush down four more flights of stairs.

For perhaps a thousand spectators there are two Turkish loos with no doors and no paper. But I have my tissues. Though depleted there are just enough. But now the flush doesn't work. On the wall it says: 'Verona, you'll always be Serie B, even when you're in Serie A.' A fascinating play, it occurs to me, with the literal and the metaphoric. Hurrying up the stairs, I find a man with a tray of wares and treat myself to a Coke and a bag of crisps. He untwists and keeps the plastic top to the plastic bottle, in case I decide to throw it down among the litter on the pitch. And maybe I would have.

At half-time I chat to the older driver. The younger is sleeping in the coach. He smiles. No, of course he doesn't mind the insults. He smoothes his big moustache. 'It's a job, isn't it. They're only playing. Actually, it's fun. We should be back around three a.m.,' he reckons, 'if everyone behaves. Not much to get excited about,' he says of the game. 'Unscathed,' I tell him abruptly. 'The important thing is to come away unscathed, so we can start the season at home.' '*Bomba*,' Fondo screams. 'On the pitch, there's a *bomba*.' But he's running out of steam.

Yes, if we come out of it unscathed, it will be OK, I'm telling myself through the second half, honestly one of the most tedious I have witnessed. Seven yellow cards have been shown. Our supposed Romanian genius, Adrian Mutu, is substituted without having done anything. Their supposed boy genius, Cassano, falls over every time he is touched. OK, no emotions, but at least unscathed, I'm thinking, when ten minutes from time the referee gives Bari a penalty.

There are no words for a decision like this. Bari's winger was crossing from the right, but he hit the ball too hard and the wind carried it high in the air. It presented no danger at all. All the same, the clever Swede Osmanovski attaches his arm to a defender, Marco Cassetti, one of the new arrivals (from Serie C!), pretends to turn and falls over. Perhaps overconscious of those television cameras, desperate to have something happen, knowing that a penalty is never wrong when given to the home side, the unforgivable referee, who has killed the game from beginning to end, whistles. Their great big Swede Andersson sticks the ball straight in the net. The Bari *curva* goes wild. The *brigate* erupt.

Now here's an interesting thing. I am absolutely furious with the referee. I'm screaming myself hoarse shouting abuse at the referee. I can't believe that not only have I not slept, not only have I breathed smoke all night, not only have I had to shit in a Turkish loo and seen no decent football, but we're not even going to get away unscathed. I have chosen to write about Hellas Verona F.C. in precisely the year that they're not only boring, but unlucky. And it's all the referee's fault.

But the *brigate* don't even seem to have noticed the referee. They are furious with the Bari fans. How can they exult when they haven't had a single shot on goal all the game, when the penalty was the most obvious of gifts? A number of fans rush past me and throw themselves at the fence. Fondo starts to climb the railing and is pulled back. Someone throws a plastic bottle without its top. At this moment, watching their faces distorted with rage, I feel they really would cause trouble, they wouldn't hold back if the opportunity for a clash came. But either side of us there are at least thirty empty yards. The police are unimpressed. Then the boys re-group and grimly resume their chanting. '*Hellas Verona segna per noi.*' Score for us. Please. We've come so far.

Surprisingly, the team react. I wouldn't have thought them capable of it. Suddenly, from nowhere, they have energy, but only eight minutes to do something with it. Substitutions are made. Gilardino, the eighteen-year-old striker, comes on. The coach has balls, I have to admit, to make a decision like that. What a moment to have the boy debut! And he brings on another player, the winger Claudio Ferrarese, a kid I've always loved because he can dribble, but a player who somehow never sees more than a few minutes of any game.

We get a corner. Ferrarese's doing. Another corner. Again Ferrarese. Gilardino is brilliant at holding the ball even with three men on his heels. But they'll never score, I tell myself. These people should have been brought on earlier. The coach is a fool. We are paying the price for having come and played for a draw, though before the penalty we had come closer to scoring than they had. If there's one thing in the world that's unfair, I tell myself, it's football. We won't even have a shot! Ten minutes' furious attacking and not even a shot. It's a miserable day.

Ferrarese wins another corner. And another. Here it comes. High, oh God, too high. But the wind is against it. The ball suddenly dips into the area. Down it plummets to where the big and totally undistinguished defender Natale Gonnella is loitering on his own. Gonnella is the immature understudy for the injured Apolloni. Has Gonnella ever scored for us? I don't think so. Without even moving he sticks his foot out and hits the thing first time.

What are the chances, even for the world's great footballing geniuses, of striking a ball like that accurately on the volley? A high long ball swirling in the wind? What are the chances, having struck it, of its penetrating the twenty players between you and the goal, one of whom, of course, can use his hands? The stadium holds its breath. But there it is. The net lifts. It must have gone in. 'It's gone in, *Dio boia!*' Gonnella has scored. Gonnella! We've done it!

All of a sudden I'm locked in a fierce embrace with someone I've never met before. He's young and drunk and delirious. The *brigate* run at the fence. 'Now bang your drum,' they chant. The Bari end is silent. The ref, I tell myself, has done us a favour. Everybody feels like a million dollars. We've had our emotions. And right at the end, with the final whistle, at last it happens: a moment's contact between fans and team, a moment's acknowledgment. Big Martin Laursen and Colucci and a couple of the others come over to stand beneath our segment. They wave, way down beneath us in this ridiculously high stadium. The fans yell, clapping their hands above their heads. Everybody is moved, they came to salute us, everybody is proud . . . and exhausted.

How quiet, how subdued the return trip is! Fondo has come off his high. Slumped in his seat, he sleeps. 'There's a *bomba*,' someone shouts, right by his ear. He sleeps. I could kill him. In front and behind, two police cars are escorting us. Quite deliberately they are driving slowly so that we will get home even later. Albe sits next to me. He explains the scar on his shoulder. 'No it wasn't a fight.' He laughs. 'Haven't you seen? Me? I'm a peace-maker me, *Dio boia*. I do everything I can to keep the peace, *Dio bon*. There are people who owe their lives to my peace-making.'

'Is it true you're a *parroco*?' someone asks me at the first service station stop. For a moment I don't understand. *Parroco* is a word I never use. It means parish priest. 'Someone told me you were a *parroco*.'

It's a dapper boy with small dark sunglasses. Behind him a couple of the younger kids are giggling.

'Are you joking?'

'*Ciao, Parroco*,' someone says. And there it is, I have my nickname. I'm Parroco, a parish priest. Is it because of my bald spot, I wonder? My father was a clergyman of course. Could it be I am like him in some way? I always thought the business of writing maintained a sort of perverted continuity with Dad's profession. 'Did you pray for a miracle, Parroco,' one of the kids asks. 'After the penalty?' 'I prayed for a fucking lightning bolt to strike the ref.'

Towards midnight, just as I'm nodding off, they begin to wake up. They start to tell jokes. Everybody is cheerful. The team are better than we thought. They reacted. They didn't take it lying down. 'Parroco, what do you think of the team? They're not that bad, are they? You'll pray for them won't you, Parroco?' Cain in particular starts to tell jokes. Mostly silent and lugubrious all the way down, perhaps reflecting on the day when he will be too old for this, too old to defend his place in the *curva*, he cheers up and starts to tell one joke after another, almost all of them at the expense of homosexuals. Funny, it occurs to me, a group of men embracing each other and sleeping with their heads leaned against each other, telling jokes about homosexuals.

'So this queer goes to the doctor. *Dottore, Dottore, Dio boia*, I've got this pain in my arse. *Dottore*, help me, *Dio can*. Right? So the doctor examines him, sticks his finger up. Can't feel anything, he says. Further up, *Dottore, Dio boia*, further up.' He's got his whole hand in now.'

Cain's eyes are shining as he leans into the aisle telling this joke to a group of adolescents with beer cans stuck to their mouths.

'He's got his whole hand in, *Dio boia*. Further up, *Dottore*, the queer says. He's got his whole forearm in. Further up, *Dottore*. Oh, right, there I've found something the doctor says. Pull it out, *Dio boia*, pull it out, *Dottore*. And the doctor twists and turns. There, got my fingers on it, got it, slowly does it, out it comes, there! And in his hand he's holding . . . a white rose! For you! *Dottore*, the queer says in a drooling voice. For you! For you! Get it, *Dio boia*! Get it?' Cain demands. He pushes his red face towards us, his thick lips. 'The queer said: For you!' Everybody is laughing their heads off when the coach comes to a sudden stop. In a tunnel.

The police had finally let us go. At last, after three hundred kilometres of expensive and quite unnecessary escorting, we were free and making good speed, beyond Pescara now, where the road along the Adriatic is a long series of tunnels and high viaducts. Until, at one in the morning, as the laughter dies down from this nth joke about queers, always with the punch line repeated amid cries of 'Get it, *Dio boia*, get it, did you?' the coach stops in a tunnel and the driver turns off the engine. Hazard lights are flashing all around. We're stuck.

After a few minutes we pile out and start walking. Only fifty yards or so further on, we come out of the tunnel and on to a spectacularly high viaduct. Over the rail to the right is a drop of perhaps two hundred feet. A hundred yards ahead, the road disappears into the next tunnel. But between the two mountains, in the centre of the bridge, is a truck, on fire. There are no vehicles around it, and there doesn't seem to have been an accident, but in the stiff breeze the thing is sending flames up thirty or forty feet into the night, and so fiercely that no one is going to risk squeezing past it. Gathering together at the head of a small crowd, the *brigate* immediately strike up one of their perfectly synchronised chants: '*Sangue, stragi, violenza sempre più, brigate gialloblù, brigate gialloblù.*' Blood, carnage, more and more violence . . .

'Move back,' a policeman shouts in a Sicilian accent. 'It might explode any moment.'

It certainly looks like the kind of thing they set up for a movie.

'If it explodes, can we shout "Re-load"?' Pista screams.

They are being deliberately childish now. Hellas didn't lose. The ref gave Bari a penalty ten minutes from the end and we didn't lose. The boys reacted.

The rest of the crowd are amused. The policeman is angry and shouts at us.

'Oh, can you repeat that in Italian?' Glass-eye says. '*Butei*, the policeman doesn't speak Italian.'

Rising to the bait, the policeman begins to say, making an effort now with his accent, that he will arrest us for insulting a public official.

'Oh the monkey *does* speak Italian,' Glass-eye shrieks, and already the others are dragging him away before the policeman can get through the crowd to him.

The truck burns on. The flames are intensely orange in the dark night. Apparently it is a vehicle that runs on GP gas, and its tanks have blown up. When the boys hear that the trailer is loaded with grapes, they strike up with a completely innocuous song, 'How nice it is to gather in the grapes with *la mia bella*.' A dull explosion has everyone running back. 'Re-load, re-load!' Pista is shrieking. The truck's doors have blown open. We fall back and stand watching. We've been here half an hour and still the fire brigade haven't arrived. Will I ever get home from this trip?

'This wouldn't happen up north,' Cain assures me. 'Up north, the fire brigade would have been there immediately.' I ask him where Fondo is. 'Why isn't he screaming, In the truck there's a *bomba*?'

'He's asleep. Fondo's a sick boy,' Cain says soberly. 'When he comes off his highs and realises what he's doing to himself, he gets so depressed he just starts drinking again.'

'Does he have a job?'

'He lives alone with his mum. His mum adores him.'

Cain is obviously sad for Fondo, he knows Fondo will not stay the course as he has.

'Pray for us to get home, Parroco,' somebody shouts. 'Pray for the flames to die down.'

'The one time', Cain says, 'we behave like angels, and this has to happen.'

When the coach finally gets on the move again all the boys at the back begin to chant, '*Sborra, autista, sborra.*' *Sborrare* is a dialect word that means 'to come' and not in the sense of coming and going, to and fro. 'Come, driver, come!' Coming, I reflect, is precisely what none of these young men have done this weekend. Such are the sacrifices of the away game.

It's getting on five in the morning when the coach pulls up at the Zanzibar. As it slows to a stop, a swarm of beer cans rolls up the aisle. After one more half-hearted chant of Hellas, the *brigate* break up and wander off into the dawn. One by one cars accelerate down the wide sensible street, ignoring the traffic lights. We are ordinary people again.

Then, before I know it, my wife is shaking my arm: 'Wake up, wake up, Tim. There's the visit to Villa Vendri,' she says. She doesn't know how late I got home. The visit is at ten. They're opening up a private stately home nearby for public inspection. The tour is limited. We have booked and paid. I *have* to go. If I don't go we will *fare una brutta figura*.

Half an hour later, bleary with sleep, my mind throbbing still to the rhythms of the coach, the strangely compulsive rise and fall of those dialect voices, I stand on the steps of a Renaissance villa looking out across driving rain on statues and stucco. 'Come, driver, come!' 'There was a complicated ongoing quarrel between the various branches of the Giusti family,' the guide is saying, 'the Tuscan branch and the Veronese branch, that is, and then between the family as a whole and other families from other parts of Italy. Someone was cheated. Someone was knifed in the back.' The guide pauses. 'Times were more violent then than they are today.'

'*Stragi sangue violenza sempre più*,' my daughter Stefi sings when I get home. She's twelve. 'Did they do that one, Dad? What songs did they sing?' The tune, I finally realise, is taken from the refrain to 'Yellow Submarine'. 'All the boys', Stefi giggles, 'stand up and sing it as soon as teacher leaves the room.'

'So what did you learn?' Michele asks more seriously. He means about our prospects, the team, can we avoid relegation? Can we dream? 'After twenty years in the Veneto,' I tell him, 'I finally understood how they pronounce *Dio boia*. And the team's not that bad either.'

IA GIORNATA

Atalanta – Lazio 2–2
Bari – Verona 1–1
Milan – Vicenza 2–0
Napoli – Juventus 1–2
Parma – Fiorentina 2–2
Perugia – Lecce 1–1
Reggina – Inter 2–1
Roma – Bologna 2–0
Udinese – Brescia 4–2

CLASSIFICA

Udinese	3
Milan	3
Roma	3
Juventus	3
Reggina	3
Fiorentina	1
Lazio	1
Parma	1
Lecce	1
Verona	1
Atalanta	1
Bari	1
Perugia	1
Inter	0
Brescia	0
Bologna	0
Vicenza	0
Napoli	0

Giove Pluvio

*I've dressed in blue and yellow, now I'll put on the
mythical scarf (twenty-one years old) and so off to the
curva. Avanti bluu!*
  Pennellone65@solohellas.net

'Hurry,' Michele says. He's meeting me off the airport bus. 'For
God's sake, Papà. We're late.'

I've just got back from Paris where I attended a festival entitled
'Écrire l'Europe'. I must, I tell myself, stop attending literary festivals.
Arranged by the Ministère de la Culture to celebrate the French
Presidency of the European Community, Écrire l'Europe was
nothing more than a complacent charade, staged around the pathetic
pretence that the authorities take writing 'seriously'. What would it
mean, I wonder, for a government 'to take writing seriously'? Are
we going to ask our leaders to read books?

By great good fortune (for the organisers) the Nobel prize for
literature was announced the day before the festival and the winner,
a Chinese dissident – already his difficult name escapes me – turned
out to have been resident in Paris for many years. He was thus
available to be fêted by the French Minister for Culture at the
opening reception (champagne and canapés) though his writing has
nothing at all to do with Europe and quite understandably he hadn't
originally been invited.

'A piece of China is European,' the Minister declared, 'indeed
French!' she added, standing beside the beaming and bewildered
winner. 'A piece of the Nobel is French!' Clearly, I thought, the

Brigate Gialloblù are not the only ones with an obsessive sense of pride in place. And, while people milled and looked solemn and bored, this elegant, ambitious woman began a substantial speech saying how much she admired the Chinese writer's commitment to human rights. Writing, at public festivals, is always construed as something committed to human rights, a sort of genteel, largely unremunerative branch of liberal politics. 'Pissing is a basic human right,' Glass-eye had screamed. 'My rights have been trampled on,' Marsiglia told the newspapers. The minister had probably never heard of the oriental Nobel until the day before yesterday. As I had never heard of our Brazilian striker Adailton till the day we signed him.

In any event, I found it embarrassing explaining to these well-meaning people that I had to abandon the festival early for a football game. I had to leave on Sunday at dawn. In a Parisian café I logged on to www.hellasverona.it but for some reason couldn't get The Wall to work. Was it the sticky mouse? For days I haven't been able to open The Wall. Why? Is access to The Wall a basic human right? 'You'll miss the main presentation to the public,' my French publisher worried. 'You'll miss the closing banquet,' one of the organisers regretted. Where was my ambition? Where was my appetite? Pray God that plane isn't late, I was thinking all the way to the airport. It's the first home game of the season. The rain was heavy and the mist thick.

'Come on, Dad, for God's sake, we'll never find a seat!'

L'Arena has announced that the curva is sold out. Considerably taller than myself, handsomely blond and blue-eyed, my son hurries ahead, entirely focused on the game, irritated by the irregularity of having to meet me from the airport. The station where the airport bus arrives is just a quarter of a mile from the stadium. People are streaming through the streets. 'We'll never get a good seat.' He is anxious, excited.

But I have to make a detour. I have to find my car and leave my bag in it. It's parked beside the canal which turns out to be full to the brink, a swollen muddy flow leaving no space at all between itself and the low road bridges. I've never seen it like this. 'We're going to miss school, Dad, if the Adige gets any higher. It's been raining non-stop.'

My son, it seems, sees an eventual flood as a chance to spend more time playing computer games. In FIFA 2000 he has bought Beckham and Zidane for Verona. We are six points clear at the top. A place in the Champions' League is assured. Dream on. The sky above us, as we join the crowd, is dense and blurred. Flying through it, less than an hour ago, the small propeller plane was all over the place. I still feel seasick.

We wait in line. The other side of the turnstiles, the police are confiscating cigarette lighters and loose coins. Once, when my wife was away, they confiscated two clothes-pegs in my pockets. I tried to explain that I always stuff my pockets with pegs when I am hanging out the washing, because I find it difficult to keep turning to the peg-bag while holding damp underwear on the line. 'My wife hates to lose good pegs,' I protested. But if the police don't fill three or four tubs with small hard objects, why are they there? And how many Italian men hang out the washing?

Then the rush up the stairs, the purchase of the plastic flag, the squeeze through the broad corridor, past the bar, serving alcohol-free beer and espresso, and at last out through the tunnel into the great spectacle of the stadium.

'There,' Michele groans. 'It's all taken.'

We usually sit towards the edge of the *curva*, above the corner flag to the right of the goal.

'Move!' I tell him. 'Go! There are still a few gaps.'

'Just people holding places for friends.'

My son is the most stubborn and instinctive of pessimists, something I thank him for, since it stimulates a rare optimism in his father. This can be particularly important after you have attended a get-together like Écrire l'Europe.

'Go!' We stumble over steps and seats and feet and are halfway across the section that ends in a high spiked fence, when a voice calls, 'He là! He là!' Pietro has saved seats for us.

I know almost nothing about this man. He must be thirty-something, tall, curly-haired, bright-eyed with a large, comically square chin of the kind usually associated with the Australian outback. Throughout the game he sits forward, rubbing his hands together with excitement and nervousness, rolling up his programme tight and beating it on his wrist. '*Dagliela bene!*' he always yells. 'Pass it well!' Inevitably the shout comes after one of our players has given the ball away. Pietro shakes his head. Sometime early last year I found myself embracing him after some particularly unexpected goal. Since then, unasked but profusely thanked, he has always held seats for us. Still, I never imagined he would do this the first day of the new season, after a three-month break. I can't understand why we are privileged in this way.

The other man Pietro holds a seat for is a sharp-looking chain-smoker with Latin dark features, black shiny jacket and black shiny wraparound glasses. They speak in dialect. They are old friends. I can only assume that they are amused by the way I occasionally break out into English imprecations, by the fact that I take the game so seriously despite not being Veronese. Certainly more seriously than any government takes writing. In any event, we like each other.

'*Ciao Pietro! Ciao tutti!*'

All the familiar faces are there. The pessimist. The boy with the copper hair. The two women to our left. They are always there, at least half an hour before the game. Once, in spring, when the days grow longer and schedules change, Mick and I got the time of the game wrong and arrived an hour earlier than usual, which is to say almost two hours before kick-off. Pietro was already there, already in the exact seat he always likes to take, with oceans of empty space all around.

'How early do you arrive?' I asked him.

'Early.' Then he added, 'Very early.'

'But why?'

'Eager,' he said.

'I bet you've been thinking of this game all week.'

The man has a charming smile. 'You bet you.'

Another day, killing time before the game, fresh from reading one of those pieces of Sunday newspaper research that claim that men think about sex at least once every thirty seconds, I asked him, 'About how often do you think of football, Pietro, I mean, our relegation prospects, the players, the goals, the next game? While you're at work, for example, how often do you think about football?'

'About every thirty seconds,' Pietro said.

Today he says, 'It's been a hell of a long time, no? Three months. *Olimpiadi di merda*. God knows what the team will be like.'

'I went to Bari,' I told him. 'We weren't that bad.' At once I'm aware of boasting.

'Bari!'

People are turning round. They can't believe I went to Bari. Eight hundred and fifty kilometres. They want to know what the game was like. They listen attentively. And Mutu? And Gilardino? What about the penalty? I can see I'm going to be treated with greater respect this year.

'Did you watch the *nazionale*?' Michele leans across to ask Pietro.

No sooner was the season finally started than it was interrupted for a week to let the national Italian team play a couple of World Cup qualifiers against Romania and Georgia.

'Couldn't be bothered,' Pietro says. He's the fifth or six football fan who's said this to me. 'No, we were in the mountains picking mushrooms,' they say, as if this were sufficient explanation. 'No, I had to go and watch my daughter play volleyball.' They would never miss seeing Verona for such trivia.

A journalist called me up from *Gazzetta dello Sport* to say he was preparing a book on the great teams of the last thirty years and had I followed Hellas Verona in the miraculous 1985. I had to admit, not without an old chagrin, that I hadn't. I hadn't had a son as an excuse at the time. I couldn't plead family matters and male bonding. To avoid the memory of one of life's great missed opportunities, I ask him, 'What do you think of Trapattoni's Italy?' The national team has a new coach. 'Couldn't care less,' the sports journalist says. 'I'm a Genoa fan.'

'I was going to watch the Romania game,' Pietro says. 'But when I saw Mutu wasn't playing, I couldn't be bothered.'

It's two weeks, then, since Verona's debut and perhaps the only interesting piece of news meantime is that The Wall, the fans' chat line, has indeed been closed down. The man sitting in front of Pietro confirms this. At once, I ask myself: is this related to the developments in the ongoing case of Luìs Marsiglia?

Plausibly, there are other reasons. With the change of sponsors, from sausages to high tech, the club's website will have to be restyled, just as the thousands of plastic season tickets, already produced, have had to be redesigned and produced again. The manufacture of dreams is not exempt from tiresome details, and in this sense the long delay of the first home game has no doubt been a godsend. It also gave the team the chance to make a last-second purchase of another under-twenty-one star, Emiliano Bonazzoli.

But despite the announced 'restyling' (an English word the Italians love to use), Net Business had promised that they would keep The Wall open so that everyone could go on sending messages like: '*Pastorello bandito*, keep your money, funerals are expensive!' Except that in the few days before it mysteriously shut down people had begun writing abusive things about Marsiglia. '*Grazie Marsiglia, ebreo di merda*', for example. Perhaps the powers-that-be have decided to remove this space for anti-Semitism until the case blows over.

The abuse was sparked off by the discovery that the Religious Instruction teacher never had a degree in theology, that there never was a fire in the library of the university of Montevideo and that the letter from a Uruguayan priest and professor claiming that Marsiglia had taken his degree was a fake. Interestingly, it has been the church authorities, not the police, who have been making the appropriate investigations. Having done so much to help the man, they feel betrayed by his public renunciation of Christianity. Inevitably, the more facts emerge to suggest that Marsiglia is not quite what he claims to be, the more the press insists, and rightly so, that none of this remotely excuses a racist assault.

Racism is very much on Italy's mind at the moment, particularly the more middle-class, ostensibly religious variety known as Catholic *integralismo*. The sentiment is best summed up in a suggestion made two weeks ago by Bologna's Cardinal Biffi that Italy should accept only Christian and preferably Catholic immigrants, since the country is in danger, the cardinal fears, of becoming predominantly Muslim.

A nostalgic dream is at work here, a dream of returning to the Italy I arrived in twenty years ago where, to my immense surprise, coming as I did then from a bedsit in Acton and an office job in Shepherd's Bush, I found that there was not a single black face on the streets. The great invasion from Africa was yet to begin. And if each town was potentially at war with the next, locked into that endless internecine struggle which is Italian unity, still each community within itself was homogeneous to the point of suffocation. Verona in particular was asphyxiatingly Catholic.

Now things have changed, dramatically. Now in the humdrum bar where I go to read the *Gazzetta dello Sport* every morning over a cappuccino, I find an earnest man called Mohammed trying to explain to the savvy old *barista* that he has three wives and is about to take a fourth. This man sits in the bar for hours, invariably wearing a black woolly hat on woolly black hair, and usually what he does is lay his cheek on the Formica-topped table and fall asleep. But today he is scribbling fiercely on a large piece of lined paper. 'To my wife-to-be,' he says, and explains his complicated family position. 'What about the mothers-in-law?' the *barista* asks pertinently. 'Do they get on?' At the next table, the pensioners arguing over their card-games can't decide whether they're envious or horrified.

And on the train, coming back late from Milan where I teach, four black prostitutes share my compartment and one of them is reading the Bible. Italian Catholics, I tell myself, watching the solemn face of this fat young woman licking her finger to turn the pages, do not as a rule read the Bible, never mind Italian prostitutes, and certainly not on the train. I have never understood why the black prostitutes of northern Italy move around from town to town in the evening and always on the train. Clearly someone is organising them. From the Bible-reader's conversation, in English, as the journey progresses, it turns out that she is a Baptist. Martin Laursen, declared man of the match at Bari, is a Lutheran. So the local paper tells me. Does either of them know, I wonder, that last September the Pope pleased many of her potential customers, many of his most loyal fans, by reasserting in an official encyclical that the Catholic Church is actually the *only* church and, above all, the only way to eternal life?

Luìs Marsiglia, meantime, having renounced that church and hence deprived himself of eternal life, continues to have his mortal existence heavily protected by the police, while a considerable group of left-wing students, arch enemies of the Brigate Gialloblù, are still spending their nights on the pavement beneath his bedroom window. Only yesterday, however, having failed to find any right-wing hotheads who might have been responsible for the attack, the police raided the very apartment they are supposed to be protecting, Marsiglia's home, and took away the threatening leaflets we have all seen him photographed with on so many occasions. Why wasn't this evidence examined at once, one wonders? And why is our trainer Perotti suddenly fielding a player we've never seen before, a player not even on the bench at Bari? Giuseppe Colucci. Another Colucci? Another southerner. Who's even heard of him?

Under the leaden sky, beneath a frenzy of banners and confetti, the teams begin to play. Not two minutes pass before Udinese hit the post, a shot through a scramble of players following a cross. Then only two minutes later Verona likewise hit the post after a move of such rapid and elegant execution that I can hardly believe it's our lot producing it. A beautiful move. All of a sudden, people sit up; the boys seem to have made a huge qualitative leap. There is that rapid patterning of passes, that sense of geometry in four dimensions, at once shape and flow, that makes football so enchanting. And now they're doing it again. They're attacking again. Giuseppe Colucci is at the heart of it. He lifts his head. He places the ball. He rushes for space and receives it again, dribbles round his man. Who the hell is he? 'From Bordeaux,' Pietro says. He shrugs his shoulders. 'Italian playing in France. Just turned twenty. He's never played in Serie A before.'

So that first quarter of an hour was a revelation. In only fifteen minutes, the inadequate-seeming Perotti, bandy-legged and bespectacled, mild-mannered and dull in interviews, had impressed the Curva Sud. The *brigate* had forgotten Prandelli, they had stopped yelling *Pastorello vaffanculo*. We have a team. The kids can play. *Facci sognare*, flutters the banner. And then it began to rain.

'*Giove pluvio*', tomorrow's *Gazzetta* will say, 'doesn't understand a damn thing about football.' *Giove pluvio* is Jupiter the rain god; it's an expression used to refer to only the heaviest of downpours, in this case an unremitting thundery grey deluge that would last right up to the final whistle. Within moments the ball has ceased to bounce. Passes stop dead. The goalkeeper fumbles. Puddles begin to appear, then ponds. It's dangerous playing in these conditions. These expensive athletes, super-trained, endlessly spoiled, are hurling themselves at each other like urchins in a paddling pool. They are falling left and right, and not on purpose for once. There are sprays of mud. Shirts and shorts are barely recognisable. 'Stop the game!' someone shouts. But the game cannot be stopped, because there are television rights; there's the Totocalcio, the pools; there are fifteen thousand spectators. Then a minute from half-time Captain Colucci (old Leo Colucci that is) goes down, his legs sliding open in a frightening split. He twists, shouts and raises a hand. Immediately, you understand it's serious. Colucci never raises his hand. Colucci is the toughest. Our absolutely key man. He's stretchered off and substituted.

During the interval the talk is all outrage that the game hasn't been stopped, and then memories of other games that should have been stopped. Do you remember Fiorentina in the fog, so thick that when we scored our second the *curva* only knew because of a roar from the other end? Or Torino in the snow? Do you remember that? The covers were taken off the pitch two hours before the game, just as the blizzard began. The game went ahead anyway, it always does, in a couple of inches of slush and ice. Torino scored, had two men sent off, then spent the rest of the match in their area defending. Successfully. That game should definitely have been stopped. It was scandalous. This game too should obviously be stopped.

But secretly no one wants it to be stopped. It's a scandal, they say, but everybody's thinking: what if *we* snatch that goal, then pack the area till the end? They'll never get through this marsh. And everybody's thinking: let them battle it out, that's what they're bloody well paid for. That's what *we've* paid for. Nobody, I would guess, and least of all myself, has so much as a thought for Leo Colucci, whom, as it turns out, we shall not be seeing again for a very long time.

The referee reappears with a player from each team to check if the pitch is playable. If you're looking for a good example of the role of the rule in Italian life, here it is. The rule states that when thrown in the air to a height of three metres or so the ball must bounce in such a way as to clear the ground. So, the referee throws the ball up in the air, the players' heads lift, the Curva Sud begins a rising roar, as when someone runs up to take a penalty, the ball peaks and starts to come down, the roar reaches its climax, the ball hits the grass, throws up a shower of water and sticks firm. The fans cheer.

Players and referee consult. The referee walks a few paces. He's put on a dry kit. He looks neat. Again he throws up the ball, again the players raise their heads, again the *curva* roars and again the ball comes down with a splash and stays put.

The referee is perplexed. What is he getting another kit wet for if they're not going to play? They have to play. The game is on cable TV. Some viewers will have paid already. Others will want to know if they've won a billion lire on the Totocalcio before five o'clock. Heads are bent in discussion. The referee walks a good bit across the pitch, testing the ground with his toes. The ball is thrown up higher, much higher. The result is the same. It's only on the fifth or sixth attempt that at last a piece of stubborn ground is found and an uncertain bounce is produced. The *curva* cheer. Anybody can see the game should be stopped, but we don't want it stopped. The problem is the rule. But a rule is there to be stretched to the limit. The referee throws the ball up again making sure it lands in exactly the same place. He watches its squelchy bounce. Good. He throws it up again, then again, always in the same place, then, at last, raises his whistle to his lips. The rule has apparently been satisfied. It's important that a rule be seen to be satisfied. And that's the referee's job. Now the game can go on. Relieved, everybody remarks what a disgusting farce this is. 'Perhaps they're supposed to play the whole game on that one square metre,' Pietro suggests.

The players troop out. During the break they have been reminded how to play in these conditions. It's back to basics. Foot under the ball, hike it up over the opponent. Don't imagine you can run with it. Just kick it on. And however remote the chance, shoot, the keeper may drop it. Above all, be physical; no, be violent! What a far cry from the first few dazzling minutes.

Perotti has taken off Mutu who doesn't know what to do with a ball if he can't dribble past his opponent. This handsome young Romanian's vision of the game must be very similar to my own when I was nine years old. It's a picture of yourself leaving four or five defenders behind, running round an impotent goalkeeper, perhaps leaping over the hand that seeks to grab your foot, then stopping the ball on the line and raising your arms to the adoring crowd who will for ever remember you as one of the great geniuses of all time. Mutu is not a man for a swamp.

So the foreign star is replaced by the new boy, Bonazzoli, a very English looking centre-forward, all height and weight and muscle and long straggly hair held tight by a bandanna. In the *curva* the wise heads acknowledge the wisdom of this decision. But just five minutes into the game, it's the more slender Gilardino, the pretty-boy blond, who surprises us. He picks up a through ball on the edge of the box, drags it along in the mud as if his left leg were a hockey stick, and simply scoops it past the approaching keeper.

Goal! First goal of the season in the Bentegodi. First goal for Gilardino in front of his new fans. The boy runs to the corner flag, takes his blue shirt off, waves it wildly over his head and is promptly shown a yellow card. Why players want to take their shirts off, I have never understood. Especially in this rain. Why isn't waving the arms enough? But then why should they be booked for the gesture when the crowd appreciate it so much? There's a sullenness to the rules of football that I have never quite fathomed, a niggardliness that is essential to the game. The fans must feel that the referee is against them, even when they have just scored.

Never mind. Like communicants in the Pope's one true church, but with a little more faith and conviction, all the fans are embracing, they're roaring. Now pack the box, Verona, pack the box in the mud, hang on forty minutes and we've done it!

Every Monday morning the *Gazzetta dello Sport* offers various sketches of the previous day's moves to goal – there are arrows and numbers and the same players will be drawn two or three times in different positions on the field. Often, in the bar over my coffee, I examine these sketches and puzzle over them and try to figure out who was where when, and every time I do so I'm bound to reflect that it's impossible to represent football on paper, or even on the two dimensions of the TV screen. Many things must flow together, knowingly, coherently through time and space and against determined resistance, before you can score a deserved goal. More often, many things will tumble together only half-knowingly, or even totally accidentally and in lucky complicity precisely with the determined resistance – a crucial deflection, for example – and you have scored a quite undeserved goal. But either way, the spectator up in the *curva* stares down at the players embracing and the goalkeeper kicking the post in anger and wonders how it happened. The day after this game with Udinese, I studied the sketch in the *Gazzetta* and shook my head. How, oh how, I ask myself, in what was now an Irish bog, did Udinese get through the eleven guys packed in the box and stick that ball in the net?

According to the *Gazzetta*, which is a serious paper, it had to do with an astute decision on the part of Udinese's trainer, De Canio. After Verona's goal he took out the Norwegian Jorgensen in midfield, brought on a no-name defender, and moved the big Ghanaian international, Gargo, hitherto at left back, up into the centre of the pitch, where Colucci was now conspicuous by his absence, thus taking control of the midfield.

The *Gazzetta* of course has a vested interest in the idea that such very precise reorganisations can bring about predictable results. Otherwise how could football be given that aura of scientific solemnity that people seem to need nowadays before they can let themselves go, before they can justify the purchase of a paper every day? How could the game be endlessly pondered over and the myth of the great manager fed? Yet, suspicious as I am when I read the *Gazzetta*'s assessments, I too spend half the game jumping up and down and shrieking why doesn't the trainer take this or that guy off the pitch. Why doesn't he bring on so and so? Move so and so here or there. I too firmly believe that if given the chance I would be an excellent manager. I would revolutionise football. Nobody will ever prove me wrong.

In any event, Gargo did make the difference. Interviewed the day before the game, this immensely talented player, black as coal, shiny as granite, newly arrived in the *bel paese*, claimed that he was going to make the Italians love him; he was going to eliminate racism from Italian stadiums, quite simply because people would admire and love him so much for the generous and gentlemanly and humble and dedicated way he played. A certain amount of delirium and narcissism is essential, I reflected, on reading this interview, for today's hard-pressed sportsman to find the dedication he needs to keep going. Much the same could be said of the novelist.

And anyway, Gargo continued to the willing pressmen, racism wasn't actually *that* bad in Italian stadiums. 'Italy doesn't have a big racist problem in the stadiums,' Gargo told the journalists. For someone in the entertainment business, I reflected on reading those words, a candid determination to please is another useful quality. Again the same is true of the novelist. I must keep my eye on this boy.

Dominating the midfield throughout the second half, Gargo was relentlessly and shamelessly taunted every single time he touched the ball. Oo, oo, oo! Invariably, whenever he passed or was passed to, the core of the Curva Sud burst out in a barrage of monkey grunts, arms pumping up and down as if they were scaling trees. It was hateful. But it only seemed to encourage the black man to do even more to make people love him, to make people see how brilliant and humble and generous he was. He pushed ahead remorselessly. He played with style. And he sent one long ball after another through the defence to the head and feet of Udinese's simply monstrous centre-forward, Muzzi.

Intimidated, the yellow-blues fell back. There is no team more scared than Verona when they are winning. The rain poured and poured and one or two areas of the pitch had begun to reflect what little light was left in the sky. Big Muzzi pushed and shoved and kicked and spat. The water splashed about him. The referee gave fouls against him and eventually showed him a yellow card, but never looked like sending the man off. He was doing his job. And then at last, in a mill of players after a high free kick that bobbed here, there and everywhere, Muzzi controlled the ball rather clumsily between shoulder and neck and struck it past the goalkeeper.

'Ferron is a Mongol!' exploded the man who sits behind me. This man, who has sat behind me at the Bentegodi for at least five years now, always has a pet hate. This season, I fear, it will be our goalkeeper Fabrizio Ferron. 'Why did Pastorello get us a Mongol in goal? And an old one at that. Hey Grandfather Ferron, you're a Mongol!' Muzzi's shot had come from a mêlée about three yards out and was slammed into the top left-hand corner of Ferron's goal. How could anyone have saved it? But I concede that there are moments when it's hard to be reasonable.

Driving home, Michele and I stopped to contemplate the Adige. 'We were lucky to get away with a draw,' I told him. The river was rolling and foaming down between its bridges, a strong brown god, untamed and intractable. Great logs and debris bobbed and dipped and banged in the flood. 'We should have had two penalties,' Michele insisted. He was sullen.

Floods were also the main subject on TV when we got home. There was flooding in Piedmont, flooding in Lombardy, a flood alert along the Po and another on the Adige. We changed channel and watched 'Novantesimo Minuto', where RAI's round-up of the day's sport always contrives to show highlights of Verona's game last or not at all.

'You see!' Michele yelled. 'You see!'

He was right, damn it! There had been two clear penalties. His eyes are better than mine. A very deliberate handball on the edge of the six-yard box, then Gilardino sandwiched and bundled over in an evident scoring position just two minutes from time. 'OK, make a note,' I said, 'we'll keep a tally of how many times they didn't give us a penalty. We'll see at the end of the season where we might have been.' Football offers unlimited opportunities for the mathematics of might-have-been, close cousin of paranoia.

Flooding was still almost the only feature on the news the following evening when I turned on the TV in a hotel in Milan. Since I teach in the city Monday afternoon and again on Tuesday morning, I stay in a hotel for the night. Huge mudslides, it seemed, were sweeping through villages not a hundred kilometres away from where I lay, remote control in hand. Cars were tumbling upside-down through the main streets of Piedmont. Bridges collapsed. Press and politicians were engaged in the usual back and forth of accusation and denial over poor environmental planning. Grim victims interrupted their mud-shovelling to talk to pretty young journalists. One clip, endlessly repeated, showed three or four buildings sliding down a mountainside. It was awesome.

All the same, on changing channel I was able to watch a more interesting programme that set out to analyse almost the whole, it seemed to me, of Inter's game the day before with Napoli, even examining in detail and from various angles things like the back pass, how to slow the rhythm of a game before half-time, different techniques for throw-ins, and so on. A small man with flappy ears and disturbingly thick spectacles leaned forward over his studio desk and became extremely excited about the psychology of 'administrating the one-goal lead'. A well-endowed blonde with a pretty lisp disagreed.

Is there anything, I wondered, as the rain fell heavily outside on the streets of Milan, as it teemed down on the dark plain of Lombardy to the south and the great lakes and mountains to the north, is there really anything more important than football? Sometimes it seems to me that all today's progress in electronics is being made only and exclusively to further a more complete, a more satisfying representation of football. Soon there will be holograms of football, miniature holograms on your sitting-room floor, allowing you to follow the game and play and replay the crucial moments. And still you'll never understand. No, I'll never understand how we let Udinese score in conditions like that, in a situation where they pretty well had to swim towards the goal. It was water polo, for God's sake. Waking in the middle of the night, a doubt occurs to me: was Muzzi perhaps offside when he received that ball? I must see the video again.

2A GIORNATA

Bologna – Milan   2–1
Brescia – Parma   0–0
Fiorentina – Reggina   2–1
Inter – Napoli   3–1
Juventus – Bari   2–0
Lazio – Perugia   3–0
Lecce – Roma   0–4
Verona – Udinese   1–1
Vicenza – Atalanta   1–2

CLASSIFICA

Roma	6
Juventus	6
Lazio	4
Udinese	4
Atalanta	4
Fiorentina	4
Inter	3
Milan	3
Reggina	3
Bologna	3
Verona	2
Parma	2
Brescia	1
Bari	1
Lecce	1
Perugia	1
Napoli	0
Vicenza	0

Rigore

SADNESS is the only word that comes to mind in this moment. Sadness not only for the club we have and the miserable squad, but sadness too for how we're treated by the national media.
  Paruca, brigate@piu–mati.it

'You might liken Patrick Vieira to an antelope, or a giraffe, or a flamingo,' writes *La Repubblica*, 'but not to a monkey. You could call him polite, reasonable, gentle, but not a "*merda*". Mihajlovic got it wrong.'

Mihajlovic, the Lazio left back and international star, has admitted that in Tuesday's Champions' League game against Arsenal he called Vieira, the Arsenal striker and French international star, a '*scimmia di merda*' – a fucking monkey. As if to remind us that newspapers also sometimes get things wrong (Vieira 'gentle'? Vieira a 'flamingo'?) the article is headed: 'from our correspondent, St Albany, Hertfordshire'.

St Albany? For a moment it crosses my mind that they might have changed the Hertfordshire place-names in these twenty years I've been away. Could this be an Americanisation, a globalisation of St Albans? One thing that's certain is that *La Repubblica* has now officially changed its position on Luìs Marsiglia. 'We owe Verona an apology,' begins the main editorial in the same day's paper. Marsiglia has confessed that he made up the whole story: no nazi skinheads attacked him; there is no need to raid the homes of the Brigate Gialloblù to find their clubs and crowbars. Meantime Mihajlovic is coming to the Bentegodi this Sunday. Verona are playing last year's champions. It's our first impossible game.

Why do football and racism keep getting mixed up? The interview with Vieira is interesting. 'What really offended me', says Vieira, 'wasn't this or that word, monkey or bastard, but that Mihajlovic really believed what he was saying. It wasn't part of the game, he wasn't saying it to provoke me, or to make me screw up and foul him. He really meant it. You could see it in his eyes.'

Vieira distinguishes then between a racism that is part of a game of insults on the pitch and a more brutal gut hatred. He isn't thinking 'racist' or 'not racist', but in shades (as it were) of racism: nominal racism, gamesmanship racism, gut racism. In his defence, Mihajlovic claims that it was Vieira started it all by calling him a *sporco zingaro di merda*, a dirty fucking gypsy. 'I am proud of being a gypsy,' Mihajlovic says, 'it's not my fault if Vieira has problems being black.' The belligerent Serb is promptly fined thirty thousand pounds and banned for two Champions' League matches.

Responding to Arsenal's complaints about the constant barracking of their black players by the Italian fans, Lazio's president, Sergio Cragnotti, all elegant suit and tie, says, 'We're not fascist, the truth is they don't want us to win.' It's interesting that *La Repubblica*, always willing to extend the racism of Verona's fans to the whole of the city, does not do the same when reporting on the Lazio game. Perhaps, in the way some people will limit sexual peccadilloes to trips away from home, Italy is eager to circumscribe its racism in the Veneto: southerners are poor and *simpatici*, northerners, or north-easterners, are rich and bigoted. This is the projected stereotype. But like it or not, it's beginning to look like tomorrow's match with Lazio will be a meeting of minds. On the same day that Marsiglia at last confesses, the Hellas website miraculously restores the famous Wall and within twenty-four hours this message has appeared:

LAZIO AND VERONA, UNITED IN THE FIGHT
ROME AND NAPLES, PIECES OF SHITE.
AGAINST NE.GROES THE ONLY TWO CLUBS
TO HAVE BEEN CONSISTENT AND WORTHY

OF RESPECT IN THE WORLD OF FAN EXTREM-
ISM: VERONA AND LAZIO. NEVER A FALSE
STEP, NEVER A RETREAT, FOR BETTER OR
WORSE [but the literal translation would be: 'in good and
in evil'] HONOUR TO THE UNMOVABLE ONES
AND THE BRIGATE GIALLOBLU.

In good and in evil, unmovable. Identity is more important than
morality. Extremism offers an excitement that moderation cannot
afford. The word negroes is written with a full stop in the middle to
avoid The Wall's censorship system. Defending political correctness
with high tech smacks of Canute rebuking the sea.

But aside from Lazio–Arsenal, another English–Italian encounter
that took place this week was Her Majesty Queen Elizabeth's visit
to Milan. To my surprise, I found myself invited to a morning
reception in the beautiful Palazzo Marino opposite La Scala. No
French blacks or Serb gypsies ruffled the cordial surface of this
encounter of thoroughbred Limeys and Eyties, but on the city
streets outside the familiar lines of policemen held back the crowd,
while once in the *palazzo* the guests showed that tendency to divide
into two camps that occurs in every stadium.

When the Queen finally appeared I was struck by the truth of
something my wife has always maintained: Elizabeth II does indeed
look rather like my mother. She even dresses the same way, though
Mrs Parks achieves the effect less expensively. So that even if I didn't
quite get to shake the royal hand (it hovered for a moment six inches
away), I nevertheless felt a keen sense of national, even racial, identity. 'The Italians are OK,' an ex-navy admiral told me, an engaging
man with all the best of the old school tie about him, 'but you'll only
regret it,' he went on, and gave examples, 'if you ever trust a Slav.'

Mihajlovic, I thought! The game. I can't wait for the game.
How dull this reception is, I soon decided, perhaps even duller – is
that possible? – than Écrire l'Europe. 'Laursen for King,' someone
was yelling after the game with Udinese. The Verona fans are
quite happy to crown a foreigner, though not as yet a black; as
the British were quite happy some time ago to accept a German

on the throne, but would hardly have brought back a tribal leader from the colonies. If my mother looks like the Queen, I reflect, on the train going home, gazing up at the mountains that divide northern and southern Europe, does that mean that I have German blood in my veins? Is there no end to the world's endless mixing? After all, it's only a month or two since a casual conversation in the family led to the discovery that my great-grandmother was Jewish. How hard it is to feel that one is any one thing in particular! The miracle is that everyone keeps trying.

Marsiglia, for one. Luìs Marsiglia claims he was obliged to leave Uruguay because the right-wing Catholic organisation Opus Dei had it in for him for his left-wing views. He was then convinced that the well-to-do families whose children go to the Liceo Maffei had it in for him because he was Jewish. Clearly at some point Marsiglia chose to assume the identity of the victim. This is his way to selfhood. As a Jew, society and history offered him the role. He worked at it, in the teeth of a world that sought to help him and kind neighbours who brought him salamis and Valpolicella when he hadn't even been hurt. Unpersecuted, Marsiglia wouldn't know who he was. In this, curiously, he is not unlike some Veronese who can't wait to be outraged when the press treat them badly, or again like so many fans from all over the world who won't feel satisfied until the referee shows his bias against them. One thing is certain: had Marsiglia ever stepped out on to the green spaces of the Bentegodi, he would have been disappointed if there were no monkey grunts for him. Reading about his background, the endless lies he has told, it crosses my mind that perhaps he is no more Jewish than I am. This man, I tell myself, may actually be no more one of God's chosen people than Queen Victoria was English, or Paul Ince African. Identity is an effort of will.

Whatever the truth of his ethnic origins, the unhappy school-teacher was unmasked as follows: the threatening leaflets that he claimed had been sent to him were carefully examined. The headline-size letters, cut from newspapers and magazines, were unstuck. By seeing what text or photograph was on the other side of each letter and then matching this presumably unique occurrence with hundreds of editions of various publications it was soon possible to establish where those letters had come from: i.e. Marsiglia's favourite newspapers, many of them Spanish.

Declaring that he was now the object of police persecution, Marsiglia confessed. At once all kinds of information began to appear in the press: the scratches on Marsiglia's forearms and the bruising on his shins were entirely incompatible, the initial hospital report had stated, with the aggressions he described. Why weren't we told this before? During his year at the Liceo Maffei, Marsiglia made a film with his students in which he played the part of a poor tramp who gets beaten up by a group of Veronese skinheads, dies, then returns to the town as an avenging angel and slaughters his assailants. Entered at a festival in Munich, the film won first prize in a competition for films against racism. Why hadn't we been informed?

'I lost my head,' Marsiglia explains to a journalist who manages to catch up with him at the airport in Milan. Accused now of simulating a crime, he is nevertheless allowed to board a flight to Uruguay, an option rarely offered to the arrested football fan. Alone, abandoned by his supporters, he must feel more than ever his victim self. 'I was overwhelmed', he says, 'by the terrible injustice done to me when they moved me away from the Maffei. Now I have to leave', he goes on, 'because I have received a number of death threats.'

'Thank you, Marsiglia, for reminding us how proud we are to be Veronese!'

'Our grateful thanks to all those who've poured shit on our city.'

'Shock horror, Marsiglia leaves Verona because afraid of the roars of the Curva Sud.'

'Marsiglia in the stocks in Piazza Bra. With his pants down.'

Such are the voices on The Wall. Still, the question that none of the fans, nor anyone in the press for that matter, is asking is: how could such an incompetent attempt to fake an assault have been allowed to generate a national scandal for more than a month? It's true the man played to accepted stereotypes: the victim Jew, the racist Veronese. Past knowledge generates prejudice, puts the mind to sleep. When Verona play Lazio, for example, anyone who knows anything about football can be excused for presuming not only that Lazio will win but also that they will play the better football throughout and deserve to win. They are after all one of the most expensive teams in the world. You would have to come from outer space, or the USA perhaps, to imagine anything different.

All the same, however strong the premises, however persuasive the prevailing myths, is there really any excuse for not opening one's eyes? How could the famously intelligent magistrate Papalia ignore the obvious about Luìs Marsiglia for so long? More pertinent to this book, though, is the question: how could the referee not see that Lazio's striker Claudio Lopez deliberately dived in the box just a few minutes from time? How could he give the man a penalty, when it would have been evident to anyone not blinded by prejudice that Verona were playing the better football and the Roman team so desperate that their strikers were constantly diving to the ground like infidels in prayer?

But let's start at the beginning. The scene was set, the packed *curva*, the swaying banners, the shower of confetti as the players came out. Mihajlovic stepped on to the pitch to rousing cheers from the hardcore of the *curva*. True to form, the *brigate* have decided to applaud his racism. At the same time, everybody's hoping that the Serb will be nervous after all the negative attention he's been getting in the press. With any luck, he will make mistakes.

And so he does. Lazio start brilliantly, as an all-star team should. What is stardom but an a priori acknowledgment of superiority? Lazio are the best that globalisation with all its mad mixing has to offer. Second minute: the Argentinian Crespo dribbles past his man and hits inches wide of the post. Third minute: our big Dane Martin Laursen just manages to steal the ball from the naturalised Spaniard Lopez as he is about to shoot at an open goal. Fifth minute: the Czech Nedved runs past a defender and crosses beautifully to the Argentinian Simeone whose header brings an unexpected reflex save from the aging Ferron, a man who spent most of his professional life in the small provincial team of Atalanta a few miles down the road in Bergamo.

The first few minutes, then, are a vindication of the notion

that what you get is what you pay for, even when it comes to
football players. Then at last our young Gilardino breaks through,
he's headed for goal, and is at once savaged from behind by
Mihajlovic. His legs are swept away. It is a dangerous and violent
foul in a last-man situation. The referee doesn't even show the
Serb a yellow card. He could perfectly legitimately have sent him
off. From that moment on, the *curva* changes tack. Every time
Mihajlovic touches the ball he gets the monkey grunt treatment,
loud, clear and remorseless. Oo-oo-oo!

The following morning *La Gazzetta dello Sport* observes: 'Without the shadow of a black on the field, the Brigate Gialloblù begin
to taunt a gypsy.' But the only prejudice this comment reveals is
that of the journalist. He has misunderstood the kind of racism that
haunts the terraces of the Bentegodi. He is making the same mistake
as his colleagues who believed that the white Marsiglia was beaten up
because Jewish. For if football is that place where globalisation and
local dreams confront each other, the one on the pitch, the other on
the terraces, then the dividing line, at least for the *brigate*, is colour.
The whole white world, Mihajlovic included, is local, is on our side.
At least potentially. A Dane, a Serb, a pale-skinned Brazilian are all
permitted to further the antique cause of the Scaligeri, to wear the
emblem of the ladder and the city's ancient colours. Likewise they
could shout from the *curva*, as I do, if they wished. An Englishman
is welcome. For years I came with a Greek friend. He too was
white and welcome. But the black who sits slumped over the table
in a suburban bar, who shivers or sweats outside the supermarket
selling contraband cigarettes, whose children go to school with my
children, this man is beyond the pale. Only the black is not permitted
to dress in yellow and blue.

So Mihajlovic was taunted throughout the game, not because he
was a gypsy, but because he was behaving badly. Lopez got the same
treatment when he split Mutu's lip with an elbow. The referee gave
the foul, but again, inexplicably, no yellow card. Why not? These
players are behaving badly because the referee is letting them.

But, damn it, the man in black is getting nervous. He *can't* give
the champions yellow cards. For Lazio are suddenly wobbling. What

is going on? Verona are attacking. They look good. As the ball curls over from a corner, Simeone places both hands on Martin Laursen's back as he prepares to receive the ball and shoves him to the ground. It's not one of those situations where two men go up for the ball together and you can't really understand what's happened but shout penalty anyway. No, it was the most evident and calculated thing in the world. The video bears me out. Tall Laursen lowers his blond head, leans forward a little. He has given his man the slip. He only has to nod the ball into the net, and instead he suddenly plunges forward on his hands and knees, Simeone is already protesting his innocence behind. The whole *curva* rises to its feet. Penalty! The referee waves his arm. Play on.

The Italian word for penalty is '*rigore*', which is to say, 'rigour', 'severity', 'harshness'. Sometimes a TV commentator will say, 'My hypothesis is that in that encounter there were indeed, technically speaking, grounds for the ultimate sanction.' Which is to say: if the rule were applied severely (any rule applied in Italy is applied severely) that should have been a *rigore*. But the referee today, a certain Signor Trentalange, is not going to apply the rules with the champions of Italy. He no more gives a penalty against them than he will show a yellow card to Mihajlovic when once again he brings Gilardino down from behind. A few moments later our midfielder Italiano tackles a Lazio player from behind and is at once shown a yellow card. The time has come to say something about referees.

Who would ever do the job? is the first question. The player plays to display his talents, to achieve, to win, to be admired by women, to make money, and then because he loves playing, or at least he used to when he was a kid. The pitch, the stadium, the TV screen, they have become the chosen arena in which he measures himself against the world, and through which he establishes his particular identity: striker or defender, constant or capricious, dynamo or sylph, team player or individual, ice-cool or eternally irascible. Every sport offers its archetypes and every player wants to embody one of them, or some novel combination. 'I want to be the new Hagi,' Mutu says in an interview immediately before the Lazio game. The older Romanian star, sly and dangerous as ever, was present at the young man's wedding. Our tiny Argentinian midfielder, Camoranesi, bought this summer from some team no one's heard of in Mexico, denies any similarity with Maradona, but admits that he consciously models himself on his idol Romario. Fulfilling the fans' dreams, the player seeks to become an idol himself, he dreams of seeing himself reflected in ten thousand pairs of dreaming eyes, arms raised to the ecstatic *curva. Gol!* At that moment, he exists more fully than the ordinary human being, his life vibrates with intensity. In this thirst for adoration, the player, I think, is not unlike the artist. Megalomania is an easy thing to understand.

But who would be a referee? Above all, who would be a referee in Italy, a country that admires flare more than fairness, that has always put style before rectitude, or conveniently confused the two, a country where there is absolutely no stigma attached to a profitable breaking of the rules, whether it be the offside trap or the VAT return?

I can only sketch a hypothesis. Wherever there is a vocation for anarchy, there are inevitably those who yearn for stability, who will support any display of authority, if only perhaps out of a spirit of contrariness. Commenting on the fragmentation of Italian politics, an editorial in *Corriere della Sera* says: 'Imagine we travel the length and breadth of this country and find a hundred people all in agreement over the same issue. We bring them together; within two hours I guarantee that we will have a hundred separate opinions. And then there will be one person yearning to *force* all the others to agree.' The referee. Perhaps he is genuinely weary of division. Or perhaps he is just a spoilsport. Certainly to deny ten thousand shrieking fans the most deserved of penalties must be a great pleasure for the person the Italians describe as a '*guastafeste*' – one who ruins parties. When our other midfield player, Mazzola, throws the ball away, the referee who has let pass a dozen brutal fouls immediately presents him with a yellow card for wasting time. That will show everybody who's boss.

The only doubt that remains is whether the authority the referee imposes is that of the rules of Association Football, or that of the status quo, the powerful teams who, with much bickering, control Italy's football league? 'The reason Roma are doing well', my small thickly bespectacled man shrieks on Monday night's football programme 'is that they now have a few saints in paradise, don't they?' By which he means, of course, that they now have powerful supporters in the Federation, people who can influence the refereeing. Knowing which saint to pray to was ever more important than the ultimate right or wrong of what one was requesting. And it's not a question here of anyone taking back-handers for this or that decision. The truth is that a referee feels genuine respect for the big and powerful team. They have spent a lot of money on the world's best players. They can influence his career track. How is he to behave if they start losing to a bunch of unsavoury provincial racist also-rans? On the other hand twenty thousand people just saw that foul.

A good referee must have an appetite for such dilemmas. Like many spoilsports, he is also a masochist. His pleasure will come when he rides a fine line, walks a tightrope with success. One favourite solution is to blow for all the fouls, but give the yellow cards mainly one way, since such decisions are rarely examined on late-night highlights. A player with a yellow card is a player in a strait-jacket. He risks going off. But above all, the referee must be able *to imagine himself fair*, no, to *know* he is being fair, when in fact he is being patently unfair. If he achieves that, if he can defend his decisions with a clear conscience against all the evidence, he will win the recognition that rightly goes to those who do a miserable job for society: the shit-shovellers, the grave-diggers, the executioners . . .

Was this, then, the game when it occurred to me that Italy should bring in foreign referees for Serie A games, men with other cultural backgrounds and mental constructs? I was proud of the idea and even thought of writing to some authority somewhere, until I discovered that the experiment had already been made in 1957. Presumably it was so successful that they had to stop it. Or perhaps the foreign referees simply adapted to the environment. Another corrective to the evident bias of refereeing was tried in 1984–85 when the referees for each game were selected entirely at random. That year Verona won the championship and again the experiment was terminated, or at least 'corrected'. Now the Federation draws up a short list of suitable referees for each game, then draws from that list by lot. The football magazine entitled, wait for it, *Rigore*, is frequently able to 'predict' which name will come out of the urn.

In any event, nil–nil still at half-time with the core of the *curva* inventing a little song:

> *Ma quanto insegna ben, il Professor Marsiglia,*
> *Ma quanto prega ben, il Professor Marsiglia.*

How well he teaches, how well he prays, Professor Marsiglia! When the fans come to the word prays they all put their hands together and bow their heads a moment. Giggling. Marsiglia, it seems, prayed to the wrong saints. Nil–nil is always a good result with Lazio.

Then only seven minutes after half-time, someone scores. Alas for Signor Trentalange, it was the wrong team. Mutu dribbled the ball down to Lazio's touch-line, hit a low cross in the middle which caught a defender on the ankle and went in. Unbelievable. And the fantastic thing about a goal like this is that there is really no way a referee can disallow it. There can be no offside because a single player has taken the ball from midfield to touch-line, then passed it backwards. What's more, there can be no foul because there was simply no other Verona player near the ball when the defender put it past his keeper. A referee can be forgiven then for awarding a goal like this. But now he has his work cut out.

One can imagine his anxiety growing. The Curva Sud are dreaming of a quite unexpected victory. The applause is deafening. Lazio attack in wave after classy wave, but without breaking through. Finally Lopez beats the goalkeeper with an angled shot. Ferron gets a glove to the ball, but only enough to slow it down. The crowd waits hushed as the ball trickles towards the net. It has about three yards to go. It is bouncing along. This is it, the equaliser. The referee is raising his whistle in eager anticipation. But he has reckoned without the young Massimo Oddo. This promising young defender, after a sprint of some twenty metres, hurls himself on his back across the muddy six-yard box, hooks an improbable foot round the ball and sweeps it away at the very last second. The referee looks at the linesman. Did it go in? The man hasn't raised his flag.

Ten minutes later Trentalange is again impotent when Verona score their second. Mutu suddenly has the ball just outside the box. Again he dribbles round his man and this time shoots cleanly into the goal. How can this be disallowed? It's infuriating. Everybody is going mad. Concentrating, the referee contrives to give Lazio a series of fouls around the edge of the area. Some of these are no doubt real and serious fouls. Apolloni and Laursen, the two central defenders, are nervous and under pressure. They are as ready to foul as any defender. But there's a lot of pushing and falling going on, a lot of pantomime. Appetising place-kicks are lined up. Shot after shot goes over the bar. What's wrong with these stars? Why can't they put the ball in the net? That offensive racist grunting must be upsetting them, though none of them is black. Then a filthy foul from Mazzola provides Signor Trentalange with the excuse to send a Verona player off and make things a little easier. Still the stars make no progress. Time is running out. If only they could get one goal, surely Verona would lose their nerve. They would be blown away in a last-minute onslaught. It's happened before.

Suddenly Apolloni and Lopez are chasing a through ball into the box. Apolloni, like Ferron, is another aging and now inexpensive player whom Pastorello wisely brought into the team at a particularly gloomy moment last year. Lopez is the young and supremely expensive striker Lazio bought this summer. No sooner have the two men crossed the line into the area than the Spaniard falls over. With what relief the referee blows his whistle! *Rigore!* 'Very generous,' the *Gazzetta* will wryly remark the following morning. Perhaps the champions can still do it.

Surprisingly it's Mihajlovic who comes up to take the kick. Lazio have any number of penalty-takers, but it's the big bad Serb who's going to hit it. Why? Why expose himself like this? Does he want to show us that the barracking hasn't bothered him? He's shooting into the goal directly below the *curva*. The whistles and monkey grunts are deafening. All around me people are shrieking and shaking their fists. Strangely I'm calm. My son is yelling to my right. Pietro is yelling to my left. While all around leap to their feet, I keep my seat and simply will the guy to miss. Miss it, miss it, miss it! I can't bear the idea that after being two–nil up we could blow it all in the last three or four minutes. Miss it, damn you! But this man is a specialist. He won't miss it. He places the ball, looks up from beneath cropped hair, narrow eyes, high cheekbones, granite features. He knows he's going to score. When has Mihajlovic ever missed a penalty? When has Ferron ever saved one? 'Filthy racist pig!' the boys in the *curva* are screaming. What a sense of humour! Mihajlovic runs up and sends the ball thundering against the post. Game over.

'Afternoons like this', is the first message to appear on The Wall an hour or so later, 'repay all the shit we've eaten over the years. PS. Thanks to the *butei* who trampled all over me at two–nil.'

The message is signed: enmancansadelcaval@trottaancaelmusso.it. Intheabsenceofahorse@evenamulewilltrot.it

It's touching to see this ancient peasant wisdom kept alive on the net and at the same time offering fair comment on the game. The Lazio racehorse wasn't there. The Veronese mule trotted home. Or maybe I'm just in jubilant mood. I feel so good when they win.

'Mont Blanc, Geneva and all the mountains around trembled to a single cry: HELLAS! Thanks to the guys with the mobiles who kept me informed and thanks Beppe. It still feels like a beautiful dream. Hellas, yellow-blue worldwide!'

So it seems those mobile phones people insist on using despite all the crowd noise are not just for the odd friend stuck in a factory. This guy is from Switzerland. Someone writes from Hong Kong thanking the *butei* for the crucial call. There's a message from Indonesia, one from Scotland, one from Germany. Xenophobic, the *brigate* spread out across the world.

'Yellow-blue orgasm in the wastes of Northern Germany! Fuck, can it be true? Greetings to the Captain in Bussolengo, to Ardu and Rensu, to Carlin, Cini and the Radish! Verona cha cha cha!'

The message is signed Mikele Briegel. The fans often sign themselves with the names of legendary heroes. Briegel was the German midfield dynamo in the year of the miracle: 1985.

But will there ever be a message from Africa? Here's a man from Turkey, with a Turkish name too, who claims he's a Hellas fan. No one replies to him. What hope for the Ghanaians? Perhaps when we see the first black in the national team, when a black family put a photo of their dead on the obituary page in the *Arena*, when a black man steps on to the turf of the Bentegodi with a whistle in his hand, perhaps then the *brigate* will think of some other, less offensive circle to draw around themselves. Meantime, forgive them for enjoying a rare moment of glory.

'Did you sleep last night, Paolo?'

The Wall is deep blue, the type is a bold yellow.

'Only after I stopped trembling,' comes the reply.

The following evening, in a bar in Milan, I was given as change a five-thousand lire note. Beside the handsome head of Vincenzo Bellini, not unlike Gilardino to look at, someone had scribbled: 'Lazio Champions of Italy!' Ludicrously – no doubt it was the coincidence of getting the thing just the day after the famous victory – I decided to keep this note as a talisman and have it always in my wallet at games to come.

3A GIORNATA

Bari – Atalanta 0–2
Brescia – Fiorentina 1–1
Milan – Juventus 2–2
Napoli – Bologna 1–5
Perugia – Parma 3–1
Reggina – Lecce 0–1
Roma – Vicenza 3–1
Udinese – Inter 3–0
Verona – Lazio 2–0

CLASSIFICA

Roma	9
Udinese	7
Atalanta	7
Juventus	7
Bologna	6
Verona	5
Fiorentina	5
Lazio	4
Milan	4
Perugia	4
Lecce	4
Reggina	3
Inter	3
Brescia	2
Parma	2
Bari	1
Vicenza	0
Napoli	0

La Partita Della Fede

*The most wonderful thing was to kiss the Pope's hand
and hear the Holy Father say that he believes in sport
as an instrument of peace and something that can bring
all peoples together.*
Martin Laursen

Bergamo in flames!
Tex-for-Hellas

Let's suppose you have been ordered to imagine the most sickly
and hypocritical misrepresentation of modern sport possible, the
most absurd and sugary pretence of what is going on when people
do battle on pitch and track. What do you go for?

Vieira and Mihajlovic embrace after the game and, hand in
hand, go to the Lazio fans to invite them to stop their monkey
grunts. As the floodlights fade, the fans hold up their cigarette
lighters like candles in the deepening shadows and start to sing,
'Red and Yellow, Black and White, All are precious in His sight.'
Or some Italian alternative.

Tame.

OK then, OK, what about a packed stadium of a hundred
thousand people to watch a charity game between two groups of
paraplegics selected from every corner of the globe? The crowd
are totally engrossed and urge on the brave handicapped sportsmen, or why not women, with strong and encouraging cries. At
half-time they drink hot chocolate and chatter enthusiastically about

improvements in artificial limb design and the capacity of the human spirit to overcome terrible hardships. At the end all participants (and possibly the crowd too) are given a medal irrespective of the final score.

Actually, this is not bad. Immediately before the Lazio game, somebody phoned one of the public radio stations – I was fretting at a traffic light in my car – to complain about the inadequate coverage for the paraplegic games in Sydney. What was fascinating was to hear a panel of sports journalists casting about for face-saving excuses. Just as nobody called Marsiglia's bluff, so none of these good people had the courage to point out the hard fact that the public wants their athletes to be physically beautiful, and their sportsmen to be as talented as ever a sportsman can be.

Especially if he's defending your goal . . .

'*Mongolo!*' the guy behind me screams when Ferron fails to come out for a cross. '*O fenomeno!* Go get your disabled pension!' Two years ago it was our unhappy centre-forward, Alfredo Aglietti, who was given the treatment every time he touched the ball. '*Handicappato! Paraplegico! Cerebroleso!*'

I turn round to see the source of this angry abuse. He's a robust sort of bloke, dark fleshy face, deep eyes, always pulling closed his big black coat against the cold. Invariably pessimistic, often witty, he sits there expecting the worst with pursed lips. When we win he pretends mere amusement, but beneath it you can see he's delighted as a child. His plump girlfriend sits beside him with the puffed-out oxygenated hair of an erstwhile dolly creature, and whenever you twist your head round to look, she raises her soft eyes in a pained expression, as if to say: 'Oh I know, he really is incorrigible.' On the extremely rare occasions when Aglietti did manage to score, I'd turn and say: 'Well, what about that, Massimo?' And he'd shake his head, trying to hide his pleasure. '*Miracolo.* Grace of God. *Un fenomeno. O fenomeno!*' he stands up and yells. '*Mongolo!* Do your trick again!'

I remember thinking once: if, in some fantasy-film scenario, Timmy Parks were to don his old boots again and get down there on the green of the Bentegodi to reinforce a faltering midfield – forgive me, but occasionally one does imagine these things –

I would doubtless hear, raised above all the others, Massimo's derisive voice shrieking. 'O fenomeno. Mongolo! Handicappato! Get back in your fucking wheelchair!' The truth is, almost all of us are andicappati when it comes to Serie A football. Massimo would be right to boo me off. I too only want to watch footballers who are infinitely better than myself. The paraplegics are welcome to sit beside me.

So, the handicapped scenario is not bad. It's wonderfully sick. But it lacks a sense of special occasion, a sense of awe. I've thought about this question quite a lot – what is the most outrageously awful politically correct sports scenario – and in the end I feel bound to accept that I personally could never have come up with something so superlatively false as the Pope's Jubilee 'Match of Faith'. Certain areas of invention, I suspect, are closed to me a priori; only a long tradition of religious orthodoxy and sleazy lip service makes some leaps of mendacity possible.

Once again, after the Lazio game, il più bel campionato del mondo was to be stopped for a weekend. Once again the national team was to play. But this time the game was a 'friendly': Italy versus The Rest of the World, a team picked from among all the star foreigners playing in the bel paese. That is quite a squad to choose from. The occasion was to be a high point in the Catholic church's Jubilee for the year 2000, a celebration which has seen great waves of pilgrims overwhelming the Holy City for imaginatively named events like, the Jubilee of the Young, the Jubilee of the Old, the Jubilee of the Politicians (for the first time I felt some sympathy for the odious Berlusconi when he chose not to attend the affair) and, just a couple of weeks ago, and rather quaintly, the Jubilee of the Pizzaioli, the pizza makers.

The sportsmen's Jubilee is to close the cycle in an orgasm of good intentions. Football needs to be made more human, we are told, more Christian! Why? In the week running up to the big event, the Pope has spoken out against doping. His timing is excellent, for at precisely the same moment a report has been published showing that throughout the eighties and early nineties, CONI, the Italian Olympic federation, which was entrusted with running doping tests in every area of the country's sport, was actually giving work to a doctor who was seeking to develop undetectable drugs.

The Pope has also surprised us all by speaking out against violence and intolerance in the stadium. However excited a crowd becomes, he says, fandom should never be offensive. 'It's *me* who feels offended, *Dio boia*,' Massimo complains to me one day after a particularly wild outburst against Ferron, 'you pay *l'ira di dio* [the anger of God] for your season ticket, and what do you have to watch? A *mongolo*! The truth is they have no respect for people who suffer for Hellas, people whose knees start to shake when they pass through the turnstiles.'

Is Papa Wojtyla aware of this side of the problem? I suspect not. There he is high up in the Olympic Stadium in his bright green stole, leaning – a little heavily, truth to tell – on his golden crook, his golden mitre on his snowy head. The crowd rises to cheer. 'What will you remember of this day?' a journalist asks a fifteen-year-old girl. 'The Pope's beautiful smile,' she sweetly replies.

But where did they find all these fine people? It's 29 October Courtesy of 'those priests who can, now and for ever, command everything', as Leopardi put it, the sun is shining after another week of heavy rain. God is good. The stadium is full of smiling faces, of happy families, men and women and children. These are not season-ticket holders, I tell myself, turning on the box. These are not the notorious Lazio racists, Roma's knife experts.

Wojtyla, decrepit with Parkinson's, had been expected to watch just half of the game, but then insisted he must see the whole thing. This has pleased the journalists immensely. 'He remembers fondly', they enthuse, 'when he used to kick around a ball as a kid.' Papa Wojtyla then confesses that he has never watched a game before, a real game in a stadium. Seeing him helped to his seat, finding it difficult to hold his head up, I can't help feeling that he's left it a bit late.

It's Sunday. My son returns from his morning game with the local village team, Juventina Poiano, furious with the referee who sent off one of his companions merely for complaining that he wasn't offside. Can you believe it? He refuses to tell me by how many they lost. A rugby score. 'Want to get angrier?' I ask him. 'Look who's refereeing *la partita della fede*.' It's Signor Trentalange.

First there's a race round the athletics track by a group of paraplegics on their specially designed racing wheelchairs. The commentator explains that the slow start is due to the inertia of the big wheels. Of course, if one thinks of all the background to such a race, it is indeed heartbreaking. And thus not the kind of sporting event you would normally pay to see. The athletes are politely applauded. Then the players come out on the field. And now the next surprise: Mihajlovic is there! For the Pope's match of faith, hope and charity! 'Siniso Mihajlovic is Russian Orthodox,' the commentator tells us, and as the team lists scroll up, he runs through all the religions of the participants: Negrouz is Muslim, Gargo is Baptist, Baggio is Buddhist, Laursen is Lutheran, Mutu is Russian Orthodox . . .

Laursen! Mutu! 'They'd better not get injured,' Michele shouts, jumping off his seat, his features suddenly alive with concern. 'If they get bloody injured just for a stupid friendly!'

'And Nakata, the Japanese star, is an atheist,' the commentator concludes.

'Be pretty bad form if an atheist scores,' the second commentator complains.

The Match of Faith begins.

Of course the unspoken subtext of the expression 'friendly game' is that other games are unfriendly. That is the long and the short of it. Even if you could never call them un-friendlies. 'You have to be really angry to win,' says Inter's new trainer, Marco Tardelli. 'Give me two grappas,' says one of the *brigate* at the station bar shortly before we set off for one game, 'it feeds my anger.' The lady serving is a pleasantly overweight grandmother figure. 'I don't know why you want to feel angry, dear,' she smiles. 'I really don't understand you young men.'

What I don't understand is how the commentators can say the things they're saying. 'The Pope is the real champion in the stadium today.' 'The Pope is an athlete of God.' 'If only every Sunday were like this, this generosity on the field, this kindness, the players constantly giving each other their hands, the fans so well behaved.'

Do they mean it?

Trentalange, meanwhile, must be having a whale of a time; he doesn't have to worry about who's winning. The church is winning. 'I use sport as a form of communication towards people who have problems,' he tells a journalist before the game. His vocation for the sanctimonious is clearly a serious one. 'This Pope is truly a saint,' he adds, safely. And Trentalange himself is truly in the spotlight, he's lapping it up, though it must be a trifle frustrating having nothing to do. I count exactly seventeen minutes before the first foul comes along.

In short, the game's a great bore. The Pope can barely keep his head up. If this is football, he must be thinking, how on earth do people manage to get excited? The pictures of him, every time the ball goes off the pitch, and sometimes even while it is still in play, are becoming embarrassing. Has he fallen asleep? Is he dying? But the genius of the kind of mentality that invents these sick scenarios is its inability to be embarrassed, a resource that arises from the complete and unquestioning commitment to an agreed façade. 'There's a flash of interest,' remarks one commentator eagerly, when a slight roll of Wojtyla's grizzled head coincides with a kick upfield.

Michele and now Stefi too have come to sit beside me and determinedly we try to watch the thing through. It's hard. Even Trentalange must be getting bored with it. The halves were supposed to be forty minutes long, but to the surprise of the players the referee blows his whistle after only thirty-five. Stefi says Laursen is terribly handsome, and Frey, the young French keeper, is fantastic. Will I let her download his photos off the web? I'd never thought of this, but girls perhaps have fewer problems with a friendly.

In the second half the substitutions are incessant. Since nothing is going on on the pitch, the commentator interviews the stars as they come off. Usually outrageously behaved on the pitch, football players tend to be the last word in conformity and caution off it. 'The most intense and special emotion of my life,' announces the young Hernan Crespo. I shake my head in wonder. Has this rich, young, handsome man never been to bed with a woman? Has he or has he not scored important goals and won trophies galore? What did he feel like when he heard that Lazio were offering 170 billion lire to buy him from Parma? Michele says, 'I've experienced more intense emotions yelling at the cat.'

Gianfranco Zola, who has been long enough in England to feel a bit out of it, isn't enthusiastic enough. Manfully, he tries to talk about the need to clean up sport. The interviewer isn't satisfied. 'How do you feel, Gianfranco, moved?' 'Yes, it is a special emotion,' Zola begrudgingly admits. 'From a deeply moved Gianfranco Zola, let's get back to the game,' says the commentator. He must have wondered for a moment whether the lad mightn't be about to say something honest.

Then something real happens at last. Poor Del Piero misses an open goal. Alessandro Del Piero has become yesterday's star. Accused of doping a couple of seasons ago, this once-brilliant striker has melted away since. Is it because they've had to go easy on the illegal substances? Who knows? Anyway, he just can't do anything right. Above all, he can't put the ball in the net. He gets in the right places, he has the 'sfera', as the Italians love to call it, at his talented feet, but he can't put it in, damn it. Already hated all over Italy because he plays for the odious Juventus, he has now become the butt of his home crowd too. People can't understand why he's playing for them any more. Not a single soul knows why he's playing for the national team. There are murmurings of sponsorship contracts.

Absolutely without charisma, Alex mumbles his excuses in endless interviews. Returning from the European Cup final which Italy lost to France, he is described as sitting alone on the plane, refusing to be comforted after missing yet another vital goal. Perhaps, it occurs to me, the Match of Faith has been named especially for him, for Alessandro Del Piero. Perhaps this game will be the turning point. There's a clever move on the right. Alex is steaming up from the left. Then, here it comes, a great through ball, perfectly paced for him to run on to, and suddenly he's all alone streaking into the box, nobody at his heels, just the keeper to beat. He hits the ball way over the bar. At once the few real fans in the crowd are on their feet whistling, outraged. '*Mongolo!*' How can a guy they've paid to see miss a goal like that? It only lasts a moment, but it's real and immediate. They're furious, derisive. Del Piero no doubt is hurt. His cruel isolation is confirmed. Shortly afterwards, at the other end Adrian Mutu, brought on only a moment before, slips his defender and slots the ball coolly into the net. Goal! The Romanian is ecstatic. Gooooooooal! He starts the regulation cartwheels. Signor Trentalange is alarmed. Mutu again! Doesn't that kid understand? He runs back, consults with a linesman. Offside, he decides.

'Offside?' Michele yells.

Offside.

'Clearly nobody's supposed to win this game,' I tell my son. 'Don't you see, Mick, it wouldn't be right for anyone to lose. Losing isn't nice. Winning is like cruelty to animals. Everybody should get a medal. This the *Partita della fede*, the faith match. Faith and losing don't go together, do they?' But Mutu is bewildered. He knows he wasn't offside. The TV, usually so avid to replay these things, chooses not to.

Mutu is upset. The commentator tries to explain this departure from script. He glosses: 'Of course, it's also right that each person should want to win a game, isn't it?' He asks help of his colleague, but the other man doesn't reply. 'It wouldn't be loyal', the commentator stutters on, you can sense he feels betrayed, 'to play if you didn't want to win. Your team-mates expect you to want to win, to put heart and soul into it. And so of course Mutu, who is Russian Orthodox, wants to win and when he thinks . . .' The speaker hesitates. For a moment it seems he might be about to tackle the immense conundrum of competitive team sports, the intense and confused emotions they arouse, emotions that lead a man to punch an old friend in another team, or alternatively to make a generous pass in front of goal to some team-mate he despises, then actually embrace the hated man when he scores.

'Yes, it's right to want to win,' the commentator repeats vaguely, 'as it's right to play fair.' Again he hesitates. How perplexing it is!

'The Pope must be enjoying these emotions,' he decides. Somehow it's as if old Wojtyla were our child for the day, a little boy we've brought along for his first game. My own impression is that the poor man fell asleep some time ago. O *fenomeno*, wake up!

Meanwhile poor Mutu is still protesting. He can't get into the spirit of the thing. He's sure it was a goal. 'I love him!' I shout. 'I love that horrible kid. I'm so glad he plays for Verona. Go Mutu! Go!' But almost at once this dangerous boy is substituted. I swear he's only been on the pitch for five minutes. The following day, after all the obligatory rubbish about how moved he was to be playing before the Pope, the Romanian tells a journalist: 'I wasn't offside though. They should have allowed the goal. How marvellous it would have been. Then every time people thought of this day, they would have thought of me!' That's the spirit!

'*Butei*, did you see?' someone writes on The Wall. 'Did you see El Pastor kissing Wojtyla's hand! El Pastor with El Pap! We have saints in paradise!'

El Pastor, the shepherd, is Giambattista Pastorello, our supposedly niggardly president. 'You can say what you like about his bow-tie, and his miserliness,' someone else writes, 'but in the end, I'd rather have a president with a head on his shoulders who knows about football and makes the right connections, than some hopeless freak with more money than sense. Perhaps the Virgin will give us a penalty in Bergamo.'

Alas no.

The next game was to be held on the following Wednesday, 1 November, the Day of the Dead and a public holiday. There is an ancient rivalry between Verona and Atalanta, the Bergamo team. Away games here have been the scene of serious crowd violence. I myself narrowly missed a shower of stones outside the stadium three years ago. But it was also in Bergamo, in the penultimate game of the season, that Verona finally made sure of winning the *scudetto* in 1985. So inevitably, just before this year's game, The Wall is awash with nostalgia.

'How I suffered in the barracks! I couldn't go.'

'I was there, I was fifteen.'

'12 May 1985, I was there, eleven years old, twelve the day after!!! Every time I see Elkjaer's goal I cry like a baby and thank God (and papà) that I was there.'

'I was serving this shitty country. In the army.'

Someone who signs himself 'Can de la Scala', greatest of the Scaligeri and protector of Dante, writes:

Tomorrow in Bergamo, the usual whirl of old emotions, I always remember that day, I was eighteen, the bus in Piazza San Zeno, heavy rain as we left, procession with orange staffs, and the Bergamaschi chased right back to the beginning of their *curva*. Then Elkjaer and . . . I'm crying. I thank God I was there. Can anybody ever understand what I feel?'

The answer is, yes.

Can de la Scala: I remember that day too. I too was eighteen. I do understand what you feel. I remember other great games. The opening game with Napoli, Maradona's debut, we killed them, the time Elkjaer lost his boot but scored with his stockinged foot against Juve. MYTHICAL. And we were there! We didn't just read about it. It's different. FORZA HELLAS. Everybody to Bergamo tomorrow. Let's kill them.

Forza nothing . . . Our documents checked and names studiously written down by the police, fifteen hundred of us squeezed into a tiny segment of a decrepit stadium to watch through grimy netting as Verona were thrashed three–nil. I will say nothing about this game. I don't want to remember it. If we have saints in paradise then they were busy elsewhere that afternoon. My son had come along with me, and he immediately understood how aberrant his optimism had been after the Lazio victory. 'I should never have hoped,' he said. 'I should have stayed at home.' He stood in bitter silence.

Throughout the match a drunken adolescent leaned against me, shouting out of tune and complaining about the referee's every decision. But the truth was there was nothing to complain about, and the crowd knew it. Why would the referee prefer one miserable provincial team to another? He was perfectly fair. We couldn't even shout *Vaffanculo* Pastorello, because Atlanta's team actually cost less than ours. There were even four or five home-grown kids in the group. They were fresh up from Serie B. They killed us. Still, we did have that hour after the match . . .

When your team lose on television, you are left in a state of extreme anxiety and disappointment. There is no sense of occasion to offer catharsis. You are on your own with no idea how to move back from these crushed hopes into a normal state of mind. I can imagine people doing serious damage to themselves and the furniture in such situations. I myself have been known to kick things, though never people or animals. At the stadium, on the other hand, there is the comfort of being part of the crowd, and after the away game there is the long forced wait in the alien stadium while the local thugs are dispersed to allow for your safe departure. This occasion was the perfect example of how disappointment can be turned into self-mockery and finally fun; how you can lose the game but still go home emotionally uplifted.

The light was almost gone. Behind the shabby stands rose a slender campanile, then the Alps. The terraces where we stood were steep so that at the bottom of the squalid corner segment they give to visiting supporters, a sort of theatre pit was formed. And as, in the stadium all around, the few remaining Atalanta fans were lighting bonfires of match programmes, while a dozen policemen and a few dogs kept watch from the pitch and took endless photographs in case of trouble, a chubby man – I hadn't seen him down in Bari – climbed on a barrier and, held there by two others who gripped his ankles – one of them was Cain – led a singing session with a megaphone.

It was supremely good-humoured and in the worst possible taste. A carnival mockery hung in the air. Perhaps because today was the Day of the Dead, an important day in Italy, a cross was made out of plastic flagpoles and the crowd sang the hymn 'Risorgeremo', we shall rise again. Meaning Hellas of course. Then they taunted a fat policewoman, without pity. I was surprised to see the girls and women among the fans joining in with this. Not only joining in, relishing. 'Let's see your fat tits!' they screamed at her. Fondo, who was prancing about at the front, exposed his torso to the icy air and tried to force his flesh into breasts.

The poor woman disappeared and it was back to singing. Everybody knew all the songs, like a congregation who have been together since birth. Perhaps on Sunday these same people will be in the congregation. Now there was certainly a religious fervour in their voices, but with a demonic inversion of sentiments. It was as if the *Partita della fede* had to be exorcised as soon as possible, together with our defeat. We bated the team of men cleaning the stadium, We bated the few Atalanta fans sitting by their rubbish fires, relishing their victory. We bated the police dogs till the poor animals had to be taken away. Then came the masterpiece of offence . . .

A few days before the game a helicopter of the carabinieri had crashed in the sea killing all those on board. The megaphone now invited us to sing the Fascist song:

> *Gira gira l'elica, romba il motore,*
> *Questa è la bella vita la bella vita dell'aviator.*
> Turn propeller turn, out roars the motor,
> This is the good life, the good life of the aviator.

With its jolly tune, the song celebrates the progress of a modern mechanised army. My father-in-law used to whistle it as he shaved. But the fans sang:

> *Gira gira l'elica, romba il motor,*
> *L'elicottero dell'arma è tornato al creator.*
> The policemen copter's gone back to its maker.

How can one laugh at such bad taste? Ten men had died. Everyone laughed. I even saw a carabiniere smile. It was the Day of the Dead and the Halloween twilight was strangely intense.

Later, as the wilder boys pushed their faces through the small open windows of the Zanzibar's bus to shout the insults and blasphemies into the streets, the good people of Bergamo, housewives and grandmothers alike, waved to us laughing, as if to old friends, their beaten neighbours. I remember in particular one tiny old man hooking his walking stick over one arm to make a triumphantly rude gesture, showing, despite at least eighty years, a vitality Wojtyla will never know again. Perhaps they're all doing each other good, I thought.

'Enough crap' is the first message to appear on The Wall after the game: 'Honour to Atalanta, a great team. No bitterness when they were so obviously better than us.'

The thrill of the generous gesture, the hand extended to the better man, this too is part of the football fan's repertoire.

4A GIORNATA

Atalanta – Verona 3–0
Bologna – Reggina 2–0
Fiorentina – Bari 2–2
Inter – Roma 2–0
Juventus – Udinese 1–2
Lazio – Brescia 2–1
Lecce – Napoli 1–1
Parma – Milan 2–0
Vicenza – Perugia 1–0

CLASSIFICA

Udinese	10
Atalanta	10
Roma	9
Bologna	9
Lazio	7
Juventus	7
Fiorentina	6
Inter	6
Parma	5
Verona	5
Lecce	5
Milan	4
Perugia	4
Reggina	3
Vicenza	3
Brescia	2
Bari	2
Napoli	1

Aborti

I didn't choose to support Hellas. They attached the team to me at birth with my identity bracelet.
Pam@Yellow–blue–from–birth

On Sunday 5 November a traffic policeman in Mantua saw the Madonna and prophesied a further and more public apparition for 8 December, the Immaculate Conception, two days before our away tie in Reggio Calabria. Putting the story among the main headlines of the national radio news, the journalists showed no surprise that the Virgin should thus respect the arbitrary Church calendar. As if Jesus had been born on 25 December after a three-week pregnancy. Will Hellas be in the relegation zone, I wonder, come the Annunciation? Will we be condemned to Serie B before Epiphany? The football calendar is tough for us now: Inter at home, Vicenza (arch rivals) away, Rome (league leaders) at home, Juve (political power incarnate) away. How many points can we hope for from that?

On the evening before the policeman's vision, the Lega Nord had arranged a 'Stop Islam' assembly in the centre of Verona. Walking with my wife to a favourite bar, we were surprised to see cars being towed from the square behind the *duomo*. The demagogical Michele Santoro, an offensively pious presenter of heated TV debates, had hurriedly set up a stage to coincide with the meeting so that Verona could be presented to the nation at its racist best. Showing unusual wisdom, the Lega cancelled the meeting. The stage with all its lights was thus useless and a man was left holding a microphone with no scandal to report. The residents are furious because they were given only a few hours to clear their cars.

The television muckrakers were luckier in Rovato, forty miles west of Verona, where the local mayor has forbidden all non-believers from coming within fifteen metres of any consecrated building on a Sunday. This probably means he doesn't want groups of blacks selling their cigarette lighters by the church doors as the good white folk walk in and out of mass. All right-thinking people are outraged. The north is insufferable. 'All cat-eaters [Vicenza supporters] and hunchbacks [Juventus supporters] and *terroni* [more or less everybody south of the river Po] should be forbidden from coming within fifteen metres of the sacred Bentegodi,' writes a fan to The Wall. 'Any day of the week.'

Over the same uneventful weekend the Vatican invites pharmacists nationwide not to dispense the day-after pill and not to stock it. The government has just included the abortion pill in its list of medicines that physicians can prescribe. The magazine *Panorama* shows two ladies coming out of mass. 'What do you think of the day-after pill?' one asks. 'Day after what?' the other replies. After losing three–nil at Bergamo perhaps. An article in the *Arena* speaks of depression and absenteeism on the morning after a lost game. But enough joking and muddling things up. 'The foetus is a human being at the moment of conception,' thunders a cardinal in a radio interview. 'And that is that.'

But is the foetus also and immediately Veronese? And if Veronese by conception, immaculate or otherwise, how could such a child, yellow-blue in the womb, ever support any team but Hellas? Alas, they can, they do. When Inter or Juventus or Milan come to the Bentegodi, the Brigate Gialloblù face a serious threat to their identity: the local turncoat who, like the impressionable referee, supports the big teams.

'Abortions!' shrieks a boy crawling up the fence at the edge of the *curva*. The object of his disgust is a knot of Veronese in the east stand wearing Inter Milan's blue-and-black scarves. 'We have your addresses! It would have been better if you'd never been born!' In my book, the only thing that really happened on Sunday November the fifth was Hellas Verona's home game with Inter. And this game I have to talk about. It outdid any appearance of Our Lady for excitement and surprise, any announcement of the Lega Nord or the Vatican for controversy, it was a dream, a nightmare that really happened.

Pietro, who keeps my place in the *curva*, once put it to me, in some half-time discussion or other, that football is essentially eleven guys trying to make something happen, and at the same time trying to stop the wrong thing happening. In some games, however generously the players give themselves, it doesn't come off. The fans will be left unsatisfied, hands thrust in their pockets, idly kicking the steps as they leave. Nothing happened. It's not just a question of scoring, of winning or losing, though a goal is an excellent spark for a conflagration and a victory is always better than a loss. No, it's the creation of a sense of urgency, of total engagement, a feeling of having been at an event where something major occurred, something collectively felt, something of which you can say: I was there.

When this does come off, it's as though team and crowd had fused together, leaving the fans with the sense that they have played a vital part in the game, the way long ago worshippers in other temples believed their sacrifices had kept the sun in the sky, or allowed a god to rise again. At the end of such a game, the players are drawn to the stand where the most energy is coming from, the core of their *curva*. They strip off their shirts, and sometimes shorts, and hurl them into the crowd. It's a token of the mixing that has taken place. For this brief space of time we have been a community. The match with Inter on Sunday 5 November was the one that fused this heterogeneous group of new arrivals – Mutu, Gilardino, Bonazzoli, Oddo, Cvitanovic, Camoranesi, Mazzola – with *il popolo dell'Hellas*. It was also the first match where we understood that we had a new genius in the team: Mauro Camoranesi. 'Bentegodi Discovers the Gaucho' will be tomorrow's headline.

An evening kick-off helped. For the first time, and quite probably the last, Verona have the star Sunday night spot. People who have mainstream pay TV will be watching on their screens. Or rather Inter have the spot. We are their chosen victims. They've made a rocky start to the season, they need a couple of easy victories. In the wonderful atmosphere of the tall floodlights, the brilliantly lit pitch and the luminous glow of faces in the dark all around, the stadium is packed and alive with tension. Packed because, despite the television coverage, Inter bring along a lot of supporters; tense because half of those Inter supporters come from Verona. How can the native-born Veronese do it? How can they live in this small proud town and support, for convenience sake, so as to be sure of winning, or at least of never going down to Serie B, one of the big rich teams? What is this phenomenon?

The funny thing is that I, an immigrant, share the indignance of the Hellas fans. I cannot feel the intensity of the ancient provincial rivalries, the local hatred of Bergamo and Brescia and Vicenza. Apart from the different dialects, I can't distinguish the inhabitants of these towns. But perhaps because it took so long for me to settle in Verona, so long to feel that this town would be *my* town, this team, for better or worse, my team, it seems outrageous to me that so many of its citizens should not only not give their support – that's fair enough – but actually come along to cheer the privileged unto whom everything has been given, the men with Pirelli on their shirts. Perhaps the kind of emotions I relish in football have to do with the pathos that you did not choose which team to support, in the way you cannot choose the personality of your children, and yet you go on supporting them even when they play awfully. '*Bastardi*,' my son yells when an Inter banner is raised. At once, magically, these are the same *bastardi* who arranged that first afternoon kick-off against Bari.

No doubt there is a certain sickness in my being attracted to this passion. Do I actually want to feel that the team I support can only win rarely, that victories will always be snatched in the teeth of fate, and that losses will be the order of the day, this so as to give a monumental importance to the occasional success? When I first came to Verona, twenty-five years old, I scuttled the streets of the centre, nervously clutching a battered briefcase and umbrella, earning a living teaching English to the well-to-do of the expensive *centro storico*. I cannot deny having felt a little excluded: linguistically, economically, culturally. These families were so settled, so well-heeled, so serenely complacent. 'I'll have to miss next week's lesson, Daddy's taking me to Cortina.' 'For my summer holiday' – I would be watching a pen slowly scribble – 'we first spend two weeks scubing in the Seishelles, then mummy tooked me to Japon.'

Without family money, or a steady job, or a book published, I felt insecure and a little frustrated. This was inevitable. When such people actually paid late, I was furious. I wrote a book, *Cara Massimina*, in which a language teacher, Morris Duckworth, becomes a serial killer. I can't remember ever enjoying writing so much. It was hard for me to get on with the heavily made-up, bejewelled and befurred Veronese. No doubt the failing was as much mine as theirs.

But in the stadium it was different. It is not that the people of the *curva* are like me. Our backgrounds are a thousand miles and many light-years apart. It's just that, if only because Verona can never be a big team, this is necessarily a population of underdogs. And there must have come a moment when, unwittingly, I linked my own battles to theirs, my own experience of, as I saw it, shovelling shit to Hellas Verona's endless fight against the flood-tide of big money. In that sense, I could feel part of their community. Had Morris Duckworth come to the Bentegodi, he would never have lifted a paperweight in anger. It would have been enough to yell *Inter Inter vaffanculo!*

The occasional visitors to the stadium, on the other hand, those well-dressed folks who buy expensive seats because they are fitful fans of wealthy teams, these people I tend to associate with all the well-fed obtusity I imagined I was up against in the early days here. I'm perfectly aware that my division of town and stadium like this is entirely unverifiable and almost certainly false. In all probability the people I have liked and hated outside the stadium are equally divided between the two sides; or more likely just not here at all. They don't give a toss about football. They find it infantile and ridiculous. But precisely the mystery of following a team is the investment of emotion where there is really no reason to invest it. Home games against Inter, Milan and Juventus are the high points of the season for me. And it's not the opposing team we have to beat, it's those complacent Veronese fifth columnists, those people who went to the Seychelles and Japan and asked if I had a proper hanger for their fur coats and always always paid me late.

Speaking of lateness, Mick and I arrived late because of the cemetery situation. Everybody eternally does the same thing at the same time in Italy – for that is what community means – and the weekends before and after the Day of the Dead bring with them an orgy of visits to lost loved ones. The circular road was blocked. Indians were selling bunches of chrysanthemums, the flowers the dead love. At the traffic lights the gypsy women were begging with their babies in their arms. It's curious how each immigrant group seems to know its niche. Two hooded figures sit over the great gate that leads into the *cimitero monumentale*. Between them, carved huge in stone, is the word RESURECTURIS. Atalanta, I thought, '*risorgeremo*', and hoped Pietro would manage to hold on to our seats, hoped the boys would have recovered their morale. In the paper, our coach, Attilio Perotti, had referred to that game as 'bringing to light a puzzling technical and psychological involution of a hitherto positive trend'. I hoped that, since anybody who can say such a thing clearly has a considerable education, Perotti would have figured the problem out.

The game had everything, fireworks at the start, fireworks throughout. As the players came on to the field, a line of glowing red smoke-bombs were lit all around the parapet of the *curva*, sending a cloud of pink into the icy, floodlit night. It was the first time the short, stocky Argentinian, Camoranesi, had been on the pitch from the beginning. It was the first time the man who had been our goalkeeper last year had returned for a competitive game. The young Frenchman Sebastian Frey has been the best loved player I have seen in my years in Verona. Enviably handsome, huge, blond, always jolly, darling of the girls, he walks over now and waves through clouds of pink smoke to his old home crowd. There is a huge chant – 'Fre-ey Fre-ey Fre-ey!' It's intriguing how some players immediately attract everyone's affection, while others will remain for ever anonymous. Frey's personality transmits itself effortlessly across the athletics track and up into the packed stands. The moment he is there, bouncing off a post to get the feel of the place, you feel you know him. He raises a big gloved hand. 'Fre-ey, Fre-ey!' Fifteen minutes later, when Verona put the first goal past him, after the huge uproar that attends any goal, there were still those, mainly women I suspect, ready to remind him of their affection, still cries of Fre-ey! It must be a strange buzz girls get from following football. The few times I've watched the women's game, I just felt confused.

This goal was the work of Camoranesi, another of Pastorello's happy discoveries, another personality immediately available to all, there to be savoured in the bright night. Small, barrel-chested, a helmet of Indios black hair, this boy is a collision of fury and talent. He loses his temper. He shouts. You can see he's going to be sent off before the season is out. Sometimes he's so determined to be clever he loses the ball too, he shuffles his legs this way and that so fast that he mesmerises himself, he can't remember what he was supposed to be doing, the way sometimes a sentence, an idea, can become so overintricate, so self-regarding in its twists and turns, it collapses in on its own conceit and already the reader is looking elsewhere. Camoranesi is left in a rage, wondering what has happened. But when intensity and cleverness combine, this boy is unbeatable.

Mutu lifts his head in midfield, picks up the little Argentinian making a run on the right and delivers the perfect through ball at exactly the speed and the angle that will cheat the defence. Camoranesi gathers it, passes his man, and suddenly there he is, running into the area, just a couple of yards from the touch-line. '*Crossa!*' people are shrieking, imperative of that old Italian verb *crossare*. Cross! He doesn't. He's heading straight for goal. Blocking his way now is the monstrous Colombian, the wardrobe-like Cordoba. With enchanting deceit, something that fools the spectators even more than the defender, Camoranesi looks up, seems to be about to cross but in fact takes on his man. Cordoba is so surprised, he trips over himself and is left on his butt.

These are the situations where time stops, the moments when you feel, far more in the stadium than ever on television, the fatal uniqueness of action and opportunity. A metre in from the touch-line Camoranesi is running at the goal. This is the vision the mind will pluck from the game like a fruit from the tree. Even years hence, however distorted, it will still be there to be gloated over. In this football is not unlike sex, which also offers its unforgettable snapshots.

But far more is at stake here! Camoranesi has to get it right *now*. The *curva* are suddenly silent. He's almost at the six-yard box. Other defenders are closing in. Frey is advancing, the miraculous Frey, voted the best goalkeeper in Italy last season, a kid who's gone from nothing to holding a regular place in one of the richest teams in the world. You've got to do it now, Camoranesi. There will be no replay. At its most intense, life is always this, everything at stake, now.

The young man doesn't hesitate. He runs directly at the keeper, fakes a shot and instead passes soft and straight across the six-yard box. The defenders throw themselves at that ball. But Bonazzoli, huge, long-haired, arrives first. Bought, or rather borrowed, for his ability to head the ball, his powerful bulk and speed, all he has to do is tap a perfect pass into an open goal.

No need to describe the crowd's response. The Inter fans are silent, especially the Veronese. There can be no one sadder than the turncoat who's made the wrong choice. When a team is a destiny, you accept anything, but when you actually chose the bastards, then hell, they'd better win for you.

The following morning the *Gazzetta* gives a full page to the game, as it must for one of the big teams. Of the referee it says: 'Rodomonti: good for the last hour, uncertain in the first thirty minutes when he fails to give a yellow card to Blanc (2'), Gresko (11') and above all Cordoba (30') who all deserved it. Applies the rules with Italiano.'

The whole game is there in this cryptic assessment. Blanc, Gresko and Cordoba are all Inter players. In the end Gresko was given a card, likewise Inter players Di Biagio, Ferrari and Farinos.

It was a wild game. The *Gazzetta* counted, I note, sitting in the bar the following morning over a cappuccino and brioche, still in a state of some excitement, twenty fouls by Inter and only eight by Verona. And those in the notebook were the few conceded by the referee.

But it was the Verona player Italiano who was sent off. 'Applies the rules with Italiano.' How eloquent. Against Atalanta, as I said, the refereeing was really pretty fair, so fair I hardly noticed it. Here it is scandalous. And surprise, surprise, it is the same referee, Rodomonti. The more I think about football, the more I am convinced that injustice is an essential part of it. The fan thirsts for injustice. The Verona fan, or indeed the fan of any small team, is lucky. He gets it.

It happened like this. With Verona all over them, the Inter defence turn nasty. The referee, worried Verona may score again, does nothing to stop the growing brutality. There are fouls from behind of the kind we were told would lead to a sending off in the World Cup. The referee gives the foul but not the yellow card.

Then Inter equalise on their first serious attack of the game. A cross headed away falls to Recoba, the defence charge at him. He passes to Farinos left quite alone and the Spaniard scores. Delighted, the handsome young man runs to salute his supporters. He has scored at the right end, under the Curva Nord, but Verona's stadium has an athletics track round the pitch, so you have to run off the grass for a moment to get near the fans. Instinctively, Rodomonti sees how he can now appear to be fair. To make up for his amazing lack of severity so far, he quite unnecessarily shows Farinos a yellow card for '*festeggiamenti eccessivi*'.

That was the twenty-sixth minute. The ball hit the net. Farinos waved to the crowd. All over the stadium Inter fans betrayed themselves leaping to their feet, waving their scarves. The Curva Sud howled. They really do hate these Veronese Interisti. Thank God for fences. Four minutes later, Camoranesi again slips past Cordoba. This time the big defender is merciless, he slays the boy, sweeps away his legs. The referee does nothing. Ten minutes after that, with Verona now attacking again, Inter make a break on the right and Italiano brings someone down, I think Recoba. The yellow card is immediate. The scene has been set for the most unusual drama.

Italiano is slim, Sicilian, of medium height. He's not the dynamo Leo Colucci is, nor does he have the ability to dribble that Giuseppe Colucci has, but he's good at the long ball and above all he has a fierce shot. This is one of his first full games after almost a year of injuries and operations, a year no doubt spent wondering whether he would ever make the first team again. Just three minutes after getting that yellow card, he collects the ball some way outside the box, looks up at the Inter players coming out a shade slowly after a Verona attack, sees his chance, hits the ball hard and low from twenty-five yards, scores. Again the Curva Sud erupts. Long starved of glory, at his first goal in Serie A, Italiano is drawn towards them. He raises his arms and rushes at the crowd like a moth to light. Fatally he leaves the field. Having shown Farinos a yellow card, the referee now 'has to' show one to Italiano. But Italiano already has a card. Second yellow card. Off. Verona two–one up, one man down. Turning point of the game. Half-time.

What turbulent and wonderfully confused emotions! Elation, fear, anger. The following day's press claims that the referee ran after Italiano, attempting to warn him. I don't remember that. The player was only off the field perhaps twenty seconds. No doubt Rodomonti feels he acted in good faith. But there have been all kinds of ferocious behaviour on the Inter side that have gone quite unpunished, while Verona are now without their central midfielder, and the midfield was already weak with captain Leo Colucci out injured. The second half will be hell. All the more so because there's another drama going on that no one on the terraces knows about.

The players return. Inter have brought on the massive Christian Vieri, his debut after a long injury. He promptly elbows his defender, Apolloni, in the face. The referee sees it, sends Apolloni off to have the blood looked at, does not give a yellow card. Vieri then hits the bar from one of perhaps a score of crosses. Inter's possession is endless, accompanied by some of the most deafening whistling I have ever heard. But for the moment Verona are hanging on. They even look organised. There are occasional rapid counter-attacks, to keep the Inter defence nervous. Twenty minutes from time, Recoba tries from twenty-five yards and Ferron makes a good save. '*Incredibile!*' Massimo shrieks behind me. 'Similaun man is still alive.' Similaun man is the 5,000-year-old corpse found in the Alps on the Austrian border. 'O *fenomeno*.' Massimo stands up. 'Similaun man, you're doing fine!' Ferron raises a hand. But not in salute. He seems to be in pain. The doctor comes on and escorts him off the pitch.

No one can understand it. He didn't seem to have taken a knock or fallen badly. Here we are, defending a two–one lead against Inter of all teams, teeth gritted, sweating blood on the field and in the stands, and all of a sudden our keeper is walking off. He's not the world's best keeper. But he is a keeper. 'The mummy's disintegrated.' Massimo flops back in his seat. He looks worried. His girlfriend hugs herself to his arm.

Tomorrow's paper will tell us that Ferron had severe stomach pains before the game and vomited at half-time. Perotti was ready for the worst. And there's something fantastic about this. Of course one knows that all kinds of things may be going on in each player's life. Someone has just fallen in love. Someone has just been dropped by a childhood sweetheart. A cold, the clap, an argument with a friend, a sick parent. You expect this. But to think that a man – the goalkeeper of all people – has been sent back on to the pitch after spending the interval retching is alarming. What's our reserve keeper like? Does nobody trust him? 'O Doardo,' someone addresses the substitute later that evening on The Wall, 'in thirty minutes you made me sweat the pains of hell.' The mistake is revealing: in fact it was only fifteen minutes. But it seemed like eternity.

Now I don't want to be mean to this boy. The season is young, I've never seen him before, it was a hard moment to come on to the pitch, I hope I will be able to eat my words, but I do suspect that Domenico Doardo may be in the wrong job. Veronese by birth, he has come back to his home town after a season as reserve keeper at Genoa, in Serie B. 'I'm tall, so high balls are my speciality,' he told an interviewer on arrival on the fourteenth of July. No sooner is he between the posts on 5 November than he goes up for a high corner and misses it. In the wild scramble that follows the ball is somehow kept out of the net. No thanks to Doardo.

The crowd are seized by an immense anxiety. Just as the handsome Frey always communicated confidence and security, even when he had let a goal in, now the equally handsome Doardo, truly a fine-looking young man with bright clean smile and shining teeth, radiates panic. He doesn't want to be there. We can feel it. He doesn't want the ball to come in his direction. But this is hard to arrange when there are only ten of you. The stadium is packed. The crowd are deafening. Inter are desperate. Doardo is terrified. We can feel him shaking. The communication is miraculously intense. 'If he doesn't shit himself,' somebody is saying, 'I think I will.'

Eight minutes after Doardo comes on, a through ball gives the Turkish striker Hassan Sukhur a chance. He's running into the area. He reaches the corner of the six-yard box with Laursen pounding behind him. Sukhur's now in almost exactly the same position as Camoranesi was when he made that sweet pass to Bonazzoli an hour ago. Now is the moment that will decide everything. Too late to beat his man to the ball, too early to respond to the direction of the shot, Doardo gathers what nerve he has and rushes out knock-kneed. Sukhur mishits it. It goes through Doardo's legs and trickles into the net.

What a dangerous cocktail of injustice and bad luck! The hotheads are rushing to the side fences to shriek at the exulting Veronese Inter fans. The rest of us have our faces in our hands. Behind me I can hear. '*O mongolo, O fenomeno*. You're not fit to drive the team bus.' And there are still ten minutes to go. Inter want to win.

I have often thought about the relation between competitive sports and aesthetics. You can become intensely engaged in the outcome of a play or opera; I still remember my adolescent horror when I realised that Cordelia was truly dead. Yet it is not like worrying about the result of a game. Visually the game offers aesthetic pleasures, and there is also the endless fascination of the interaction between personality and skill, the interlocking of the players within the team, their hostile confrontation without.

All this is guaranteed to engross for at least ninety minutes. But when my own team is playing, the result becomes important, and tonight in particular the result could be bad, awful, and without any catharsis. Not that to lose is difficult, but to lose like this, with a man sent off for nothing, with their team constantly protected, with a sick goalkeeper and an incompetent reserve and a mishit ball that barely managed to roll into the net. Yes, I could actually leave this stadium, it occurs to me, feeling more appalled by Verona being beaten than by watching the representation of a young woman cut down in the prime of life. Or indeed any other narrative awfulness. Forget *Silence of the Lambs*, watch Hellas lose. And suddenly I'm telling myself: really it would be too too aesthetically awful if we lost now. It would be too *ugly*. It wouldn't be *right*. For morality and aesthetics are twin sisters. Doardo goes up for another high cross and again fails to touch it. Again there's a hopeless scrambling to get the thing away. Clearly this is not the moment for tackling philosophical conundrums.

But, though it's our goal under constant pressure, the last touch of irony (all at our expense) comes not from Doardo but from Frey. Three minutes from time, an exhausted Hellas launch a valiant counter-attack. Giuseppe Colucci dribbles into the area on the far left and sends a low cross to Mazzola arriving on the right. Suddenly, incredibly, we have a player absolutely free in front of Frey, perhaps four yards out. He takes the ball on the volley and hits a thundering shot. Upon which Frey reminds us what it is to have a serious goalkeeper. His body is quicksilver. The ball spins off for a corner. Unbelievable.

'How can you spend fifty thousand to see something that you wish would be over as soon as possible!' Such the comment of one of the guys sitting in front. He's shaking his head. But it is at last over. Two–two. At least we didn't lose. But we could have won! Or maybe it's precisely because we didn't win, and because that second half was such a nightmare, that we feel so close to the team as the final whistle blows. The players all come to toss their shirts into the crowd. In the car, I'm still trembling. 'What do you think,' one commentator is saying to the other as I turn the radio on. 'Two points lost by Inter, I'd say.' I turn it off. '*Bastardi!*' Michele shouts. Though we get home late, I crack open a litre of beer and pour some for him and for perhaps fifteen minutes we both sit at the table shaking our heads, occasionally muttering '*Bastardi.*'

'Applies the rules with Italiano,' the *Gazzetta* tells us next morning. And adds: 'Though the rules should be changed.' The *Arena* says Italiano was infantile. Italiano says he was overcome by joy. He uses exactly the words Marsiglia used: 'I lost my head.' On The Wall, someone is furious:

'It's a sacred right of us fans to see the players celebrate with us beneath the *curva* when they score.'

Sacred! I tend to agree.

5A GIORNATA

Bari – Parma 0–1
Brescia – Roma 2–4
Fiorentina – Perugia 3–4
Lazio – Bologna 2–0
Milan – Atalanta 3–3
Napoli – Vicenza 1–2
Reggina – Juventus 0–2
Udinese – Lecce 2–0
Verona – Inter 2–2

CLASSIFICA

Udinese	13
Roma	12
Atalanta	11
Juventus	10
Lazio	10
Bologna	9
Parma	8
Inter	7
Perugia	7
Fiorentina	6
Verona	6
Vicenza	6
Milan	5
Lecce	5
Reggina	3
Brescia	2
Bari	2
Napoli	1

I Magnagati

Camoranesi one of us.
McDan

I have been halted beneath a huge poster showing Silvio Berlusconi's strange smile. This immensely powerful man, owner of a vast media empire and leader of the main opposition party, has something of the beaten dog about him. It's an expression I have never figured out. The lips are lifted in a smile, but the eyes are pained, as though anticipating that you won't trust him. I don't. I always feel uneasy about posters of Berlusconi, though never so uneasy as when I realise we have a panicking keeper between the posts. Before this book is finished and more or less around the time that we will know whether Hellas Verona have escaped relegation or not, Berlusconi will probably become Italy's next Prime Minister.

We are being marched about two kilometres from station to stadium through Vicenza. There are about three thousand of us in a long snake, with the beautiful city centre to the left and the imposing sanctuary Monte Berico on the tall hill to the right. '*Vicenza, Vicenza vaffanculo!*' we yell. Police in riot gear prevent anyone from breaking out on either side. Occasionally, as now, they order everybody to halt. In quotation marks beneath Berlusconi's unhappy smile are the words: '*Adozioni più facili. Ogni bambino ha diritto a una famiglia.*' (Easier adoptions. Every child has a right to a family.)

Adoption is necessarily a major issue in a country that prizes local identity but has one of the lowest birth rates in the world.

The population of Verona apparently remains stable at 280,000 only thanks to the virile contribution of its immigrant population. Meantime, and much to everybody's relief, it has been announced that Italy has willingly adopted Mauro Camoranesi. Yes, Hellas's young gaucho has been granted dual nationality because one of his grandfathers, it seems, hailed from the *bel paese*. This is important because only three *extra-comunitari* (citizens from outside the EC) can go on the field at the same time. Now the boy can be more easily sold on to one of the big teams who are full of *extra-comunitari*. Pastorello no doubt foresees a profit.

Things have not gone so well for Lazio's Argentinian Veron whose claim that his grandfather was Italian has been found to be based, like Marsiglia's theology degree, on forged papers. The star player is under investigation for fraud while at the same time the police have declared that Mihajlovic is under investigation for inciting racial hatred. To complete the picture a Nigerian who plays for Reggiana (Reggio Emilia) has taken the Federcalcio, the footballing authorities, to court because when his team was relegated to Serie C he found himself without a job. No *extra-comunitari* are allowed to play in Serie C. The judge recognised that this state of affairs was contrary to the Italian Constitution. Immediately, the sports director of AC Milan, Galliani, demanded that the restriction to three *extra-comunitari* be removed from Serie A. Milan, it seems, could field a whole team of *extra-comunitari*. 'Death to the alliance between blacks and big money!' someone responds on The Wall. Blacks and big money! The more intense the mixing, the con-fusion, the more the heat given off and the greater the nostalgia for some simple local identity. But when did the long slide start? When did this infernal process begin? Who can say, but certainly the day that Hellas Verona made their first trip to Vicenza was an important turning point.

Formed in 1903, Hellas was little more than a group of friends for the first few years. Who were they? Schoolboys at the Liceo classico Maffei, workplace of Luìs Marsiglia. The more I learn about the club the more the Maffei won't go away. Unsure what to call themselves on their way to their first game, the boys accepted the suggestion of the Greek teacher: Hellas. The team would be their *patria*. One can only hope the man had his degree and his papers in order.

All the same, the public weren't interested at first. Matches were sporadic, interest fitful. Then in 1906 a game was arranged in the Arena, the Roman amphitheatre in the centre of town. The *Gazzetta dello Sport*, already a major publication, commented: 'Most of the Veronese didn't even know what football was about before this game: but the experiment carried out in front of three thousand people confirmed the impression already dominant in other countries: football will be the athletic game of the future.'

Prophetic words. That was in February. Two months later Hellas were being invited to travel the forty long kilometres to close neighbours Vicenza for a small four-team tournament. They declined, complaining that the fifteen lira inscription fee was too high. Ninety-four years later, picking up my ticket for the game, I hear the guy in front of me complaining, 'Is it possible these shitty cat-eaters want us to pay thirty-seven thousand lire to get into their miserable shitty stadium! It's a scandal.'

An old dialect saying runs:

> *Venessiani gran signori*
> *Padovani gran dotori*
> *Vicentini magnagati*
> *Veronesi tuti mati.*

> Venetians lords and earls
> Paduans learned scholars
> Vicentini gobble up cat
> Veronese are all quite mad.

But in the end Hellas decided to pay and go, as today three thousand people have chosen to pay and come to Vicenza, though inexplicably Vicenza have made only 1,500 tickets available.

In 1906 Verona lost two–one. They played a return match

shortly afterwards in Verona and again lost two–one. At a similar tournament won by Vicenza in 1908, Hellas retired halfway through protesting exhaustion. Occasionally one still sees teams who might do well to exhume this option. It wasn't until 1912 that Verona finally beat their oldest and nearest rivals. Reporting the crowd response, the local journalist was clearly witnessing for the first time a new way of expressing group-identity and antagonism.

> Hellas won! Nothing we could write to express our joy, if such a thing were possible; no declaration we could ever make as to the indisputable talent of each single player, none excluded, could be so eloquent as the powerful, almost savage yell of the crowd each time Hellas scored a point. The shouting slowly subsided to be replaced by a confused never repressed clamour rising and falling with the anxious and diligent inspection of every move on the field. Hellas won! A victory too long desired.

In the 1960s the Romanian philosopher Emil Cioran wrote: 'The civilising passage from blows to insults was no doubt necessary, but the price was high. Words will never be enough. We will always be nostalgic for violence and blood.'

It's strange, it occurs to me, being escorted through the streets of Vicenza, as the boys yell insults at the blacks, at the Vicentini, at the police, as scuffles break out and a few stones are thrown and the crowd heaves this way and that confused by conflicting orders from various megaphones, strange that a Romanian of all people, a man from the country that bred Hagi and the adorable, impossible Mutu, would not have realised that football offers an ambiguous middle ground between words and blows.

In his nineteenth-century *Discourse on the Game of Florentine Football*, Giovanni Maria de' Bardi defined the sport thus: 'Football is a public game of two groups of young men, on foot and unarmed, who pleasingly compete to move a medium-sized inflated ball from one end of the piazza to the other, for the sake of honour.'

'Unarmed' is the crucial word here. That day in 1912 the

Veronese crowd, unarmed, discovered a new way of expressing their antique rivalry with their neighbours. And for the first time they had the upper hand. For the first time they could take pleasure, unarmed, in their neighbours' discomfort. They could taunt and gloat and be cruel. Football offers an arena for experiencing all the passions, positive and negative, and escaping unscathed. Hopefully. Perhaps five minutes after thinking these edifying thoughts, I was struck in the face by a whirling flagpole. Moments later the crowd broke around me and a policeman exploded into the empty space, truncheon raised above my head.

You beat the neighbouring town at football and a collective dream is born: to impose yourself on all around, not in battle, where you couldn't hope to prevail, not even commercially, where perhaps you couldn't compete, but in this heraldic and athletic festival, for honour let's say, which is an attractive word. In 1911 Verona joined the north-eastern region of the football league. Now they could beat Bologna and Venice as well.

Yet the moment the dream is dreamed, the complications begin, the hard work, the contradictions. There are not enough good players in Verona to make Hellas great. Or if there is a good player, somebody invites him to go elsewhere, to Milan, Juventus, to Pro Vercelli. Today the best native-born Verona player, Damiano Tommasi, plays for Roma. So the team's first manager immediately sent out scouts to 'steal' players from other provincial teams. In 1912 a Swiss boy stopped by at the club and claimed to be a good central defender. He had played for Young Boys, Zurich. So a foreigner was invited to bear the banner of Veronese honour. He could barely speak Italian, never mind dialect.

In 1920 gunfire is heard during crowd violence in a game against another local side, Petrarca. Since football must hover at the brink of violence, but never fall into it, the game is suspended. In 1921 Verona is allowed into the Northern League, playing teams as far away as Turin and Genoa. In 1926 the league goes national and now Hellas can take on Rome and even Naples. Sitting opposite me in the train on the way to Vicenza, a wizened old man warns me of the dangers of away games down south. He has a small shrivelled face and an incongruous fuzz of Hendrix hair. 'Those kids don't fool around,' he says in a dialect I can barely understand. 'Our *butei* have their *telefonini*, the Neapolitans their guns.'

It's a constant scramble to compete in a bigger and bigger league, to impose local pride on a larger and larger, ever more mixed-up world. And each time a new horizon is opened, a few old names will disappear. Where now Audace with their red-and-black shirts? And Edera? Where is the once formidable Pro-Vercelli?

But Hellas Verona are still there, just, despite, in 1941, a brief descent into the 'inferno', as the official history of the club would have it, of Serie C. In 1946, the writer tells us, they earned themselves a place in purgatorio, Serie B, but then would have to do eleven years' penitence before winning their first promotion into Serie A, paradiso, 1957. After which what remained but the goal of that new heaven and new earth, Europe? In 1983 the club finally won the right to participate in the European Fairs Cup, and on an extraordinary autumn evening Hellas Verona extended their Yellow-Blue reign across the Adriatic, beating the mighty Red Star Belgrade in their home stadium. 'You're all filthy Slavs, as far as I can see,' writes a Turin-based Juventus supporter, invading the hyperspace of www.Hellasverona.it.

Yet, however far afield the Yellow-Blues may travel, stretched and overstretched, however many Brazilians and Germans and Danes and Slavs may play or have played in their team, in the end it always comes back to this, this old old game with the *magnagati*, our *cuginastri* (nasty cousins), this re-enactment of the first mixing of all, when Verona went to Vicenza. This is the game that generates the most heat, the one no one wants to lose, the one that will attract the most away-game supporters. No distinction is more urgent or more arduous than that between ourselves and those who most resemble us, the guys down the road. And how much more difficult the distinction becomes when Verona is now owned by the Vicenza-born Pastorello and Vicenza by an anonymous consortium of British investors. It's one of those puzzling moments when you must '*aggrapparsi ai colori presi dallo stemma della città*': cling to the colours taken from the city's coat of arms. 'VERONA, CITY AND STATE!' one banner says. On The Wall someone writes: 'Since 1200, whenever the Scaligeri go to Vicenza, the ground trembles.'

The scene as we leave town might be an expensive cinema reconstruction of some moment in 1916 when the Alpini and Bersaglieri were cheered off to war. The railways have laid on a special cut-price train made up of ancient but rather charming carriages, a good twenty of them. The big windows pull right down. The boys are hanging out in the damp air with their scarves and banners and flags, shouting and waving. 'Cheer up!' a voice shrieks at me. '*Dio boia!*' A huge man comes stumbling into the compartment. 'It's our party!' He's high. He has a bottle of *limoncello* in his hand. '*Alè Verona!*' He waves his hat out of the window. Then turns to my worried face, disgusted. '*Facciamo festa!*' he orders. 'Party time! Look out of the window! Cheer up.' He grabs me from behind and pushes my head outside. 'Isn't it fantastic! Isn't our party beautiful!'

He's right. The train is grinding out of Verona Porta Nuova in a tight left-hand curve which takes it over the big circular road where the black prostitutes hang out, then across the Adige, still spectacularly swollen with this autumn's constant rain. It has rained ever since that evening we gathered outside the Zanzibar for the away game at Bari. For a moment I have the wonderful vision northwards that seduces every arriving tourist: the red-and-white brick embankment of the fast brown river, the stone bridges, the bristle of towers, *palazzi* and *campanili*, the ancient fortifications zigzagging up the steep cypress hills to Castel San Pietro on the right with its picture-book battlements, the Sanctuary of Our Lady of Lourdes far away to the left, and behind, just visible beneath a grey sky, the already snow-capped Alps. Gazing out at the scene beside this man waving a bottle beside me, I'm struck by the fact that I have spent twenty years here, my whole adult life really. All the taxes I have paid I have paid here, *Dio can*. A fortune! I have brought up my kids here. I too have a right, I tell myself, to this civic pride. I too can party.

'Sing!' the new arrival orders me. He starts into a song to the tune of Verdi's *'Va' pensiero'*. 'Bang on the window!' he orders. *'Veronese!'* And we bang time on the window. *'Gran figlio di troia sei tu, sei gialloblù, sei gialloblù.'* Veronese, great son of a bitch you are. You're Yellow-Blue, Yellow-Blue.

It's fun banging on the window as the train fizzes with excitement. Then, tall, unshaven, blond, drunk and coked to the eyeballs, the new arrival bounces out as suddenly as he bounced in. Without him to order me about, I collapse on my seat. The old man opposite tells me about the Neapolitans with their guns and knives and then the boy in the far corner proudly announces that he was knifed in Rome. He tells his story. He took the Eurostar, and was walking drunk through the city singing at the top of his voice when all at once someone stabbed him from behind. 'In the butt. Police took me to hospital. Thirteen stitches.' Deep down you can see he's delighted. 'A game of two groups of young men,' I reflect, 'unarmed, for honour.' When I ask him whether it was worth missing the game for, he tells me, yes.

At Vicenza station, the American and Japanese tourists, fresh from their visits to Palladio's masterpieces, to Giotto's frescos of the damned, look on with wonder as these damned boys march out of the station chanting blasphemies. Everybody is promisingly aggrieved. Everybody pulls their hats over their faces as we pass the policeman with the video camera at the top of the stairs. There's an old guy covered with medals, a fat woman in her sixties dressed in yellow-blue rags from top to toe. Gathering in the street, we give Vicenza notice of our arrival with a rousing performance of *Chi noi siamo*.

Then things turn sour. The walk is too long. There's too much stopping and starting. The police are overstretched. They are trying to keep our crocodile compact and to fight off attacks from stone-throwing Vicentini who rush up quite suddenly from desolate side-streets, hurling a few pebbles at us, nothing serious, and dash away again. A policeman bangs his truncheon on the back of the van that's supposed to be leading us. 'Move, asshole!' He's dented his own van! The boys jeer. We shuffle on.

A cloud of ambiguity hangs over these scenes. You can never know quite what's happened or why. How is it that some boys are suddenly fighting the police on an island of flowering shrubs in the middle of the road? Plastic flagpoles are being used as swords. Some of the kids are mad. Others are smugly urging them on, but keeping out of trouble. 'Why does nothing ever really happen? What's wrong with these kids? Go on, do it!' When the police lay into someone, the boys are indignant. We haven't done anything! Thugs, Fascists. When a stone hits a helmet there are cheers.

Suddenly the whole crowd shifts violently. I'm almost knocked over. Where there was a solid mass, there is nobody. On the ground before me a boy is being beaten. A stout moustached policeman looks me in the eyes, his truncheon raised. I'm lucky, it doesn't come down. A firework sizzles over our heads. A few yards away the police are beating two youths on the ground. Their truncheons come down again and again, fast and rhythmical, as if this were some kind of wearisome manual labour. Other people light cigarettes, leaning against a fence, bored.

Finally we reach the stadium just twenty minutes before the game to find only one small gate open. It's narrower than a regular door in an ordinary house. Strait is the gate and narrow the way. And they're trying to check all the tickets, one by one! This is crazy. We'll never get in. The game will kick off without us. Half the crowd haven't got tickets. The police are trying to turn them away. The crowd behind won't make room. Behind the narrow gate, a policeman is standing on a box or raised platform of some kind so that he can loom out waving his truncheon. Other police hang around the fringes uncertain what to do. One or two of them are selling tickets. How can this be?

'*Issa!*' the crowd began to shout. '*Issa!*' Heave, heave! Those at the door are being crushed, forced through the gate. A group of police are trying to hold a barrier. It's ridiculous. And how strange, at the edge of the crowd some fans are calmly chatting to the policemen, while others stand only inches away shrieking the most obscene insults right into their plastic visors.

'We were at Brescia yesterday,' a policeman tells me. For the

Saturday game with Atalanta. 'There was lots of trouble. Much worse than this.' Only now do I realise that these men are part of a specially trained force. They're not locals at all. Perhaps they actually volunteered for this. Perhaps they look forward to a little trouble.

'Why don't they just let us in. Is there space?'

He shakes his head. 'Sure there's space. Plenty of it. If it was up to me, I'd just let you through. Mad, isn't it?' He seems resigned, unimpressed. For reasons I can't imagine a tear-gas canister is fired. People lift their scarves to their faces. But no one wants to lose his place in the crush. We hang on, gasping. Then I'm just two yards from that narrow door, hand over my mouth, when I become aware of the fence. There's a low railing to force people into line against the wall. It's between ourselves and the door. How could we have known? Thousands of people are forcing themselves against this railing. It's jammed against my thigh. *Issa. Issa.* Afraid I'll be crushed, I lift my knee, get a foot on the top bar and push. The force of the crowd behind sends me shooting up, and suddenly I'm crawling over heads and shoulders right through the door and into the dark of the entrance. Others are following. As I drop down I can't help bursting out laughing.

In the stadium the ambiguity persists. '*Salutiamo i nostri cugini*' says one banner at the Vicenza end. And beside it two smaller ones: 'VERONA MERDA', 'HELLAS A.I.D.S.' Meantime the *butei* are hanging up a banner at the back of our paddock. 'VAFFANCULO MANGIAMIAO'. Fuck off miaow eaters. They start to sing: '*Vicentino maledetto, hai mangiato il mio micetto.*' Damned Vicentino ate my cat.

As if to give the lie to this, a man dressed in a huge red and white cat outfit (Vicenza colours) appears from the players' tunnel and goes round the pitch to general cheers and mirth. He waves his paws and waggles his whiskers. When the teams come out, each Vicenza supporter holds up a huge red card, perhaps half a metre square, so that their whole *curva* is a solid block of red. What an effort to orchestrate this! The *brigate* clap slowly.

The game is the most violent of the season so far. The *Gazzetta* will describe it as very 'English': the muddy field, the brutal, low-quality football under a 'London smoke' of a sky. Verona play better and get nowhere. At the beginning of the second half, against the run of play, Vicenza score. Only sixty seconds of gloom before our equaliser. The Vicenza fans are furious because they're convinced that Bonazzoli, our centre-forward, pushed the defender out of the way. Looking at the video later, I suspect they're right. Dodging police, a fan rushes on to the field and makes straight for the referee. From under his coat he produces the huge red card used for the show earlier on. He points the referee to the dressing room. Off! There are general cheers at this show of wit as the police drag him away.

Surely now we are going to win. We are the better team. We have equalised. But their centre-forward, Luca Toni, keeps falling over. He wins a free kick outside the box. They score again. Two–one. And now there's real despair. We'll never equalise twice. To make matters worse, the Vicenza supporters to our right are throwing coins at us. I turn my back to them. Suddenly a big red firework comes spinning and fizzing through the air and down into our paddock. A man picks it up and hurls it back. But then it comes back to us again, turning over and over in the air. Yet again it's thrown back. Each time it passes the fence a great shout goes up. This time it lands right on someone's head and there's a shriek. Applause from the crowd. The police have got the thing, and it's eyes back to the pitch.

'Shit,' the man next to me is muttering. 'Shit shit shit.' For the whole game I have had to listen to his monotone litany. Perhaps my own age, grim, tense, unhappy, this sharp-faced man grumbles on and on under his breath. The referee is biased. The stadium is shit. The pitch is a bog. The police are thugs. The Vicentini are subhuman. He joins in none of the songs. He never cheers. He never claps. He seems locked into some terrible gloom. To his other side, an over-made-up woman in a rather smart jacket holds his arm tight and smiles, but she knows it's pointless to interrupt. 'Merda, merda, merda,' he's saying. There's a curious pathos, a compassion, in the way she accepts his misery. She lays her dyed hair on his shoulder. It occurs to me that perhaps a man like this should not be supporting a team like Hellas Verona. Perhaps it would be forgivable for a real depressive to support Milan or Juventus. Have psychologists latched on to this kind of thing?

Then miraculously, from a corner, Camoranesi pays us back for his recent adoption. Unbelievably this small boy, just a metre seventy-four the official website tells me, jumps higher than all the huge defenders and puts the ball in. For just a moment my neighbour is a volcano of happiness. He's yelling. '*Rete!*' Goal. He embraces everyone, the people behind, the people in front, myself, his wife. Then she resumes her position as his face sets in intense anxiety again. '*Merda.*'

Two–all. Both teams are possible relegation victims. Both teams are determined to get those three points. As the floodlights come up, the last fifteen minutes are savage. Martin Laursen, in particular, seems finally to have met his match in the giant Toni, a mountain of a boy who either pushes him out of the way or falls over at once to win a foul. There are more dangerous free kicks. The usually calm Danish boy is getting wild. He's forgotten all the noble words he spoke when interviewed after the Pope's game. We need these points! Even more importantly, we mustn't let Vicenza have them. He slides across the filthy pitch with studs up. It's dangerous. But he just can't hold his man. Toni is strong, he's talented. He defends the ball with great cunning. Laursen is tiring. Finally he hacks the striker down from behind and is justly sent off. A glimpse of his distraught face suggests he's lucky not to be armed. And luckily there was only a minute left. Two–all it is. An away point is money in the bank.

6A GIORNATA

Atlanta – Brescia 2–0
Bari – Milan 1–3
Bologna – Fiorentina 1–1
Inter – Lecce 0–1
Juventus – Lazio 1–1
Parma – Udinese 2–0
Perugia – Napoli 1–1
Roma – Reggina 2–1
Vicenza – Verona 2–2

CLASSIFICA

Roma	15
Atalanta	14
Udinese	13
Juventus	11
Lazio	11
Parma	11
Bologna	10
Milan	8
Perugia	8
Lecce	8
Fiorentina	7
Inter	7
Verona	7
Vicenza	7
Reggina	3
Brescia	2
Bari	2
Napoli	2

Al Vincitore

Hellas is a feeling, a faith, not a cheque to stick in your pocket, Pastorello.
    Zio Preben (Elkjaer)

How consistent is character? Coming back from Vicenza I observed a strange scene. Slumped at last in a train compartment, I was listening to the man and wife opposite me assuring their families on separate mobile phones that they had not been involved in any of the violence that was apparently being shown on television. A boy came rushing across the compartment and slammed down the window. He was slim, handsome, perhaps seventeen, with blond hair expensively cut round a centre parting and a fine chiselled face. Leaning out of the window, be began to shout at the line of policemen only a yard or two away. 'Shits! Thugs! Worms! Turds! Communists! Go fuck yourselves!'

If a young man were to do this on any ordinary day in any ordinary street of northern Italy, the abused policemen would arrest him at once. Instead, within the framework football provides, the men in uniform gazed back impassive, their padded jackets full of weapons. 'Fascists! Slavs! Kurds! Bastards! *Terroni!*'

Then the boy realised his mobile was ringing. He pulled it out of his jacket pocket. 'No, Mamma, we're still in the station at Vicenza.' How sweet his voice was now, how empty of tension or anger! 'No, we didn't have much homework this weekend. I've already finished.'

But as he was speaking, the carriage began to pull out of the station. '*Momento, Mamma.*' Putting his hand over the microphone, he leaned out of the window again. '*Vaffanculo stronzi di merda vergogna di tutta l'Italia.*' His face was livid with rage. The policemen were motionless, inscrutable. The other people in the carriage barely noticed. 'Sorry, Mamma,' the boy goes back to his phone, 'the *butei* are making a bit of a racket.' He laughs. 'Anyhow, we're just leaving the station now, so if you put on the pasta round, what, six-thirty I should be back when it's cooked. *Ciao, Mamma.*'

In the late 1920s, observing the behaviour patterns of the Iatmul Indians of New Guinea, the British anthropologist Gregory Bateson invented the word schismogenesis. He was trying to define the process by which the individual assumes a personal identity in a larger social dynamic. In the case of the Iatmul he noticed that whenever one of the men began to show off, which was often, the other men would immediately compete with him. Meantime, the more the men became exhibitionist and boastful, the more the women in response grew quiet, admiring and contemplative.

The pattern was endlessly repeated. Bateson, who knew nobody ever reached a conclusion without jumping to it, quickly decided that any behavioural gesture would provoke either competitive or complementary reactions on the part of others and that this would generate a schismatic process, with one person assuming one role, one another, but always in relation to each other. It was no time at all then before the anthropologist was talking about schismogenesis in marriages and families, in the workplace, in politics, in the arms race.

But Bateson did not call his book on the Iatmul *Schismogenesis*. The more he watched those men showing off, those women admiring, the more he realised that this business of action and reaction, whether competitive or complementary, was not a process that could go on unchecked. Otherwise it would surely lead to wild behavioural extremes, perhaps to conflict, perhaps to a crippling sterility. For, if behaviour was for ever thus conditioned, an individual's range of experience would inevitably be lamentably narrow. The Iatmul men were interminably exhibitionist and competitive, the Iatmul women contemplative to the point of catatonia.

Bateson called his book *Naven*. It was the name of a bizarre series of religious rituals the Iatmul engaged in at regular intervals. Here the normal behaviour pattern was emphatically reversed. The men dressed up as women and vice versa. The women now assumed, with great excitement and relief, extremely aggressive and exhibitionist postures, the men became abject and passive, and even submitted to simulated anal rape. Bateson suspected that it was this release-through-reversal in carefully controlled conditions that allowed the society to remain sane and stable.

It would be all too easy to see something of the same thing going on at the stadium. Aside from its immigrant population, Verona has the most homogeneous and conservative society imaginable. My children complain that they cannot arrange to see friends on Sunday because they all without exception visit their grandparents. They all go to catechism. 'Francesco never missed his catechism,' Totti's mother announces to the *Gazzetta* during the European Finals. When each Saturday night brings its frightening death toll on the roads around Verona, people say, 'But Roberto was always such a careful driver.' 'Matteo was a quiet, ordinary boy,' protest the respectable friends of a young man who has knifed two prostitutes in the back of his car. 'Perhaps our children have two souls,' says a father, reacting to the news that his son is among those arrested for disturbances outside the stadium.

Two weeks after the Vicenza game, in another train, on my own this time, travelling to the game with Juventus, a man comes into my compartment. He has seen the yellow–blue cover of the book I'm reading, *Il calcio a Verona*. Born and brought up in Trento, but of Veronese parents, this young man follows every Verona away game on his own, being forced to scrounge and beg tickets on arrival, since, by law, tickets for Verona supporters can only be sold in Verona.

'Yes, all my friends are amazed,' he admits. His name is Mirko. 'They say, you're such a calm ordinary bloke. What are you doing messing with the *brigate*?' He admits it's become a drug. I ask, 'What about your girlfriend?' He tells me a sad story. 'Never again', he winds up with some bitterness, 'will I let the need to say I have a woman get in the way of what I really want to do.' He really wants to go to away games. He wants to stand in the *curva*. 'When the chanting begins,' he laughs, 'it's something else, isn't it? *Chi noi siamo!*' Half-humorously he raises a fist in the air.

But this sort of behaviour is not Naven. Among the Iatmul Indians the assumption of a different role, the extension of normally limited personality in a frenzy of aggression (our young blond boy yelling insults) or an acceptance of humiliation (our policeman) was underwritten by the gods. It was a duty to welcome this invasion of new emotions. An experience of ecstasy was inseparable from an act of faith. It had meaning. Could we ever say the same of the football fan?

The week after the Vicenza game, Verona were thrashed four–one at home by league leaders Roma – it's not a match I want to report on – and in the crush on the stairs leaving the ground I spotted Andrea, the man who is selling me a new computer system. 'How can they play that badly?' I wrote him an e-mail half in fun, half in desperation. 'How can they expect us to watch them when they're so pathetic?' 'Hellas is a faith,' Andrea wrote back at once. 'You must never ask why.' During the game, even as we were being thrashed, the fans had sung: '*Hellas, la nostra unica fede.*' Our only faith. Their arms are raised in the air, their faces bright with worship.

But just because people use this inflated vocabulary doesn't mean that football is a faith for them in the way Naven was for the Iatmul. After all, Hellas Verona clearly *is* a commercial concern and Giambattista Pastorello does well to keep a sharp eye on his wallet. *Il calcio a Verona* is full of the tales of those who, drunk with dreams of glory, lost the shirts off their backs for the club. 'I made a mistake after Verona won the *scudetto*,' says ruined ex-chairman Chiampan. 'I should have sold all the big players at once and started from scratch.'

Preben Elkjaer was no doubt the biggest of those players, the most valuable property. But he wasn't God. Or if he was, then there's a vertiginous turnover of deities these days. 'Frey is God,' I heard last year. But this particular idol was on loan from Inter. The Iatmul's divinities were not so easily replaced or traded, their faith not so frequently lost and found; indeed it was probably so solid they didn't even realise it was a faith at all. They didn't have to try.

But most of all, in a ceremony like Naven, or any traditional religious ritual, the complicity of all the participants is total. They know that without the ceremony the world would stop. The Aztec sun would die and fall from heaven if a victim wasn't sacrificed. The victim knew this and accepted his fate. The killing went ahead uncontested.

Unfortunately, the policeman at today's stadium doesn't see it that way. He's there to stop two groups of hooligans from tearing each other apart. He doesn't think of himself as engaged in a ceremony. On the contrary, he probably supports the football federation's evident desire to discourage fans from coming to away games, to convince them to stay home and dial up the match on the new system that allows you, once you have bought the right equipment, to watch any game you like. Why don't these idiots stay at home? the policeman is thinking. You can see it in his eyes. Why do they insist on these impossible journeys, this theatre of outrage? 'Stronzo, pezzo di merda!' The policeman believes that insults and obscenities are uncivil. He is getting angry. He doesn't like the idea that in certain situations certain laws are suspended. If he stays put and soaks up the young man's abuse it's only because his training tells him that any other approach will lead to havoc.

Havoc. Football is a hybrid constantly seeking to become something it is not, something pure. Its fans want it to be a faith, they want it to offer that delirium of escape into a different realm of experience. But without a God to underwrite the ceremony, it can never quite become that. Meantime the temple and its owners try to cool the fanatics' fervour. They know that the game's bottom line is business, and they would like it to be no more than that: a contest between two groups of young men, on foot, unarmed, for TV rights and cash.

So however carefully set up, the ceremony at the stadium always risks breaking down. Not knowing quite what football is, the various participants aren't sure how they should behave. The event can never quite achieve ritual status. The crowd believe in Hellas, but then they don't believe. They can dream, but they don't really expect to go to heaven. Alongside the passion there is always irony and ambiguity. 'O Parroco, have you prayed for our Verona?' a kid asks me. I recognise a boy from the Bari trip. The one who sat opposite me and munched the endless sandwiches. 'Sure I've prayed,' I tell him, and we both laugh. The *curva* raises a forest of arms in adoration, but immediately afterwards we all clap ourselves. We're clapping our capacity to dream, perhaps. It's uplifting, but never quite uplifting enough. From time to time something gets out of hand, out of bounds. All ancient religions concur that when a ceremony is profaned and a sacred space invaded, havoc and bloodshed will follow. In football, where the space was never quite sacred anyway and where the ceremony always needs the unlikely alibi of healthy outdoor entertainment, violence is recurrent and probably inevitable.

At more or less the same time as we were leaving the Bentegodi after our defeat against Roma, a certain Massimiliano Ferrigno, captain of the Serie C team Como, punched Modena player Francesco Bertolotti. The two, once close friends in the same squad, had quarrelled during the game. Ferrigno had been sent off. His team lost. The punch, when he saw his old companion in the dressing-room corridor, was sudden and violent. Bertolotti fell back, banged his head on the floor and did not get up. He is in coma. He may die. Monday's *Arena* reported the story on page 23. In a rather larger article complete with colour photo on the front page, the paper reports that, to deal with her fiery temper, Naomi Campbell has taken up boxing.

And now, only a week after that startling news, in an unrelated incident, a group of Verona fans, including women and children, were savagely beaten by the police as they left the Stadio delle Alpi in Turin after Hellas's game with Juventus. There were six arrests. But before we tackle this unhappy incident, let's read the poem that, along with *Il calcio a Verona*, I took with me that day in the train to Turin.

To a Winner with the Ball

By Giacomo Leopardi, November 1821

Of glory the face and the jocund voice,
You must learn, blessed boy,
And know how much the sweated virtues
Surpass effeminate indolence. Be alert
Generous champion (from the swift
Flood of the years may your skill snatch
The spoil of your name), be alert and bend
Your heart to greatness. The echoing
Arena and the circus, the roaring support
Of the crowd call you to illustrious deeds.
Today our dear country is
Coaching you to repeat the examples of the ancients.

After this first stanza, I should assure the reader that the original is written in beautifully rhyming verse. But however cumbersome my translation, I think it's worth looking at the thing. Leopardi's ball-player throws himself into the game in search of glory, immortality even. The ancients are in the background, though their deeds were of quite a different nature. The crowd urge the player on. Somehow they will share in his achievement. Travelling to Turin 179 Novembers later, I and the man opposite me, his nose now joyously buried in *Il calcio a Verona*, were certainly hoping to share in Mutu's glory that afternoon, or Gilardino's, or more likely our goalkeeper Ferron's. But at the same time we were eager that Juventus strikers Del Piero and Trezeguet and Zidane be denied glory. We would love for them to leave the pitch humiliated. Sport is a cruel business, as Leopardi's next, horribly contorted, verse reminds us.

He did not dip his right hand
In barbarian blood at Marathon
Who could look lukewarm at the
Naked athletes and their arduous trials

On the Olympian field, or, seeing
The blessed palm and victor's crown,
Not feel his pulse race to emulate.
In Alpheus, perhaps, the hero who led
The Greek ensigns and wielded Greek steel
Amid the Persians, earlier cleansed
The dusty manes and flanks of the victorious horses,
So that, tired and terrified, the pale legions
Fled, and the deep waters of the Euphrates and
The enslaved shore beyond echoed
With inconsolable grief.

This is difficult, isn't it? Why did Leopardi, who was no fool, make a poem about a ball game so hard that today your average Italian reader needs a crib to approach it? Struggling to translate the thing, some days now after the Juventus game, I begin to suspect that that high poetic tone and extravagantly archaic syntax are partly there to hide the cruelty and pessimism of what the poet is saying. Let's see if we can gloss.

Alpheus was the river that flowed by the Olympian fields, home of the Games. Before the battle of Marathon the Greek general looks for inspiration by washing down his horses in the river of athletic achievement. The link between military glory and sporting prowess, between ancients and moderns, is thus established. Meantime, anybody who could be indifferent, the poet tells us, to ball games would also have been useless on the battlefield. The same aspirations are involved.

But, aside from glory for the winners, what do these aspirations lead to? The immediate result of the Greek success is 'inconsolable grief' for the losers. Leopardi, singing of glory, has nothing to say to alleviate the sufferings of those who pay the price of another's fame, those who face relegation. But when Hellas go to Juventus you have to be prepared to lose. 'We are not going as sacrificial victims,' Attilio Perotti tells the newspaper the day before, confirming that this is what everybody believes: we are going as sacrificial victims.

No comfort for the losers, then. But the poet's pessimism is only just beginning. In the next verse, read between glances at swamped rice fields between Milan and Turin, Leopardi reveals that it is precisely because he has no religion and believes in nothing at all that he can think winning with the ball is so important. As so often, it's hard not to see some uneasy relationship between the phenomenon that is modern sport and the decline of religion.

> Shall I call vain what unlocks and stirs
> The hidden sparks of native virtue,
> Reviving in sickly breasts
> The lost fervour of our vital
> Spirit? Since Phoebus first shifted
> His chariot's sad wheels, has human effort
> Ever been but a game? Is truth any less
> Empty than falsehood? With delightful deceit
> And happy shadow-play, Nature herself came
> To our aid: and now that unhealthy custom
> No longer lays its bait to lure errors of greatness
> People have turned glorious pursuits
> Into bare and humdrum hobbies.

It's funny here seeing how the Italian crib (without which I would never have understood those final lines) tones down what Leopardi is saying. 'Nature comes to our aid', it explains, 'by filling the emptiness and meaninglessness of life with delightful fantasies and happy dreams. But because our senseless modern way of living offers no fuel to feed the great illusions of the past, people have transformed the endeavours that once brought glory into squalid, ignoble leisure.'

This gives the gist, but not the grim grit of it. Leopardi used the word 'error'. The pursuits that brought glory, the grand illusions of the past – military prowess, artistic endeavour – were in fact errors, because nothing is worth anything at all, nothing was ever any more than a game. What we most admire comes from what is *erroneously* granted meaning. Or to put it the other way round: football is as meaningful as anything will ever be. So go for it! There is nothing else. Our national sport, in this reading, is the tropical bloom of modern decadence.

The person capable of swinging from extremes of joy to extremes of depression, Schopenhauer told us, is living in the thrall of an error. The austere German shakes his head in disapproval. But better a thrilling error, the Italian Leopardi had already decided some decades before, or any error at all for that matter, than the truth that the world is a 'solid nothingness'. Better to kneel before the TV in ecstasy when Scholes scores and bang your forehead against the wall when Kanu equalises, than simply watch a blank screen. All of a sudden you realise that the purpose of any culture is to foster collective self-deceit, to provide an enchantment within which we can live out our thrills and fears in a pageant of colour, to dangle the bait that will lure 'errors of greatness', in short, to 'make us dream'. 'Fantastic,' Mirko whispers over a photograph in my book. 'Do you remember Galderisi?' 'Before my time,' I tell him. 'Galderisi was a genius,' he says. If we had Galderisi today we could kill Juve.

Could we? I'm not convinced. Modern man – this was the conundrum Leopardi endlessly set himself – no longer believing naturally in anything at all, no longer born into a world where illusion is compact and homogeneous (as was Naven for the Iatmul), has *to make a big effort* to deceive himself *consciously*, he has to *decide* to be in error, he has to go *in search of illusion*, and this is a very tough prospect. Certainly it is a tough prospect to imagine Verona winning in Turin. Turin is hard. All the same I know that when I get into the stadium, when the rousing chants begin, when the players start passing the ball and Verona perhaps hazard a strike on the break, then, foolishly, wonderfully, I will start to hope. '*Giochiam' con voi!*' the *brigate* will sing to the tune of 'Auld Lang Syne'. 'We're playing with you!' It's easier to believe things when there's more than one of you at it. Perhaps that is the logic of all religious proselytising. If I can get others to believe, I'll be more convinced myself. In the station in Verona, as I was buying my ticket for the trip, I noticed a new advertising space. A four-metre-high black pillar had been set up in the middle of the big foyer. In letters the pink of *La Gazzetta dello Sport* it announced: 'To the Arena to sing. To the Stadium to

Dream.' Only the combination of place and crowd make a certain mental state possible. '*Buon viaggio, tifosi gialloblù,*' the ad finished, and underneath. 'The *Gazzetta*, your daily pleasure.'

But before the dream of the stadium or the pleasant after-echo of the daily papers, we still have two stanzas of Leopardi's nightmare to get through. Here he imagines that if the athletic and military *virtù* of the past is not recovered then Italy will soon descend into ruin.

> The time may come when herds trample
> The ruins of monumental Italy
> And the seven hills are offended by
> The plough; nor perhaps will the Earth
> Circle the sun many times before
> The fox slinks in our cities and dark woods
> Rustle between once high walls:
> All this if fate does not free perverse minds
> From the fatal forgetfulness of our country's
> Destiny, if the heavens, made merciful
> By the memory of deeds past, do not snatch
> Our abject people from imminent ruin.

Leopardi joked in letters to friends that, glancing through the titles of his poems, his father, Monaldo Leopardi, would never have been able to guess what was in them. He was twenty-three when he wrote 'To a Winner' and still financially dependent on the right-wing Monaldo who was worried about his eldest son's revolutionary politics and pessimistic philosophy. On The Wall somebody who signs himself Alcohol remarks 'thank God Papà thinks I'm using the computer for homework!'

All the same, reading this odd poem on the train, I'm convinced that Leopardi was trying to talk seriously about sport, or rather about winning. If you can't, against your better judgment, he seems to be saying, believe in your team, your country, or in fact anything, if you can't, in essence, be *infantile*, then it (team, country, whatever) and you yourself may disappear from the face of the earth, for you will be left with no resistance to nothingness.

To believe in something, knowing it can't be so, that is the ultimate achievement and also, far beyond the incursion of black players in white teams, it is the ultimate mixing: the superimposition of two contradictory states of mind. I know we're going to lose in Turin today, and I believe we're going to win.

'*Stronzi! Merda! Ciao, Mamma.*' Would a frenzied devotee of primitive rituals ever have managed the mental shifting back and forth demanded by the interruption of the *telefonino*? What religion could survive a priest who answered the phone while officiating the sacraments? Yet in late November I read in the *Arena* of a football game where a referee did indeed answer the phone. His shiny black referee's shorts began to trill – Pronto? – the man answered – Ciao! – and the players – it was a youth team – and the small crowd of vociferous parents (how vociferous those parents can get!) were jerked out of the mesmerism and passion of the game to stare amazed as the man resolved the problem of when to toss in the pasta, or where to meet for a drink. Then he blew his whistle and they began again. Only football can survive this kind of outrage, only something we believe in and don't believe in, simultaneously.

Leopardi concludes his poem by reflecting how hard it is to live in an age where all sense of nobility is gone.

> Admirable boy, how painful for you
> To outlive your unhappy country.
> You would have shone for her then
> When she glowed with the crown that –
> The fault is ours and fate's –
> Is lost. A season past:
> No one boasts being Italian born now,
> But, for yourself, raise your mind
> To the sky. What's life for?
> To be despised: blessed then when by danger
> Beset, of itself forgetful, not measuring
> The damage nor attentive to the flow
> Of slow and putrid hours

Blessed when the foot
Pushed even to the banks of Lethe
Comes back the happier.

Yes, he actually says that! Life is to be despised! So don't think about it, young sportsman! Raise your mind to the sky! Do it for yourself (but for us too!). Push your antagonism to the banks of Lethe, yes, to the very brink of death; it's the only way to chase off emptiness and boredom and come back the happier, with a sense at least that something *extreme* has happened.

This is tough talk. Clearly the anodyne arabesques of the Pope's misnamed *Partita della fede* will not do. Something more vigorous, more violent is required. Marathon was not a friendly. And perhaps the melancholy tone of the poem arises from the fact that the young Leopardi knew he could never thus participate. He himself would never push a game to extremes and be adored by the crowd. ('*Adesso fuori i coglioni,*' the *brigate* scream. 'Show some balls, *Dio boia!*') Leopardi was *gobbo*, hunchbacked, perhaps from too much reading and writing. He never played any sport at all. And the supporters of Juventus are known all over Italy as hunchbacks. For in popular folklore a hunchback is supposed to be lucky (how the unlucky Leopardi must have cringed every time this belief was mentioned). '*Gobbi di merda,*' the Veronese will shout as soon as they are in the Stadio delle Alpi. '*Torino in fiamme.*' These guys are dying for a chance to push their feet to the banks of Lethe.

But despite my reading of Leopardi, I'm not thinking so negatively as I get off the train and pull on my yellow-blue cap. 'We're going to kill them,' I assure Mirko. 'Three–nil,' he agrees. Is he laughing? Does he half-believe it? We have exchanged mobile numbers. I remember a few lines from Mallarmé:

Yes, *I know*, we are nothing but vain forms of matter – yet sublime too when you think that we invented God and our own souls. So sublime, my friend! that I want to give myself this spectacle of a matter aware, yes, of what it is, but throwing itself madly into the Dream that it knows it is not, singing the Soul and all those divine impressions that gather in us from earliest childhood, and proclaiming, before the Nothingness that is the truth, those glorious falsehoods!

'*Alè Verona!*' comes a shout from further down the train. A blue and yellow flag appears. Then the song: '*In Italia, Hellas, in Europa, Hellas, e ovunque Hellas, per sempre gialloblù, per sempre gialloblù!*' In Italy, Hellas, in Europe, Hellas, all over the world, Hellas, for ever *gialloblù*. With this glorious falsehood in mind, we set off for the stadium.

7A GIORNATA

Brescia – Juventus 0–0
Fiorentina – Vicenza 3–2
Inter – Perugia 2–1
Lazio – Milan 1–1
Lecce – Bari 2–0
Napoli – Atalanta 0–0
Udinese – Reggina 3–0
Verona – Roma 1–4
Bologna – Parma 2–1

CLASSIFICA

Roma	18
Udinese	16
Atalanta	15
Bologna	13
Juventus	12
Lazio	12
Parma	11
Lecce	11
Fiorentina	10
Inter	10
Milan	9
Perugia	8
Verona	7
Vicenza	7
Reggina	3
Brescia	3
Napoli	3
Bari	2

Numbers

*Miserable Veronese, the only way you'll get out of
Turin is with a police escort.*

verona merda (Torino, Italia)

*Slave of Agnelli, shut up and screw the next bolt on
that Cinquecento.*

Aiooogalapagos (Verona, Italia)

Another way you can look at the game of football is as a series of
numbers. If I said goodbye to Mirko on the platform of the station
at Torino Porta Susa, it was because this match was to be different
for me. No *brigate* today. In exchange for an article, my first ever
piece of sports journalism, an editor at *La Stampa*, the Turin paper,
has offered me a pass to the press gallery.

So a quarter of an hour before kick-off, here I am, sitting at a
numbered typing desk, high above the half-way line. To my right
and left, along a long row of identical desks, are a score of grim,
businesslike men in heavy winter jackets, smoking and tapping on
their portables. But there are women too, equally grim, equally
intent. Immediately beside me is a plain young creature who works
for a frothy mid-week TV show called 'Quelli che il calcio' – The
Football People. Laid on each desk, courtesy of the Juventus press
office, is a folder containing three sheets of paper giving every
possible statistic on Verona, Juventus and the referee. So I read
that, born in Ravenna on 22 August 1960 (it's always important
to know where a ref is from), Danilo Nucini has presided over

62 games in Serie B and 7 in Serie A, blowing the final whistle on 33 home wins, 23 draws and 13 away wins. He has sent off 30 players, but only 3 in Serie A, conceded 35 penalties, but none in Serie A. 'How can I know', I ask Stefano, the journalist who's accompanied me and is sitting on my other side, 'if he's biased in favour of Juventus or not?'

Stefano laughs. 'Aside from the fact that they're all *tendenzialmente* biased towards Juventus,' he says, 'you have to check the bit that says how many times they've reffed each team and with what results.' He points to the place at the bottom of the page: Verona 4 games: 1 victory, 1 draw, 2 defeats. Well, that sounds pretty much like our average performance over four games. No clue here. And Juventus . . . 0. The man has never refereed Juventus! It's a first. 'So you can't know,' Stefano tells me. And he explains that his speciality and passion is Formula One, not football. 'There's still some humour in Formula One,' he tells me. 'The drivers are capable of a joke or two. But football is death. We're not here to enjoy ourselves.' Again he laughs, as if to demonstrate that he is exempt from this sickness. Just beyond him, wearing black woollen gloves cut off at the fingertips, a colleague is hunched over his laptop, jaw clenched, typing furiously. He will not smile or laugh or exchange a relaxed word all afternoon.

Stefano's job, it turns out, is to cover the after-game interviews. He isn't doing the match report. His paper sends four journalists, each tackling different angles, dividing the game up into different areas of experience in much the same way as the press release breaks down the encounter into a series of neatly drawn boxes filled with numbers and surrounded by the colourful logos of a dozen sponsors.

It's wonderful the illusion of understanding that all this hard information confers. I read attentively through the statistics of past matches from 1939 on, home and away, in league and cup, of encounters between the two trainers throughout the course of their careers, achievements and ignominies, goals conceded, goals scored, biggest victories, worst defeats, percentages of all the above, comparisons of performance with the same moments in previous seasons. 'Without a continual falsification of the world by means of numbers,' Nietzsche wrote, 'mankind could not live.' Perhaps. But today I feel I could very easily live without the numbers. For the bottom line is that Verona have never, but never, beaten Juve at Delle Alpi. Not even in the magical '85. I can't imagine that today will be the day.

Dutifully, I study the team formations and check the numbers everybody's going to be wearing on their backs in case, in my article, I need to mention them: Van der Saar 1, Birindelli 15, Montero 4, Iuliano 13, Conte (Captain) 8, Tacchinardi 20, Davids 26, Pessotto 7, Zidane 21, Inzaghi 9, Trezeguet 17. How much easier it was at school and college when we all wore one to eleven!

But all of a sudden what's annoying me is that Del Piero is among the reserves. He's going to be on the bench, not on the field. It's infuriating. Del Piero is a player I love to hate. I revel in his inability to come to terms with lost celebrity. I had been looking forward to leaping to my feet and shrieking with disgust when he tripped himself on a defender's foot in the box and fell, rolling over into the now-notorious sitting position, both hands raised, palm upwards, demanding his penalty. Only now do I realise how much I had been looking forward to these emotions. What numbers could explain that?

A sudden drop in the noise levels causes me to look up from the press release. The game has started. They've already kicked off and I hadn't noticed! How is that possible? Is it me? Is it the press gallery? Or could it be this famous stadium?

I had been looking forward to seeing Lo Stadio delle Alpi. Alongside Milan's San Siro and Rome's Olimpico it's one of Italy's big three. Certainly the view as you approach doesn't disappoint. About twenty minutes north of the town centre, the stadium stands out like some sportsman's Pompidou centre, wrapped in orange pipes and coloured girders. The snow-topped mountain backdrop and the motorway just a few hundred yards away increase the sense of visual drama. It was conceived to be an art object of epic proportions.

Inside, too, the first impression is of elegance on a vast scale. The pitch is surrounded by a big athletics track and the curved slope of the terraces is broad and shallow so that the circumference of the whole structure, if circumference is the right word for an oval, is considerable indeed. It's impressive. On TV, it looks fantastic. Way above my head, two great girders run across the pitch bristling with cameras and loudspeakers. And yet . . .

A chill wind descends from those mountains. Despite the elegance of its form, the place is cold and alienating. You're too far from the action. You look down from an impossible distance at players toiling on a field that, after all the money spent on the structure, is just a muddy bog with marsh grass to mark the boundaries. The Juve fans are all sitting comfortably and empty spaces are numerous. For all the team's fame and national popularity, the stadium is far from full. Perhaps Verona are not considered an adversary worth losing a Sunday afternoon for.

But what is most disconcerting of all is the PA system. Right up to the starting whistle an unbelievably powerful battery of speakers has been drowning the stadium in rock music. So this is the first game of the season where I have heard no pre-match warm-up of chants and insults. Nothing could be more soulless. The fans come to hear themselves. They want to join vocal battle. The players might be our representatives, but the real battle is between the two towns. Wasn't this how football started: a ball pushed back and forth between one village and another in a parody of war? How humiliating, then, not only to be trapped in a cage of fences and Plexiglas, but to find that even when you yell your heart out your sentiments are crushed by deafening Euro-pop.

Anyhow, it was this PA system, I think, that fooled me. I just couldn't imagine that the game might be starting without some crowd excitement. Only a few moments after the kick-off, with the music turned off, did I finally pick up a remote chant of '*Juve Juve vaffanculo.*' It was this that lifted my head. But the voices were muted; it was as if you were just catching a cry from a distantly drifting lifeboat of exhausted survivors. Sound evaporates in this shallow saucer; it floats up into the grey sky like a soul freed from its body.

My eyes rove to find the *brigate*. Where are they? There! A knot of yellow and blue, edged by a sharp line of black. First there were only a handful, now, fifteen minutes into the game, a couple more busloads must have been let in. Surrounded by the police, they have been herded into a large empty paddock the other side of the stadium way over to the left. It's so far away that I can't make out any individuals, or even the banners they've brought. Yet again and again throughout the game I find myself turning to them. I know that if I were among them, the noise would be rousing, and the game, seen from the skew of that angle, would be more urgent and exciting. Every offside decision would be outrageously unfair. Every ball in the area would be a possible goal. I would be warmer, angrier. Only fifteen minutes into it, I've already decided that I shall never sit in the press gallery again. It's as if the game were not really taking place. '*Merda!*' I let out when the referee gives a foul against Laursen just outside the box. 'Isn't your language a little colourful?' the lady journalist beside me enquires.

To watch five minutes of a game like today's Juventus–Verona is to appreciate why contemporary football squads have to be so much larger than in the past, why we see numbers like 30 or even 50 on a player's back. It's dangerous out there this afternoon. It's brutal. Ten years ago, the difference between a big team and a provincial rag-bag like Verona, or Piacenza or Brescia, would have been one of talent. Elegant players like Baggio and Donadoni would invent previously unimagined trajectories in a complex pattern of feints and dummies and rapid changes of direction and speed. Under the spell of this skill, the opposing spectators would be somewhat anaesthetised and gradually resign themselves to the inevitable. Sometimes you might even feel a little ashamed of the way your own team's sole resource was to break up the star players' fluency with a weary repertoire of pushes, shoves and shirt-pulling.

But this is no longer the case. Today the big celebrities are quite as ruthless as the no–name provincials. Talented no doubt, they are also monsters of athletic preparation and amoral determination. Above all they are willing, Leopardi-style, to push things to the limit, to stretch out the foot in a slide tackle that could take them, or more often their opponent, to the very banks of Lethe. So much is at stake. So much money has been paid for them. It's as if, with the crowd violence that characterised the seventies and eighties now largely under control, that energy and urgency had migrated on to the field to be lived only vicariously by the fans.

Everybody deplores this state of affairs. Everybody is appalled. In hospital in Modena, the *Gazzetta* constantly reminds us, Francesco Bertolotti is still in coma. Yet for all the breast-beating and anxiety, it's hard not to feel that actually we are all getting exactly what we want. The game may be less attractive this way, but the drama is heightened. From the moment the player was allowed to turn professional, he became as much a gladiator as an entertainer ('A gladiator without a helmet,' says German player Marcus Babbel). His livelihood is at stake. Why else would he be so determined to win for us? Meantime, we amuse ourselves by following his ups and downs, enjoying his success or gloating over his failure. 'Doardo: go sell soap powder!'

But simultaneous with the warnings that the game is deteriorating, there is always a chorus of voices, often the same voices, insisting that the players *aren't trying hard enough* because they've already been paid too much. 'They should all be kicked in the arse,' said Marcello Lippi of Inter's all-star squad shortly before being fired. 'Hellas must learn to be more '*cattivo*' the *Arena* endlessly repeats. Exasperation is of the essence in football. If we've decided to invest emotion, and money, in these men, above all if we've allowed them to fill our heads and dreams, they'd better be willing to die for us. We want to see that foot pushed to the edge of Lethe, *Dio can*!

And in the ordinary way it is. It's not the occasional off-the-ball aggression that's so surprising in your average Serie A game, but the sheer ferocity of the general engagement. Today is no exception. Juventus have started the season poorly. They are only fifth in the table behind such minor names as Atalanta and Udinese. Today they *have* to win to stay in touch with the top. Uninspired, but lightning quick and above all ruthless, they are trying to overwhelm Verona with sheer physical force. The midfield is a constant angry fizz. Zinedine Zidane in particular has a crazy bullish anger about him, a head-down tension and animal violence that no doubt goes far beyond football, reaches back to some profound personal quarrel this man has with the world, his days as a poor immigrant's son in the white man's France, perhaps.

Likewise the black Dutchman Edgar Davids. Evidently Davids considers the centre circle his own personal property. Dreadlocks swinging behind, he runs round and round chasing others out. You can't come in! This place is mine! Behind him the Uruguayan, Montero, is frightening. 'Gilardino versus Montero = David against Goliath,' tomorrow's *Gazzetta* will say, 'only yesterday the boy wonder didn't get to use the sling.' Again and again the striker goes down. Every tackle Montero makes will stop his man even if it doesn't make contact with the ball. All in all, it's a situation where players are simply bound to be lost. Bones will crack, muscles tear, tendons snap. Over the length of a season the team with the bigger squad of fitter, more talented, more violent players is going to have the edge. Especially if referees are selectively lenient with the yellow cards.

In response to Juve's fury, Verona look well-organised, but timid and lightweight. They've already lost Leo Colucci in that torrential rain against Udinese. He was our only bulldog. They lost Bonazzoli with a back injury against Roma, and Mutu, who was stretchered off during that match, only started training again yesterday. Now it seems they are more or less resigned to losing this game. At best they're hoping against hope for nil–nil. It's depressing. As Ferron saves a second time, then a third, everybody in the stadium is just waiting for Juventus to score. To make matters worse, they'll deserve it. The Verona fans won't even be able to feel they've been robbed when the ball goes in.

For the truth is that whenever a provincial side come to Turin, they arrive expecting to be cheated. More than they would anywhere else. We'll lose, they're telling themselves, but at least in Turin we can enjoy the consolation that we lost because there is a conspiracy against us. Why is this so?

Sit down at the computer, hook up to the net and type in

www.antijuve.com. An extraordinary site appears giving information that will never appear on any Juventus press release. Going back to before the war, it lists all the occasions on which half of Italy is convinced that the Turin club bought their way to footballing fame with their owners' – Fiat's – money. You learn that Juve were the only club involved in the betting scandals of the eighties not to be seriously punished, the only club never to have agreed to random dope testing. As you get to more recent seasons, there are videos showing amazing refereeing decisions. A ball that clearly and for some two or three seconds crosses the line, is not given as a goal. The Juve keeper whips it out. Play proceeds. Or a ball does not cross the line, but a goal is given anyway. The ref blows his whistle. Juve have won!

So the provincial team's supporters arrive in Turin complacent in their contempt, braced for injustice. Yet today when Juve's goal comes there is, alas, nothing to complain about. Martin Laursen, who has controlled everything in the air, suddenly slithers in deep mud around the penalty spot. He totters and, exactly as a cross comes over from the right, goes down on his butt. Unmarked for perhaps two seconds, Trezeguet has no difficulty jumping to head home. 'Verona are a bunch of also-rans,' comments the prim woman to my right. It is a terrible thing to watch a game with people who are not eager to create the same illusion you are. Like trying to worship God with an atheist. I am tempted to tell her to fuck off.

After a dull cold half-time break during which the journalists redouble their writing efforts, the inevitable happens. Verona attack, Juve score. The tricky Inzaghi collides with Laursen and goes down. Zidane sends a wonderful place-kick just over the wall and curling into the net. We were now deep into the second half. Camoranesi, having irritated his man by dribbling him a couple of times, had been stretchered off after a determined tackle. At once I knew that we would not see him again for a long time. Another key player had gone. To console myself, I chose to keep my eye almost exclusively on Massimo Oddo, who was now the only exciting talent we seemed to have on the field.

Hailing from my wife's town of Pescara, on the Adriatic,

twenty-four years old, cropped hair, clear eyes, bits of beard and moustache that seem to have been stuck on his young face in a Marsiglia-style montage, Massimo Oddo is in the curious position of doing his obligatory military service while at the same time earning a big salary in a major football team. So from Monday to Thursday this young man is in the barracks, cleaning guns and lavatories, generally doing what almost all Italian conscripts consider a complete waste of time and certainly the furthest thing imaginable from Leopardi's (or anybody else's) vision of military glory. Then on Friday he is allowed out to train with the club. On Sunday he plays, then on Monday it's back to the barracks. Sometimes, late at night, my wife and I hear the heavy tramp of boots clumping up the hill past our window. It's the soldiers on an overnight hike. If you go out on the balcony you can see them pass by, torches and maps in their hands, their faces blackened. I always pray that Massimo Oddo is not among them. How can he possibly play if he's tramping about all night?

Oddo was bought from Naples during the summer. Naples had just been promoted from Serie B and Oddo had never played in Serie A before. When the news broke that he would also be doing his military service and would have to spend most of the week in the barracks, the *Arena* suggested that Pastorello hadn't known, he'd been tricked by those dastardly Neapolitans. Others thought the shrewd Pastorello knew all too well and got the player on the cheap, since no other club in Serie A would want the man.

But whatever the truth of the matter, this was one decision Pastorello got absolutely right. Today, with every minute of the game that passes, Oddo is looking like the best defender *and* the best attacker Verona have on the pitch. Cooler than the tropical storm of Zidane and Davids, certainly less commanding, less physically threatening, you can nevertheless see the boy thinking and working and reacting incredibly fast. It's always such a pleasure to see a player *think*, to see the man raise his eyes and, despite the pressure of feet and bodies hurtling toward him, place the ball in *exactly* the right space at the right speed for his companion. As the game wears on, the team begins to revolve around him. He's lifting them. He's communicating hope. And when Davids and Zidane start to tire, Oddo is suddenly in complete command of the right side of the field. He's even dribbling defenders and pushing into Juve's box. Juventus's trainer sees the danger, takes off Davids and brings in another volcano of vigour, Gianluca Zambrotta. But it's too late, the damage is done. It has occurred to the boys in yellow–blue that they might actually score. And at the ninetieth, they finally get there, a scrappy goal after a mess in the box. Two–one.

There are three minutes left. Three minutes of injury time. They are the only exciting minutes of the whole game, the only moments, for me, of total engagement with what is happening on the field. All of a sudden the result, the only number that counts, is at stake. All of a sudden Juventus are a mess. They panic quite as badly as Verona do when they're defending a result. They collapse. Desperate, the all-stars are kicking the ball high into the crowd. In the dying seconds Martino Melis, who's replaced Camoranesi, sends in a scorching shot from just outside the box. In goal Van der Saar is beaten. Montero hasn't even seen the ball, but it just brushes the top of his head and is deflected inches over the bar. Game over, a game that lasted, for me, exactly three minutes.

After the final whistle I'm used to standing with the fans and waiting till the players come over to salute the *curva*. It seems a necessary gesture before returning to the humdrum life outside the stadium. But today, no sooner has the referee looked at his watch and raised his whistle than the desks around me are deserted. The journalists are racing to the press room. They plug their computers into phone sockets. They're writing and smoking and muttering to each other from the sides of their mouths while high on the wall the TV runs through reports from all the various games. Some miserably dry sandwiches and flat soft drinks are brought. Pouncing on the trays, everybody begins to ask each other what mark they are planning to give which players. So tomorrow I will read:

Birindelli 6.5, mixture of left-back and left-half, he 'puts his signature' on the cross that Trezeguet heads in.

Camoranesi 6, hard to get the ball off him, excellent

control, but filthy temper. If he kept calm he might be more useful to the team.

Cvitanovic 5 (Verona's Croatian left-back), neither fish, flesh, nor fowl.

Zidane 7.5, Turin should erect a statue to him.

How do the journalists do this? How can they watch twenty-two players all at once and reduce such a complex group experience to a series of numbers corresponding to individuals, as if a player's performance wasn't largely determined by those around him and against him? One answer, I discover in the press room, is consultation: 'Do you think 6 is OK for Inzaghi?' 'Oh God, he missed a sitter again. He hasn't scored for weeks.' '5.5 then.' 'I'm giving him 5.' 'But he did get into a few good scoring positions.' 'What about 7 for the ref?' 'Too high. Those yellow cards for simulation were over the top.' '6.5 then.'

My children complain that when they get marks from one to ten for tests at school, the teachers never give any pupil less than five or more than eight, even when the subject is something as clear-cut as maths. The same is true of these sports journalists. They want to judge, to take control of the experience, to dress even the most elusive impressions and complex dynamics in the peremptory authority of numbers; but no one must be offended too greatly, nor praised too highly. For that would expose the judge to criticism.

Stefano grins at my amazement. 'The local journalists always give their home team the highest marks', he explains, 'because they want the players to be friendly in interviews.' On Monday night a TV programme will collect all the marks together from all the papers for all the matches of the day, and then all the days of the season. They take an average and set up a table. Who is the best striker? Batistuta 7.89, Totti 7.73. It reminds me of the way, at school, we used to give the girls we knew scores according to their various physical attributes. Character was not the obstacle it is in Miss World competitions. Monica: tits 5, arse 7. 'Davids 6.53,' the Monday night programme will tell us, 'Italiano 5.85.' It's funny how little difference there appears to be between these two.

Davids's salary and transfer fee must be at least ten times Vincenzo Italiano's.

A door bangs open. 'Zidane in the interview room!' But it might be action stations on a battleship. The man claps his hands. '*Zidane, signori, Zidane!*' Half the journalists stay glued to their computers, the other half rush for the door. I follow them. With rows of well-upholstered chairs, the place looks exactly like the conference hall where my students defend their dull theses before the degree commission. As it turns out, after-game interviews are even less interesting. Eager to be awed, I sit down beside Stefano, who has his laptop on his knee.

Zinedine Zidane, European champion, World Cup champion, is wearing a heavy grey quilted hiking jacket, zipped to the neck, collar turned up. On his head, incongruously, given the warmth in the room, is a simple black woollen cap with the letters D&G on the front. Is it a sponsor? Pulled low on his forehead the thing serves to emphasise the bushy black arch of thick eyebrows and the aggressive forward thrust of the man. There's almost a hunch to him as he leans forward over the desk up front, fingers knotted together. Hugely talented, hugely rich, he is ill at ease and impatient. When he speaks, he apes timidity and respect.

'The pitch is a disgrace. It penalised us more than them.'

His Italian is not perfect, but he has the commonplaces off pat. It's very important for Italians that their foreign stars make an effort with the language. How much more endearing they are making mistakes than using an interpreter. Zidane says what he has no doubt said a thousand times before:

'We are improving but we're not there yet.'

'We have to stay humble and do a lot of work.'

'Yes, I'm glad I was declared man of the match, but it's the team that counts.'

Two or three older journalists in the front row give the impression of being serious sophisticates. They stand up while the others stay in their seats. One strokes a full grey beard, another holds an expensive pen poised in the air. They call the man by name, with a mixture of familiarity and fawning respect. 'Zinedine, did

the *innesto* [grafting in] of Zambrotta come too late in the game?'
'Is it Juve's plan to occupy the *centro nevralgico* [the nerve centre] of
the pitch as quickly as possible?' 'What made you decide to *imporre
quella traiettoria rientrante* [impose that inswinging trajectory] to your
free kick?'

'Well,' Zidane says. His smile is nervous. He thinks about it.
Finally he decides: 'We've still got a lot of work to do before
we're at our best. The pitch is a disgrace.' And in the middle of
the next question he gets up to leave. To my surprise, I see he
has a small suitcase on wheels and hurries out, hunched forward,
cap down over his ears, pulling his case after him, looking for all
the world like one of the thousands of unemployed North Africans
who haunt the railway stations of southern Europe.

'You didn't ask a question,' I say to Stefano.

'Would it have made any difference?'

Then we are all called out to see something on TV. There has
been crowd trouble in Reggio Calabria. The team was losing its
sixth successive game. The score was three–nil to lowly Brescia.
The fans invaded the pitch and the game had to be abandoned.
Frankly, I'd feel like invading the pitch myself if Verona were to lose
three–nil at home to Brescia. Now the screen is showing angry men
hurling themselves against the transparent barrier between terraces
and pitch, tossing their flagpoles over the top at the police, setting
fire to their plastic seats. Clearly terrified, a father is trying to steer
two small children through the worst of the crowd. The journalists
shake their heads. Somebody still isn't sure whether to give Oddo 7
or 7.5. And the curious thing is that even as we are able to watch,
live, from almost a thousand miles away, this violence going on at
the other end of Italy, in the very same structure where we are
now standing, the departing Verona fans are being beaten up by
the police. And no one knows, no cameras are watching.

Monday's *Arena* carries three pages of reports, interviews and
statistics on the game, but only the smallest mention of any trouble
afterwards. Six Verona fans were arrested and others claim to have
been beaten by the police, it tells us. It is not until Wednesday, on
page 36, one of those sections dedicated to the various godforsaken

villages of the surrounding countryside, that we get a chance to learn any more. An interview appears with Marcellina Canazza, a forthright woman in stout middle age who runs a small supporters club of her own in the lowland town of Cerea, hiring a coach week by week for the games not too far away:

'They made us leave from a single exit,' she says, 'a corridor with barriers on one side and a line of riot police on the other. We all had to go through and as we did they beat and kicked us. Everybody was hit over and over, even girls, even kids. I saw a little blonde girl with her head stained with blood.'

Marcellina agrees there are hotheads at the stadium, but insists that none are ever allowed on her buses. 'Sunday evening it was as if we were coming back from a war. More than half of us had to go to hospital for dressings. One was missing, presumed arrested.' She has phoned the managing director of Hellas Verona and claims she is willing to bring charges against the policemen involved. A small article below speaks of the parents of the arrested boy who weren't allowed to contact him for three days.

There is something extraordinary about all this; not so much the event itself, but the way it is being reported. The front pages of the *Arena* – the local, proud and specifically Veronese paper – are full of stories of violence at the French frontier where Italian farmers are refusing to let French cows enter the country for fear of BSE contamination. By Saturday of this week the same pages will be showing scenes of even more serious violence as Italian left-wingers protesting against globalisation are refused entry to France to demonstrate outside the European leaders' summit in Nice.

But at the same time a large number of local Veronese citizens have been beaten up by the police. Six of them are still being held in Turin, and the paper doesn't even send a journalist to find out what happened. It's as if there were some radical uncertainty as to what is scandalous at a football match and what isn't. Perhaps it is all right for the police to beat football supporters. In any event, the *Arena* clearly isn't eager to take the side of fans against police. Respect for authority is even greater among journalists than it is among referees.

At the next home game on Sunday, there will be a huge banner, perhaps thirty metres long, in the Curva Sud complaining about legalised beatings. Plus a new graffito has appeared over one of the main entrances: '*Giustizia italiana, figli di puttana.*' But nothing is said in the club programme. A further two weeks later, at the next home game, the club programme does speak cautiously of a possible court case against the police at the stadium. Meantime, the *Arena*, now a good month after the event, has at last given some kind of account of what was happening while I and a score of other journalists were listening to the inanities of Zidane. Cautious as ever, the paper presents the story only in the form of a letter to the editor.

I was in Turin for the Juventus–Verona game at which six Verona fans were arrested. There were about three hundred of us and everything was quiet right up to the end of the game when a few nutcases went wild and threw their plastic seats into the adjacent part of the stadium which was empty.

Everybody had got up to go. It happened very quickly. We saw the seats flying and at the same time, before we knew it, we were being charged by the police. We were beaten with tremendous violence. No one escaped. I saw girls falling under truncheons, children hit over the head. There were about twice as many police as fans.

We were given some medication on the spot, but then we went to the casualty ward in Turin for the more serious wounds. I heard a policeman say: 'They brought us in from Genoa because we're the best when it comes to beatings.' On the way back the bus looked like a hospital ward: people with ice on their heads and bloody bandages.

There is no justification for this massacre. If we were treated like this without having done anything, you can imagine what the police did to the ones they arrested.

Andrea Valentini, Verona

And that's it. Nothing more. No valuable journalistic time has been spent on the matter, after the oceans of space dedicated to the Marsiglia affair, to a man who claimed he was beaten up for racist motives, but in fact wasn't. A friend of my son's, who turns out to have been a student in Marsiglia's classes at the Maffei, tells me, 'The point about Marsiglia is that he was really charismatic, we really believed him, we did, right to the end, however incredible it seemed.' Nobody, it seems, ever believes a football fan, even after the hospital has medicated a score of them.

'Honour to the fallen of Turin,' announces The Wall.

'Honour to our comrades who were beaten.'

How they love this solemn rhetoric. Inevitably, events are drawn into *brigate* folklore. Somebody called Franz, who supports Juventus, sneers: '*Conigli* [rabbits], you let yourselves be beaten up by a couple of *sbirri* [pigs, policemen].' An interminable back and forth begins, with Franz maintaining that the Veronese are in fact racially Slavs, famous only for their Pandoro, a kind of panettone. The Veronese reply that they have sent a couple of Slavs to Turin with a truckload of poisoned Pandori. It is approaching Christmas after all. Meantime the front page of the paper learnedly discusses the expansion of the EU, our European home, and the complex new voting procedures that leave Germany firmly in the saddle after the Nice summit. As the mad cow battle continues at the French border, inside pages show an excavator digging a trench to prevent gypsies, Slavs and Albanians from using a piece of land destined for redevelopment, while the public prosecutor Papalia – that man again! – has spoken of his own personal concern with new and more sophisticated forms of racism.

In short, everything is returning to normal. But sitting in the bar where day by day I read my *Gazzetta*, the polygamous Mohammed opposite me half-asleep by the paraffin stove with his hat over his face, I feel upset that I wasn't among the *popolo gialloblù* that day in Turin. I feel the pull of the event and its squalid drama. I should have been there with the boys. I should have been part of what happened. Camoranesi, the paper tells me, will be out for at least a month.

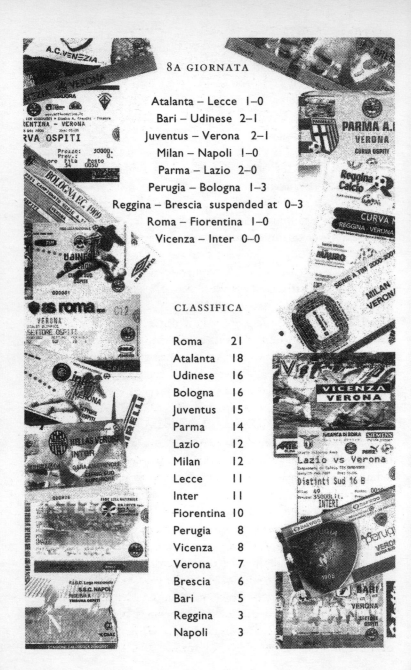

8A GIORNATA

Atalanta – Lecce 1–0
Bari – Udinese 2–1
Juventus – Verona 2–1
Milan – Napoli 1–0
Parma – Lazio 2–0
Perugia – Bologna 1–3
Reggina – Brescia suspended at 0–3
Roma – Fiorentina 1–0
Vicenza – Inter 0–0

CLASSIFICA

Roma	21
Atalanta	18
Udinese	16
Bologna	16
Juventus	15
Parma	14
Lazio	12
Milan	12
Lecce	11
Inter	11
Fiorentina	10
Perugia	8
Vicenza	8
Verona	7
Brescia	6
Bari	5
Reggina	3
Napoli	3

Il Verdetto del Campo

Win for us, Hellas Verona . . . and these miserable peasants will magically disappear.
    can de la scala, sav@l.it

'Ancelotti Gets It Right' was the headline to the *Gazzetta*'s match report the day after Verona–Juventus. Ancelotti is the Juventus coach. But what if Montero's scalp had not accidentally deflected that final shot? 'Ancelotti Goofs Again', the paper might have said. I accept '*il verdetto del campo*,' Perotti tells us: 'the field's verdict' – a favourite platitude. The final score exorcises the game, decides the paper's headlines, clears the way for the next encounter.

But if every match report is written under the spell of the official result, then as the season progresses every game is played more and more under the spell of the accumulation of those results, the ultimate verdict towards which the whole season is tending. After losing two games in a row, it's time to take a look at the league table.

There are eighteen teams in Serie A, hence each team plays thirty-four games, seventeen home, seventeen away. So we're now about a quarter of the way through. At the end of the season the top two teams will be admitted to the Champions' League, the third and fourth will play off with some similarly positioned foreign club for a further place in the Champions' League while the fifth and sixth teams, together with the winner of the Coppa Italia, will be admitted to the UEFA Cup and the seventh and eighth will play off for admission. If any of the top teams actually wins a European competition, they gain admission automatically and this will make another place available for the ninth and even the tenth teams, if we assume that the winner of the Coppa Italia is one of the top clubs.

Meantime at the bottom of the table four teams will go down into Serie B. Unlike the English league, then, the whole thing is carefully arranged so that almost all the teams will finish the season in a state of elation or misery. Asked to comment on what he has learned in his first months of Italian football, the Croatian Mario Cvitanovic, a worried-looking boy with dark, close-set eyes beneath a fashionable centre parting, reflects: 'Here in Italy, after every game, you are either in paradise or in hell.'

He's right. This is what Italians want. A constant alternation between *trionfo* and *tristezza*; *vittoria* and *vergogna*. When you think about it, even those four or five teams that finish the season with neither a negative nor positive result, neither in Europe nor in Serie B, will either be appalled that they just missed entry to the big competitions or elated that they have just escaped relegation. It is this last emotion that the Veronese are dreaming of.

In any event, the slow accretion of the league table is the glue that from week to week holds together the intense experience of each Sunday's game, prevents it from becoming a mere super-imposition of the same emotions, gives it direction and purpose. After day eight, then, Roma are top. They've won seven and lost one. It's an extraordinary performance. Inevitably the papers are full of pseudo-political headlines of the variety 'Balance of power shifts from north to south'. Fresh from Serie B, Atalanta haven't lost a single game: five wins and three draws. This is even more remarkable. Udinese and Bologna have also performed beyond expectations. 'Revenge of the Provincials' is the papers' line here. Everything must be seen in terms of established rivalries, the ever-vibrant force-fields of Italian national life – north/south; big city/small city. There is nothing that can happen in Italian football that will not be seen in terms of an ancient quarrel. Meanwhile, the individuals – players, coaches, even owners – are interesting only in so far as they further an old cause.

Or fail to further it. Napoli's Slav coach Zeman, so famous for his complicated schemes and all-out attacking style, has been fired. Reggina's coach will surely be the next to go. And most likely Bari's. With the gearing that gives three points for a win and one for a draw, even the drawn game can be seen as a disaster, especially if a direct rival is winning elsewhere. Now at the stadium as the game progresses the eye periodically glances up at the screen above the Curva Nord that will flash out a new result whenever someone scores in Serie A; now every game is understood and interpreted in the light, or gloom, of all the other games. It's a complicated business. The whole country is united in mutual tension, an invisible criss-crossing of envy and *schadenfreude*. Cheers are raised that have nothing at all to do with the game in hand: Vicenza are going down again. The crowd groans, even as their players perform well: Napoli have scored. And week by week the spell grows stronger. 'We must win the game against Brescia,' announces the mild-mannered Perotti. 'There is no alternative.' He is growing more tense, more obsessive. Good. That's how we want him.

As it turned out, the next three games, like the game against Roma for that matter, all started in exactly the same way, with Verona scoring within five minutes of the kick-off. After which all of them offered only the agony of hoping the result could be defended, the dismal business of watching the yellow-blues milling and flailing around the edge of their area with fluttering knees and feverish minds. The team is getting worse.

Against Roma, Verona had opened with a beautifully fast move that ended, in less than a minute, with Gilardino being pulled down by the goalkeeper and Oddo scoring from the spot. For half an hour the boys had hung on, but were finally overwhelmed. By the time Roma's equaliser came, the fans were resigned. The three goals that followed were no more than expected. We didn't suffer much.

Against Brescia an unlucky rebound from a defender set up Bonazzoli alone in front of goal. This was about five minutes into the game. He shot perfectly into the far corner. For the rest of the match the crowd sat in utter misery as Brescia outclassed and outplayed us. Roberto Baggio, in particular, seemed to put our defenders under a spell. At half-time, despite being one–nil up,

everybody around me was convinced that Verona were bound for
Serie B. How could we play this badly? It was painful, enthralling. In
the second half Brescia poured in everything, substituted attackers
for defenders, seemed interminably on the point of scoring, though
without ever quite getting a shot at goal. Five minutes from time,
quite undeserved, Verona snatched a second on the break. The *curva*
rejoiced. 'Bye bye Brescia,' they sang (in English!) to the tune of
'Auld Lang Syne'. 'Serie B, Serie B, Serie B.'

At the ninetieth, with Verona already celebrating and the
so-called fourth referee indicating a full five minutes' injury time,
Brescia got one back. All of a sudden, the match was a replay in
reverse of the Juventus game. Verona collapsed completely. With
seconds to go Brescia hit the post, and when at last the final whistle
went, a curious combination of elation and disgust settled on the
ground. We had played our worst game of the season and won.
Should we be applauding or whistling our contempt? Boasting of the
efficiency of Verona's police force, tomorrow's paper will publish a
picture of one of the town's specially armoured, rigorously glass-free
buses taking the appalled Brescia fans away. Their faces can be seen
pressed against the wire netting that has replaced the windows.
'Africa', someone has written in spray paint on the outside.

'O *butei*,' a message appears on The Wall, 'our next game's in
Africa.' With Reggina's pitch disqualified after last week's crowd
trouble, their game with Verona has been moved from Reggio
Calabria to Catania, Sicily.

This was a crunch moment for me. All kinds of things were
going on. When I wrote my article for *La Stampa* I had made it
clear to the editor that I wanted no mention of the fact that I was
planning a book. The paper published the piece under the headline:
'Writer among the Hooligans: Parks Writes Book on the Brigate
Gialloblù.' The next day, without contacting me, the local *Arena*
reproduced this 'news' and much of my article in four generous
columns. I was nervous. How would the *brigate* react? Would they
feel spied on? Would they feel irritated by this apparent claim to
be one of them? Could I travel with them again?

And did I want to? Catania is 1,200 kilometres from Verona,

about as far as you can go in Italy. I have never been there before. Tentatively, I phoned the Zanzibar, hoping that there might be a plane chartered. 'They're going by bus,' the barman tells me. 'Leave a phone number and we'll contact you.' A young woman called. After explaining that the bus would leave at six-thirty Friday evening, taking a total of sixteen to eighteen hours to reach Catania, she suddenly said, 'But you have an accent. You're English.' 'Yes.' 'You must be Tim Parks. I saw in the paper.' 'Yes.'

An hour later she phoned again. 'There's only one seat left and three people on the waiting list, but the place is yours if you want it. We want you to come.' There was genuine excitement in her voice. I declined. But at the same time I realised I'd have to go to the game now. It would be a fraud to write about the season without going there. These people, who weren't writing about it, were going to every single match at great effort and expense. 'I'm going by plane,' I invented, and asked, 'Why can't we all go by plane?' 'Too expensive,' she said. The bus price would be 200,000 lire, the plane cost 700,000. 'They might give us a group reduction,' I suggested. 'They'd never take us,' she said. No doubt she was right.

No sooner had I put the phone down than I thought: 700,000 is too much for a football game, a miserable game between two desperate teams scrapping over relegation in an empty neutral stadium. '450,000 if you stay over Saturday night,' the airline told me. It was the decisive moment. Don't go, I thought, watch it on TV. Saturday games are shown on pay TV in the bars. I could walk to the Stonehenge, a wonderfully fake English theme pub run by a busty transsexual on the hillside near our village. They have a huge screen surrounded by paraphernalia of the ship's cannon and ancient trombone variety. It would be full of fourteen-year-olds wearing blue-and-yellow bobble hats and shouting *Diaolo boia* over glasses of Coca-Cola. That too could be an experience.

But if Catania was a crunch game for me it was also surely a test case for the whole question of Italian national unity. Verona–Catania. I looked again at the map. From the Alps to Etna, the two extremes of Italy, north-east to south-west. One tends to forget how long this country is. Past Bologna, Florence, Rome, Naples, Reggio, the Strait of Messina. Could these be the same people? I booked my ticket and at seven in the morning, with the fans no doubt toiling and blaspheming in a drunken haze down the Amalfi coast, I flew right over them across the blue water of the Ionian.

This is 9 December. At the airport it is raining heavily. It just will not stop raining. Buckling into my seat, I stare out of the window at the rain, thinking about Perotti and the wonderful job of being a football coach, of being paid, handsomely paid, to reflect on all the possible combinations of twenty and more young and talented men, each with his different psychology, his different strengths and weaknesses. The plane rises through thick cloud. The Alps are invisible, but as we cross the Apennines the familiar landscape appears. Strands of mist shine like fresh snow on the ancient hills, then the sea is liquid copper under the morning sun. You fly directly over the Eolie islands, until, dropping down, there is Etna, a picture-book volcano, taller, more majestic than I had imagined, its high crater topped with Christmas icing. Beyond, at the bottom of long slopes of vines and lemon trees, right on the dazzle of the coast, is Catania.

Italians will always insist on the differences between north and south. How could they so incessantly complain about each other if there were none? And up to a point they're right. When I ask for a granita I don't get the crushed ice of the northern version, but a sort of liquid almond ice-cream, more an Arab sherbet. And the croissants here are always served hot. There's a difference. White-jacketed, a warm sun on his face, the waiter is a charming caricature of southern vanity. It wouldn't do up north. I'm sitting at a table in one of the central squares. I'm outside, for heaven's sake, in December. How wonderful. But there's more noise in the street here than in Verona, I tell myself critically. More children screaming. You can't help noticing that. And the traffic is constantly on the verge of deadlock. I look up. Whereas Verona, through its foggy winters, has warm ochre walls and pink marble pavements, Catania under its blistering summer sun is lava grey, a monumental mix of volcanic rock and white limestone. That's something that would take a little getting used to.

I take a bus east along the coast to check out the fishing village of Aci Trezza where Giovanni Verga set his great novel *I malavoglia*. Stone angels on the church façade blow their judgment-day trumpets right in the noses of the painted trawlers pulled up in the port. With its glare and shadow and Saturday morning leisure among pots of oleanders and lemon trees, the place is so beautiful it's hard to see how Verga could have been such a pessimist. But those were the days of poverty and malaria.

Sitting in a bar I read a local newspaper that draws a parallel between Sicily's hosting first a game from Serie A (a rare occurrence) and then next week a United Nations Conference on Criminal Organisations. These are good signs, the paper thinks, indications that Sicily is not to be for ever left out of everything. Perhaps soon they will have a team in Serie A themselves. Perhaps soon they can be thought of more for crime prevention than Mafia.

How familiar this regional perspective is with its paradoxical mix of self-regard and malcontent! A long article proudly describes the restoration of the capitol of the Greek Temple of Concord in Agrigento, built around 450 BC. An editorial complains that last time the Veronese played in Catania, when Etna was erupting and the city threatened, the Veronese fans brought banners saying *Forza Etna!* 'We should put local rivalries aside and support our cousins across the water,' the journalist decides. 'We must form a common front against these northern barbarians.' Well, here is a real difference. I can't imagine the Veronese supporting Vicenza or Brescia under any circumstances, not even against a team of extra-terrestrials.

There's been a strangely balmy feel to this morning, I decide, folding up *La Sicilia*, watching the slower, slightly dragging gait of the shoppers, listening to their drawling voices that stretch and soften the vowels. Is it a caress or a whine? 'We mustn't be always whining like those miserable *terroni*,' somebody wrote on The Wall, apropos of what, I can't remember. Then the distant sight of the old Norman castle back towards the town, high and solid on a rocky outcrop above the coast, suddenly makes me nervous. The Normans in Catania! The Greeks in Agrigento! There were a pair of away games and no mistake! Time to get to the stadium.

On the one occasion when I made the mistake of accepting an invitation to a big Italian talk show, I was immediately attacked by a rumbustious 'expert' who accused me of knowing nothing about Italy. He turned to another guest, an octogenarian Neapolitan actress, and fired a question, to which she replied at length in the Neapolitan dialect of sixty years ago. 'What do you think of that?' he demanded. We were speaking in front of a theatre audience who had all been bussed in from Naples. I understood nothing and was thus quickly and entirely discredited before a giggling public, though perfectly aware that almost nobody born north of Rome would have understood, while the lady herself would have got nowhere with the Brigate Gialloblù. 'Italy', the man insisted, 'is divided by its different languages.'

He was right. There's always a comic moment at the stadium when the fans get on to the language problem. 'Pà-à-uh-a! Pà-à-uh-a!' the Veronese chanted in Bergamo, imitating the way the locals pronounce that key word *pastasciutta*. And then they broke out into the song that at some point gets sung at every game. The tune is the old favourite 'Guantanamera'. The song has but one idea.

> *'Non si capisce ma come cazzo parlate,*
> *Non si capi-i-i-sce ma come cazzo parlate!'*

Which briefly translates as: 'We can't understand what the fuck you're saying.' And implies: the centre of the world is our city, our language, our accent.

In any event, as I pushed through the turnstile of the *sezione ospiti* at the Cibali stadium in Catania, the boys were already singing it. Less than a hundred of them, but in excellent voice, immediately declaring their racial superiority, punching their fists in the air, tightly hemmed in by the inevitable riot police.

'Get ready,' I told my companion, for I was not alone.

The moment I knew I was going down to Catania, I called a friend who has worked down there and asked him for the number of someone who could find me a hotel. Daniela teaches English in primary schools. On the phone she duly recommended a place to stay, then showed amazement that I should be going to a game. She has never been to a game. 'Come along,' I told her, 'come and see the *brigate*.' She wouldn't dream of going to see a bunch of uncouth northern racists. 'I dare you,' I said. So here I am being driven to a game by a dark, slim, well-endowed woman in a dress that is short, tight and generously décolleté. Curious that, thinking as she does of these fans, she should come thus attired. '*O Dio*,' she shivers when she hears those voices. '*Non si capisce ma come cazzo parlate.*'

Emerging from the stairway I see to my surprise that the small stadium is packed. Perhaps fifty busloads of fans have come across on the ferry from Reggio Calabria, plus there are all the local Catania enthusiasts who never get a chance to watch top-level soccer. Ranged around the terraces of a very pretty little ground they stand watching the barbarians wave their blue and yellow flags and insult them. '*Non si capisce!*' Then, rising to the challenge, Calabrians and Sicilians came back with one voice, urgent and derisive: '*Merde siete e merde resterete.*' It's the staple chant of all football grounds: 'Shit you are and shit you'll stay.' So despite the attack on their way of speaking, not only have they understood the Veronese, but they are making themselves understood. Perfectly. Overwhelmingly. Immediately, I felt justified in saying that this was one nation. Even if everybody has a different way of speaking it, the need to insult, not to mention the need to talk about football, has established a lingua franca.

Nervous, Daniela insists on standing to one side, beside a policeman. All the boys are there. Fondo, Il morto, Forza, Cain, the pleasant young man with the short phocomelic arms. They notice me, give a nod of acknowledgment. It was presumptuous on my part to imagine they would give a damn about my presence, about my writing books.

'How was the trip?' I ask one of the youngsters. He grimaces. 'A nightmare.' Although they're working hard at their chants, none of the group seem high or wild. The drink must have worn off before they got here. Daniela smiles. 'They're rather charming,' she says.

Reggina play in claret and white. Verona have changed their standard dark blue for white and yellow. The sun is full in our faces.

'Is this the Red Sea or what,' the man beside me laughs as the referee starts the game. 'I'm scorching.' And he starts to take his sweater off. Before he has got it over his head, Verona have scored. 'You didn't miss anything,' I console the man. 'None of us saw it.'

They have put us in a corner and the goal was at the far end. Only later on video would I understand the dynamic of the thing. A lucky rebound and a perfect long shot. My son is under instructions to video all the goals this season.

So now, once again, we face ninety weary minutes of watching Hellas Verona trying to 'administer the one-goal lead'. And once again it is unutterably painful. Reggina attack endlessly. Their fans are going crazy. At half-time we are showered with small metal objects, screws, nails. One hits the phocomelic boy on his shaven head. He's bleeding. The police shrug their shoulders. Daniela is appalled and starts to show solidarity with the *brigate*. Ten minutes from the final whistle, with Ferron beaten, alone on the edge of the six-yard box, their centre-forward shoots wide. Five minutes later the same man hits the underside of the bar. 'If ever a result was robbed,' laughs the man beside me, now bare-chested, 'this was it.'

But the game isn't over. With thirty seconds to go to the end of injury time, Reggina's goalkeeper, the towering Taibi, runs all the way to Verona's goal in the hope of gathering a free kick from the centre circle. Everybody is in Verona's area. The defence lose their nerve. Oddo heads a ball that is going safely out back into play and after a ferocious scramble somebody sticks it in the net. All the players run off the pitch to celebrate under their fans. None of them is shown a yellow card. The referee whistles the end. One–all.

Daniela is surprised at the calm reaction of the Verona fans. 'They sensed it was coming,' I explain. 'They knew a win would be robbery.' And I added, 'In the end, they accept *il verdetto del campo*.' But what the boys weren't going to accept was that the police should throw them out on the street at once and unprotected. Cain is furious. 'You can't let us out now!' The police are trying to move people to the gates. 'They'll fill us with bruises,' he protests, using a Veronese expression. 'They'll swell us up like canoes.' The police relent. Meantime, Daniela and I manage to slip out, me hiding my blue-and-yellow scarf, feeling protected by the young woman's totally southern look. But all the way back to the car she is repeating those two very Veronese expressions, 'They'll fill us with bruises. They'll swell us up like canoes.' She savours the strange accent, trying to get it right. And over dinner that evening with her husband and various friends she insistently and improbably praises the Brigate Gialloblù. She sings a couple of chants for the company: *Non si capisce ma come cazzo parlate. In Italia Hellas, in Europa Hellas.* I sense she has been seduced by their mad energy.

Later, shortly after one o'clock, I turned on the television in my hotel room and discovered a programme where an astrologer analyses the chances of each Serie A team on the basis of their collective birth charts. 'Reggina have too many Aquarians,' he says, shaking his head, 'and this is a bad moment for Aquarians, but it will get better after Christmas.'

Trying to sleep, it comes to me that there was a wonderful symmetry about the game; it held the opposites of north and south in perfect balance: a goal at the very beginning, a goal at the very end. Though one thing that is definitely different about the south is how late the street life goes on. At two-thirty, when I last looked out, the traffic was still jammed on the street outside. Open car windows offered a selection of the music I usually hear tinkling on my son's Discman. The south drags things out, I thought. They walk slowly, they speak slowly, they dine in the early hours and they leave scoring till dangerously late. The *brigate*, meanwhile, would be between Naples and Rome. I slept with earplugs and a pillow over my head.

9A GIORNATA

Bologna – Vicenza 1–1
Inter – Juventus 2–2
Lazio – Reggina 2–0
Lecce – Fiorentina 1–1
Napoli – Bari 1–0
Parma – Atalanta 2–0
Perugia – Roma 0–0
Udinese – Milan 0–1
Verona – Brescia 2–1

IOA GIORNATA

Atalanta – Perugia 0–0
Bari – Bologna 2–0
Brescia – Napoli 1–1
Fiorentina – Inter 2–0
Juventus – Parma 1–0
Milan – Lecce 4–1
Reggina – Verona 1–1
Roma – Udinese 2–1
Vicenza – Lazio 1–4

CLASSIFICA

Roma	25
Juventus	19
Atalanta	19
Lazio	18
Milan	18
Parma	17
Bologna	17
Udinese	16
Fiorentina	14
Lecce	12
Inter	12
Verona	11
Perugia	10
Vicenza	9
Brescia	7
Napoli	7
Bari	8
Reggina	4

Incanto

*Sunday we'll climb once again the mythical steps of
the Curva Sud! Remember, we must be the 13th,
14th, and 15th man on the field. Sing, butei, sing!
Let's hear the curva's cannons! Ever and only Hellas
Verona!*
Paruca brigate@piu-mate.it

In canto. In song. *Incanto*. Enchantment. To enter into song is
to enter into a spell, the thrall of the music. Individuality and
discrimination suspended, you throw your weight behind the yoke
of the rhythm, bound together like beasts of burden for the
extension of the song. Shortly after the game with Brescia, I
received the following e-mail:

Dear Mr Parks,
    My mother – a highly respected professional woman – just
called me on the phone, shouting, 'Eugenio, get on the net,
find *La Stampa*'s site and check out the article by a certain
Parks on Juventus–Verona. He's a nutcase like you!!!'
    And in fact I must admit that after reading that article, I
told myself, 'See, you're not as strange as friends and relatives
have always painted you.'
    But I should give you the facts.
    My name then is Eugenio, I'm thirty, and I'm a journalist
for CNN. I work in Atlanta, Georgia, at the network's
head office. But first and foremost I'm a *BRIGATISTA*

GIALLOBLÙ, I've been sick with 'Hellas fever' ever since I was a kid. And, what makes matters more complicated, like you I'm not even Veronese, I'm not even from the Veneto, and I don't have any relatives from round there. I'm from Asti, Piedmont, and my family is from Tuscany. One day, when I was small, they took me to see Juventus–Verona in Turin. I don't remember anything about the game. I spent the whole time watching the *brigate* in their *curva*, they sent shivers up my spine. That night I decided that one day I would become one of them.

And so I did. For years, first by train, then car, I followed the Brigades all over Italy and finally became one of them, as I had always dreamed I would ever since I was a kid. How many times, in Pisa or Cremona, Como or Perugia, I'd be there in the middle of the gang and suddenly find myself wondering, 'What the hell are you doing here, Eugenio?' And how many times my friends and family would ask, with horror in their voices, 'Verona? Why Verona? How on earth can you support Verona?' As if a fan needed any justification! As if anyone not supporting Juventus or Milan were some kind of pervert or subversive. They gazed at me with a mixture of pity and amusement as if to say, 'That's Eugenio. A born joker. He likes to provoke.'

To provoke! I want to know what's provocative about singing till your voice cracks in the oppressive heat of a Terni June, or the freezing cold of an Udine November, trying to understand – just to give you an example – what kind of awful family tragedy must have plagued Graziano Battistini [an ex-keeper] every time he took a goal kick. He never got one right, not one.

The crunch came last year when, at the end of a long training course, I was taken on by CNN and given the job in Atlanta. Despite having worked towards this for years, I immediately thought: And Verona? And the stadium? And the games against Milan? And insulting the southerners?

In the end I took the job out of a sense of respect for my

mother's mental health, and she consoled me saying, 'Not to worry, you can see the games via satellite.' Well thanks a lot, as if it were the same thing. In the Curva Sud I used to shout, 'No to TV football.'

But between nothing and the satellite, I settled for the satellite. In fact I have two satellites here on the balcony, one for Rai International and the other for Fox World Sport. Sometimes they show a Hellas game.

So there's a condominium in Atlanta in the southern United States where every Sunday morning at nine a.m. people ask, 'Who is that asshole rolling around on the floor screaming in three languages?' and 'Who the hell is this Bonazzoli he likes so much, or that Cvitanovic who doesn't press enough? And what does press enough mean anyway?'

Now my friends and work-mates here look at me with that same mixture of horror and amusement I used to get in Italy, and every now and then one of them stupidly says, 'Not to worry, you've got a good job, haven't you?'

I know I've got a good job. But already I'm organising my holidays around the Serie A calendar. At least I can make it to the last game of the season. I absolutely can't miss that.

This e-mail is signed: 'Eugenio, for ever *gialloblù*', and reading it I can't help feeling what a dangerous thing it is to be taken to a football game as a little kid and to enter into the song of a group like the Brigate Gialloblù. They may not be sirens, but their enchantment certainly seems able to hold people in its grasp. Daniela felt its power. And she was from Catania and had never watched a game of football in her life. Mirko from Trento is still climbing on the train every Sunday. We exchange phone-calls from time to time. He says he would sacrifice any job or girlfriend that did not allow him to join in the chant. There are a group of Germans who drive down from Munich once a month, two or three rather melancholy guys from Rome who regularly make it to away games south of Bologna, an English couple who fly over from London when they can. The core of the *brigate* accept these strays with a mix of pity and incomprehension. These people have been enslaved by the song, by the rhythm it gives to their lives, and this without even knowing Verona the town, or speaking its dialect, or sharing its blind civic pride. These people will never sign a message *Verona città e stato*, or *Lo Scaligero*. They can never feel the same sense of ownership, the way the fan born in the shadow of the Bentegodi feels he owns the team far more than Pastorello. But if they shout loud enough and raise their arms when the chant leader tells them to, they are welcome. 'It sings in my ears for hours afterwards,' Mirko assures me, 'for days. I know it's stupid, but I can hear them while I work. *Per sempre gialloblù.*'

I too had a powerful experience of entering into song as a child, of succumbing to the enchantment of the group. But this song was different and even more dangerously coercive than that of the *brigate*. Eventually it had to be rejected. And when in adult life I discovered the football chant, the spell of the crowd and the stadium, it was as a pleasant surrogate for an intoxication that had been too mad and possessive.

From as early as I can remember, I was a treble in the choir at St Mark's Church, Layton. The choir was perhaps forty-strong. There were more than twenty boys, too many for the stalls, so that stiff wooden chairs were added on the stone floor towards the Lord's Table. As you grew older you graduated from these chairs where you sat with the hymn and prayer-book in the lap of your cassock, to the stalls where you could hide your hands under the music ledge and make pellets from the peelings of old book bindings to flick at those opposite. Then we stood in the gloomy cold to sing Bach or Handel, or just the descant to a Christmas carol, as the choirmaster strutted up and down between two lines of white surplices, overenunciating in a would-be castrato and pouncing on anyone, often myself, who was however slightly flat. Once a month after Sunday Service probationers got a sixpence, the next grade up, with the surplices, whose name I have forgotten, got a shilling, and the choristers with the blue and red ribbons round their necks got half a crown.

This was a beautiful way to be in song, though you could only let yourself go and feel the elation of the music when the choirmaster turned his back to sit at the organ. Otherwise we were too frightened of hitting a wrong note. But even this had its attractive side; it made for solidarity, complicity and giggles. We giggled at weddings and we giggled at funerals. We were disinterested spectators at life's great events, more ball-boys really than fans, contributing our unbroken voices (*le voci bianche*, the Italians beautifully call them, white voices), but never participating the way you do when the chant leader shouts, 'Now!' and everyone hurls the scraps of paper they've prepared into the air and claps their hands and begins: '*Alè Verona alè!*'

There were no girls in the choir. The choirmaster refused to accept them. Their voices weren't pure, he said. And girls didn't play football either. Or at least I'd never heard of such a thing. I was sweeper in the school team at the time, an enthusiastic player in a family where no one had ever kicked a ball in their lives. Every now and then some sidesman, or perhaps it was the father of a school friend, would take me to Bloomfield Road and even Old Trafford. I was not captivated by the fans' voices. I remember only the geometry of the big stadium, the intense green of the pitch and, still in my mind's eye, the wonderful tangerine shirts that Blackpool played in.

The truth is that my thoughts, or prejudices, about football crowds had already been formed on what must have been a Saturday evening in early infancy. Unusually, we were to be treated to fish and chips. We were about to set out for the shop. Perhaps this is an apocryphal memory, but none the less intense for that. Hearing on the radio that Blackpool had lost at home, my father, who as a clergyman knew what he knew, remarked that the chip shop would be full of women and their children who didn't want to go home. They would be afraid of being beaten up, he said. Then I realised that football crowds were ignorant and working-class and got drunk and swore and that we in St Mark's choir, singing 'Adam lay y bounden', were infinitely superior. I later discovered that my father, who couldn't have cared less, always checked the football results to know what humour his congregation would be in on the Sunday morning.

Another thing that was superior in those days was Northern

football. So much so that no sooner had the family moved down to London than I was made captain of my new class team. It was the last year at primary school. I was ten. To prove myself worthy of this honour, I played furiously, shouting encouragement to my team-mates throughout, so that if there had been a choir I most likely wouldn't have been able to sing in it. But Christ Church North Finchley lacked this glory, as the dull London suburb lacked brass bands and Whitsuntide processions and May Queens and wild Bonfire Nights and all the ways that the North had learned to express its identity in a collision of raw energy and muddled heraldry, whether Christian or pagan. Now instead our family was immersed in the stagnant lily pond of the Southern middle classes, a gloomy world of quiet and cautious repression. When my old Blackpool schoolmates came south on a school journey and I went to meet them at their hostel, everybody expressed amazement at the change in my voice. How quiet you are, they said, how soft-spoken. I was doing all my shouting on the field.

My mother, a Londoner, expressed great satisfaction at having escaped at last from the barbaric North. She felt at home here. She liked the propriety, the better taste, the more closely drawn curtains. She would have been happy, it has often occurred to me, with the stiff decorum of the well-to-do Veronese. Yet whenever some inconvenient wild beast is slain, or monstrous emotion suppressed, you can be sure it will turn up again elsewhere in some other guise. In the end the defining characteristic of the monster is the number of heads he has. And the moment, shortly after one head is cut off, when another appears, the moment when it first snorts its fierce fire and gnashes its sharp teeth, that moment is often far more frightening than the ugliness you were used to. Monsters should be bridled not slain. This is what football violence is all about. So, when the choir-less Christ Church in polite North Finchley did begin to sing, the experience, at least for a thirteen-year-old, was terrifying.

In 1968, with revealing simultaneity, exactly as the too-well-behaved children of the diligent professional classes finally exploded in a clash of guitars and naïve political revolt, so my father's congregation was swept off its stolid feet by the charismatic movement.

People were baptised in the spirit, spoke in tongues, were granted prophecies and Words of Wisdom and even performed exorcisms. My father, my mother, the handsome curate, the intellectual curate, the sidesman, the youth club leaders: they were all swept away by a wild and terrible enthusiasm. Only the ancient verger who had first taken me to White Hart Lane and who, I later realised, laid his hand on my knee too often, seemed immune. And now in church, instead of the stilted rehearsal of 'Love Divine' or 'The Church's One Foundation', these hitherto wooden suburbanites entered wholeheartedly into the enchantment of song; of awful songs with trite Billy Graham words and hurdy-gurdy melodies. And where before people had kept their eyes down on their hymn books, or stolen concerned glances at their watches, now they raised their joyful faces to the chancel steps and even the roof, as if struck by the bright light that hit Saul of Tarsus on the road to Damascus. Certainly a general blindness seemed to afflict them. Eyes shining with tears, they began to lift their arms as they sang, their hymn books tossing in the air, swaying in ecstasy. Sometimes the sound, as we reached the sixth verse or the seventh, was more of chanting than of song, the way in the Bentegodi something that starts out with some old and famous tune – 'La Marseillaise' perhaps – suddenly resolves itself into an insistent cry of Hellas Hellas!

I wasn't immune to this enchantment. I was still obliged to go to church at the time and felt its pull. Church in the end, for me, had always been an extension of family; it was the community I most intimately knew, and I wanted to be part of it. All around, people of my own age were singing and swaying in a kind of frenzy. And I would join in up to a point. I would try to go beyond that point. But then something blocked me. I couldn't do it. Not only would I suddenly find myself outside the spell, but I would be in a sweat of resistance against it. I would be quite desperate to be out of that room, that church, that prayer meeting, and what's more I would be willing the collective spell to fail, willing for people to realise how ridiculous they were being. Charismatic religion is ridiculous, I thought, its demand for total submission is obscene. How can I be asked to believe that this babble is really speaking in other languages, how can I ever accept the idea that the greengrocer's wife has really been given the gift of prophecy? How can I give myself wholeheartedly to folly? Rather than offering a welcome release from the experience of separateness – the pleasure, for example, of singing a descant over the solemn voices of tenor and bass, perhaps with the occasional smile flashing back and forth across the stalls, boy with man – these frenetic encounters actually increased my sense of being alone. I could not and would not believe in this silliness. I was like a Milan supporter who finds himself by accident in the Curva Sud, asked to join in some improbable song claiming Hellas is about to win the Champions' League. He opens his mouth, but he can't do it. It's crazy. And he knows he has been caught out. They've seen he isn't singing. They've spotted his scarf! *Dio boia, Milanista di merda!* Be sure your sins will find you out. Now they are going to tear him to pieces, or make him a convert.

Obliged to read the Bible daily, I discovered that my problem was intellectual pride. But I didn't seem able to do anything about it. Oppressed, I eventually managed to pull away from the church, though in my case this inevitably involved distancing oneself from family too; all kinds of emotions became mixed up. And for years afterwards I overreacted by refusing to join in any group singing. I taught at a summer camp in the USA and could not join in round the camp fire. Hitch-hiking companions sat cross-legged on the beach in Spain singing Bob Dylan. I could not join in. Religious music in particular was impossible for me. 'Jerusalem' sung at some official gathering was at once too beautiful and quite impossible. I opened my mouth, but then was overwhelmed by ungovernable emotion. I could not sing at friends' weddings, nor, when alas they began, at friends' funerals. I love singing and frequently, cheerfully, sing on my own, too frequently and too cheerfully for those who live with me. But from age fifteen on I had lost the ability to lose myself in the spell of group song. For me every meeting was revivalist, and hence impossible.

What a pleasure then, at the Bentegodi, to rediscover the crowd and its choral pandemonium. I could even, after a while, raise my hands at the appropriate moments. Like the church, the *curva* embraces all comers. In particular, I love the ragged end to almost all the songs and chants; you launch with great gusto into something inanely repetitive – *nella pioggia e sotto il sole, nello stadio ci saròòòò!* ('in rain or shine, I'll be there' – the tune is 'La Marseillaise'). You sing it once, you sing it twice, then all of a sudden it breaks off, there is no predetermined end, you can never know when it is going to stop, so that someone will be left with his arms in the air when all the others have lowered theirs, somebody's voice will be heard loud on its own when all the others have sunk away. That person looks round, amazed, faintly embarrassed. I remember in particular a man in his forties on the station platform when we arrived in Vicenza. Bundling out of the train, the fans were yelling *Vicenza Vicenza vaffanculo!* and so taken was he with the excitement of yelling fuck off into the faces of people he didn't know, that he went on a good thirty seconds after all the others had stopped. His voice at last trailed away. His face was a picture of embarrassment. Then he burst out laughing. In the football crowd one moves constantly in and out of the spell, in and out of the group, in and out of the law. Singing together you are all-powerful, singing alone you are a fool. People are aware of this. And however stupid they may be, at least the songs are not addressed to God. They are not *that* stupid. Then, once in the stadium, they have a definite purpose: to incite the team, to raise these mercenaries' adrenaline levels. Dark-eyed, sharp-nosed, chinless and turkey-necked, Captain Leo Colucci says: 'For us the fans are like the motor in a car, without them we wouldn't get any mileage. It's they who give us the drive when things get tough, and if it wasn't for them I don't know how we could manage.'

'Will they manage?' I ask Pietro, arriving for the game with Milan. This is 17 December. Leo Colucci is still out. Camoranesi's injury gets more serious every time I read about it. His knee is bust. Now Mutu too is injured it seems. My son as ever is tiresomely pessimistic. 'Be a great game,' Pietro says. He rubs his hands. 'Great game, always a great game when Milan come to the Bentegodi.'

How reassuring this man is. How wonderfully cheerful with his big-jawed smile and his bright eyes. And today he has tradition on his side too. Verona have an uncanny tradition of beating AC Milan at the Bentegodi. Twice the big club actually lost the championship here on one of the last games of the season. In 1973 Hellas beat Rivera's team five–three, this after Milan had just won the Cup Winners' Cup. As a result Juventus took the championship. In 1990, with Verona doomed to relegation, Arrigo Sacchi's Milan, with Van Basten and Gullit in attack and Rijkaard midfield, went down two–one. This time Napoli popped up to take first place. And even in 1997, the most miserable year I've held a season ticket, Verona still managed to beat Baggio's Milan three–one, almost the only important victory of the season.

Why does history repeat itself like this? Why hasn't the great AC Milan, a team built with the resources of Silvio Berlusconi's vast media empire, scored a victory at the Bentegodi in a decade? Is it that an initial fluke is then followed by a subversive, self-fulfilling desire for the jinx, a sort of infantile thirst for the supernatural at any cost? 'If we keep losing against those second-raters that means there must be something more to the universe than blind mechanics.' Is that it? So that even the new star player from Brazil perhaps, or from Spain, someone who has never played at the Bentegodi before or even heard of it, nevertheless, by some curious mental contamination, expects things to go badly when he steps out on the pitch beneath the Curva Sud. Today Milan are headed by the man who last year was Serie A's top goal-scorer, the Ukrainian Andrij Shevchenko. The *rossoneri* (red-and-blacks) as they're called have just won three games in a row. Verona must play what jinx value they have for all it's worth.

They do. '*Milanisti!*' the PA system booms out. 'Welcome to the fatal Verona.' The *curva* goes wild. In fact the thing I remember most now of this game is the fantastic scene that followed that announcement, the enchantment of the *curva* in full voice. To the tune of 'Guide me O thou great Jehovah', a tune I first heard no doubt in the pews or choir stalls of my father's church in Manchester or in Blackpool, the *butei* sang: '*Quanti scudetti avete voi?*' (how many championships do you have?). And then came the refrain, *sotto voce* but growing louder as the music shifts up the scale: '*Due di meno, due di meno.*' Two less, two less.

Why do I find it so moving? Why is it so easy for me to join in? And as a line of red smoke-bombs is lit around the edge of the terraces, every single man and woman, boy and girl in the Curva Sud hurls a roll of (generously provided) white ticker-tape down into the bowl beneath us, so that for a few moments the whole area seems to have been caught in a blizzard framed in burning red. The spell is cast. A magic circle has been drawn. The players are in the middle of it. Waving to us, they do not realise they have been enchanted. The whistle blows. In less than three minutes, Bonazzoli has scored.

'Too soon!' Everybody said it at once. 'Too soon!' Why do we score so early? Three minutes later, entirely alone in front of the goal, our young Cassetti, fresh from Serie C, tall, stooped, long-haired and timid, rose to a perfect cross from Martino Melis on the left and headed it down hard. The goalkeeper froze, beaten. The ball struck the ground in the six-yard box and bounced over the bar. Oh. The spell had already broken.

'That's it.' Everybody shook their heads. That was the moment to take control of the game, to sew it up. There won't be another. Sure enough Milan equalised after about twenty minutes. But we were already resigned. And fifteen minutes into the second half, with the Verona defence split apart, the great Shevchenko was running on to a low cross that came skidding and bouncing along the top of the six-yard box.

This is the only clear picture I have of the whole game, though the action was at the far end and my eyesight isn't perfect. Wrong-footed, Ferron had already gone down. He was beaten. Already Massimo, behind me, is yelling, '*Mongolo!*' It was so obvious that the Ukrainian was going to score. In a moment the great bank of red-and-black scarves and banners behind him will erupt, and likewise the fifth columnists hidden in the more expensive seats to our right. Yes, they will jump to their feet and then sit quickly down again when the *curva* around me roars out for their blood. The ball keeps coming. Shevchenko keeps running. It is like the one time I was involved in a serious car accident. From the back seat I saw the impact coming a surreal split second before it did.

And that fraction of a second was silent and infinitely long. The Curva Sud is silent. Even the cry of *mongolo* has died away. The stadium holds its breath. Ferron looks up from the ground. The white ball and the blond man are about to meet.

Now!

And somehow Shevchenko contrives to miss it. This star player, fabulously rich, fabulously talented, contrives to screw up this most open of open goals. For some reason his foot doesn't connect with the ball. It seemed he was already tapping it in. But somehow the ball continues in the same direction. The Verona fans stood and hugged. It was as if we'd scored. It was a miracle. It was proof that Verona is indeed fated when it comes to AC Milan. And in fact the draw was played out now with only four or five more scares. We knew the ball wouldn't go in. At the end I returned home exhausted and hoarse, complaining as ever in the car to my son about the referee's leniency with the yellow cards when it came to the big teams. Giuseppe Colucci had been stretchered off after an unpunished foul. Another key player gone. '*Bastardi!*' Michele agreed. But back home, watching the evening's round-up, we saw that if any team had been favoured it was Verona. Our goal was outrageously offside. Once away from the *incanto* of the crowd, it was clear we'd been a very lucky team that afternoon. 'I accept *il verdetto del campo*,' I announced. All the same, with Vicenza winning at Parma and Napoli beating Reggina six–two, we are now only two points clear of the relegation zone.

IIA GIORNATA

Bologna – Atalanta 0–1

Inter – Brescia 0–0

Lazio – Roma 0–1

Lecce – Juventus 1–4

Napoli – Reggina 6–2

Parma – Vicenza 0–2

Perugia – Bari 4–1

Udinese – Fiorentina 1–3

Verona – Milan 1–1

CLASSIFICA

Roma	28
Juventus	22
Atalanta	22
Milan	19
Lazio	18
Fiorentina	17
Bologna	17
Parma	17
Udinese	16
Perugia	13
Inter	13
Lecce	12
Verona	12
Vicenza	12
Napoli	10
Brescia	8
Bari	8
Reggina	4

Calendario

Forza Verona, how can I go a Sunday without you?
Ricky@semprehellas

The ambition of every enchantment is to extend itself everywhere and ad infinitum. Only when it fills your whole mind, always, only when you think from inside the spell and never see it from without, never even realise you are bewitched, only then does it hold you completely in its thrall.

Open any Italian diary, even the desktop business diary that I use, and it will give at least one saint for every day of the year. Today, for example, the twelfth of January, is San Modesto, not a popular name these days, and certainly not a nickname you would want to give to a footballer. Who knows now what San Modesto did? No one. But once that name would have meant a story; once every day had a story and every story contributed to the overarching enchantment, the spell Christendom then lived in. The Aztecs did the same. Every day was dedicated to a god and every god had a festival. What was polytheism for but to fill the world up, top time to the brim, a deity a day? There was always something to celebrate, never a moment for reflecting, as the hunchbacked Leopardi so often did, on life's nothingness.

So on 11 November, the day before we played Vicenza away, amid all the insults flying back and forth on The Wall, someone remembers to write: '*Auguri per il tuo onomastico Martino Melis!*' Best wishes for your saint's day! For a moment the Christian calendar and the football calendar embrace. Born in Hungary in the fourth century,

186

Saint Martin was pressed into the Roman army at the age of ten. Sixteen hundred years later, aged fourteen, Martino Melis left his home in a small village of Sardinia to go to a football college on the mainland. Saint Martin asked to be allowed to leave the Roman army because he was a Christian. He was Christ's soldier and could not fight a secular war. Martino Melis is also a practising Christian, though fortunately his beliefs don't prevent him from joining the weekly fray. When charged with cowardice, Saint Martin is said to have offered to stand in front of the Roman battle line armed only with a crucifix. The dark and dapper Martino Melis, whose face now appears on the local paper's full page ad for Pocket Coffee, always touches the crucifix nailed above the changing room door before entering the battle ground of the Bentegodi. Or so the team masseur told me. But sitting, as I and my son do, directly above the corner flag, we often see from close up how, having completed a run down the left wing, Melis faces his defender. It's the moment when he must dribble or cross. But he seems to freeze. We can see his thick jet-black hair, his fussily trimmed beard. He shifts his weight from side to side, hesitating. The seconds are ticking by. The area is filling with defenders. '*Punta l'uomo, Martino!*' the crowd shrieks, 'Pass your man!' and beside me Pietro sighs. 'He hasn't got the courage. Since his injury he won't take on his man. He's scared of the foul.' Saint Martin, it seems, was the first example of a Christian becoming a saint without undergoing martyrdom. Martino Melis, perhaps, is eager to emulate that achievement.

But if there are analogies between football and religion, hero worship and saints' days, there are huge differences too. And one is that while Christianity does, or did, really fill every day of the year, football on the contrary, however hard it tries, hasn't yet extended its calendar over the whole year. Not quite. It's true that when there's not the league there's often the cup; Verona, alas, was knocked out of the Italian cup in September in a manner so distressing I chose not to mention it. It's true too that when there's neither the league nor the cup there are the European cups which are now carefully dosed out to occupy Tuesday, Wednesday and Thursday, with the result that there are many weeks in October and November which actually offer an important match *every single day*: that is, to recapitulate: the two *anticipi* for Serie A on the Saturday, afternoon and evening; the main fixture programme of Serie A and Serie B on the Sunday afternoon with a big match delayed to the evening, the *posticipo* of Serie B on the Monday, half of the Champions' League on the Tuesday, the second half on the Wednesday, the UEFA cup on Thursday, and the *anticipo* of Serie B on the Friday. There! The whole week has been filled. Quite an achievement when you think that the number of saints' days people actually remember are now as sparse as the vandalised seats in the Curva Sud.

Such blanket coverage is the result of very serious planning. Talented administrators are hard at work to make sure that we are never without football, as once the bishops no doubt worked hard to spread the saints across twelve months and fifty-two empty weeks. In alternate years we will even get the European Cup or the World Cup to fill the summer. So another arid, empty space blossoms with colour and heraldry.

And yet it stops. Try as they might, they can't quite fill the whole year. Or perhaps they could. They could, but there's something that prevents them from doing so: a modesty, a *pudore*, a residual sense of realism and measure, a fear of hubris, perhaps, the kind of common sense no religion can countenance. Perhaps this is part of the modernity of football: that unlike the other transporting experiences whose function it unwittingly seeks to replace, giving shape and direction to our lives, football is nevertheless something we all stand outside of from time to time. Then, like the man who hears his voice after all the others have already stopped chanting, we feel vaguely embarrassed and say: it's only a game. Ridiculous words! There are other more important things, we say. Absurd! At which, we sense a sudden emptiness. It's the emptiness of the temple robbed of its gods. The world has stopped. In Italy, which unlike England still imagines itself a Christian country, one of those stoppage times is Christmas.

On Monday 18 December, Saint Graziano's day, I lay on my narrow bed in my Milan hotel and, eating (despite the mad cow craziness) a burger bought from the McDonald's in Piazza

Duomo a hundred yards away, I tried to watch from beginning to end the TV football programme called 'Il Processo di Biscardi' (Biscardi's Trial). To my surprise, I saw that sitting beside the asinine Biscardi, a belligerent loud-mouthed fellow, all extravagant tie and unwarranted self-importance, was a cappuccino monk. Theatrically bearded and bespectacled, this holy man smiled with bland complacence. His name, so it seemed, was Padre Antonio, and 'he is here', the presenter Biscardi announced, 'to bless us all before our Christmas break.'

Break? Christmas? Fighting hard, I tugged a wallet from a tight pocket, pulled out my Hellas calendar and discovered that there was indeed a hiatus in the otherwise seamless calendar: from 23 December (away to Florence) until 7 January (away to Lecce) the fans were to be left entirely to their own devices. So Sunday by Sunday the football calendar superimposes itself on the religious calendar, with optional ceremonies during the week 'for several occasions' as the *Book of Common Prayer* puts it. But then, come Christmas, the old calendar surfaces, the Christ dinosaur raises his thorny head, and we are obliged to savour together the aftertaste of His lost enchantment. Yes, for a full two weeks we will be quite defenceless against everything else that is encroaching on our mental space: the massacres in Palestine, a fresh crop of deaths on the road, the endless and incomprehensible election campaign, BSE, global warming, and even the bomb that this very night someone is placing behind the gargoyles of the Milan *duomo* exactly opposite those golden arches where ten minutes ago I paid for my burger. But for the moment let's concentrate on Biscardi.

Together with the monk he has a couple of 'experts' in the studio, most frighteningly the fellow with the thick glasses and flappy ears whose name is Maurizio Mosca. This barrel-chested little Neanderthal is always hunched over his desk in attack position. When not talking, he fiddles in frustration with a pen whose purpose remains obscure to me. Can he write? Does it squirt poisoned ink? But these periods of agitated silence don't last long. Mosca treats a conversation the way Zidane and Davids handle the midfield. It belongs to him. If he hasn't been passed the conversational ball, he will simply go out there and grab it. His oratorical talent is to be measured in decibels. One day I suspect they will find he is doped.

Meantime outside the studio, but grotesquely present on the sort of huge screen Mussolini would have loved, are a few top executives from the major clubs: Moggi from Juventus, Galliani from Milan, Cragnotti junior from Lazio. Why, one wonders, are these presumably intelligent, certainly powerful men going to submit themselves to what is a three-hour (I repeat, three-hour) shouting match about football, a scenario where everything they say will be contradicted before they have said it, with Mosca jumping to his feet and gesticulating wildly and the fatuous Biscardi yelling, 'No no no, that's not true!'?

Why do they do it? 'Because', an ex-president of Roma football club eventually explained to me, 'if you don't go on these TV shows, they, the TV companies, who after all are football's paymasters, find ways of making you and your team suffer for it.' 'So you act out of fear,' I asked this once-powerful man. 'Of course!' He was dismissive. How foolish of me to ask. Power and fear are part of the same experience. Power is fear of losing power.

'It's an outrage,' Mosca is shrieking. His glasses gleam blindly. He and Biscardi are insisting that sports judges should be able to look at TV proof to punish players whose violent actions the referee hasn't seen. Moggi, the Juventus representative, is complaining that it is always Juventus who are punished, never the others. Is this possible? A youngish and admirably solemn studio audience looks on, chins in cupped hands, brows knitted, as if the outcome of this battle were absolutely essential to them. Where do the television studios find these people? One can only assume that this is the man in the street.

'Just because you see it on television doesn't mean you actually understand what happens,' Moggi reasonably remarks. 'Workable and demonstrably transparent regulations must be put in force,' he says.

'Transparent' is an oft-repeated word in the murky world of Serie A.

'Technology!' Mosca shrieks. 'You are resisting technology because you're scared it will interfere with your power! You won't be able to fix the games!'

Again and again, while all these men holler at each other and accuse people they refuse to name of seeking to influence the sports judges and referees, the TV viewer is constantly being shown and re-shown three violent incidents, as follows:

On day 5 of the first half of the championship – 5 November, that is, in the Christian calendar, Roma's Batistuta is harried by Brescia defender Siviglia in a touch-line situation where nothing particular appears to be at stake; eventually the two go down together; Batistuta reacts to what he considers a foul; there's a vigorous brawl with kicks and punches; the referee doesn't even give a yellow card;

also on day 5, at the Bentegodi, Inter's Vieri, jumping for the ball, pushes away our Apolloni then very deliberately elbows him in the face; his lip is pouring blood; a foul is given, but no yellow card;

on day 9 of the championship, 10 December, while Juventus form a wall to deal with an Inter free kick, ugly Montero is seen giving a punch in the side of the head to Di Biagi, who staggers but keeps his feet; the referee doesn't notice.

The images are endlessly repeated. The experts yell. Mosca bangs his fist on the table. When he speaks he sprays saliva. The various presidents must be relieved that they are in distant studios. The audience watch solemnly. Just occasionally the camera pans round the panel to bring in Padre Antonio, who smiles on the scene with condescension, twiddling his holy thumbs, presumably waiting for the moment of closure when he will be allowed to assert the superiority of his calendar to theirs.

I change channel. If this is the level of debate, I tell myself, football will never enchant our whole lives. We will always find ourselves thrown back on such threadbare spells as Easter and Christmas. Of about ten other channels available on the fuzzy set of this cheapest of cheap hotels in central Milan, four are discussing or showing football and three are involved in fortune-telling of one kind or another. There's a Spanish league game, a discussion with the coach of the team now top of Serie C, and a chat with a referee about his training programme. Meanwhile a woman with a turban does phone-in tarot and Mago Maurizio (mago means wizard) gets in contact with the dead for you.

Mago Maurizio is far more charming than anyone on the 'Processo di Biscardi'. Handsome, unshaven, with thick wavy hair and solid square jaw, he smiles seductively at the camera. He is young, wise and psychic, an unbeatable combination. Almost all the callers are women. 'Can I speak to my brother? He was killed in a car accident.' Signora Mara is crying. 'Is it too soon to get in touch with my husband? He died last May.' This is Signora Assunta. 'I would like his advice about a problem we're having with the inheritance.' 'His date of birth, please,' Maurizio asks. He is businesslike and reassuring. 'Right, good, and now the exact date of death. Thank you.' How strange that these calendar numbers allow Maurizio to get in touch with the lost spirit at once! As if one were to say: Fabrizio Ferron – first appearance in Serie A day 3 of the Championship 1988, last appearance day 10 . . . But now I'm suddenly reminded of a large graffito right above the central tunnel that leads out into the heart of the Curva Sud: '*Oltre la morte!*' it says. 'Beyond death.' What can it mean for a football fan to write that?

I zap back to the 'Processo di Biscardi' to find them slow mo-ing Montero's punch for the thousandth time while off-camera someone is screaming, 'But this will only lead to more and more players faking and falling down every time anybody touches them.' This programme, I decide, is a trial above all for its audience, like a long and impossibly dull sermon. Why do people subject themselves to these things? But then why do people travel all night in coaches to see their teams lose away? Is it that you can't convince yourself that something is important unless you suffer for it?

Zapping back, Mago Maurizio has fallen into a trance and as his eyes gaze blank beyond the tomb his hand is scribbling with insane speed on a block of A4. The letters are huge, the writing aggressive and forward-slanting, not unlike my own. As he does this trick, the portentous kitsch of the *Carmina Burana* swells up from the background while various telephone numbers flash on and off the screen, exactly as on the telephone sex channels. 'No waiting!' it says. '24 hours a day.' Surely not. The boy looks as if he sleeps as well as a footballer. He writes. He tears off sheet after sheet of A4. Signora Assunta's heavy breathing, perhaps sobs, can be heard in the background. Maurizio's pen suddenly stops. He looks up and unleashes his most seductive smile. His unshavenness somehow makes this more sincere, more authentic. Then he reads: 'Know well my dearest one that I bring you joy. The troubles you have been passing through are almost over.' It's a formula you get used to if you watch Mago Maurizio for more than ten minutes. It's as automatic as his writing. If I called and asked him to get in touch with some dead football star to enquire about Verona's relegation prospects, he would say, 'Know well, insane fanatic, that I bring you joy. The injury problems that are plaguing Hellas Verona are almost over.' And he would be right of course: of whom or what, in the end, might it not be said, with a small shift in perspective, that their troubles are almost over? 'You can also look at life', Schopenhauer wrote, 'as an episode unprofitably disturbing the blessed calm of nothingness.'

Going forward a channel, the disturbance is massive. Valencia have scored. I have to cut out the audio for a moment. I think it's Valencia. I couldn't care less about the Spanish league. There are limits. The goal is being shown again and again. Goals occupy more space than other moments in life. Going back two channels the coach from Serie C has been substituted by a city councillor from the town of Lodi explaining why they are insisting on a referendum about the granting of cheap land to the Muslim community for the building of a mosque. It must be a local channel. First the team, then the councillor. It seems protestors have dumped a ton of pig shit on the proposed site. And how strange, having heard the word *moschea* – mosque – to think that the loudmouth on the 'Processo di Biscardi' is called Mosca, which in Italian means 'fly'. Certainly he offers the same unprofitable disturbance as the fly buzzing about on your car windscreen. 'We need more technology,' the man is still yelling when I zap back to him. 'More, more, more! There is no reason why we shouldn't understand everything that happens on a football pitch. Everything.'

This is Mosca's style. He stabs his pen at a piece of paper. Perhaps that's what it's for. I zap back to compare it with the *Mago*'s pen and as I do so it occurs to me that his name too is Maurizio. Mosca and the *Mago* share the same saint's day, but the latter uses a more impressive pen, a fountain pen. 'Could you tell me whether my grandson is going to survive?' asks a quavering voice. 'He was born last Thursday, two months premature with a hole in his heart.' Just as people are willing to take their most intense emotions to football, so they will bring their most intimate grief to TV sorcerers. 'Know well that I bring you joy,' Mago Maurizio says. What is impressive about him is how, when he goes into trance, he always scribbles in a different style of handwriting, as if there truly were some alien spirit moving his wrist. I don't think I could do this. '*Sia serena, Signora Anna.*' Be serene. 'The boy will live and grow strong.' 'May Christmas bring serenity,' Padre Antonio is saying. At last the 'Processo' is over. 'Your sport is a wonderful thing, but I fear it lacks serenity.' Paid to yell scandal and goad the big executives into saying something they shouldn't, Mosca and Biscardi bow their heads in wise agreement. 'May God bless you all this Christmas season.' The monkish smile is as empty as the Arctic north.

I turn off. I will never, I decide, *never* watch 'Il Processo di Biscardi' again. There is a limit to the research one can do for a book. Lying down to sleep it occurs to me that if the world has become a madder and madder mixing of absolutely everything, then it is with the remote control pointing at the TV screen that this becomes most apparent. The remote control, I tell myself, the practice of zapping around dozens of channels, has made it impossible for any one calendar to assert itself. Didn't somebody send me an e-mail entitled 'Happy Divali'? Didn't Lodi's councillor say we should be more aware of Muslims during Ramadan? Armed, disarmed, by the remote control, it has become impossible to be solemn about the way we fill up time. It's getting harder and harder to distinguish Christmas from Easter, Spanish teams from Italian, the Panettone from the Colomba. Where once there was rhythm, a dignified division, now there is quantity and noise. Yet at the same time we now feel obliged to *appear* solemn about *everything*, so as not to offend those still inexplicably locked into the doomed worlds of old religions, or, even worse, the kind of well-wisher who gave me a 2001 diary where, alongside the saints' days, are all the UN celebration days: 8 March – women's rights; 21 March – for the elimination of racism; 23 April – for books and the respect of copyright. Can you imagine? Respect of copyright! If ever there was a spell stillborn, here it is. For myself I keep my Hellas calendar in my wallet. Often I pull it out to reassure myself of the emotions that stretch before me or, just occasionally, to savour again those that stretch behind. But I always feel a bit embarrassed when non-believers see me with my blue-and-yellow calendar. I always pretend football's a bit of a joke.

In any event, more or less at the same time as I was pondering these several imponderables in my hotel bed in central Milan, a few hundred yards away a workman spied a brown paper package behind one of the gargoyles on the floodlit façade of the *duomo*: a bomb. And in the morning, when I turned on the TV for the news, something one does only in hotels, the reaction of the political parties was not unlike the reaction of the executives of the powerful clubs to any proposed change of the rules. 'I don't know who did this, but the intention is clearly to damage our cause,' says one. 'It's a right-wing plot to destabilise the country before elections.' 'It's a left-wing plot to give people the impression that the right wing is seeking to destabilise the country before elections.' At once you sense that no one will ever get to the bottom of this.

A few days later, on 22 December, San Francesco if you will, a bomb actually did go off, this time outside the offices of the left-wing newspaper *Il Manifesto* down in Rome. 'This is a pre-election strategy of tension designed to damage the centre parties of the left.' 'This is clearly designed to split the centre-right coalition and keep the left in power.' As I read these statements, I can hear Fondo's raucous voice: 'In the election campaign, *c'è una bomba!*' And turning, as I always quickly do, to the sports pages, it's to find that the Football Federation is delaying the start of all the weekend's pre-Christmas games by fifteen minutes in order to protest against those who threw two Molotov cocktails against the Inter players' bus after the team went down six–one to Parma in the cup. 'The players must defend their right to lose!' the Federation announces. 'Fuck off,' someone responds on The Wall. 'We're only two points clear of the relegation zone. We can't fucking-well afford to lose.'

But however unpromising this attitude, it has to be said that Padre Antonio would have been proud of the Brigate Gialloblù during the away game at Fiorentina on 23 December. It turned out to be exactly the thing we needed to prepare for the serene – that is emotionless – two weeks to come. For the curious thing is that Verona fans, who always insist on shouting and writing '*soli contro tutti*' (alone against everyone), have a *gemellaggio*, or twinning, with Fiorentina fans. That is to say, where normally there is the theatre of hatred, here we have a theatre of friendship and even brotherhood. Where normally we shout 'Juve *merda*, Vicenza *vaffanculo*', today we chant 'Forza Viola', for Fiorentina play in purple. And the authorities are aware of this different charade. They know we are friendly. So instead of being kept rigidly separate by lines of riot police, the fans are allowed to mingle freely with each other outside the ground. Little boys run in and out of the crowd, asking if you will swap your Hellas scarf for their Viola scarf. There are smiles and embraces.

Why? In what way are the people of Florence different from the people of Milan or Bologna? 'Tradition,' Beppe tells me. I'm driving down to the game in a minibus with the group who call themselves The Maddest Ones. 'But when did it start?' I ask. What's the story behind it? Nobody knows. Can I shout, 'Fiorentina *vaffanculo*'? 'Not if you don't want to be lynched.'

The stadium was freezing. We were herded into the only corner not in the sunshine and obliged to watch the game through a grim cage of Perspex and netting, something even more galling when the fans were so friendly that we might just as well have watched the match holding hands. After an hour's shivering wait, the players come out on to the field and Fiorentina at once confirm their recent form by creating five scoring chances in the first few minutes, all of which Ferron amazingly saves. I wish Massimo could see him now.

I like Ferron. I like his courage, his manly calm, his concentration. I think he's a great keeper. Again he saves what should surely have been an easy goal. Who knows, perhaps today is going to be the day. But no. To show that we are not short of Christmas spirit, Fillipini, one of the reserves drafted in at the back for the suspended Apolloni, handles the ball for no reason in an empty penalty area. *Rigore*. One–nil. The stupidest goal of the season so far.

As the second half opens, Bonazzoli heads against the post. A few moments later we have a promising free kick just inside the Florence half with all players moving upfield to put the pressure on. Standing on the ball, the young Marco Cassetti – he who gave away the penalty in Bari – looks around. Is it that his irritatingly long hair gets in his eyes? Why can't the manager insist that a player get his hair cut? Instead of kicking directly towards goal and the waiting head of Bonazzoli, Cassetti taps the ball sideways across the centre circle to where he imagines Anthony Seric, another rarely seen reserve, is expecting it. He has not seen that Rui Costa is standing between them. And Rui Costa is only one of the world's fastest and most talented strikers. In a few seconds he and Enrico Chiesa are alone in front of Ferron and this time there is nothing the keeper can do. Cassetti is in tears. I am outraged.

It is at this point that I am obliged to acknowledge the superiority of the much-maligned *brigate* to my irretrievably neurotic and rancorous self. While I, in the centre of the crush, was shrieking at the idiot in front of me whose monstrous flag was blocking my vision of our pathetic attempts to equalise, the *brigate* had already understood that the game was lost and that since this was Christmas and what's more we were twinned with Fiorentina, we should do our best to put a brave face on it. About fifteen minutes from the end, the game now quite dead, the chant leader shouts through his megaphone: 'On the count of three, we score.'

I didn't understand. There were about a thousand of us, all with our scarves and hats, though some had switched blue-and-yellow for *viola*. As always at away games we were standing. We were packed together for warmth, all stamping our feet on each other's toes while the icy air round our heads steamed and smoked. We were shivering. We couldn't see properly. We were losing two–nil. What did the man mean, on the count of three we score?

'One.' Everybody fell silent. 'Two.' They opened their mouths grinning. 'Three.'

'*GOL!!!*'

The whole throng all around me went quite mad, shrieking, embracing. '*Rete! Gol!*' On the pitch a couple of players looked up from whatever mundane administration they were involved in. What was going on? '*Gol! Forza Verona alè!*' Across the stadium, when the Fiorentina supporters finally understood, they joined in the cheering. There was a loud crackle of applause. Five minutes later the megaphone said: 'Now we hit the post. One, two, three. Ooooh! No!'

'And now, *butei*, we equalise.'

'*Gol! Gol! Gol!*'

In the end, or in cloud-cuckoo-land, Verona won the game three–two, an illusion within the general illusion that is football. Congratulating themselves, the *brigate* sang '*Buon natale, buon natale, buon natale gialloblù*' – Happy Christmas blue-yellows – to the tune of 'Clementine,' as if the game were already over. It might as well have been. For myself I was shocked by such unwarranted good spirits and didn't recover my equilibrium until I heard someone saying, 'What a cripple Cassetti is! *Che natale di merda per lui.*' A shit of a Christmas for him. Yes, Cassetti will have an awful Christmas, I thought, and likewise Filippini who gave away the penalty. They deserve it.

Then driving home, the world stopped. Isn't this what the ancients always feared at the winter solstice? Descending from the frozen Apennines, we found the Po valley under the thickest fog and crept back the last eighty miles at a snail's pace. Verona was icily still, the temperature well below zero. No football for two weeks. Nothing to do but detoxify oneself with rich food, strong wine and sloth.

I honestly dread the days between Christmas and New Year. There is no rhythm to them. Initially excited about their presents, the children grow restless. You have to drag them away from their computer games. Or play computer games with them. Having discovered that in 'Superstar Soccer' Sweden play in more or less the same colours as Verona, Michele and I take on all the best teams in the world – Germany, Brazil, France – pretending we are Hellas Verona. Needless to say, we win. 'The right to lose is one thing,' somebody writes on The Wall, 'but the right to relegation is quite another.' Hellas Verona are fifth from bottom.

When the papers re-appear on the 28th, I am cheered by a tidal wave of kitsch. In a nearby village, at midnight mass, a priest read out all the SMS messages he had received on his *telefonino*, then invited the whole congregation to get their *telefonini* to trill together at midnight exactly. Perhaps the *brigate* should do this when we score a goal. Meantime there are articles on the so-called charity calendars that so many sports teams produce. This year all the athletes are getting themselves photographed naked. 'They may be bottom of the league,' – this about a girl's volleyball team – 'but they're the top men's choice when it comes to a calendar.' The money goes to the needy somewhere or other. It always does. The mixture of charity and prurience, it seems, is unbeatable. If *Playboy* and *Hustler* said that half the cover price went to Save the Children, they would double their sales. An incredibly long article discusses the case of the San Martino Buon Albergo team who planned such a calendar but then found that some players refused to get their kit off. 'Behind the ball the centre-forward has his pants on,' the journalist complains.

Oh but this is a hopeless week. No work, no peace to read with the kids in the house, no football, the roads too choked to drive anywhere. Why don't the Italians have Boxing Day matches like the English? The English never stop playing football.

As the frustration mounts you begin to hear fireworks going off at all times of the day and night. Italy is preparing for New Year's Eve, an explosion of pent-up, pyrotechnic energy released into the nothingness of the winter night. This year stops *now*, everybody is screaming. We're fed up; let another one begin. Turn solstice turn! Isn't it enough that we invented that story with God coming into the world? Isn't it enough that we've suspended the football season? Let this dead time end. All over Italy, but above all in Naples, the police are confiscating home-made fireworks. A child has lost his hand.

What can the Parks family do to add their weight to the general effort to shift the earth a little on its axis? On New Year's Eve we drive up to the mountains to walk in the snow; anything to get the circulation going. Not to the skiing areas – that would be impossible – but the depopulated desolation of upper Lessinia: San Rocco, Rovereto, Velo Veronese. On all the road signs out of town, a yellow sticker proclaiming 'Republica Veneta' is evident. This is serious Lega country. Everywhere there's the poster that announces in dialect: *'DIME CAN MA NO TALIAN!'* – Call me a dog, but not an Italian.

We park the car above Velo at 3,000 feet and walk up towards the high plateau: my wife, myself, Michele, Stefi, Lucia. Michele, gloomy as ever, disappears ahead. He wants to walk on his own. The girls roll in the snow, two feet deep here. But an hour later, as we climb up higher and higher, the wind takes you by surprise. It's quite bitter. Rita turns back with Lucia, while I must press on with Stefi to find where on earth Michele has got to. Going over the top of the ridge on to the plateau, we're suddenly in Scott-of-the-Arctic conditions. The wind whips hard flakes of ice across an expanse that is hugely white, with the range of Monte Baldo to our left, the tall peak of Carega to our right. But where is my son, my firstborn?

Bent to the wind we stagger on, and find him at last where the path, marked by poles in the deep snow, passes a little hollow that the farmers use in summer as a watering hole for their cattle. Now the water is frozen solid into a tiny round lake. On his knees Michele is scraping letters on the ice with a stone. In the huge nothingness of the landscape, beneath a white and empty sky, on the last day of the year 2000, he has etched *'HELLAS VERONA, VINCI PER NOI'*. And immediately beneath this: *'JUVE MERDA!'*

I2A GIORNATA

Atalanta – Inter 0–1
Bari – Lazio 1–2
Brescia – Lecce 2–2
Fiorentina – Verona 2–0
Milan – Perugia 1–2
Napoli – Parma 2–2
Reggina – Vicenza 1–0
Roma – Juventus 0–0
Udinese – Bologna 3–1

CLASSIFICA

Roma	29
Juventus	23
Atalanta	22
Lazio	21
Fiorentina	20
Milan	19
Udinese	19
Parma	18
Bologna	17
Perugia	16
Inter	16
Lecce	13
Verona	12
Vicenza	12
Napoli	11
Brescia	9
Bari	8
Reggina	7

Lecce

Italy, land of a hundred cities, that unites love of my home town with love of my country and love of Europe. There is more that unites us than divides us.
President Ciampi, New Year's address

Italian unity = Roma merda, Inter merda, Milan merda, Napoli merda, Vicenza merda, Lecce merda. Need I go on?
Dany-for-Hell@s.it

By the age of ten their skills are evident. Their mothers are shrieking on the sidelines. Talent scouts are offering advice. By the age of fifteen they are in a football college. They survive one selection after another. They see other boys leave, hanging their heads. Sensing they are destined for glory, they go to bed early, dreaming of the turf at San Siro, at the Olimpico. On the telephone Mamma and Papà urge them on. Their few old friends urge them on. They don't drink and they don't smoke. Their diet is controlled. The training is exhausting. By seventeen or eighteen they are playing in Serie C, or sitting on the bench in Serie B. Solemn men in heavy coats gamble on their future. They are bought and sold. A billion lire this year, five billion next. They are shunted up and down the length of the *bel paese*, Treviso, Taranto, Palermo, Turin. They know no one outside the world of football now. They hardly know what to say to a person who is not a player or a manager or a journalist. Or at least a fan. Is there anybody who is not a football fan? They are simultaneously proud of what they have achieved and afraid of seeming stupid. They haven't studied. They haven't had time for a social life. Always supervised, they haven't had time to develop a character. Before each game their bags are prepared for them, three shirts with name and number stitched on the back, three undershirts, three pairs of shorts, three pairs of socks, three pairs of shoes, the club tracksuit, the spare all-white kit just in case. Their travel is booked for them, their meals are prepared for them, their days are planned out for them. Five days a week they train, one day, if they are lucky, they play, and one day they are free to read the papers about how they played. Before and after each training session they are weighed. They are told their optimum weight and must maintain it. They mustn't have sex before a game. They are fined if they are late for training. They are fined if their *telefonino* rings when the coach is speaking. They are fined if they don't wear the club uniform when travelling with the team. Yearning to be picked for the game, what can they do but agree with everything the coach says? What can they do but try to carry out his every wish? Picked, they are proud and relieved; left out, they suffer all kinds of anguish. Dreading injury, they become hypersensitive and hypochondriac. They have a twitch in the calf, a tingle in the wrist, a swelling in the neck. What is it? The team doctor examines them, the team masseur revives them. Surgeons of international renown perform the most routine orthopaedic operations. Yearning to be adored, they are afraid people want their company only because they are famous. They watch pornography in anonymous hotels. When they win they are worshipped. Standing arms raised beneath the *curva*, they are drenched in glory, their faces resplendent. Their clothes have become sacred objects. People seek to touch them in crowds. When they lose they are spat on. The whistles are deafening. They make for the tunnel with head down. Lonely, they marry young. An old girlfriend perhaps. Perhaps a young model, lost and vain as themselves. Or in the claustrophobic autism that reigns in this world, they turn to team-mates for sex. It's a men's world and the men are young and attractive. Waking with a headache in the middle of the night, they have to call the team doctor before they can take anything. There are dope tests. They cannot put drops in a stuffy nose. They cannot inhale Vicks. They cannot think about anything but the game. The next game is crucial. The next game is always crucial. The night before the game they are too tense to sleep. The night after the game they are too excited, too furious. The whole body is inflamed. The muscles are swollen, the joints are stiff. They cannot sleep. With amazement they read about players in other countries who drink heavily and smoke and smash up restaurants and aeroplanes. How can this be? What would the *Gazzetta* say? Italy is a Catholic country. They read that English players check the horse-racing results at half-time. They do not believe it. It can't be so. Like Spartan soldiers, they are truly themselves only on the field of battle. Only when they run out through the players' tunnel into the big green stadium can they unleash all their pent-up emotion. Only here can they show their genius. Only before a huge crowd can they at last behave appallingly. They clutch their opponent's shirt. They crash into his legs before he reaches a scoring position. The crowd applaud. Pull him down! They constantly pretend that they themselves have been fouled. They fall over when they haven't been touched. They deny the most evident truths, insisting they didn't touch a ball when everybody has seen that they did; claiming a ball didn't go out when everybody has seen that it has. Winning, they toss the ball away to waste time. They clutch it and refuse to hand it over. Fouled, they writhe in pain when they feel no pain at all. Substituted, they cross the turf as slowly as possible, despite the whistles of the opposing crowd. They are simultaneously infantile and mature, petulant and courageous. When they score they lose all sense of control. They tear off their shirts, they go wild. When their opponents score they collapse on the ground in dismay. They protest vigorously. They kick the goalposts. After the game they phone their mothers. Interviewed by the television, they are cautious and conformist: we did our best, our compliments to the other side, we must work hard to improve, we must be humble. Next day they check their marks in all the papers. They check their hypothetical value in the fantasy transfer market. Will I still be here next year? Will I be playing, will I be on the bench? Immensely privileged, they are hopelessly deprived. They have no ordinary life. Above all, they are paid huge salaries. And right now I am waiting to meet them, or some of them, in the foyer to the Marco Polo airport, Venezia.

It is 5 January, three p.m., and I am sitting in the departure lounge of Venice airport waiting to meet the Hellas Verona team. I am going to fly with players and coach first to Rome, then Brindisi, way down on the heel of the Italian boot. Then a car to Lecce where I will stay with them in the hotel on Friday and Saturday nights. On Sunday I will watch the game with the owner, Giambattista Pastorello, and the sports director, Rino Foschi. I am beside myself with excitement. When I saw Her Majesty the Queen, it occurs to me, a couple of months back now, I was completely offhand. It meant nothing to me. The only thing I was curious about was how far Her Majesty did or did not resemble my mother. Now I am like a little boy on his birthday, or at an important exam. Why?

I first contacted the club back in October. I expected, to be honest, the kind of self-satisfied obtuseness I grew used to in my twenties and early thirties when working as a translator for the Veronese business world. Gruff, hard-working men would quiz you as to why your translation was slightly longer or shorter than their original. Many of them couldn't distinguish between Italian and dialect. 'Why don't you use the same number of words?' they asked.

But Saverio Guette, Hellas Verona's marketing man, turned out to be quite a different figure. The first thing that took me aback was when he courteously returned my phone-call. 'By all means let us fix an appointment, Signor Parks.' So a few days later I discovered Palazzo Pancaldo, the new office block to the west of the city where the club has just moved. Stepping out of the lift and into a hushed, blue-upholstered reception on the fifth floor, the feeling was more like corporate America than the provincial improvisation I'd expected. The floor is an imitation grey-blue marble. There are the flags of Europe and the United Nations.

I tried to explain to Guette the kind of book I was planning to write and the sort of help I was hoping the club might give me. He nodded. My opening remark on the special mix of quasi-religious emotion and wittily distancing irony was taken as common knowledge. 'You should be reading Philipe Ariè and Mikhael Bachtin,' was his immediate advice. 'Bachtin's book on laughter and the spirit of carnival.' I wrote down a title. 'The two clubs whose fans most embody this combination in Italy', he told me, 'are Verona and Inter.'

He answered the phone frequently as he spoke, but politely tried to show how eager he was to get back to me. 'The general transfer of the public libido to football has gone hand in hand with its availability to a wider public through pay TV,' he remarked between finishing one call and starting another. 'The point being of course that football can both generate and manage sharply contrasting emotions.' He offered me two hefty university theses to read on finance and marketing in Italian football. 'They will help you understand the nitty-gritty.'

I wondered if he was trying to impress. Apparently he tutors at a private university. 'Football merchandising has never really caught on here. People find it difficult to associate fashion and football.' His Italian was clipped and elegant. 'Poems about football? Yes, Leopardi of course. "Al vincitore". And then Umberto Saba, you know?' I didn't. He began to quote:

> *'Il portiere caduto alla difesa
> ultima vana, contro terra cela
> la faccia . . .'*

> Fallen in a last vain defence
> The keeper hides his face
> Against the ground . . .

'A little sad, though,' Guette laughed, 'don't you think, for a poem called "Goal"? Please don't write a sad book about football. It's a joyous thing.'

Humbled, I was already wishing I could spend hours and hours with this man, not just to pump him for everything he knew, but for the unexpected pleasure of his company, at once fussy and accommodating. 'I was hoping, perhaps,' I tried cautiously, 'just vaguely hoping, you know, that perhaps, maybe, the club might, well, help me out with maybe just one of the distant away games, perhaps just once I could travel with the team.'

'That will be our pleasure,' Guette smiled.

I was introduced to his assistant, Massimiliano, a tall, absurdly handsome, absurdly polite boy. For a moment I imagined myself with a priest and his eager acolyte. 'I went to Bari on the bus with the *brigate*,' I said to try them out. Guette laughed. 'Our fans are marvellous,' he said. 'If only they would stop their racist chants.' With a clear reference to their opposition to his boss, Pastorello, and the choruses of '*Pastorello vaffanculo*' that characterised the last games of the previous season, he said, 'As you can see, we make no attempt to influence them, or to buy off their leaders with free tickets as some clubs do. They are entirely at liberty to think what they like.' I would never have imagined, before he said this, that clubs tried to sweeten their fans with free tickets.

Then very briefly I was introduced to Pastorello himself. Again there was a strangely American feeling to it all. A tall, slim, bearded man rose from behind a battleship of a desk with huge glass windows behind. He shook hands, smiled warmly. He was tanned, elegant, endearingly vain. With some difficulty I tried to match this image of urbanity with all the negative things I'd heard and read of Pastorello: his interminable meanness, his aloofness, his coldness, his supposed disdain for the fans. 'I saw El Pastor jogging in a Hellas tracksuit,' a voice writes on The Wall. 'Shame on him. He has no right to wear blue-and-yellow. If I catch him alone, I'll give him a good hiding.'

'How interesting,' Pastorello was saying. 'Yes, it will be an honour to have you write about us. By all means come on one of the away games.'

But to have opened one, or even two doors is not to have opened them all. Not in a football club. The curious nature of the football club is the way the owner delegates, or should delegate, enormous powers to those who work for him: first to the sports director, as the Italians call him, the man who plans which players to buy and sell; and then above all to the coach, who must carry the can when things go wrong and in return has complete control over who goes on the pitch. This breakdown of authority is designed to overcome, or at least paper over, the essential contradictions at the heart of football: that the sporting result is very often in stark contrast to the financial result; that it is a team sport in an era that thinks only in terms of individuals.

So quite often what the *presidente* may feel is good PR, or just generosity, the coach may interpret as a dangerous intrusion into the group psychology of the team. I had asked if I could interview a couple of players; I was told I could, but the coach would have to be consulted first. Officially, I was given the go-ahead, but then the players seemed unavailable. I was told I could travel to the game with Reggina, but at the last moment this offer was cancelled. There were logistical problems. Like anyone in Italy who is thwarted, I immediately suspected, wrongly as it turned out, that there was a plot against me.

Then four days before the game in Lecce, first of the New Year, I found myself being invited once again to Hellas headquarters. 'We need to get to know you, Signor Parks.' We who? 'I'll come over at once.'

I was shown into the office of the acting managing director, Luigi Agnolin. And here one has to explain a peculiarity of Verona football club. Until the end of last season, Pastorello dealt directly with his employees, the press, the fan clubs. He was the undisputed boss. But despite the fact that in just two years of ownership he had taken the club back into Serie A and then up to ninth position, the *curva* hated him. They hated his smart gentleman's jackets, his superior air, the fact that he was from Vicenza, the fact, above all, that he was planning *to make a living* out of his job. Pastorello is not pouring money into the club from the car industry, from petrol refineries, from a media empire. He does not have a treasure chest in his pocket. On the contrary, he plans to get his own and everybody else's salaries out of the club's success. '*Pastorello mercenario di merda!*'

was the fans' response. When it became clear, towards the end of last season, that he was in direct conflict with the beloved coach, Cesare Prandelli, then the opposition became hysterical, the chants of *Pastorello vaffanculo* interminable.

Verona ended the season with the right to play off for a place in the UEFA cup. But Pastorello withdrew and put the club up for sale. He wanted out. His considerable vanity couldn't bear these public insults. When no one would offer the cash he was asking, he decided to hang on, but to detach himself from the running of the show in a cocoon of wounded pride. He would own it, make money out of it, but have nothing to do with it. Hence he appointed Luigi Agnolin as his acting managing director.

'Professor Agnolin,' announces the company secretary, 'this is Mr Tim Parks.'

This man (professor?) is handsome, solid, thickly bearded, clear-eyed, cautious, in his early fifties I would guess. His voice has a pleasant gravelly sound to it. Very noticeably, he thinks before he speaks. Yes, about my coming to Lecce. 'Hmm. Yes. Well, we are a little worried, to be frank, about what your plans are.' He mentions an American writer who has written a book about a season with the Serie B team Castel di Sangro. 'He lived free with them, all expenses paid for the whole season, then filled his book with unpleasant details about their private lives.'

What can I say in reply? My own feeling is that in a world that considers everything but the impeccable scandalous, then thirsts for news from the gutter, I personally would never invite a writer to anything I was involved in. No biographies please. The very *raison d'être* of the contemporary writer is to expose, to give the impression that whatever is examined is outrageous and must change at once. I said, 'All I really want, Professor Agnolin, is just this one chance to meet the team on one away game. Nothing else.'

Such was the mixture of urgency and infantile pleading in my voice that Agnolin was disarmed. He handed me a typed schedule. Venezia, Roma, Brindisi, Lecce. 'But there are certain rules,' the professor warned me sternly. 'Rules to which we cannot make exceptions. Most importantly, no outsiders can ever, ever travel in the team bus. You will have to get to Venice airport on your own.'

I was still thanking him when a head was poked round the door. 'Professor Agnolin, the president is here.' What is he professor of, I wondered? Agnolin stood up and apologised that he would have to cut our meeting short. 'The bishop is arriving to bless the club,' he explained. 'Let's hope he blesses the boys well,' I said. 'We need the points.' 'Oh he blessed the players long ago,' Agnolin replied. 'It's the building he's blessing now.' As if to say: how could you imagine that we would leave the players unblessed so many matches into the season?

Then going out I noticed the crucifix over the corporate door. Common as a door-handle or thermostat, crucifixes rarely catch my attention these days, whereas when I first arrived in Italy I felt overwhelmed by them. The miracle of Catholic Veneto, I told myself driving home – there was still an extravagant nativity scene in a side-street by the stadium – is its ability to combine a genuine desire to be upright and morally correct with the awareness that the world is an evil place and that all kinds of compromises are necessary if one is to keep one's company afloat, one's wife in furs and one's team in Serie A. *Il calcio a Verona*, for example, is full of stories of games bought and sold, of corrupt officials, convenient nil–nil draws, bent referees, betting scandals. But Agnolin doesn't want me to suppose that any of this is presently going on at Hellas. He doesn't want an investigative journalist travelling with the team. Then I remember that of course for most of his career Luigi Agnolin had been a referee, an international referee. And who more than a referee knows that what has happened is what you decide has happened when you blow your whistle? When the referee doesn't blow his whistle, nothing has happened at all, however many pages some tin-pot journalist may choose to write.

The air was cold in Venice, the wind icy. My blue-and-yellow scarf and woolly, official-merchandising Hellas hat were appropriate, if unfashionable. Shivering, I kept them on in the departures lounge. I was an hour early. I took out the book I'd brought along. Acting on the principle that when one is thinking intensely about a subject it is sometimes better to read something altogether different, I was trying to get through Thomas Bernhard's *Der Untergeher*, which tells of a pianist destroyed by his all-consuming desire to be Glenn Gould. But I couldn't concentrate. I kept looking up, anxious to see the players. 'Wertheimer always wanted to be someone else,' Bernhard's narrator announces. I put the book down. Was my nervous excitement about meeting the team, I wondered, to do with my own desire, at least as a child, to be someone else? How I envied the better football players! Oppressed by choir practices and Sunday services and the need to be for ever on one's best behaviour, I played football obsessively and was widely feared as one of the most aggressive of players. 'The animal', I remember being called. On the first occasion that a Cambridge college game was refereed by a woman I was sent off for reacting to a foul with a wild kick and a torrent of filthy language. Football, for fan as well as amateur player, combines the need to vent one's anger with the vicarious dream of being someone else. '*Giochiamo con voi!*' When Bonazzoli puts the ball in the net, so do I.

And suddenly there he is, Italy's under-twenty-one centre-forward: a tall hulking boy with straggly long hair, dressed in a dark blue tracksuit. They are all dressed in dark blue tracksuits. Hellas Verona! They have the magic badge with the ladder of the Scaligeri. And all their big blue bags have it too, the yellow-blue badge and the player's name: Italiano, Mazzola, Salvetti. Hardly talking to each other, apparently preoccupied, even abstracted, they look quite unlike your normal group of young men on a trip. They are terribly sober. That is my first impression. Like so many Mormons. Having piled their bags up by the check-in, they spread out to empty seats and begin to fiddle with their *telefonini*. Where is Laursen, I ask myself. Where is Mutu?

Eager to introduce myself, I accosted Attilio Perotti as he came out of the lavatory. He didn't understand who I was. Fair enough. Then young Massimiliano, Guette's assistant, took me to meet the assistant coach, Agostino Speggiorin. We were standing by the bar. Agnolin, Professor Agnolin that is, appeared in the background chatting to a couple of pretty air hostesses. He seemed charming and avuncular. I glimpsed Rino Foschi, the sports director. Massimiliano was saying how professional the players were, how seriously they took their commitments. Tall, a little austere, a little defensive, Speggiorin hesitantly agreed: Italian players were indeed better-behaved and regimented than those of other nations. Is it because I'm English that they're saying this?

Then on the plane I found I was sitting next to Perotti. Yes, the coach himself. My chance had come. I was at the heart of it. They had put me next to Perotti. I had an hour to talk to the coach, to understand the workings of top-class football.

Attilio Perotti is a small, stocky man, with straining eyes behind metal-rimmed glasses. He was dressed in a blazer with the club badge. I quickly took my place beside him. But no sooner had we settled than he pulled out a book. He folded back the hard covers and ran his finger down the crease of page one. Then he lowered his head. It was a deliberate statement of withdrawal. Shortly after take-off, I asked him, 'What is it you're reading?' Reluctantly, he showed me the cover. Ken Follett: *Il codice zero*. 'I need the diversion,' the coach explained and returned determinedly to his reading. Everything in his manner suggested he would rather I hadn't been invited.

On my other side was Flavio Fiorini, a tall handsome white-haired fellow, in his late fifties or early sixties, smartly moustached, vain and cheerful. His job was *accompagnatore*. He carries everybody's tickets and makes sure they are all present and correct. Once a footballer himself, now a rep for various industrial products, he does the job for free, he says, just to be in touch with football still. 'Oh only Serie B and C,' he explains. 'Nothing big.' He played for Reggina during the famous revolt of 1971. 'You know, when the city rebelled against the decision to move the regional capital to Catanzaro.' I didn't know. I felt I should.

After about half an hour, I turn to my right. 'Can you really see what's going on on the field from the bench?' I demand of Perotti point-blank. It's an old curiosity of mine. 'I mean, you're level with the pitch, can you see what's going on at the other side of the field? Can you get a sense of the geometry of it?'

Perotti blinks. He looks up. 'Not really, no.'

'You can't?'

'No.' He reflects. 'Actually, a little while back, watching a game, not Verona, from the stands, I was thinking just that, how much better I could see.'

I'm concerned. 'So how on earth do you give advice, how do you decide the substitutions?'

'Well, you do your best. You get a sense of a situation that is static, or not in your favour, so you introduce a different player, someone with different characteristics, to see if that will shift things. It's always a gamble. Sometimes it works, sometimes it doesn't. Sometimes things get worse.'

This isn't reassuring.

'Why don't you, maybe, have someone in the stands, someone whose judgment you respect, connected by radio, so you can consult on how it looks from somewhere else.'

'Nobody seems to do that,' Perotti says vaguely, and he goes back to his book. I ask, 'So what's Ken on about this time?' That cheers him up. He begins to describe Follett's complicated plot. There's a missile. A Londoner wakes up in a public toilet in Moscow without knowing how he got there. There's a girl. I'm amazed to see he's already read thirty pages.

At Fiumicino, following the Connecting Flights sign, I find myself side by side with Rino Foschi. Here is a completely different man, bull-headed, Roman, in heavy dark overcoat, complexion scraped pale, hair unkempt and lank, the gait aggressive.

'That was just a joke,' he begins to explain.

A few minutes before, as we stood crammed in the aisle of the plane waiting to get off, he had been proposing some complicated scam whereby a player, I can't remember which, bought a car from him at one price and sold it back to him after a year at an even higher price. How this would work I have no idea.

'You have to joke a lot to create a sense of camaraderie. You know. The group is all-important. I try to be with the team all the time. It's all just fun.'

I'm nodding my head in agreement. He begins to explain that

in fact the hardest work is done in the pre-season retreat when the team train together for a couple of weeks up in the mountains above the Valpolicella.

'It's hard living together all the time, getting to know each other. Give and take. Becoming a team. Perhaps that's the most important part of the year. Nice group of boys, don't you think? Well behaved. The retreat is very important.'

He speaks intensely. He has put his arm round my shoulder in the friendly way older Italians do. I like that. He does the same with the players.

'*Duro, durissimo*,' he insists. Very hard.

I point out that when they were on their retreat, they still hadn't bought their two star strikers, Gilardino and Bonazzoli. Or the keeper, Ferron.

He shakes his head. 'A team the size of Verona, you know, we can't usually clinch a deal till the day the football market closes right as the season starts. Always the last minute. Question of *portofolio*.' He taps his pocket. 'Very hard for us to find the right people at the right price, drive the bargain, bring them home. You'll see now, the market opens again as of Monday, closes the 31st of January. Let's hope we can bring a couple of reinforcements into the team. But it'll be the very last-minute. It's hard.'

'But exciting.'

He shakes his head. '*Durissimo.*'

'I mean, exciting *because* it's hard. You wouldn't want a job that was easy.'

He looks at me as if I hadn't understood. We're walking through the airport. His eyes are intense and slightly glassy.

'*Durissimo!*' he repeats. His lips are large and pale, loose and mobile. 'The point is, we must think of making money. We have to get the kind of player we can sell on at the end of a year or two. And that means you've got to reconstitute a group every year. And groups are hard, hard, hard.'

'But you've done wonderfully well these last two years.'

He nods. 'It went well with Prandelli. Fourteen games without defeat. You know that?'

This is now the third or fourth time I have heard someone praise last year's coach. One begins to appreciate why Perotti buries his head in Ken Follett.

I ask, 'What is the club's budget for salaries?'

Surprisingly, he tells me. Twenty billion lire. About seven million pounds. I suspect he's shooting low. But it's the ostentatious frankness of the man that is so attractive. Foschi is full of nervous energy.

'So why did Cesare Prandelli leave? We were all so disappointed. A question of money I suppose.'

'No, no!'

'I thought he'd done so well that everybody else was offering him more. And Pastorello insisting on his working out his contract. Rightly . . .' I added. I didn't want to seem to be criticising his boss.

'No, it wasn't that!'

Then his phone rings. It's someone calling from Spain. There's some talk about an interesting player. I take a step or two back, not to seem indiscreet, but Foschi doesn't lower his voice. He says a few forthright things. 'Don't take no for an answer!' You can see at once how much he enjoys it all. He must be hell in a quarrel.

'No.' He takes me by the arm again. Agnolin is standing a few yards away. Is the professor worried about what I'm being told? What is he a professor of? PR?

'No, it was a question of recognition, of who was responsible for the team's success. Prandelli thought *il presidente* was trying to take all the credit. There had been an interview somewhere, Pastorello had said "my team" or "the team I built". You know. He was getting all that stick from the *curva*. He wanted some credit. Well, Cesare thought he was trying to steal all the glory.'

Unwisely, I object, 'But that's infantile. Everybody knows it's a joint effort. They'd been together two years, it looked like the beginning of something fantastic.'

Foschi shakes his head. 'Great trainer, Prandelli. Really great. But vain. Needs the recognition. He'd failed in the job before you know. Been fired. So Pastorello is saying, it's me gave you this chance. Without me you wouldn't be in this position.' Foschi sighs. 'It's hard keeping these people together. I did everything I could. Cesare was worried about the players Pastorello was selling. I said, Cesare, I'll find you some new players. There are plenty of players out there. I got the two of them together at last for a reconciliation, I was there to mediate, and Cesare just comes out with a torrent of insults. You wouldn't believe it.'

Tall, bulky, head bent down over me from the top of his overcoat, Foschi shakes his head. 'I've had the same problem too, you know. The *presidente* says something that gives people the impression you don't exist maybe. Your work is irrelevant. You have to say, *Presidente*, this is our team. I did the work too. I built the team too. *Presidente*, I told him once, I could go to Juventus tomorrow. I could go to Inter tomorrow. So everybody has to feel they're being recognised. It's hard. People are vain. But we have to stay together.'

'So why did Pastorello decide to sell?'

'Oh, it was just a bad moment. The stick from the fans was upsetting. I went to talk to them. Leave off, I said, if you don't want the team to fold completely. You see they've left off now?'

Suddenly I remember Glass-eye's curses that night in October waiting for the bus to Bari: 'The boss says: OK *ragazzi*, explain yourselves! And nobody answered. Nobody answered.' Was the boss perhaps Foschi?

The sports director raises his head and looks around. Again his telephone rings. This time I think it must be a woman, he lowers his voice. Suddenly afraid that my moment of grace will run out, I'm desperately trying to think what I should ask. '*Il presidente*.' He taps the phone. 'Coming down tomorrow night. He's watching the *anticipo*.' Vicenza are playing Bari Saturday afternoon.

'Is Mutu really injured?' I demand. 'Is that why he isn't here?' On The Wall everybody has been wondering if Mutu has really been out of the team because he insists on playing prima donna.

Again Foschi insists on how difficult it all is. '*Durissimo*.' Mutu, it seems, is immensely talented, but thinks he's God. 'You have to be diplomatic. If I'd told Adrian what I thought of him, you know, these last couple of months, he'd have walked out and we'd never have seen him again.' Foschi repeats this concept two or three times. 'God, if I'd told him what I thought of him. But you can't. You leave him on the bench for a few games. You have to make him understand he has to work for the team.'

'And Laursen?'

'Laursen injured himself training over Christmas.'

Agnolin comes up and begins to talk about *Il presidente*. '*Professore!*' Foschi exclaims, embracing him. '*Professore!*' My moment is over. 'I'll talk to you any time,' Foschi tells me, 'any time,' and the two of them walk away together.

'I need to play,' Piovanelli tells me very frankly.

On the flight from Rome to Brindisi I have once again been seated next to Perotti. Again he has the window seat, though this time to my left. Again he very determinedly pulls out his book. Glancing over his shoulder, I see he's already up to page 70. I can't remember when I last read so many pages so quickly. At this pace the weekend for him will mainly take place in Moscow, and not in southern Italy at all. On my right, Marco Piovanelli, twenty-six years old, is one of those who almost never plays. It was only thanks to the seven injuries and a couple of suspensions that he was brought on in the second half against Fiorentina, in left midfield.

'I thought you were good.' I'm being diplomatic, but honest too. He seemed solid and vigorous. He gave the feeling of being more experienced than the young Cassetti. Piovanelli has a mischievous pink face, bright eyes, spiky hair. 'Yeah, I played well. But you need to play regularly. Not just half an hour once a year.' 'Will you be playing Sunday?' 'Doubt if I'll even be on the bench.' He is slumped back in his seat, eating from a crisp packet and he keeps turning to talk to Seric who is just across the aisle. He too got his first game of the season in Florence.

'Does it get depressing?'

Piovanelli shrugs. 'There are thirty people in the squad. The Mister has his own ideas.'

Perhaps because the modern game was brought to Italy by the English, the coach is always referred to as the Mister.

Then Piovanelli added, 'You see, the club has its plans for particular players. That's inevitable. Someone's going to stay out.'

I didn't understand what he meant by the club having plans for certain players, but felt I'd look stupid if I asked.

'Are you English?' Seric leans over to ask. It turns out that though officially Croatian, Seric actually grew up in Australia. Anthony Seric, he's called. We switch languages. How strange to be suddenly hearing this Sydney accent.

'Italians. They take it all so seriously,' he laughs.

Perotti has reached page 90. I ask him for a summary of the plot and get confused by all its complexities. 'A book has to grab me in the opening pages,' the coach explains. In that regard it's like a game of football, if you're not supporting one of the teams. It has to grab you in the first few minutes or you don't bother. But he doesn't always read thrillers. 'I really enjoyed *The Name of the Rose*. Film was rubbish though.' He sighs, then returns to his drugs and missiles and beautiful spies. Still nobody has mentioned Sunday's game. Nobody has said what they think of Lecce, nobody has reflected on our chances.

All the same, in the car driving from Brindisi to Lecce, Agnolin is informative about money. Lecce is about fifty kilometres south of Brindisi. The team have a bus which is waiting for them under police guard. We are travelling in a hired car.

'Is there anything you need to know?' Agnolin asks. The professor/referee has a forthright way of driving. He brakes hard, stops in the middle of a fast road, buzzes down the window and shouts at a cyclist to have directions. Someone honks loudly as he tries to quiz the driver in a car coming the other way that has stopped to make a left turn. Again he buzzes down his window. The guy behind is going mad. It's unnerving. 'The roads are much better down south,' Agnolin confides. 'A well-kept secret. The government spends so much here on public works. Keep people busy.'

'Tell me about the club's income and expenses.'

The professor is concerned at how little I know in this regard. He brushes aside my preconceptions. 'Running costs around forty-six billion lire. OK?' A billion lire is about 330,000 pounds.

'Of which the biggest part is the players' salaries, twenty-five billion.'

'Twenty-five? I thought around twenty.'

He looks at me. 'No, more than that.'

Aside from the players there are only about ten employees. 'For the stadium, owned by the town – you know that Italian teams don't own their stadiums – we pay a percentage of the gate and above all the garbage collection tax, which is based on the same principle as for any industrial space, that is we pay by the square metre, which is ridiculous. Don't you think? For a stadium. Drives us mad. Where's the sense in paying the same price for garbage collection as a huge factory that produces tons of waste every day?'

Indeed. Everybody in Italy hates the garbage tax, one of the few the government manages to collect.

'OK, so how are the costs met?'

The professor is now driving south at a speed of a hundred and sixty kilometres an hour.

'Fourteen billion from pay TV. Every Serie A club gets that, for games televised throughout the year. Then seven billion from the Football Federation. That's money state TV gives the Federation and they share out between the clubs. Then about eight and a half billion from the gate.'

'Not much.'

'Not much. Then one and a half from the sponsor.'

This is far less than I expected.

'It depends on the club and the sponsor. For a club like Verona that's not bad. Anyway, altogether the income is about thirty-one billion, which means that every year the company has to make fifteen billion in buying and selling players.'

The countryside is flat and nondescript. The evening is warm compared with Verona, a thousand kilometres to the north. Remembering what Piovanelli said about the club having plans for particular players, I suggest, 'Doesn't that mean that the coach will be under pressure to field the players the club has bought young and cheap in order to increase their value rapidly on the market? I mean, we get to a situation where we're more worried about long-term club finance than the game in hand.'

Agnolin hesitates. 'No,' he sighs. Is he a Professor of Economics, I wonder. Or Marketing perhaps? I know that referees even at the highest levels hold other jobs. Finally, he says, 'All things being equal, one might sometimes act that way. I mean, if there's no other reason for choosing between two players. But remember the coach's job is to win the game.'

Then he starts to explain that when you sell a player, that goes on the balance sheet this year, but when you buy him it's deducted from the balance next year. Naturally that can effect the timing of a lot of decisions. But now we're getting into town. The car stops abruptly. Agnolin leans out of the window and asks two pretty young girls if they could tell us the way to our hotel.

At the buffet in the dining room I introduce myself to Adailton and Melis. We're choosing from a generous selection of salads and cooked vegetables. Adailton says his girlfriend's English. He met her when he was playing for Paris St Germain. 'Worst year of my life,' he says happily. More soberly, Melis admits that after only a couple of years he's become one of Hellas Verona's senators. 'With all the buying and selling there's not much continuity.'

Then I'm just turning to sit with these two friendly players when Massimiliano touches my shoulder. Another sacred rule is that the players eat separately, all together round one long table. No one shares their meals with them. There is no wine at that table. No temptation. They are being set apart, purified for the sacrifice.

And now comes one of the most difficult moments in this process of saying what happened at Lecce. How can I write down what was said at Friday dinner, without appearing to be ungrateful, without appearing to write the merest gossip, above all without Professor Agnolin shaking his noble grey head and saying, I knew we should never have invited that writer?

Let's do it this way. Let's say that there are eleven staff accompanying the players on this trip: Agnolin, Foschi, Perotti, Speggiorin, Fiorini, Beppe the masseur, Marco the work-out expert, De Palma who trains the keepers, the older man who handles the gear, Fillipini the team doctor, and Massimiliano who handles the press. Then let's say that I'm sitting at a table with five of these guys of whom I will name but one, Agnolin himself. And I name the professor for the simple reason that he took no part at all in the conversation, but concentrated, somewhat gloomily, on maintaining his diet. 'Nearly all my life I've been trim,' he explained to me, 'as a big-time referee should be.' But since his wife's sad and sudden death he has put on a bit of weight. Now he has set himself a couple of months to get it off again. While the others go for three courses – the pasta, the fish, the sweets – Agnolin stays with his salad and looks on with the referee's critical eye as everybody starts to talk about . . . sex.

It begins, childishly enough, with the word *pompelmo*, a grape-fruit. Someone says that grapefruits are particularly good for you because they eat up negative cholesterol. Someone replies that *pompini* are even better for getting rid of negative energy. A *pompino* is a blow job. But isn't a blow job only a poor second best when one can't actually fuck? In the car for example. In your car! Oh the stains in his car! For heaven's sake. I don't know how you could even find a woman who would sit in that car. Well, someone says, his fossilised mistress, maybe. Better an old mistress than none at all. You need 'turnover' with mistresses, someone says, using the word usually used to mean putting in different players for midweek and Sunday games to give the stars a rest. The girls at the discotheques these days, somebody else announces, they just want it. Not from you they don't. They lean against the wall, they're dying for it. Not from you they're not. A guy just comes and rubs up against them. How about it? That's it. Not with you it isn't. Picking up girls at a discotheque, someone else rebukes, is like shooting farm-bred pheasants. The real challenge is to hunt down a bird in the wild. Wild? Who's wild?

Etc. Etc. It goes on and on with spiralling scabrosity. It's actually one of the funniest group male conversations about sex I've ever heard. And participated in. I wouldn't want to be left out. And even as it's happening I'm furious that I won't be able to report it with the flourish and detail it deserves, won't be able to characterise the various approaches, attach this or that phrase to this or that person. Because this is such a tediously Catholic country and the press would scream scandal, the *Gazzetta dello Sport* above all would say, how scandalous! How immoral! 'After being knocked out by Romania, instead of going to their hotel rooms to meditate on their miserable performance, the English players were out drinking until four in the morning. Shame!' Thus the *Gazzetta dello Sport* during the European Cup. As if one should wear sackcloth and ashes after losing a game of football. The same edition ran a two-page feature on how important Inzaghi and Totti felt it was to have their mothers near them during the competition.

So no, I can't say who said what on this occasion, or even exactly what was said, only that the conversation fizzed with wit and tease, and all the more so because it was immediately clear to all of us that no one was actually *thinking* of sex at all. Not even remotely. They were thinking of the game. They know the season is about to turn a corner. We've won only one point from the last three games. The team can either break out of it, or begin its descent into the underworld. Talking about sex, like Perotti's reading *Il codice zero*, is just another way of admitting how important this game is.

'I'm going to bed,' someone suddenly says. He stands up. The temperature around the table seems to have dropped about ten degrees. In just a few moments everyone has gone to bed. They can't keep up the pretence. They want to be alone. But it's only nine-fifteen! 'Doesn't anybody want to walk into town?' I ask as people hurry across the lobby. 'No. We're tired.' The players, it seems, all went to bed half an hour ago. 'Don't you need to watch them, see they don't slip off and go out on the town?' 'No, they've brought their play-stations and computers. They play games, get on chat lines. Ten years ago you had to watch people, not now.' Only Agnolin has hung on a moment. He accosts me by the door. 'That was just to release tension,' he explains of the dinner-time conversation. 'It wasn't serious at all. None of it's true.' Is he a Professor of Psychology, perhaps, I ask myself.

I wander alone into town. All I have to do is follow a straight street that takes me back in time through various architectural periods, from the seventies to the fifties, then the thirties, the nineteenth century, the eighteenth century and finally the baroque. As in Catania I'm struck by the predictability of it all. The *passeggiata* tugs me into the centre. I don't have to ask where it is. The first piazza is full of stalls selling dry fruit, candies various, nuts, toys. Exactly as in Catania, or Verona for that matter. Perhaps the people are slightly smaller, the shops less obviously fashionable.

But there is nothing 'less' about Piazza Duomo when I get there. It's a revelation. With only one narrow opening on to the main street the whole generous space is built in a sugary yellow-white limestone carved into a textbook rehearsal of every baroque flourish and motif: columns, saints, angels. In the evening floodlights the stone is luminous, almost too bright, the sky black above but for a full moon. On the cobbles two or three couples are kissing, as if this were the only appropriate thing to do here. I retire to a bar.

It's a smart place with granite and chrome fittings. Elegant young customers occasionally raise their groomed heads to a huge screen on the back wall showing a series of fashion parades. Presumably it's a video. There are collections of various levels of prurience, collections where you look at least partly at the clothes, or perhaps faces, and collections where you can only see the astonishing bodies of people who, like football players, can rarely spend the evening drinking in a bar. I order a whisky. One spends half one's life, I reflect, watching those who in some way deprive themselves for our sake. The music is loud. It's hard to study local physiognomies, with these perfect buttocks dipping and bobbing on the wall. Some sequences, like goals, are repeated ten and even twenty times. We mustn't lose this game, I tell myself. I order a second whisky. 'Lecce, Lecce,' I mouth at the mirror behind the bar, '*vaffanculo!*'

La Befana

*Isn't there some Arab sheikh interested in buying
Verona? Our presidents are always crap. I can't
handle it.*
Franco (Verona, Italia), Fuckingfedup.it

Please, Bill Gates, buy Verona.
Desper@do

L'epifania, tutte le feste si porta via – Epiphany carries off the last
holiday. So goes the proverb. It's 6 January, the Twelfth Night,
the last flicker of the Christmas–New Year binge. Crossing the
street before breakfast with the local newspapers in my hand, I read
the headline: *La Befana ci riporta il calcio.*

Befana is another word for the same festival: 'Epiphany brings
back football.' More exactly, the Befana is the name of a legendary
old woman who was too busy to see the Magi when they passed
by on their way to Bethlehem. She would catch them on their way
home, she thought. The Magi returned by a different route and two
thousand years later she is still roving the world looking out for them.
On 6 January, her busy day, she brings presents to Italy's children.
So her missed opportunity becomes our gift. Today *La Nazione*,
a southern paper, subverts the old proverb about carrying off the
holidays to say that in fact La Befana is bringing us children our
football back. My suspicion of a complicity between the Christian
and Serie A calendars is confirmed. When one enchantment wearies,
the other kicks in again: Vicenza and Bari are playing this afternoon,

Juventus and Fiorentina this evening. I'm going to watch them on TV with the players of Hellas Verona.

Meantime the local section of the paper gives three full pages to a 'far west' shootout in a village just a few miles from Lecce. Ten minutes of heavy gunfire. Over breakfast in the hotel, the news provokes the inevitable reflections on the south. 'They shoot at each other, then whine about it.' Certainly this would be rare news indeed in Verona.

I find myself at table with Beppe the masseur, Vincenzo the man who trains the keepers and Marco the kit man. Beppe had tried to be a footballer as a kid. At fourteen he was selected for a football college down in Rome. It didn't work out. When they sent him away he was so depressed he couldn't watch football for ages. Eventually he came back in via massage. All three of them agree that twenty years ago the players were more skilled. 'When we trapped a ball, we trapped it dead. If it escaped even half a metre from your feet you were out.' Thus Beppe. 'But today. Half of them can barely trap the ball at all.'

I sense the man is still bitter about the day they told him his trial was over.

'So what are the trainers looking for now?'

'You have to be strong as an ox and then mentally willing to fit in with all these rigid schemes and mechanisms they have these days.'

But having said this, Beppe goes on to praise ex-coach Cesare Prandelli for the complicated patterns and strategies that he taught his players. As soon as the men start talking about Prandelli, you can hear an excitement in their voices which is also a resentment. They are proud to have worked with him, feel betrayed by his departure. In the still air of the dining room, you can sense the charisma he transmitted to them; it's as if a ghost had sat at the table: Cesare Prandelli still haunts Hellas Verona.

'You should have written your book last year,' one of them says, 'when Cesare was here.'

This can only be bad news for Attilio Perotti.

'So what was so good about him?'

'Everything,' Beppe says. He thinks, then explains, 'He used to train the players without the ball.' The older men nod. 'It looked crazy, but it was brilliant. He would make them play without the ball. If Melis moves here then Italiano automatically moves there and Falsini overlaps there. And the moment they're even a metre out of place, stop and start again. Stop, start again. You do it without the ball so that you're not distracted by it, you don't keep looking out for it, letting it condition your movements. You're only thinking of your place in relation to the other player, to all the other players. Then when you've got it exactly right, a dozen times, OK, you add the ball. That's why things began to work so well.' Beppe is earnest. 'You remember Melis and Falsini on the wing?'

How could I forget! The last two seasons were galvanised by a fantastic partnership on the left wing, an endless duet of triangles and overlaps. Again and again these two men, neither star players, would pass through even the most surly of *catenaccio*s with a rapid, ever-varied series of movements that must have seemed miraculously unpredictable to the hapless defenders. It was Prandelli's imagination coming to life on the pitch, a projection of the coach's mind. But Falsini has gone now and Melis is only half the man without him.

Beppe sighs. 'You have to do that complicated stuff now. The game's too fast otherwise, and then you have all these demolition men in midfield. They're just waiting to destroy you. When one man goes out you have to have another who knows exactly what to do when he comes in.'

'The game is choked by red tape,' the masseur goes on. He begins to explain about the anti-doping situation. For every game two people from each team are selected, 'supposedly randomly', for a urine test. There are three possible results. Positive, negative and 'not negative'. 'What can "not negative" mean?' Two players from Perugia were recently found 'not negative'. They are under investigation, suspended, but without anyone being sure what they've done. Before the game a representative of the team has to give the referee a sealed envelope, with a signature across the seal, detailing any medicine taken by any member of the team over the past week. This will be opened in the event of a positive test to see if the result can be legitimately explained. The problem is that the team doctor is criminally responsible if the test is positive. And that could mean no more than that some player has used some hormone cream on a skin problem. And maybe he hasn't told you. Or worse still, he is taking some illegal substance, but you don't know. And you're responsible.

Beppe goes on and on. The others nod. It's fascinating how many details there are that you would never have thought of: reminding the players not to pee directly after the game in case they've been selected for the dope test. 'Of course sometimes a player forgets and then you're waiting for the poor guy to pee and he can't pee and you've got a plane to catch and everybody saying pee, pee.'

'Beppe! Oh Beppe!'

It's time for the morning training session. The masseur is required. The boys are already hanging around in the foyer. All the time we are here, there are two policemen on guard in the lobby and a police car outside beside the bus. I want to go right out to watch them train, but Agnolin is against it. We can go along later. He suggests we see the town. Taking the same route I walked yesterday, he talks about the history of the place. The Romans, the Norman invasion. 'The Venetians used Brindisi as a convenient place to replenish a ship and so had a big effect on the architecture.' Is he a Professor of History, I wonder.

Since it's a bank-holiday there's almost no one about. Although there can be no possible difficulty in finding the centre, Agnolin stops to ask directions of three pretty traffic policewomen who are turning away cars from the restricted historic areas. Piazza Duomo, when we arrive, is all but empty. Agnolin insists on exploring an exhibition of contemporary art under the porticoes of the seminary. Garish and incomprehensible, the paintings are for sale. Suddenly I realise that the thickly bearded Agnolin looks a little like John Ruskin. He likes the play of light and dark in this picture in particular, he says. Could he be an art professor?

Finally, and to my immense relief, we make it out to the

training ground, a pleasant sports club in the suburbs. The inevitable policemen are guarding the team bus. One has a machine gun. The boys are already well on with their practice game. I glue my nose to a green fence and leave Agnolin to take a phone-call.

It's not the first training session I've seen. Any midweek afternoon you can watch the boys working out on a pitch behind the stadium. There's even a tier of rotting wooden benches to sit on and in the winter twilight perhaps fifty or a hundred people will be scattered around worrying and arguing about our chances of avoiding relegation. 'Cassetti and Italiano are barely up to Serie B, never mind A!' An old man flicks his lighter on and off. 'It's not the players, it's the coach!'

Most of the talkers are pensioners, they pull their trilbies over their eyes and smoke. But there are some younger men too. They talk less and stare hard. And of course there are a few girls hoping to see the young blond Gilardino. 'Does anyone have Alberto Gilardino's address?' one girl writes endlessly to The Wall. 'Can someone introduce me to him?'

For some reason these training sessions always remind me not so much of my own time kicking a ball about in the cold, but of the evenings when I followed my father round the church as he prepared to lock the place up on winter evenings after choir practice. It's the sense of being admitted backstage that links these moments, the awareness that you're witnessing the humdrum mechanics that make a dream possible. And as in the past when I watched my father pottering among the pews, footsteps echoing in the empty nave, so now, seeing the players fuss with their socks or shin-pads, or pull a woolly hat down over an unwisely shaved scalp, I'm struck by how fragile the foundations of those dreams are. When the choir launches into its processional hymn to the thunder of the organ, when the players burst in bright colours on to the field, then everything seems possible, the blood thrills. But when you see them milling about in the drizzle, or complaining about a backache, you appreciate that you mustn't count on them. The smart fan does not go to training sessions.

Still, at least the boys come to life on a football pitch. In the lobby

they looked like zombies. 'Adda Adda, here, Adda!' Adailton traps
and passes. They are playing two-touch in the tight space of perhaps
a quarter-pitch, showing skills they would never risk during a game.
'Gili, Gili, Gili, now!' Salvetti takes a pass and lets it spin up his shin,
then twists round and catches it on his heel before side-kicking it
into the path of Mazzola. Were they really more talented years ago?
Ferrarese tries an overhead shot. He connects, but not quite cleanly
enough. As he goes down he seems to bounce back off the grass.
'Bona! Bona!' someone calls. You can sense their energy, the rush
and thud of their weight, things you can't get up in the *curva*. All
the same, from ground level you get none of the sense of geometry
you have higher up. Agnolin comes to stand beside me. 'I wonder',
I ask him, 'who was the first person to realise how beautiful football
would look when seen from above.' He seems annoyed. 'Gonnella
moves too early,' he says.

They're practising free kick routines now. The ball is more or
less at the top-right corner of the box. Oddo and Adailton stand
either side of it. The Italian can strike it right-footed curling high
across the goal. The Brazilian can strike it left-footed curling low
towards the goal. If Oddo is to strike, Bonazzoli makes a sudden
decoy movement at the near-side of the area while Gonnella must
run in for the high header on the far post. If Adailton strikes it,
Gonnella makes the decoy run while it's Bonazzoli who must
move sudden and late to flick the harder lower cross into the
near corner.

'Gonnella is moving too early,' Agnolin repeats. At once I sense
that this is a criticism of Perotti, who stands with his back to us just
the other side of the fence in stony silence. Each time the kick is
taken, he shakes his head then nods towards the spot to have them
repeat it. Nobody, it occurs to me, has yet had a word of praise
for Perotti.

They try the free kick at least twenty times. If Adailton raises
his arm, Oddo is to take it. If no arm is raised, Adailton is to take it.
Sometimes the strikers get the cross wrong. Sometimes the attackers
move out of sync. Gonnella must count two after Adailton raises
his arm. Sometimes the defenders hustle the attackers off the ball.

But of course the defenders know what is going to happen, so it's not like a real game scenario. Sometimes the attackers reach the ball but head it straight into the arms of the keeper. Is it really possible, I wonder, to impose these plans on the unpredictable nature of the game? But how else can you train? After fifteen minutes they still haven't got the ball in the net and Perotti moves them on to corners, then penalties. I'm surprised how little he speaks, and when he does there's a sort of resigned, sardonic tone to his voice.

Adailton has three penalties saved by the reserve keeper, Doardo. Oddo scores every time, a low, hard, thundering shot. They joke. They don't seem to have any method. Perhaps, I think, there's really no secret to playing football. You try to get close to the action, hoping for some revelation, but there is none to be had, just guys kicking the ball, businessmen spending money. Adailton runs up again, stabs the ball hard, waist height. Standing right behind the net now, I see how impossible it is for the keeper to make contact. The posts are so far apart, the penalty spot so near! Yet Doardo does it again. His glove tips the ball round the post. Perhaps I've been too hard on this boy. Perhaps one day he will make the vital save that keeps us in Serie A.

Massimiliano comes over and warns me that I probably won't be allowed to watch the Vicenza–Bari game with the team. 'The Mister likes to be alone with the team at these moments.' I'm disappointed. 'Ask him,' Professor Agnolin encourages me in the car.

'Can I see the game with you?' I ask Perotti back at the hotel. Again he has his slightly dazed, worried look, as if there were no moment of the day when he is not trying to arrive at some impossible solution to his selection problems. 'Sure,' he says. It seems he can't imagine why I should think I might be excluded.

So after lunch we file into the TV lounge. I have the stern and handsome Ferron on my left, the young Doardo on my right. Perotti is just two seats away. I'm expecting that every now and then the coach will point out things to his men, tell them to make a mental note for some future game. They'll be planning the appropriate strategy to use, I tell myself, when they meet them. I'm intrigued. I feel privileged to be here. But nothing. Absolutely nothing. The twenty-odd men watch an irretrievably dull game in total silence. I'm hugely disappointed.

'Filth!' Foschi announces coming to the dinner table that evening. 'Take it away.' This of a dish of antipasti. 'Filth.' He puts his elbows on the table and sits forward aggressively. 'What have you got, waiter?'

The rest of us have already ordered. Foschi is late. He has been talking with his opposite number in the Lecce staff about players to buy and sell. While the fans love to hate each other, the managers are all doing business together.

The waiter parrots a long list of dishes as Italian waiters will. The fish and fowl are in his mind, much as Prandelli would see a series of overlapping triangles all down the wing. 'Is the bass fresh?' Foschi demands. He has hollows under bright eyes. '*Signore, sì.*' 'Fresh from the fridge, you mean?' The waiter is patient. His list is long. He finishes with the various meats. There is foal steak, beef carpaccio. 'Bring me a cappuccino,' Foschi says brutally and puts his head on his hands.

Perotti suggests a minestrone. Foschi waits until the waiter is perhaps ten feet away then calls him back. 'A minestrone.' Five minutes later, the waiter brings it together with a plate of fresh basil leaves. 'What are these?' Foschi demands. 'Take that filth away.' The waiter does so, winking at the others. Everybody is chuckling. Perotti and Foschi begin to talk about their minestrone. 'Not a bad minestrone,' Perotti is saying. 'Filth,' Foschi says. He's extremely nervous, but hamming it too. The players are eating quietly behind us. A more subdued group you couldn't imagine. 'You haven't put enough parmesan on,' Perotti says. Then Perotti calls the waiter to tell him to take the wine away. 'This wine is awful.' The waiter does so. Perotti orders a different bottle. 'Much nicer with the parmesan.' Foschi agrees. Then when the waiter comes back with the wine, he says, 'You know, waiter, this minestrone is really excellent. I don't think I've ever had such an extraordinary minestrone. I can't thank you enough for recommending it.'

Wondering when Agnolin is going to tell me that this is just a way of dealing with stress, I ask Foschi, 'Do you think I should try some minestrone myself?' He stops mid-spoonful, looks at me as if he'd only just realised I was there. 'Waiter,' he hollers across the restaurant. 'Waiter, another plate of minestrone for the Englishman. But none of that filthy basil.' So despite the fact that I've already eaten my pasta, I'm now back on minestrone. 'Fantastic,' Foschi insists shaking his head with wonderful earnestness. 'The secret is in the parmesan, the quantity of the parmesan.'

As soon as I have the plate in front of me, he begins to spoon on cheese for me. 'Enough!' 'No, Mister Parks, you need more.' He's extremely earnest. 'You need more.' 'Enough!' But I let him do it. A huge coagulating slick of parmesan is sinking heavily into the soup. 'Isn't it wonderful?' Foschi demands as I dip in my spoon. I reserve judgment. I pretend to be thinking. 'Isn't it marvellous?' I won't be swayed. 'Give me time.' As I expected, it's a completely ordinary vegetable soup. 'Oh don't eat it if you don't like it,' Foschi shouts. Everybody is laughing. The waiter is laughing. Agnolin is laughing. Massimiliano is laughing. 'Not bad,' I finally decide. I pause. 'Except for the parmesan. The parmesan is stale.' 'Stale! The parmesan? Waiter, this parmesan is stale!'

Right at that moment, something echoes in the back of my mind. '*Autista! Autista di merda!* Turn off the light. *Autista*, shame on you, why did you turn off that light? Steer straight, *autista*. Accelerate! Slow down!'

Driver and waiter play the same part: punch-bag for stress release. Prompted by this reflection, I look at my watch and remark, 'The *brigate* will be in their coach. They'll already be on their way.' But the comment is lost. No one's interested. 'I've some good sleeping pills if you need them,' Perotti is telling Foschi. But Foschi, who previously complained that he didn't sleep last night, now claims he has the best sleeping pills anybody ever invented. Again he turns to me. 'You want to try one.' He pulls a huge pill out of a box in his pocket, it's almost an inch in diameter, frightening. He begins to describe how they work. Nothing for ten minutes, then sudden and unexpected unconsciousness. 'Lasts eight hours. No after-effects. If you want one I'll give you one.'

I decline.

The evening *anticipo* is at 8.45. Juventus–Fiorentina. Disappointingly, most of the players have already gone to bed. Only six or seven file into the lounge for what should be a much more interesting game. The policemen who are supposed to be guarding us from the attacks of opposing fans come in to watch. Sitting alone right at the back, Perotti predicts a three–nil win to Juventus. After ten minutes Fiorentina are two–nil up. He goes off to bed.

'You need a camomile tea,' Fiorini tells Foschi. The older man seems genuinely worried by the sports director's nervousness. Foschi turns to me. 'Do you want a camomile?' 'I'd rather have a whisky.' 'A whisky, bring this man a whisky, waiter, at once!' As he speaks, I'm filled with an enormous affection for Foschi. 'Terim [Fiorentina's coach] is one of the luckiest men in the world,' he grumbles. The game is sparkling, electric. 'We could do with a bit of luck ourselves,' I say. '*Taci*,' he says quickly, putting a finger to his lips. '*Taci!*' Shush.

The game finishes three–all and afterwards I'm left taking an evening walk on my own again, the only man not to go to bed before ten. I think of the fans who will be travelling all night in the most uncomfortable conditions. Yet they seem to have so much more fun than the players. I wish I was with them.

Scaramanzia

*After weeks of scrupulous market research, Attilio
Perotti has been chosen as the right man for the
forthcoming advertising campaign for the Sweet Dreams
Camomile Tea. Go for it, Attilio!*
Aiooogalapagos

'Ow arr yoo thees morning?'

Agostino Speggiorin tells me he's learning English. It's Sunday
morning, the game is just a few hours away. In the lobby the players
seem even more inert and listless than ever, sprawled over armchairs
and sofas.

'OK, I'll give you a quick lesson,' I tell Agostino at the breakfast
table. It's an excuse to fire a series of questions.

'Where are you from?'

'I am from Vicenza.'

'Like Pastorello.'

'Like Pastorello.'

Agostino is tall and gives the impression of being a little stiff,
as if every move were studied. He looms over me, standing with
his hand on the back of the chair. 'Sit down,' I insist. 'Speak some
English.'

He sits straight-backed, concentrating fiercely. 'I live on my
own in a flat in Vicenza.'

'And how long have you been there?'

His story is typical of so many who work in football. He was
himself a player in the lower divisions, for Treviso. Then he was

transferred; his new club was bought and sold; suddenly no one wanted him. He went home. For a while he couldn't bear football. He studied for the appropriate certificates and became a gym teacher. He loves teaching. Then he began to scout for Verona. He tells me about scouting. At short notice you are told to go to Stockholm, to Madrid, to see a player. You set off at once. You watch a game, write a report. For example, he had suggested the Vicenza centre-forward Toni to Verona years back when the boy was only sixteen. The president at the time responded to his positive report by sending a friend, actually his barber, to watch the boy. The barber thought Toni was useless. Agostino is full of contempt. 'You have to understand potential and character. Toni was too tall to have total control of his body at that age. But already you could see how intelligently he moved, you could see he had enormous determination. Now he's worth a fortune.'

Pastorello, Agostino claims, is much more canny than the previous president. 'When I recommended a Swedish centre-back to him, he went to watch the boy himself three days later and after the game immediately made a big offer. That's what you have to do. Make up your mind fast. We have to get in one week before the richer clubs.'

'Who was that? I don't remember a Swede in Verona.'

'The Swedish club turned the offer down.'

Speggiorin's English is slow and endearingly precise. He likes to study grammar books, he says. He does lots of written exercises and rarely makes mistakes. I suggest that he has a control obsession, he should relax, try to absorb without understanding, reply without thinking. 'I'm not that sort of person,' Agostino objects. 'I do it this way.' Then I recall that his job now, as assistant coach, is to teach the players individual skills, not the game as a whole. During training sessions he takes them aside one by one and has them trap the ball a thousand times, first with the right foot, then with the left, now with the chest. He breaks things down into their separate parts. 'But surely football,' I put it to him, 'like language, requires an element of Zen. The game has to play itself through you. Rather than controlling everything, you have to give yourself to it.' Agostino shakes his head. Everything he has achieved he has achieved only and exclusively by meticulous study.

And he says one of the problems the players have these days is that they don't study enough. 'A player with an all-round education will play better in the end. He has more confidence in himself. Unless you're a natural-born genius it's important. Most players are completely lost when they have to leave football.'

Speggiorin is rightly proud of himself for having overcome the crisis of having lost a team, having crashed out of his dream career. Listening to him, I can see that his whole attitude is admirable. I even agree with him. Yet somehow I begin to feel that, together with Perotti, it doesn't add up to charisma or inspiration. I fear there's no real motor behind Hellas Verona, no dynamism. Where there should be ferocious appetite and huge egos, we have only something well-meaning, calculated, even accountant-like: two men getting on sensibly and modestly with a job they've learned. '*Il ragioniere tira le somme*' is a typical headline when the *Arena* is talking about Perotti: 'The accountant does his sums.' I fear this doesn't bode well. I fear that this group lacks a megalomaniac. Only Foschi seems to have that kind of drive. Of all the people I've met, he's the only one I would sweat blood for.

But now it's team talk-time. Perotti is going to announce the team and give them their pre-match briefing. This is strictly confidential. This is sacred. Nobody, not even Agnolin or Foschi, can penetrate this mystery. I head up to my room and jot down the following reflections on a sheet of headed hotel notepaper:

'Personal stories: it was a mistake to think you could understand football through a weave of personal stories: Agnolin, Perotti, Cvitanovic, Agostino, their personal lives are quite insignificant beside the phenomenon of the stadium, the banners, the chants, the hypnotism of the game.'

I suck my pen, but that's it, that's all I've learned.

Turning on the TV to kill a little time, I find that they're discussing the riots in Reggio Calabria that Flavio Fiorini talked to me about yesterday. It seems it's the thirtieth anniversary of the revolt. The national government had moved the provincial capital of Calabria from Reggio to the smaller Catanzaro. Obviously there were private interests involved. Then the politicians tried to blame communist agitators for the uprising. They sent in the army. But the rebellion was quite spontaneous, the ex-mayor is explaining. He's an old man now. Black-and-white film footage shows dramatic clashes between troops and mob, something far beyond anything that happens at football matches. The uprising was brutally suppressed.

'So it was a failure,' the interviewer provokes. 'Not at all,' the old politician responds. 'We learned so much from those days. We learned that we were a community. That we had the energy to make our voice heard. But most of all we learned that we were on our own. We had to get on and help ourselves without any help from Rome.'

How Italian this is! After every defeat a player will say: we have to '*stringersi come gruppo*': get closer together as a group. 'We can't expect the help that others get from the referees, we'll have to do it on our own.' After the defeat at Juventus, someone wrote on The Wall: '*Siamo sempre più soli, sempre più gialloblù*' – we're ever more alone, ever more yellow-blue.

But don't think about defeat, Tim! I kill the TV. It's time to meet Pastorello.

'If we win today you can travel with us to every game,' he says generously. He's very tall and gives a powerful impression of how much care he takes over self-presentation: the groomed beard, grey and white, the coifed hair, the perfect jacket and tie.

'Perhaps we'll win five–nil.'

'One–nil, own goal at the last minute would be quite sufficient, thank you very much,' Pastorello says. 'Then we'll take you with us everywhere *per scaramanzia*' – as a good luck charm.

I hadn't thought of this. I see myself travelling all over the country with Hellas Verona as they achieve a miraculous series of away wins. I'm interviewed by all the papers, I begin to ask for money.

'Have you met Agnolin?' the president asks.

'He's been telling me how much he enjoys it when the crowd shout *sei un bastardo, arbitro*.'

This was exactly the wrong thing to say. 'Well I can assure you', the president tells me coldly, 'that it's no fun at all hearing the *curva* sing Pastorello *vaffanculo*.' He turns on his heel and heads for the dining room.

The players ate at elevenish so as to have digested before the game. They have already left for the stadium. Foschi and the rest of the staff have gone with them. At lunch there are just myself, Agnolin, Pastorello and two friends of his who have actually driven down from Verona.

Pastorello starts to tell us how his sciatica has kept him awake all night. He can't find a comfortable position. Everybody offers advice. But there's only so long you can talk about insomnia and sciatica. There are a few moments of embarrassed silence, a few uneasy remarks tossed back and forth in the hope of finding a conversation that isn't football.

Then unexpectedly Agnolin says, 'How is Matarese taking it?' Matarese is the president of Bari and an important figure in football league politics. After yesterday's loss, his team are bottom. Pastorello flew down south with the beaten team.

'Well,' *il presidente* nods, becoming serious. 'I thought he took it well. He said he felt *"sereno"*. He wouldn't make the mistake he'd made with Boban. He'll go on as he is.'

I ask, 'What mistake was that?'

Pastorello explains that in the past Matarese had tried to solve his team's problems by paying a lot of money for a big-name star, like Boban, but that in the end this strategy doesn't work with the small provincial team. Doesn't work money-wise, that is. If you're lucky you might just stay up, but the only thing that's certain is that either way you'll be broke. He reflects, 'The only thing we can do is to train up younger players and sell them on.'

'And the team?' Agnolin wants to know.

Pastorello says that he noticed one or two behaviour patterns among the Bari players that looked bad. For example, some of them were wearing the team uniform, but some weren't. Then the sports director had scolded the players for their arrogant behaviour with the check-in staff. 'He was right to tell them off, but not in front of me. And really of course he was complaining about their having lost the game.'

As in the conversation with Foschi yesterday, I'm struck by how these men, who have never studied psychology, are extremely sensitive to group dynamics.

'With all the pressure,' I ask him, 'are you still able to enjoy the game?'

'When we win,' Pastorello says grimly.

Agnolin already has his fingers over his lips. 'Don't talk about the game. Brings bad luck.'

And so up to our rooms for our luggage, then out to the cars for the match. Much to my surprise it now emerges that the sleepless Pastorello has made the twenty-minute walk into town this morning and bought two paintings from the awful exhibition in the *seminario*. Not on the advice of Agnolin, I trust. 'I have a big collection of paintings,' he says offhand. 'I like paintings.'

At the stadium we're shown up to our expensive seats right above the halfway line. The structure is small and low, but attractive. Unfortunately, like Bari's bigger stadium, the concrete bowl has gaps and a brisk wind is blowing through. It's cold. Way over to the right the *brigate* have arrived, only fifty or sixty of them. They are busy hanging up their banners. One very long one says: '*Nicola, anche assente, sei sempre con noi.*' Even absent you're always with us. Nicola, I later discover, is one of their number who has recently died. Such commemorations are part of stadium ritual. There's a slow hand-clap, then it's business as usual: '*Acqua e sapone, ci vuole acqua e sapone.*' Soap and water, it takes soap and water (to wash a southerner). '*Lecce, Lecce, vaffanculo!*'

Ten minutes before kick-off the staff and the four or five players who aren't even going to be on the subs' bench come up to join me in the stands. I find myself with Claudio Ferrarese sitting on my right and an ageing Lecce supporter on my left, his wife beside him. In front of me are Foschi, Pastorello and Agnolin, all grey and grim.

I hadn't thought of this. I hadn't imagined that the owner of a football club would be obliged to watch his team play among alien supporters. What could be worse? In the opening five minutes Lecce have three wonderful scoring chances. All around us people, mainly old and well-to-do, leap to their feet in enthusiasm. Pastorello & Co. hunch smaller, pulling their overcoats about them in the nagging breeze. This is cruel. These men have done all the work they can: they have bought the players, chosen the coach, made sure every facility is available, and now they must sit back and watch and hope among an ocean of people just waiting to laugh at them if they got it wrong. It's a strange way of doing business. I'm feeling nervous.

Then about twenty minutes into the game Verona score. The referee awards a dubious free kick in the very place the team were practising kicks from yesterday. Oddo and Adailton go up to the ball and consult. Adailton raises his hand. Oddo's going to take it, I tell myself. Oh shit, Gonnella's moving too soon. Too soon! But no, Adailton takes it after all. Gonnella is the decoy. Bonazzoli lunges forward at the near post and flicks the ball in. Incredible. They must have changed the signalling system in the pre-game talk, in case some spy was present at the training session yesterday. And it worked! In the midst of a sea of gloom all around us, the Verona contingent leap to their feet embracing. My estimation of Perotti soars. Verona hold on with no trouble at all till half-time, and this despite the absence of Laursen in defence. I begin to hope.

Espresso at half-time. 'What if I bring good luck,' I joke to Foschi. His whole body shudders. He covers a grey lip with a white finger. 'Not yet,' he says. 'Too soon.' When I get back to my seat Ferrarese is talking on the phone. He's vociferous. He doesn't stop me overhearing. 'A brilliant training session yesterday and I'm not even on the bench, *Dio buono*! All defenders on the bench. All defenders! What's he going to do if he needs to put an attacker on?'

The whistle blows. For ten minutes all is well, then it happens. Ferron kicks upfield. In the centre circle, a Lecce player miscalculates. Perhaps the ball is ballooning a little in the wind. Instead of taking it on his chest, he has to lunge. This is purest chance. The ball just strikes his knee and leaps forward right between Verona's two advancing centre-backs. Standing on the edge of the offside trap, Lecce's striker, Osorio, is suddenly running for a ball which has fallen exactly to his feet in a way no calculated pass from the midfield possibly could have. Ferron doesn't have a chance.

'Fools!' Foschi shouts. 'Idiots. They've been begging for Lecce to score for the last ten minutes.'

How sad to have to watch all around you exulting. Clearly I will never be able to speak of bringing good luck again. I should never have mentioned luck at all. Verona collapse. Lecce suddenly look brilliant. They score a second. Hellas press forward, desperate to equalise. Salvetti shoots from point-blank range. The Lecce keeper saves. 'All defenders on the bench,' Ferrarese had said. Munching biscuits, the boy is watching grimly. He should have been picked.

Immediately after Salvetti misses, Lecce score a third. At which Pastorello's guests get up in a hurry and leave. 'May as well start driving back early.' The old couple beside me are gloating over our discomfort. '*Vai Lecce vai!*' The home crowd are in full throat. No sooner have the two men gone than the floundering Seric brings down a striker in the box. The referee points at the spot and it's four–one. In the confusion of joy among the Lecce tribe, Pastorello leaps to his feet and hares off down the stairs. How can one envy a man who has to put up with this kind of experience?

To make matters worse, the news now comes through that Napoli, who had been fourth from bottom, have actually won at the Olimpico against Lazio. And Reggina have won at Parma. These results seem impossible, surreal. How can Napoli beat Lazio? It would be like Charlton Athletic winning at Old Trafford. Verona are in the relegation zone. We're the fourth from bottom now, *Dio boia*. As all around me hurry off to the dressing rooms, I'm left alone to enjoy a prolonged choral performance from the Lecce fans exulting in their *curva*. 'Serie B Serie B Serie B!' they're chanting at the miserable gaggle of *brigate* fenced off in their cage eight hundred miles from home.

I retreat to the poorly lit security compound by the team bus, where I'm obliged to hang around for almost an hour. The players come out of the changing room one by one. There are a couple of palm trees in pots, a low wall with a patch of grass. Cassetti has tears in his eyes. 'But you were only on the field ten minutes,' I tell him.

'It can hardly be your fault.' He pulls out his *telefonino* and slinks off. 'But you scored a wonderful goal,' I tell Bonazzoli. Glazed, he pulls out his *telefonino*. Soon they're all perched on the wall or among the palm trees, like so many sad pigeons on a winter evening, and each one of them has his *telefonino* out, explaining the lost game to mother or girlfriend. Finally Agnolin appears, grim, professorial. 'Let's get out of here,' he says. It seems Pastorello has fled in the car with his two friends and his newly purchased pictures. 'He couldn't face the airport scenario.'

What is the airport scenario, you wonder? The egregious commiseration of gloating strangers: 'Don't worry, it'll go better next time.' People are approaching the team as they huddle by the check-in, offering words that cannot possibly give comfort. 'You did your best, we were too good for you today.'

On the plane I'm next to Perotti *again*. At last it occurs to me that more than a way of initiating me into the mysteries of football, it might actually be an attempt to isolate the coach from the others. No one wants to sit next to him. Out comes Ken Follett. *Il codice zero*.

I turn to the left, where fortunately I seem to have the only member of the group not in a state of deep personal crisis: Marco, the kit man. He's solid, paunchy, balding, sensible. 'The trouble is,' he sighs, 'some of them won't want to play in that shirt again. I might have to change the lot of them.'

Often, when a game ends particularly badly, the players don't want to use the same kit. A question of *scaramanzia*. In response to my questions, Marco explains how it works. On Monday he counts out how many shirts have been given away. If a player gives away his shirt, either to opposing players or to the crowd, then he has to pay for it. About 100,000 lire. Then there are always a few shirts given at the beginning of the game to the linesmen and the referee. And sometimes they come and ask you for more than you've given them. Yes, the president of each club always gives the referees and linesmen something before the game. Obviously if it's Roma and you can give them Batistuta's shirt, all the better. The ref is flattered, he's reminded that this team has famous players and really ought to win.

'But what do they do with all the shirts?'

'Collect them. Sell them.'

He talks for a long time about all the presents the club is constantly making and how complicated it makes his life. 'Of course there's an unspoken blackmail to it all,' he says. 'There's always the feeling that if you don't give them what they want, they'll take it out on you somehow.'

'*Damiano, ciao!*'

'*Ciao, Michele!*'

The gloom starts to lift at Fiumicino. Big Michele Cossato waves to someone he knows. The huge thoroughfare that links all the gates at the airport is buzzing with football teams all changing planes at more or less the same time on their way back from their various games all over the country. Players wave to each other, they exchange notes on their games. With telling and retelling, the defeat, at least for some, begins to sink into the past.

But not for Foschi. Perotti has disappeared. He's taking a plane home to his wife in Genoa. Monday is the footballer's day off. But why, I wonder, does his wife live in Genoa? Why didn't she move to Verona for the year? It can't be good, this feeling of detachment from the town. The players drift towards the self-service restaurant where it seems a section has been cordoned off for us. And as each boy goes in through the glass doors, he has to pass by Foschi who has taken a seat right outside in the corridor, whence, huddled in his overcoat, he glares accusingly at them as they pass. As soon as he's through the door, Seric giggles and says in broad Australian, 'Oh these Italians are so bloody gloomy when they lose.'

Certainly Emiliano Salvetti is gloomy. I find his strange and haggard face beside me on the plane back to Verona, the last leg of the trip. Salvetti is the quietest of all the players and, on the pitch, one of the most curious, capable of inspired runs, brilliant through balls, but also of entire games of listless non-engagement. Studying him as he stares blankly at the seat in front, it seems impossible that this man is only twenty-seven. His skin is sallow, his hairline has drastically receded above each temple leaving a fuzzy central brush high on the top of his head. His nose and chin are both long and pointed, his mouth small and still. Above all he has huge, softly sad, doggy eyes.

'You didn't play badly,' I finally suggest.

He raises an eyebrow.

'It was a brilliant shot you got in at two–one.'

He shakes his head. With a little more prompting, he tells me about last year when he was doing his military service at the same time as playing for the club. As Oddo is doing now. After the game on Sunday, he would drive down to Bologna with his girlfriend, then get the plane to Rome and be in the barracks there by ten p.m. Only once in the whole year did he hold a gun. And only once on that occasion was he allowed to pull the trigger. Every other week he cleaned the kitchens or the toilets. That was his military service. Otherwise it was just training to keep fit for the weekend.

'So you're forced to do your service, to show the law is equal for all. But then you don't really do it, you just waste your time?'

'I suppose so,' he says. 'I never really thought about it.'

I think of the way Pietro, who sits beside me at the Bentegodi, hates it when Salvetti plays. 'Wake up, wake up,' he shouts at him. 'Move your arse. Do something!' Maybe the trouble with getting to know the players is that you can't so easily shriek insults at them any more. Will I ever be able to yell at Cassetti, after seeing the poor kid emerge from the changing rooms in a state of such dejection?

'Princess in Goethe,' comes a voice from the seat in front. 'Can you help?'

Melis, Piovanelli and Oddo are doing crosswords again.

'Sorry.' Melis turns back disappointed. What on earth is the point of bringing a writer on a trip if he can't even help with the crossword?

Then suddenly it's over. The plane's landing. No sooner have the doors opened than Agnolin hurries off. He barely touches my hand, doesn't look me in the eye. The players have a bus waiting, I take a cab to the train station where my car is parked. Then lying in bed I try to sum up the weekend. And, yes, I have to admit it, I'm disappointed. When I went to Bari, I expected nothing but a dull bus ride in the company of yobs, at best a hard-fought game, maybe a result, then the ride back. Instead I came home with something I didn't expect: a rhythm that drummed in my ears for days, a strange and exhilarating cocktail of theatrical transgression and studied irony, an intense sense of community always ready to defend itself with self-parody.

Instead from Lecce I bring back only the massacre of my illusions. There is nothing special about these people except what they can do on the pitch. And this time they did nothing on the pitch. Then, damn it, I can't sleep. Why? Because I'm feeling sorry for them. It's ridiculous, I suddenly realise. Tim, you're feeling sorry for a group of kids who earn more in a year than you do in ten. Not only do we lose the game, but they're robbing me of my sleep too! They should be sorry for *me*, for Christ's sake, not me for them.

Careful not to disturb my wife, I slip downstairs to the *taverna* where we keep the computer. What are the fans saying? I open The Wall.

'The club is considering whether to take the team away in retreat to overcome this difficult moment,' writes someone who calls himself McDan. 'Good idea. I would suggest the new multi-functional sports facility of Dachau.'

'A deaf mute in charge of a herd of human vegetables,' comments Il Bandito.

'Electrocardiogram of Hellas: flat,' writes Pam. 'Bile of fans: record for world production. *Diavolo porco*, if you don't want your cars smashed, let's see some balls!!!'

'PIGWHORESLUTBASTARD.'

'For sale, section of the Curva Sud of the Bentegodi Stadium, Verona. Seats upholstered with human skin . . .'

After about ten minutes I'm laughing my head off. Good. Having re-established the proper distance between myself and the boys in yellow-blue, I at last went to bed with a smile and slept deep and sound.

'Just calling to thank you,' I told Guette the following afternoon for getting me on the trip. Naturally he was depressed about the result. 'By the way,' I ask, 'what exactly is Agnolin a professor of?'

'Agnolin? He was a referee of course.'

'Yes, but everybody calls him "professor".'

'Oh right,' Saverio Guette says. He pauses. He's trying to remember. 'Of *ginnastica*. That's right. Gym. He was a gym teacher.'

13A GIORNATA

Atalanta – Roma 0–2
Bologna – Brescia 1–0
Juventus – Fiorentina 3–3
Lazio – Napoli 1–2
Lecce – Verona 4–2
Milan – Inter 2–2
Parma – Reggina 0–2
Perugia – Udinese 3–1
Vicenza – Bari 1–0

CLASSIFICA

Roma	32
Juventus	24
Atalanta	22
Lazio	21
Fiorentina	21
Milan	20
Bologna	20
Udinese	19
Perugia	19
Parma	18
Inter	17
Lecce	16
Vicenza	15
Napoli	14
Verona	12
Reggina	10
Brescia	9
Bari	8

Magic

Go magical Hellas!
Paruca

'*Dagliela!*' shouts the girl behind me. 'Pass it to him.' She's on her feet screaming. '*Dagliela BENE!*'

On the pitch Martino Melis lifts his head. But he can't hear her. She's only one voice. Thousands of others are chanting: '*Su Verona, su Verona, dai, dai!*' Melis is dithering again.

'*Ma dagliela!*' she weeps. '*Dagliela bene!*' Give it to him right!

Too late Melis sees the opening and passes. The ball runs long. The girl collapses in disappointment. A moment later she begins again: 'Pull him down! Pull the bastard down, *Dio povero!*' She's suffering. Mazzola can't hear. '*O mongolo*,' comes the familiar call from a few rows further back. '*O fenomeno*, go back to Cloud-cuckoo-land!'

On The Wall, as Sunday's game approaches, the exhortations flow thick and fast:

'ODDO, YOU MISERABLE MERCENARY,
LET'S SEE SOME BALLS TODAY.'

'*PEROTTI, MERDA!* ENOUGH DRAWS
AND DEFEATS. SEND 'EM OUT TO WIN,
DIO BOIA, AND DON'T PLAY CASSETTI.
HE'S A CRIPPLE.'

Why do people write messages to those they know are not going to read them? Why do people shout at players who they know can't hear?

'Shoot, shoot, shoot, *porca miseria!*' The girl's on her feet again. 'Shoot *now!*' But never for a moment does she imagine that Bonazzoli can hear her. She knows his world is quite separate. What is going on?

The Saturday before the game there is always a full page advertisement in the *Arena*. Right across the top, a broad grey band bears the slogan:

FORZA GIALLOBLÙ FORZA GIALLOBLÙ

Immediately beneath are the names of the teams:

H. VERONA vs NAPOLI

Then, right across the centre of the page are two large diagrammatic football pitches laid side by side, each giving one of tomorrow's teams and the formation they play in. Here for example is what's on the left diagram today. The team reads from left to right:

H. VERONA (4–4–2)

	Seric	Melis	
	Apolloni	Italiano	Gilardino
Ferron			
	Laursen	G. Colucci	Bonazzoli
	Oddo	Salvetti	

But now comes the curious thing. Right in the middle of the page – squashed, that is, between the two football pitches and their teams – there is just about room for one elongated vertical advertisement, which thus takes pride of place and becomes the focal point of the whole layout. It reads:

CENTRO
ZEUS
Giuseppe Strano:
Tarot, Astrologer, Spiritist
Specialist in matters of the heart
Consult him for:
Love, Business and every *forma negativa*

Placed between the two teams, in the conundrum of their eventual engagement, we have a *mago*, Giuseppe Strano, which is as much as to say, Joseph Strange. He's in the right place. 'Magic exists as a primitive explanation of the world,' said the anthropologist Evans-Pritchard, 'and continues to flourish wherever science is unable to offer reassurance.' Certainly there could have been no reassuring, scientific explanation on that bitter cold Sunday afternoon, 14 January, when, on a sodden pitch, without having done anything to deserve it, Napoli scored fifteen minutes from time to go one–nil up. Doubtless many in the Bentegodi who witnessed this injustice felt convinced that Verona were the victims of a '*forma negativa*', a jinx.

'As a historian of civilisation,' wrote the German scholar Aby Warburg in 1923, 'what interested me was how, in the midst of a country that had developed its technical culture into a remarkable precision weapon in the hands of the rational man, nevertheless there survived a small enclave of primitive pagans who, while facing the struggle for existence with absolute realism when it came to their hunting and their agriculture, all the same went on practising with undiminished faith magic rituals that we tend to look on with contempt as a sign of complete backwardness.'

Primitive pagans? Warburg was speaking of the Pueblo Indians of New Mexico, their tendency to exhort a sky that couldn't hear them to rain, an earth without ears to be fertile, but the paragraph might as well refer to the Brigate Gialloblù, or any fan praying to someone who can't hear. Warburg goes on to talk of magic as a stage lying between totemism and technology; it involves, that is, an intense desire to manipulate events through a process of cause and effect, but without having developed the technological means to do so. You do a certain dance to make the clouds come. You wear your old blue-and-yellow scarf for forty-eight hours before the game in the vague hope that this might prove propitious.

'This coexistence between fantastical witchcraft and rational utilitarianism seems to us to be a symptom of scission,' reflects Warburg. 'But for the Indian [or football fan] there is nothing schizoid about it at all. On the contrary: it amounts to the liberating experience of an unlimited possible correlation between man and the surrounding world.'

'*Dagliela bene!*' the girl is screaming again. This time Melis passes at once, a perfect through ball to Mutu. 'There,' she claps her hands. 'There, see that, ESP! He heard me.'

'*Vai magica Hellas!*' is Pietro's favourite shout. 'Go, magical Hellas.'

Having agreed that magic is an attempt to manipulate the world, the anthropologist Sir Edward Burnett Tylor tackled the thorny question, why does the believer in magic keep at it when it clearly doesn't work, when the scarf wrapped round the neck for forty-eight consecutive hours is followed by such a miserable drubbing you feel like hanging yourself with it? When you pray to Perotti to behave sensibly and he never does.

The conclusion the anthropologist came to was that the practitioner of magic could explain away its failure only by positing the greater power of some opposing magic: we deployed all our spells, but somebody else cast a counter-spell, a *forma negativa*. One can see the logic of this, but it has to be said of that game on 14 January that, although the Neapolitans are committed fans and notorious believers in magic, they were nevertheless hopelessly outnumbered at the Bentegodi. How could their influence be more powerful than ours?

The anthropologist Sir Alfred Radcliffe-Brown had a different take on this loyalty to the futile formula. More important than the efficacy of magic, he felt, was its social function, which was 'to underline the importance to the group of the desired or protected event'. Writing threatening messages to Pastorello, or begging Adailton to shoot, you express how absolutely crucial it is to all of us that Hellas win.

In this regard, Radcliffe-Brown mused on, magic offers a way of 'ritualising optimism'. You insistently repeat what you most desire and thus tense yourself and others towards a happier future. Before each game that Hellas play, someone signing himself Zeno (Verona's patron saint) writes to The Wall predicting the day's result, always in our favour. 'Verona 4, Napoli 1: goals by Mutu, Bonazzoli and Melis. All in the first half. Penalty to the filthy *terroni* early in the second. Final goal in the closing seconds from the mythical Gilardino.'

But ten minutes from time, on this miserable afternoon of 14 January, it was still one—nil to Napoli. From almost thirty yards out — their first serious shot of the game — Bellucci had struck a ball that curved hard and fast into the top left-hand corner of Verona's goal. It was perfect. No magic of Ferron's could have resisted it.

At despairing moments like this, what I always ask myself is: why do people invest this enormous desire for control, for magical cause and effect, in an area where they know they can have no such control? After my week at the bank, at the school, in the factory, why don't I choose an entertainment where I can enjoy some reassurance as to the outcome? Computer games, for example. A little wine-bottling.

Or again: having chosen an entertainment where we have no control, why don't we sit passively and just suffer or enjoy it? Why do we seek to influence events? Here I am on my feet again, screaming, 'Cassetti, for Christ's sake, don't pass back. Fuck and shit, Cassetti, attack!' Is it that we actually want this exhibition of helplessness? Perhaps the theatre of the stadium allows us to act out our most intimate intuition: that in the end and in all the truly important things of life — where we were born, who we are, our passions, our children, our illnesses and aging — we never had any control at all.

Down but not beaten, the *curva* rallies with bitter determination. Sing despite everything is the rule. '*Tu sei il Verona, il mio Verona!*' I make a brief attempt to join in but I can't do it. I feel sick. Your book is going to be a book about relegation, I tell myself. That's the bitter truth. Perhaps writing about things brings bad luck. In just a few minutes from now Hellas Verona will be third from bottom.

Support for Radcliffe-Brown's vision of the social function of magic comes from further studies on the American Indians. 'The Zuni tribe under strong pressure from Spanish explorers and Franciscan missionaries to repudiate its indigenous customs, would, figuratively speaking, draw a magic circle around their innermost belief and ceremonies, above all their mask dances.'

Masks! As we had filed into the Bentegodi that afternoon, it was to find that the *brigate* had provided not flags, nor ticker-tape, as on previous occasions, but, on every single seat of the *curva*, a small white surgical mask of the variety American cyclists wear in city traffic: to protect ourselves from the smell of those terrible Neapolitans. There is a local song that runs:

> *Senti che puzza,*
> *scappano anche i cani*
> *sono arrivati i napoletani.*

> Get that smell,
> Even the dogs are running
> The Neapolitans are coming.

So as the teams ran out into the stadium, it was to find ten thousand people wearing small white masks and singing, '*Siamo i tifosi dell'Hellas e abbiamo un sogno nel cuore, bruciare il meridione, bruciare il meridione.*' 'We're Hellas fans and we have a dream in our hearts, to burn the south.'

Until fifteen minutes from the end of the match it seemed that, at least in footballing terms, that dream might come true. For all the first half and most of the second, Hellas had attacked and Napoli had defended. In Napoli's goal, Mancini had saved well on two or three occasions. Five minutes after Napoli scored, Verona won a corner. Martin Laursen rose to meet a high ball at the far post and crashed it down . . . against the woodwork. That's it, I thought. We're jinxed.

'We're going down,' muttered Pietro.

'We're already down,' said the pessimist who sits in front.

In the past, when I used to hear people talk of their fear of relegation, I thought it was a mere question of footballing prestige they were worried about, of seeing a high-quality game. Only recently did I realise that what is really at stake is the taboo thought: what if our community disintegrates? Imagine: the club goes down first to Serie B, then to C; the Hellas fans dwindle; the Juve and Milan and Inter fans multiply. When the *brigate* sing, 'When Hellas are in Serie C, in the stadium we will be,' what are they trying to do but ward off the terrible suspicion that maybe they won't be there at all? The *brigate* will be gone, swallowed up in the world of modern entertainment where football means nothing more than an afternoon's cable viewing. If this isn't cultural harassment, what is?

Under threat, the Zuni drew a magic circle round themselves. I've often thought of the Bentegodi as a magic circle. The opposing fans are admitted into one small segment only in order to be driven out by a Hellas victory. A ritual exorcism. But today even our gas-masks can't protect us from the heavy smell of defeat. With ten minutes to go and the tension in the stadium almost unbearable, *Ragioniere* Perotti at last decides to take a risk. He pulls off Melis and throws in a third striker, Adailton. '*Vai Ada!*' shouts Pietro to the boy who can't hear. To our right three older men get to their feet and head for the stairs. They have lost faith.

The game was drawing to a close. The Napoli players, quite naturally, were wasting time, falling over and shrieking in fake pain, raising their hands to call for the team doctor, taking for ever to set the ball down for a goal kick. And at this point there came a sudden roar of pain that seemed to have nothing to do with anything happening on the pitch. At once I raised my eyes to the big screen over the Curva Nord where an electric ribbon of light was bringing the results of other games. As at Lecce last week, the news so far was all bad. Brescia were winning, Reggina were winning. But now worst of all came a revised score-line from

Serie B: a team called Chievo Verona had equalised at Salerno. As one man the *curva* groaned. The misery was too much. And so, just as we reach this crucial and desperate moment of the season, the last five minutes against Napoli, I fear I shall have to interrupt my story to talk about an even greater threat to the Hellas community: Chievo Verona seem to be headed for Serie A.

I admit I've been putting off this part of my tale. I should have mentioned it way back, perhaps at the very beginning of the book. Then I could have said, 'Actually the city of Verona has two football teams, one in Serie A and one, rather surprisingly, in Serie B, rather than Serie C, or D where it belongs.'

That would have done it. That would have prepared you. But the truth is I had imagined I could get right through my story without ever mentioning Chievo. Chievo are irrelevant, I remember thinking, to the scope of this book that I have decided to write about the glorious Serie A team Hellas Verona. Chievo are a quiet backwater, a bunch of parochial nobodies. You don't want to waste your reader's time with Chievo.

The decision was rash. For some weeks I have felt the problem creeping up on me. For some time now I have been observing, ruefully, that when you write a book as a diary, you just can't know at the beginning what may turn out to be monstrously important at the end. Here we are nearly halfway through the season and Chievo Verona are actually a couple of points clear at the top of Serie B. While Hellas plummet into the abyss, Chievo rise meteorically. Something will have to be said.

Chievo is a small suburb of Verona, sometimes nicknamed 'the dam' because it's situated by the dam that controls the flow of the Adige through the city. Their team was little more than another parish club until the 1960s. Then slowly but surely, despite boasting only a handful of fans, they worked their way up. In 1994 they finally made it to Serie B and were admitted to the Bentegodi. Hellas play there one Sunday, Chievo the next. When you go to watch the boys from the dam, you find the terraces empty and just a few old folks with their picnics of salami and polenta.

Well, it was bad enough when Hellas were relegated, having to play Chievo in Serie B. It will be even worse having to welcome them into A. But in the end even that is not the problem. The growing fear is that Chievo will get into A while Hellas Verona crash into B. And this fear is galvanised by the apprehension that the world at large, the great wide world of TV and political correctness, finds Chievo Verona a more palatable phenomenon than Hellas Verona. Chievo have a couple of black players. Chievo supporters do not indulge in racist chants. They never attack the police as the Hellas fans are about to do in ritual fashion as soon as this miserable game with Napoli is over. Chievo fans are cheap to manage, easily dispersed and rarely irritate the authorities by travelling to away games.

If Chievo go up to A and Hellas down to B, I ask myself, as the dying minutes of Verona–Napoli tick by, could this really be the beginning of the end of the Hellas community? I think it could. And don't be fooled by pleasant appearances! No doubt many readers are thinking: how quaint to see a tiny parish getting its boys in Serie A! Maybe. But the quaintness is only part of the truth. Like anyone else, Chievo's managers have to pay their players salaries. How do they do this without supporters? With money given by the television channels for the rights to show the Serie B *anticipo* on Friday and the *posticipo* on Monday. Chievo are actually a by-product of modern TV football, proof that fans in the flesh aren't essential. For anyone eager to eliminate the unruly crowds who haunt the stadiums, the promotion of Chievo and the relegation of Hellas Verona would be a most welcome event.

Today, 14 January, it had seemed that Chievo had at last met their match. They were losing at Salerno. The news of Salerno's goal had been met with a great cheer. Perhaps one loss, people thought, would pop the Chievo bubble. But now, no sooner do we start losing than the news comes up that our execrable neighbours have equalised! Never has the gloom been more intense on the terraces of the Bentegodi.

Then someone scored.

It was hard to say at first who it was or how it happened. Napoli had taken off their one striker, Bellucci, and were packing the box.

It looked easy. They had only a few minutes to hang on. But Verona were at least putting the work in today. And at last in a mêlée, even before the girl behind me had time to tell him to shoot, somebody finally stuck the damn ball in the net, right beneath the *curva*.

'Cassetti' – the name flashed up on the scoreboard. In the midst of the exultation, I couldn't believe it. I always curse Perotti when I see he has fielded Cassetti. Every Saturday the team is announced, in the *Arena*, without Cassetti – it seems impossible we should need Cassetti – and every Sunday we find him there on the pitch, sweet, long-haired, adolescent and incompetent as ever. But in a sea of mad embraces, I shouted aloud, 'Cassetti, I forgive you. I forgive all your utter uselessness for that one goal.' My son too was shouting, '*Grazie, Cassetti, grazie.*' Then the scoreboard made a correction. 'Mutu.' I felt better.

The ninety minutes were up. The fourth man produced his little glowing board to announce injury time: three minutes. But Verona couldn't be satisfied with a draw. Not against Napoli. '*Vai Verona vai,*' shrieked the crowd. And when the whole *curva* shouts together, then there is a real psychological pressure. Then it is no longer a question of the single imprecation lost in the storm, the voice unheard. Now it is a rising tide of sound. And Napoli were crumbling. They had lost their nerve. My opinion on supporters changed again. Fans are vital! If Chievo had supporters they'd be in the Champions' League! '*Su Verona su!!!!*' The chant was steadily deafening. Until, from the left, Mutu sent the ball in high to Bonazzoli on the corner of the six-yard box. Caught between two defenders the big boy swivelled his torso to chest down to where Adailton was storming in unmarked. He didn't even need to hit it hard. It was so easy. *Rete!*

I cannot recall another moment of such complete promiscuity on the terraces. People were tumbling every which way in huge group embraces. And as they stumbled to their feet at last, the *brigate* began to sing. All myths and fables tell us that what the hero must do after he has killed a monster is steal its magic power, the Gorgon's head, the aegis. So, having at first defended themselves with gas-masks, the Hellas fans now stole what the Neapolitans are most famous for, their song: '*Ohi vita, ohi vita mia,*' they sang. Ten thousand people. Life, my life. '*Ohi core, 'e chistu core.*' O heart of this heart. '*Si stat' o' primmo ammore, O' primmo e l'urdemo sarraje pe'mme.*' You were my first love, oh first and last you'll be for me.'

This is Italy, the north singing the south. Giuseppe Colucci, himself from south of Naples, was so excited he tossed his shirt in the air and was promptly sent off. A few seconds later Mutu was sent off for reacting with a punch to a foul by a Napoli defender. Both players will miss the next game. But who cares! The crowd flowed out of the Bentegodi ecstatic. Today at least the magic had worked. In extremis. Hellas exists.

14A GIORNATA

Brescia – Perugia   1–0
Fiorentina – Milan   4–0
Inter – Parma   1–1
Juventus – Bologna   1–0
Lecce – Vicenza   3–1
Reggina – Atalanta   1–0
Roma – Bari   1–1
Udinese – Lazio   3–4
Verona – Napoli   2–1

CLASSIFICA

Roma	33
Juventus	27
Lazio	24
Fiorentina	24
Atalanta	22
Milan	20
Bologna	20
Udinese	19
Perugia	19
Parma	19
Lecce	19
Inter	18
Verona	15
Vicenza	15
Napoli	14
Reggina	13
Brescia	12
Bari	9

Insulti

Bolognese, you're useless at insulting, something even
the terroni *know how to do.*
  Black Dog

On Monday 22 January, two days after a miserable one–nil defeat at
Bologna, I returned late to my cheap hotel in central Milan, turned
on the television and saw, to my immense surprise, the face of Luìs
Marsiglia, would-be *professore*, not of *ginnastica*, but *religione*. Another
important development was at hand. The man is doomed to haunt
Verona and my book.

  Having wound up my tutorial around seven o'clock, I had
spent the evening with a friend who is professor of psychology
in Turin. She had recently organised an international congress
and was laughing at the incredulity of her English and American
colleagues when she tried to explain to them how politicised the
Italian academic world was, how absolutely important it is in Italy
to understand which political grouping has which appointment in
its gift. I responded by telling her how, on arrival at Bologna's rather
pretty little stadium, the *brigate* had started the afternoon's insults
with a hearty chant of '*Communisti! Vergogna!*' – since Bologna was
ever a left-wing town – followed by a chorus of '*Rossi di merda, voi*
siete rossi di merda.' 'Shitty reds, you're shitty reds.'

  'Football is politicised too,' I said.

  Sensibly, Valeria said this wasn't quite the same thing. So I told
her that Giuliano Amato, our present centre-left prime minister,
had recently given an interview saying, 'This year I'm supporting

Rutelli and Roma, both capable of beating the people I don't like.' Since Francesco Rutelli, ex-mayor of Rome, is the candidate whom the centre-left have chosen for the forthcoming national elections, and since the man he has to beat is Silvio Berlusconi, President of AC Milan, the remark was considered as giving unfortunate political significance to the Milan–Roma game played at San Siro yesterday: as if the match were somehow a rehearsal for the elections.

Valeria shook her head. 'It's still not the same thing as having political parties who carve up power in areas that shouldn't have anything to do with politics.'

I told her that according to market research, Milan's championship victory some years ago had been worth half a million votes to Berlusconi in the general election that followed, whereas it was calculated that a loss against direct rivals Roma might cost him thirty thousand votes in this spring's election.

'Thirty thousand votes,' I repeated. 'If it's a cliffhanger like the Bush–Gore contest, Milan–Roma could decide it.'

'Did you say the game was yesterday?' Valeria asked at once. 'How did it go?'

'Berlusconi won, three–two.'

'Shame.'

'There's always the return match.'

'And when's that?'

I pulled the championship calendar out of my wallet. It would be the same day as our return match against Bologna: 'May twenty-seventh.'

'*O Dio*, that might be right around the election date.'

'You see! You take it seriously.'

Valeria laughed but insisted that it still wasn't the same thing.

How could I persuade her?

'Did you know that last week', I tried, 'Andreotti [ex-prime minister] proposed Franco Sensi, the *presidente* of AC Roma, as candidate in the forthcoming election for mayor of the capital. With Roma six points clear at the top of Serie A, the club president couldn't lose.'

'Now we're getting there,' Valeria admitted. Then she frowned. 'Though it would probably be a mistake to propose Sensi if Roma have just lost to Berlusconi's team.'

In Italy one doesn't so much discuss politics, in the sense of what this or that party is actually proposing, or what it might be better to do for the country. No, you discuss who is controlling what, why and how. During such conversations you enjoy a sense of outrage at what is happening and of complacency at the thought that you are one of the few who have understood.

But such weighty matters were not on my mind as I walked back to my hotel in heavy rain. Nor was I even thinking seriously about football. Under my umbrella I was humming, '*Stevanin! Stevanin! Sepeliva le putane nel giardìn, col badil!*' And what I was wondering was: why do I laugh at such awful things? Why did even someone serious, someone left-wing and feminist like Valeria burst out laughing when I sang her this unforgivable song? 'Stevanin! Stevanin! He buried whores in his garden, with his spade.' I had learned it Saturday afternoon on the Zanzibar bus. Every single person I have repeated it to since has burst into laughter.

The game with Bologna, as I said, had been dull beyond belief. After only a few minutes, Verona allowed the striker Locatelli to walk through their defence and curl a shot into the top corner, after which nothing was done to remedy the deficit for the rest of a sleepy afternoon. The players gave the distinct impression of not really wanting to be there. When the final whistle blew, I felt quite sure that we were doomed for relegation. And Chievo had won again!

Yet the ride back to Verona was hilarious. And in fact, if ever you have to swallow a bitter pill in life, even something as awful as relegation, I can suggest no better way to do it than to ride with the Brigate Gialloblù. The truth is that I now look forward to these bus trips. I love the din, the confusion, the shambles of beer cans and bottles and abandoned newspapers and smoky air. And above all the riotous, desecrating songs:

L'autista va, senza capelli,
Sull'autostrada sfonda i caselli!
Indifferente! Brutto pelà!
E che la vaca che te l'ha cagà.

How can I convey in English the mad hilarity of such a song?

The driver drives, bald as a coot,
On the road he crashes through tollbooths
Indifferent! Egghead brute!
Cow of a mother that shat you.

This image of the ruthless aging driver, ploughing with grim contempt through the feeble fencing of the law, is completely at odds with the reality of the tame young man who is steering us back to Verona under police escort in a bus incapable of exceeding 100 kilometres an hour. The song is a celebration of impossible transgression, a celebration that mocks both driver and singer. Join in and you're guaranteed to collapse in a gale of laughter. That said, how can one possibly defend the Stevanin song?

Stevanin – does anyone remember his Christian name? – was/is a serial killer. He lived just outside the small village of Terrazzo in the foggy plain south of Verona. His particular perversion was to pick up prostitutes, strangle them as he achieved orgasm and bury them in the family's smallholding. He killed eight in all, or at least eight were dug up: blacks, Slavs and Italians. The judge refused to recognise diminished responsibility. Thinking of his poor victims, of the horror of their deaths, the gruesome midnight burials, how can you laugh? How can a middle-aged, respectable family man like myself giggle over such a song, I wondered, splashing up the Via Matteotti in heavier and heavier rain. It just will not stop raining this year. 'The pitches of northern Italy are a disgrace,' says the magazine *Rigore*.

The tune is jolly, with a sort of brass-band, marching-song base to it. It begins with a flourish, 'Stevanin! Stevanin!' as if announcing the name of some celebrated centre-forward. Then there is the rapidly rhythmical narrative: '*Sepeliva le putane nel giardìn.*' After which we have a thundered addition, banged on at the end of the line like the beat of the big bass drum: '*COL BADIL!*' With his spade! You can almost hear the hard steel whamming down the earth on another grave.

This brusque reminder of a story everyone in Verona knows is followed by a chanted couplet:

> *E scava scava scava,*
> *Si è trovata un' altra Slava.*

And shovel shovel shovel,
We've dug up another scrubber [actually, Slav woman].

Yes, this is truly awful! Cleaning my teeth in front of a cracked mirror, shortly before turning on the TV and finding Luìs Marsiglia's sanctimonious face, I'm determined to understand why I actually enjoy these and other songs so much. Or at least, I enjoy them *on the bus*, in the context of the trip, the carnival din of voices, the fatuous Fondo, wearing pink skiing goggles beneath his gialloblù cap, the kids hauling back the window to yell, '*Bolognesi comunisti!*' The faint sound of the answering cry from the street: '*Veronesi, razzisti di merda!*'

Then, drying my face, I remember the French author Lautréamont, or at least Roberto Calasso's essay on Lautréamont, which I recently translated: 'on reading his work,' Calasso said, 'the reader is infected at once by an insane hilarity and a vast sense of unease.'

Wasn't this exactly what I felt when I heard the Stevanin song? Hilarity and unease.

Lautréamont. I settled on the bed with the TV remote control in my hand. Here was another man who didn't seem to have a Christian name. Or rather, Lautréamont was a pseudonym, the way all the *brigate* have pseudonyms, and all those who write on The Wall enjoy masquerading under false and ferocious identities: Black Dog, Ivan the Terrible, Il Bandito.

In 1869, after a long battle with censorship, Lautréamont finally

managed to publish his *Chants de Maldoror*, the story of an unbelievably cruel and perverse serial killer. And the book was as hilarious as
it was horrible. The reader finds himself seized, as the critic Julien
Gracq put it, by 'the most embarrassing of nervous giggles'.

One of the advantages of having translated something is that
with an effort you can remember long chunks of it. I lay on
my bed in Milan trying to exhume Calasso and relate it to the
burial and exhumation of Stevanin's victims. *The Songs of Maldoror*,
Calasso claimed, 'was the first book ever written on the principle that
anything and everything must be the object of sarcasm'. Isn't that, I
thought, more or less the guiding principle of the Brigate Gialloblù,
especially after the team has lost? 'Everything is reduced to the same
level,' Calasso goes on, 'in the obsessive sound of the same voice,
that reaches us as though amplified by a faulty microphone.'

The microphone! Where did I hear the Stevanin song if not
through the crackle of the bus's faulty PA system? One of the fans
had gone to the front, taken the driver's microphone and between
swings of *limoncello* was singing all the scandalous songs he knew.
'*Son' greso! Pisso cago scoreso!*' (I'm gross, I piss, shit, fart).

Another trick of Lautréamont's was to publish a short book of
poems that were actually adaptations, desecrations, of the greatest
and most sacred lines of French verse. Calasso comments:

'The premise that lies behind such methods is that the whole
world is inevitably cloaked in a poisonous blanket of parody.
Nothing is what it claims to be. Everything is already a quotation
the moment it appears.'

Again it fits. What do the *brigate* do but take every famous piece
of song or opera or even religious hymn, and adapt it immediately to
any situation that occurs, the burning truck on return from Bari, the
crashed helicopter of the carabinieri, the championships Milan have
lost at Verona, the farce of the supposed beating of Luìs Marsiglia.
But everything is farce. '*Vi vogliamo così*,' I remember them singing
once as Verona went down six–nil. We love you like this.

So you sit – I'm almost ready to turn the TV on now –
half-inebriated, semi-suffocated, in the beery, smoky community of
the coach after yet another away defeat – Florence, Lecce, Bologna

– and through these scandalous songs you are allowed to touch, just for a moment, Leopardi's world of utter nothingness, of no truth, no moral substance, the futility of all illusions. The bald and brutal driver crashes through the tollbooths; Stevanin sweeps away every public piety. *Col badil!* With his spade! Every value is dismembered and buried in this moral midnight. And what are you left with? Only the insane thrill of life itself, a fizz in a void. You burst out in a long nervous giggle. After which, on arrival in Verona, you are restored to your beloved wife, your darling children, your challenging work, somehow fortified, ready once more to take everything around you as seriously as you possibly can.

Good, right, resolved. End of problem. I click on the TV and there is Marsiglia, exact antithesis of the bawdy *brigate*.

It's a documentary programme called *Sciuscià*, produced by that man Michele Santoro, he who sent his cameras up to Verona to capture the Lega at their most xenophobic, only to find that they had cancelled their meeting. A *sciuscià* is, or was, a Neapolitan urchin who made his pennies shining shoes. The programme, then, a RAI production, which is to say, Italian public TV, is on the side of the poor, or the victim (but in the modern world the poor are always victims, and vice versa). Santoro, robust and jowly, is the implacable champion of the wronged. Which means he is constantly in search of scandal.

Today's scandal is the way the city of Verona treated Luìs Marsiglia. The programme is called 'The Liars'. 'So who was lying?' the presenter demands. And he means, not Marsiglia, but the Veronese. It's a fascinating retelling of the story, or rather of the background to the story, since almost nothing is said of Marsiglia's account of the fake assault on himself, the weeks of false testimony to police and media, etc., etc.. Rather we must understand why an intelligent and sensitive man would resort to such a ruse. Because he was persecuted.

Marsiglia, it seems, in talking about the Holocaust, offended the extreme and racist Veronese right. They were out for his blood. The claim that Marsiglia was not in possession of a degree was the merest excuse for dumping him. This is demonstrated by the fact that once the *Curia* had removed him from the Liceo Maffei, where the well-to-do folks go, it was nevertheless willing to have him go on teaching elsewhere. Anyway, the presenter claims, even if Marsiglia didn't have his degree certificate, he had completed all his studies. And suddenly we are in Uruguay. Public TV has forked out the money to send cameramen, interviewers and producer all the way to South America to interview the one or two ancient priests who were teaching at the Theological College of Montevideo when Marsiglia was there many years ago. They assure the presenter that Marsiglia had studied quite enough to teach religion (though what he actually taught was the Holocaust).

Hilarious here, for an Englishman lying on his bed after having taught a day at a university in Milan, is the implication that in order to teach anything you merely need to be capable of doing so: a dangerous, *laissez-faire* notion. Far from it. Actually, you don't need to be capable at all. To teach you need a certificate. You need a degree. Italians spend half their lives getting certificates, not learning how to do things. The document is crucial.

Documents! When the programme breaks for ads, I fiddle in my bag, pull out my newspaper and hurry to the sports pages. '*Documenti falsi!*' is the headline. There is a list of foreign players, mainly South Americans, whose European passports are considered fake. Veron, Recoba, Cafu. Mountains of paper are under scrutiny. Only the official certificate, thoroughly stamped and dated and validated, makes appearance reality in Italy. Life is so evidently without substance that everything must be certified. When the certificate is counterfeit, confusion reigns. Has the whole of Serie A been falsified this year?

But now the programme has started again. An old friend of Marsiglia's is introduced as South America's finest young novelist. I have never heard of him. 'I will say, brother, welcome back!' the writer declares of an eventual meeting with the hounded *professore*. Unaccountably, the famous man hasn't actually seen Marsiglia yet in the two months he's been back. But they are the closest of friends. To his credit, Marsiglia himself has refused to be interviewed. He has learned enough about the media to keep away. But we are invited to believe that he is unable to appear before even *Sciuscià*'s friendly cameras, because so damaged psychologically by the terrible people of Verona. To convince us how terrible they are, we are shown the local bishop saying mass in Latin with a bunch of diehard Catholic traditionalists, a couple of bigots from the Lega Nord and a group of thugs outside a discotheque.

Only in Italy, it occurs to me later as I settle down to sleep, would a whole city be isolated and stigmatised in this way, as if it were radically different from the cities around it. I can already hear the swelling chorus of complaint that will be filling the Veronese papers and The Wall over the coming days. The *brigate*, I tell myself, are bound to become involved.

In an extraordinary couple of pages in his *Discourse on the Present State of the Customs of the Italians*, Leopardi, in 1828, came to the conclusion that society in Italy, so far as it existed, was above all 'a school for insult'. 'In Italy the main and most necessary talent for anyone who wants to engage in conversation is the ability to show through word and gesture every kind of contempt for others, to destroy their self-esteem as completely as possible, to leave them dissatisfied with themselves and consequently with yourself.'

If I had read this out of context, my first thought would have been that the writer was describing the exchanges between football fans. But Leopardi meant life in general. And sure enough, the day after the *Sciuscià* programme an interminable slanging match begins. The centre-right mayor of Verona, a lady called Michela Sironi, accuses Santoro of arrogance, bad faith, intellectual dishonesty and prejudice. Santoro says that he is willing to come to Verona to debate the xenophobia issue, but adds, 'So long as the debate is not in Latin.' I can hear the fans singing, 'Can't understand how the fuck you speak.' The Church rebuts all the criticism in the programme and invites the Veronese not to pay their TV licence: why should we pay for public TV if the money is spent on insulting us? Inevitably, court cases are begun. It was in this atmosphere, with the city of Verona enjoying an orgy of collective indignation about the way it is being presented in the national press, that Hellas entertained Parma at the Bentegodi on 28 January.

I5A GIORNATA

Atalanta – Fiorentina 0–0
Bari – Reggina 2–1
Bologna – Verona 1–0
Lazio – Inter 2–0
Milan – Roma 3–2
Napoli – Udinese 0–1
Parma – Lecce 1–1
Perugia – Juventus 0–1
Vicenza – Brescia 1–1

CLASSIFICA

Roma	33
Juventus	30
Lazio	27
Fiorentina	25
Atalanta	23
Milan	23
Bologna	23
Udinese	22
Parma	20
Lecce	20
Perugia	19
Inter	18
Vicenza	16
Verona	15
Napoli	14
Reggina	13
Brescia	13
Bari	12

I Più-mati

Oo! Oo! Oo! Oo! Oo! Oo! Oo! Oo! Oo! Oo! Oo!
Oo! Oo! Oo! Oo! Oo! Oo! Oo! Oo! Oo! Oo! Oo!
Oo! Oo! Oo! Oo! Oo! Oo!

Ringoboys, Reggina

It was before the game with Parma that I discovered that Pietro, who keeps our seats for us, still plays football regularly, well into his thirties, and is in fact president of the football club of the village suburb of San Giovanni Lupatoto. He plays Sunday morning and watches Sunday afternoon. I suggest to him that we do an away game together. He tells me he used to go to lots of away games but has now stopped. 'Is it family commitments?' I ask, the common Italian expression for wife trouble. Pietro shakes his head. 'If you do the away games, it takes you over. You lose a sense of proportion. It fills your whole life. It's too strong.'

At once I'm aware that he is describing something I have felt growing in myself, a sense that I am losing control of my thought patterns. My mind is full of chants. I'm constantly whistling the triumphal march of *Aïda*, '*Alè, forza Verona alè*' or 'Guantanamera', '*Non si capisce ma come cazzo parlate!*' Even at the breakfast table, even in the corridors at the university. *Forza gialloblù, gialloblù, gialloblù, giallobluuuuu!* And after every away game the bus rumbles on longer and longer in my head. Stevanin! Stevanin! The bottles clink backwards and forwards on the tidal run of my thoughts. *In Italia Hellas! In Europa Hellas!* This is it, then, I tell myself, as the players come out of the tunnel, the enchantment the *brigate* live under: the background noise of the mind is for ever *gialloblù*.

The game starts. There are the usual yellow-and-blue smoke-bombs. The bang of a big firework is vastly amplified by the concrete circle of the stadium. Then the ritual insults. Parma have recently fired their manager and Arrigo Sacchi, ex-Milan, ex-national team, has taken over. Sacchi means bags in Italian. '*Sacchi di merda*,' the crowd sings. Bags of shit. You're bags of shit. I love it.

Then comes the one thing that for me always breaks the enchantment. The majestically black Lilian Thuram, French international, European and World champion, touches the ball, and the *curva*, or a small part of it, begin their monkey grunts. 'Oo! Oo! Oo!' The rest of the stadium falls silent. 'Oo! Oo! Oo!' A new tension is in the air, corroding the happy spell of the encounter. The crowd know this is trouble. What could more effectively confirm Santoro's thesis that Verona is a hateful, xenophobic, racist city than a bunch of fans taunting a black? These monkey grunts, I tell myself, will prove that Marsiglia was hounded out of Verona by right-wing barbarians.

Before the game, all the talk had been of last year's victory over Parma when Morfeo took us from three–one down to that famous four–three victory. If football is so successful at generating community, it must be because it offers such vivid episodes around which the collective memory can build its myths, and then frequent triggers for recalling them. But no one will ever wish to remember Verona–Parma, 28 January, 2001. Bonazzoli missed an early chance. Ferron was stretchered off after a collision. Doardo once again wasn't up to it. Parma scored. The racist taunts grew louder. Fifteen minutes into the second half, just when Verona were applying maximum pressure, Anthony Seric made a terrible error. The pitch was again sodden after heavy rain. Running back for a long ball, he slid on the mud and let it slip under a leg. Di Vaio went on to score. Next time Thuram got into the action, the monkey grunts were louder still. Mutu won a penalty, took it himself and hit it over the bar. The grunts were furious. But by now the game was dead. People were already leaving. Needless to say Chievo, with their two black players, had won away.

Before turning on the TV for 'Novantesimo minuto' that evening, I knew that the sanctimonious presenter, Fabrizio Maffei, would make a meal of the affair. I knew he would shake his well-groomed head, and grimace beneath his fashionable glasses, and talk about 'real' fans who were only interested in football and those ugly racists who only went to the stadium to insult and knew nothing at all about sport. It's wonderful how simple the world is to the pious mind. And this unctuous, entirely predictable fellow would then no doubt mention – it has been all over the papers – that when the second half of the season begins, on 11 February, new rules are to come into force allowing the powers-that-be to impose a stadium ban on any club whose fans have indulged in racist chants. Forced to play on neutral ground, Verona, who never win away, will be doomed. In the event, what Maffei actually said, with excited earnestness, was: 'Let's hope these new rules are applied rigorously!'

All this I had expected, but not the suicidal interview that Giambattista Pastorello was at that very moment giving over the phone to a local TV station in Parma. Perhaps because our top scorer Bonazzoli is on loan from Parma, the journalist asked Pastorello if there was any truth in the rumour that Parma wanted to have Bonazzoli back now in exchange for their Cameroon striker, Patrick Mboma. Pastorello replied:

'If I made a swap like that I'd have to go and buy a team in Finland or somewhere: the fans here in Verona would put me on the rack. Add to that that I'd be exchanging Bonazzoli for a coloured player, well, enough said.'

Within minutes the entire world of sport – the president of the football league, the president of the Italian Olympic confederation – was condemning Verona, condemning Pastorello for his lack of courage in facing the racists. By seven o'clock we even had a strong condemnation from the centre-left Minister of Sport. The smell of elections grows stronger by the hour. Determined to be tougher on racism than even the left, Verona's Mayor Sironi announces she will definitely close down the stadium if this goes on. The chief public prosecutor Guido Papalia declares that he is considering an investigation into racist crimes at the stadium. Has Pastorello been threatened? he wants to know.

Next morning pages and pages of the national press are given over to racist Verona – 'and this less than twenty-four hours after Holocaust Commemoration Day,' thunders the *Gazzetta dello Sport*. Small incidents like a drunk driver killing a mother and two children are all but overlooked. It was inevitable. But now events took a surreal twist. Towards ten-thirty on Tuesday morning, I left my dusty office to grab a coffee and check the papers in the local bar. Yet again a whole page was dedicated to the 'Verona crisis'. In the middle of it all was a small article entitled, 'In the Curva Sud, *brigate* in command.' A subtitle promised: 'Map of *il tifo gialloblù*' – the Verona fans. After a summary history of the famous *brigate*, the article tells us:

> As well as the *brigate* in the *curva*, there are a number of other groups, the most important of which is 'Gruppo primo Febbraio 1987' led by Tim Parks, an English writer who has lived for many years on the banks of the Adige. This is a fringe group that broke off from the *brigate* because it didn't agree with either its ideology or behaviour. To distinguish themselves, its members abandoned the *curva* and took over an area at the top of the West Stand.

Tim Parks! Me! I lead a group of fans. It's written there in the dreamy rose-pink of the *Gazzetta dello Sport*. I am an important person in the world of Veronese football, though I have no idea what the significance of 1 February 1987 might be.

No sooner have I finished reading this news than the mobile is ringing. My wife tells me that three national TV stations have called inviting me to participate in talk-show debates on Verona, football and racism. Naturally, I refuse. 'But who would have told them such a ridiculous thing?' Rita asks. 'It must be a joke.' All at once it occurs to me: 'I Più-mati' – which is to say, The Maddest Ones.

How can I explain? After *La Stampa* published my article on the Juventus game in November, after the *Arena* then followed this up with something particularly inaccurate about me, shortly before Christmas, I put a little note – my first – on The Wall, disclaiming various things they had said and winding up with the obligatory *FORZA GIALLOBLÙ*. The immediate response was a message of solidarity from Il signor Pennellone (Mr Paintbrush). He was the webmaster, he explained, of Solohellas.net. Only Hellas. I checked it out. The site is a testimony to the lengths people will go to spend absolutely *all* their time thinking about football. The graphics are rich and jolly, unlike the frozen solemnity of the official site. There are pictures of the fans at all the games. There is a wonderful insulting machine. You type in the name of the object of your contempt, sex, place of birth, and above all football team, after which, at the click of the mouse the software offers a range of insults at once both appropriate and preposterous. Did Leopardi foresee the invention of such a thing? But above all, I found that Solohellas is the spiritual retreat of the most frequent writers to The Wall – Lo Scaligero, McDann, Pam, Paruca (wig), Cris-do-I-bother-anyone, Only-Hellas-I-hate-the-big-teams, Aiooogalapagos, Ash, Alcohol. Here these people hold court in brief and brutal articles on the game, the players, the now-evident national plot to banish Hellas to Serie B and replace the club with Chievo. After a brief exchange of letters, Pennellone invited me to join the group for dinner. 'We call ourselves I Più-mati,' he said.

So it was that I found myself standing outside the Bar Bentegodi, opposite the stadium, at nine o'clock of a Friday evening. It was raining again. My book is going to be rained off, I thought. Nobody will believe it can rain so much in Italy. Waiting, I remembered some of the messages these people had written: invitations to storm Hellas headquarters, to burn the players' cars, to descend on Vicenza and lay waste its ancient centre. I remembered challenges to the fans of rival teams to meet and fight at specific places at specific times. I was a little nervous. And instead the people who turned up were a bunch of regular if oddly heterogeneous folk on a night out. The ferocious Pam in particular, who I had imagined was a man (since Pam isn't a normal name in Italy, and Pam's messages are particularly masculine), turned out to be a peroxide blonde in her early thirties with a husky voice and an acid wit. The terrible Alcohol was a sweet if overweight sixteen-year-old. The grim Cris-do-I-bother-anyone was a polite, well-spoken charmer. Pennellone, or Mr Penn, wore a carnival hat with moose antlers and turned out to be an insurance broker.

I should have expected this. It was all there in the name of the group, which is a play on words, a play between Italian and dialect, between public identity and private delirium. *Piumati*, in regular Italian, means 'the feathered ones'. The Solohellas homepage has a yellow-blue feather that flutters down across the screen. To say 'the maddest ones' in Italian, you must say: *i più matti*, with a double *t*. But in Veronese dialect the double letters are neither pronounced nor written. So to the ear *più-mati* could be either feathered ones or nutters, either light-hearted sane folks, or ferocious hooligans. In this way the Più-mati flutter between Italian and dialect, between their everyday office identities and their monstrous projections in yellow-blue hyperspace. Like the stadium, the net is a *zona franca* where one can be anyone and say anything.

It was through the net that the Più-mati had come together. Of widely different ages, from widely different backgrounds and income brackets, they have three things in common: they are Veronese, they support Hellas, and they never take themselves seriously. It's a pleasing cocktail. When we staggered out of a hillside trattoria towards one a.m. they invited me to continue the evening in a bar by the lake fifteen miles away. I declined.

'The Più-mati must have done this,' I told my wife, seeing this bizarre news in the *Gazzetta dello Sport*: Tim Parks, leader of the 1 February 1987 group. They love to spread silly rumours. The following day, for example, I had a sneaking suspicion that the Più-mati might be behind a letter published in the *Arena* and quite improbably signed by the 'Association of Cameroon Students for Hellas'. It was about racism, of course, and Pastorello not being able to sign Mboma because of the *brigate*. 'We hope', the letter finished in perfectly pompous Italian, 'that soon this outstanding Cameroon player can come and give his contribution to the success of our Hellas Verona.'

Can there really be a group of Cameroon students who support Hellas Verona? I wondered. Or is someone trying to demonstrate how unfounded and stupid half the things written about sport are? For sports journalism, I realised, as I watched events unfolding the week after the Parma game, is a sort of extreme parody of journalism in general: a clatter of exciting misinformation.

Meanwhile, in the opinion columns and phone-in radio-shows the racist debate rages on. 'I'm proud to be Nazi,' one member of the Loma Band phones to say. 'How the hell can they call me racist,' Aiooogalapagos writes on The Wall, 'when I work alongside someone from Vicenza?' 'Oh forget politics,' comes the response. 'Let's play, fuck, eat and *Forza magica Verona*!'

But sadly politics won't be forgotten. And as the days pass the feeling grows that things are coming to a head. The Hellas fans will be punished, the stadium closed. A man from Channel Five, one of Berlusconi's TV stations, comes and rings twice on my doorbell. They need to interview me. Then the German national channel arrive. They want to know why I support a racist club. The Germans! My wife tells them all I'm out.

'The truth is,' a laconic voice cuts through hyperspace, 'they don't want us to stop the monkey grunts. They love calling Verona racist. They want to close the Bentegodi. We crash into Serie B. Chievo come up and replace us: the acceptable face of the Veneto. *Butei*, when we go into the stadium on 11 February, they'll be auditioning us for scapegoat.'

The 11 February game is against Bari, who usually field two blacks. The stage is set for a dramatic afternoon.

But before that there is Perugia away and another week of tension.

16A GIORNATA

Brescia – Milan 1–1
Fiorentina – Lazio 1–4
Inter – Bari 1–0
Juventus – Vicenza 4–0
Lecce – Bologna 0–0
Reggina – Perugia 0–2
Roma – Napoli 3–0
Udinese – Atalanta 2–4
Verona – Parma 0–2

CLASSIFICA

Roma	36
Juventus	33
Lazio	30
Atalanta	26
Fiorentina	25
Milan	24
Bologna	24
Parma	23
Perugia	22
Udinese	22
Lecce	21
Inter	21
Vicenza	16
Verona	15
Brescia	14
Napoli	14
Reggina	13
Bari	12

Puliero

I am a football enthusiast writing from Australia. Who are Verona's best players at the moment?
  Simon Simon, Sydney, Australia

Simon Simon . . . the best player at the moment is Preben Larsen Elkjaer or Hans Peter Briegel . . .
  Solohellas@odiolegrandi.it

'*RETE! GOL! ALÈ ALÈ BOOM BOOM BOOM! BRAVI RAGAZZI, FORZA HELLAS!*'

Long before I actually took to going to the Bentegodi, this was the siren shout that tugged at me, that reminded me I had once been a football fanatic and that one day I would have to yield to my baser instincts and head for the stadium again.

'*Alè! Alè!* Boom boom boom! *Gol!*'

The voice came across the air. Rita and I would be walking up on the hills above the city on some crisp cold day, ice on the cypresses, the sun dazzlingly low, when all of a sudden it would explode from around a hairpin, or behind a barn, or within a thicket. *Rete!!!!!!* An elderly gentleman, perhaps, was holding his fur-coated wife with one arm, while the other pressed a small radio against his ear. *Gol! Goooool!!!!* The gentleman turned to his wife and embraced her. Or on a warm spring day it might be boyfriend and girlfriend on their stomachs in the meadow grass beneath the cherry trees. Briegel . . . Galderisi . . . cross . . . Elkjaer, *RRRRREEEETEEE!* The boy jumps to his feet and runs two or three times around a tree, trailing his yellow-blue scarf behind him.

Hoarse and compelling, the voice was that of Roberto Puliero, perhaps the most recognisable man in Verona. Almost twenty years after I first heard him, ten years after I myself became a regular listener to his nail-biting accounts of Hellas Verona's vicissitudes, I find myself sitting beside him in the back of a big black BMW Series 7, headed for Perugia. Roberto is worried. He doesn't usually ask the radio station to provide him with a fast car and a driver. But once again Verona have been given the Saturday afternoon losers' slot. And on Saturday evenings Puliero has to be back in Verona by quarter to nine at the latest. As well as being the radio commentator for all Verona's games, he is also the director and lead actor of La Barcaccia, a small local theatre company. At nine-fifteen he must be on stage for a rendering of a work by the eighteenth-century playwright Carlo Goldoni.

Here is an irony then. Notorious throughout the peninsula for its supposedly brutish fans, Hellas is most frequently associated in the Veronese mind with a highly cultured man, warm, liberal and charismatic, a man recently invited by the centre-left to stand as town mayor against Signora Sironi. 'I'd enjoy the campaign,' he admits. 'I'd like that, speaking to people in the piazza. But what would I do if they elected me?' Sensibly, he has declined.

Roberto Puliero is built tall and square. In his early fifties now, his broad, wrinkled, mobile face is the result of years of extravagant mimicry and clowning. He wears his fuzzy hair long and absolutely unkempt, but then, with improbable vanity, he dyes it coal-black. His voice, strained with overuse, rich and nasal with dialect intonations and generous with emotion, is absolutely distinctive, immediately seductive. Halfway into the journey we stop at an *autogrill* where he stocks up with biscuits and chocolates for the return trip. Perugia is three hundred kilometres away and high in the Apennines. The sky is threatening snow. 'I'll need energy for the stage,' he explains.

Roberto is worried that he won't make it back in time. 'We must be out of the stadium the moment the final whistle blows.'

He's worried about all the political hullabaloo surrounding the team; it must be affecting them, he thinks. He's worried about the incredible number of injuries. Mazzola has mumps. He's worried that Pastorello hasn't used the New Year's window in the transfer market to bring any really good players to the team. Last year at least we got Morfeo. The big clubs have stars on their benches who they're eager to lend out for a few months to give them some match experience. And this year, who? Teodorani, a 22-year-old left-back from Roma to replace the disappointing Cvitanovic and Seric. And a kid, a child almost, Lanza as a possible centre-back when Apolloni is out. Apolloni is out again today. But who has ever heard of these people? Meantime Brescia and Atalanta have both picked up big players. Napoli have bought the Brazilian, Edmundo. Why can't we have people like that? The defence is weak. He shakes his head. The midfield has neither skill nor stamina nor character. When on earth will Leo Colucci return? And now he has heard that the players are all arguing and Perotti hasn't got a grip on things.

'I don't like Oddo's attitude,' he says. 'I'm not convinced by Oddo.' The underlying problem, he feels, is that Pastorello is only in it for the money. Puliero, it turns out, has an instinctive aversion to the figure of the entrepreneur. He is a child of the '68 students' revolution, one of those people who are physiologically left-wing. 'The man should spend more. But he's tight. The players are all on loan or half-owned by other clubs. It's difficult to establish a team spirit.'

I am fascinated by this attitude. On the one hand there is a resentment of money – football has been ruined by money! – on the other hand the insistence that money be spent lavishly, beyond the point of folly. Behind it all is the suspicion that the owner doesn't suffer emotionally as much as the fan does, the fear that someone else is considering in merely money terms what for you is immensely important, even sacred. The only way for the rich person to demonstrate real passion is to throw his money away, as does the president of Inter, Moratti, with the most unhappy results. Inter change players and coaches faster, more expensively and less effectively than any other club in Europe. 'But the fans respect him more', Puliero says, 'because they know he cares.' Then he adds, 'Even though he's obviously an idiot.'

The chauffeured car climbs into the hills above Bologna. The vineyards and olive groves are bleakly grey-green in the winter light. From pessimism it's an easy step to nostalgia. Puliero begins to remember the better days of the mid-eighties when Hellas were always in the top five or six teams. He knew all the players in those days. They would often have a pizza together. He laughs. 'People would stop me in the street and congratulate me on the team's success, as if it was me playing. During the second half of the '85 season when it became clear Verona had a chance of taking the *scudetto*, loudspeakers were set up in Piazza Bra and crowds listened to the away games in the square.' I remember this myself. I remember standing by the Roman Arena with my wife, feeling drawn to that urgent voice, eager to stay and listen, and her saying, 'Tim, come on, let's get home, it's freezing.'

'And the funny thing is', Puliero tells me, 'that officially it was illegal for me to be broadcasting. Private radio stations weren't allowed to broadcast the game. There was a state monopoly. I had to sneak into the stadium with a walkie-talkie and heavy batteries. Once my wife wrapped the batteries in gift paper and said we were taking Christmas presents to friends after the game. Or if it was a low stadium I'd see if someone would let me use a balcony overlooking the ground.'

As with so many Italian laws, officials would go through the motions of telling him that what he was doing was illegal, then let him get on with it anyway. The important thing is that illegality be established, not prevented. Meantime, in Verona thousands of people, including policemen, were standing in Italy's biggest piazza listening to an illegal broadcast sanctioned by the town hall.

Why is Puliero such a successful radio commentator? Other local stations now offer game commentary, but no one listens to them. The agony of football on the radio is that your anxiety about the result isn't mediated through the attraction of the spectacle. It is suffering or elation of the rawest variety. What Puliero does is to bring a theatricality, a sense of performance to the occasion that in part at least substitutes for the absent spectacle of the game, and thus makes the result more acceptable. His voice is full of grand gestures. He suffers as much, no, *more* than you do. And, like the experienced fan on the terraces, he combines complete partisanship – he *really* wants Verona to win – with a determinedly objective vision of the game. He never pretends the team is playing better than it is. He doesn't imagine there's a penalty every time a Verona player falls over in the box. In this he is the exact opposite of the standard Italian commentator on public radio who pretends he is impartial but then constantly insinuates that the team he is rooting for is being hard done-by.

Most of all, though, and this is uncanny, Puliero has a way of hinting to you what is about to happen. He reads the game so well that you are already prepared for the goal when it comes, particularly the opposition's goal, which is the one that is so hard to bear. His voice begins to fall, you can sense that he barely wants to talk to you, so appalled is he by what is happening on the pitch. '*Attenzione, attenzione pericolo a sinistra.*' Danger on the left. Then there is a brief silence, a barely whispered phlegmatic '*Gol*'. More silence, then the repetition: '*Gol. Gol di Pippo Inzaghi.*' Then the verbal head-shaking: '*Ahimè, ahimè, amici sportivi veronesi* – alas, alas, my Veronese sporting friends – once again our poor Hellas have demonstrated all their many, many limitations!'

But almost immediately, his voice picks up. And as the *brigate*, staggering from the punch, quickly gather their wits and renew their singing to rouse the team, so Puliero switches from addressing the public to exhorting the players: '*Coraggio ragazzi! Coraggio!* Perhaps there is still time. Perhaps all is not lost. *All'arrembaggio! Forza Hellas!*'

'*Arrembaggio*' is a wonderful word. Try repeating it a few times, throwing all the stress on the *ba* and making sure you linger over the soft double *g*. The dictionary definition is: 'the action of boarding and attacking an enemy ship once grappling hooks have been attached'. It's an all-out assault. You imagine the blue-yellows swarming into the opposing team's arca, determined to equalise. You turn up the radio volume a little, you begin to hope. And then a low voice from the Radio Adige studio interrupts. 'Roberto? Roberto?' Puliero stops. 'Just to say that Chievo have scored. It's two–nil.' Damn! The boys from the dam are winning again!

High on the snow-driven Apennines now, Puliero agrees that being a good commentator has a lot to do with acting. 'You're playing a part. You have to do it with complete conviction.' Laughing, he tells me how once when one of the Veneto teams had had their stadium disqualified and were obliged to play a game with Avellino at the Bentegodi, he was asked by an Avellino radio station, whose commentator hadn't made it to the ground, if he would do the match for them. 'No problem. I had no problem at all sounding completely fanatical about the team. Supported them breathlessly the whole ninety minutes.'

I'm appalled. Avellino! It would be like pretending enthusiasm for Scunthorpe.

We drive through an Etruscan gateway and up a narrow, cobbled street. Perugia is a very beautiful town, cluttered about the steep slopes above Lake Trasimeno and the Tiber valley. Naturally, we're going to see nothing of it, except perhaps the few *campanili* and rocky hilltops visible above the stadium's stands. Among other things, the place is famous for having a university for foreigners with excellent facilities for learning Italian. It's the only one in the country. A couple of years ago they even set up a special school for helping foreign football players to improve their Italian. It appears that to date not a single player has actually signed up. Perhaps the transfer market really is too fast and they're afraid they'll be in another country before they've mastered the inflexions of the present tense.

I wanted to watch the game with the fans; Roberto was going to the press room. We parted in a car park outside the small attractive ground and met up again less than two hours later to jump into the BMW and roar away into what was now heavily falling snow for Roberto's appointment with Goldoni. In the meantime absolutely nothing of any interest had happened. For if football is a sport where everything can happen and emotions may be wound up to fever pitch, it is also a pastime where the utter dullness, the endless repetitiveness of human existence can be held in the palm of the hand for an interminable ninety minutes. Perugia played badly and scored, once. Verona played badly and failed to score. Even the fans seemed short on energy. The *brigate* arrived late, their buses held up in a traffic jam. The Perugia fans raised a long banner: 'An anti-racist town is always in Serie A.' It was a provocation too banal to elicit any response. 'No comment,' Roberto said, hurrying back to the car from the press room. I made none.

And four hours later I was in the theatre watching a play called *La cameriera brillante*, which might be translated, 'The Canny Maid', or 'The Witty Servant', or 'The Brilliant Housekeeper'. We had raced through the snowy hills, the dull plain, shaking our heads again over the enigma of highly paid players who didn't seem eager to play, a coach who had no idea who to put on the field from one game to the next. Would Perotti be fired? We ate our chocolate biscuits. By eight-forty we were in Verona; my wife and elder daughter, Stefi, were already waiting at the theatre in a dingy back-street near San Zeno. And now here we are in the front row, with the actors' feet hurrying to and fro at the level of the eyes, far closer than you can ever get to a football field these days. Thank God I don't have to worry whether they'll win or lose.

We are back in the eighteenth century, somewhere in the Veneto. People are wearing long velvet coats, lace ruffs, extravagant hats. The plot is simple, schematic and effective, qualities that Perotti might do well to reflect on. An aging widowed landowner, Pantalon dei Bisognosi, alias Puliero, is reluctant to marry off his two daughters to two rich young men. One daughter is modest and undemanding, the other demonstrative, arrogant and worldly. The grooms-to-be are fantastically unsuitable: an extravagant southern fop is to marry the modest daughter; a gloomy, misanthrope farmer is promised to the society girl. The fop does nothing but boast previous successes with countesses various. The farmer thinks only of getting back home to watch his peasants at work. What unites the two is a tendency to think of the girls as nothing more than dowries and social convenience. The cantankerous father has seen through them and is determined to send them packing. But he has a weak spot.

He is in love with his young housekeeper, a woman of flashing wit and great manipulative genius. Constantly flirting with her master, interminably working on the daughters and their suitors, only she seems capable of making something happen.

I lie back in my seat. How different from the stadium! No fences, no police hemming us in! And yet . . .

'I can't understand you when you speak that blasted Tuscan!' the old man complains to his maid. She is teasing him. He speaks in a fierce Venetian dialect; the fop speaks Tuscan. The two servants are from Bergamo. Argentina, the housekeeper, demonstrates her intellectual superiority by her ability to switch back and forth between dialect and Italian. She coerces all the characters to take part in a play within a play, where the old Pantalon will have to declare his love for her. In Tuscan. And he can't do it. He can't get his tongue round it. Soon all the familiar language insults are flying back and forth. '*Non si capisce ma come cazzo parlate!*'

The purpose of the housekeeper's little *commedia* is to have everyone act out a personality opposite to their own. The fop must learn to be humble, to say he is not worthy of his lady's hand. His modest *fidanzata* must be imperious. Needless to say, they all balk at their lines, introduce vicious asides, throw down the script in disgust. Yet in the end the housekeeper wins the day. Everybody marries. Everybody is persuaded that they have more to lose by opting out than by compromising their instincts in the collective theatre of community.

But is this a happy ending? These people are marrying for money and convenience, aren't they? Or are they? Perhaps deep down they were just waiting for a chance to compromise, to leave their more intractable selves behind. Goldoni is ambiguous. We don't know quite what any of these people are thinking, or what the future will bring. We only see what's there on stage. We see that romance is beautiful but that only a fool would ignore economics.

And towards midnight, at the pizzeria where the actors always eat together after the play, I put it to Roberto that actually this is the same ambiguity that surrounds Pastorello and so many of the people involved in the business of football. We would like the coach and the players and the owner to be more passionate, more sentimentally attached to their clubs, but we know that football, like marriage and families, has also largely to do with money. And then maybe they *are* more sentimentally attached than we think. Maybe they have to fight against their sentimental attachment so as not to be ruined financially. How will we ever know how much Pastorello cares? Of course he bought the team to make money, the players only came to the team to make money, but maybe, as in the ideal marriage of convenience, affection *sets in*. Didn't Bari-born Leo Colucci recently say in an interview: 'This yellow-blue shirt is my skin, these colours are in my blood'?

'Perhaps Pastorello will learn to love Hellas.'

We are in the upstairs room of a pizzeria in the outlying village of Quinzano. The waiter is black, something that would have been unthinkable when I myself lived in this village twenty years ago. The actors are jolly and friendly, but, like football players, less glamorous than one expects. They have little to say about acting or Goldoni. Roberto remarks that as theatre director he has often thought of himself as being like a coach, or rather a player–manager in the English tradition. He has to choose his team, get the right actor for the right part. Over ice-creams and *limoncello*, all the actors begin to talk football. They are well-informed; and everybody agrees: Bari, the first match of the second half of the season, will be make or break for Perotti, and make or break for the *brigate*. If we lose, if the stadium is disqualified, it's all up.

17A GIORNATA

Atalanta – Juventus 2–1
Bari – Brescia 1–3
Bologna – Inter 0–3
Lazio – Lecce 3–2
Milan – Reggina 1–0
Napoli – Fiorentina 1–0
Parma – Roma 1–2
Perugia – Verona 1–0
Vicenza – Udinese 1–2

CLASSIFICA

Roma   39
Juventus   33
Lazio   33
Atalanta   29
Milan   27
Fiorentina 25
Perugia   25
Udinese   25
Bologna   24
Inter   24
Parma   23
Lecce   21
Brescia   17
Napoli   17
Vicenza   16
Verona   15
Reggina   13
Bari   12

Moo-too Moo-too

IF YOU INFERNAL FASCIST SHITHEADS GET
THE STADIUM BANNED I'LL HAVE YOU ALL
KILLED. BRAINLESS BASTARDS, LEARN TO
KEEP YOUR MOUTHS SHUT FOR HELLAS.
PREBEN ELKJAER
hell@s.it

A dull, flat voice, neither masculine nor feminine, drained of any expression, bereft of communicative energy, reads out, over a metallic PA, an official announcement carefully phrased to generate the maximum indifference, if not contempt:

> Hellas Verona football club advises the sporting public that in accordance with regulations introduced by the Italian Football Federation every racial or territorial insult inside and also outside the stadium will be penalised with the application of fines of ever-increasing severity and eventually with the disqualification of the club's home ground. We would therefore wish to appeal to the civic sense and collective responsibility of all fans, inviting them to behave in a correct fashion throughout the game.

The announcement is met with a gale of whistles. The *curva* is packed, the weather gloomy. Hopefully more effective than the PA's saccharin homily is the huge banner that announces, black on white:

CIVIL VERONA SHOUTS 'FORZA HELLAS'
NO TO RACISM
NO TO THE DEMONISATION OF OUR TEAM

But this message is hung along the parapet of the expensive stands on the east side of the stadium, and the fans in the *curva* have no time for the polite and seated season ticket holders, who, of course, are never to be seen at away games. The moral capital of the *brigate* is built on the sacrifice of all those away games. Only three points in eight matches and thousands of kilometres, but they, and I, have been to all of them.

More nervous than ever, my son and I take our places. Once when he was very young, I had to forbid Michele from joining in racist chants. Now he is their fiercest opponent. 'I hope to God they shut up,' he keeps saying. 'I hope to God they don't ruin everything.'

The players stream out on to the pitch, all wearing yellow tops over their club colours. 'FIDAS', the shirts announce. It's the name of the blood donors' society. They always advertise at the stadium. Apparently many fans give blood. Perhaps they leave the stadium with their pressure unbearably high. The players line up for photographs. Beneath the name FIDAS is the message: 'Blood has no colour. Love . . . say no to intolerance.' That pious slogan, I'm sure, will be a red rag to a bull for the fans.

As the players strip off their politically correct tops and prepare to do battle, I think of Pastorello, of my conversation with him yesterday, and marvel once again at the enormous gap that separates the administrators of football from its most determined disciples.

'Just hang on while I take these drops,' he had begun.

Rather surprisingly, *il presidente* had agreed to talk to me the very day before this crucial game: Bari bottom and desperate, ourselves third from bottom and terrified, the race issue looming.

'Sciatica,' Pastorello explained. 'It's crippling. Though probably a win tomorrow would do more for it than any painkiller.'

Was this a subtle hint that he somatises, that he really does suffer for the team? We sat down either side of his monumental desk and

I asked him how much time he gave to this racist problem and these political issues.

'Very little. We do what we can, which isn't much. It's the fans who have to change.'

I suggest to him that the frequent talk about 'defeating' racism on the terraces is a mistake. The word 'defeat' only provokes the hardliners. They don't come to the stadium to think of themselves as defeated.

'Good point,' Pastorello says earnestly. He's elegant in sober suit and tie. 'Words are important.'

I know the comment will be promptly forgotten. I ask him, 'Why do the fans hate you so much?'

He takes this on the nose. 'I've absolutely no idea.' He gives me a brief history of his career. He grew up supporting Vicenza. He was sports director at Parma for many years but never had any trouble with their fans. They were always very well behaved. He even bought AC Siena a couple of years ago, took them from C into B, then sold them again. 'It was just a favour I did for old friends.' And at the same time he bought Hellas Verona.

'Nobody welcomed me when I arrived,' he remembers, more with puzzlement than complaint. 'The club was going through a crisis and I stepped in. I had a good record. I assumed people would be pleased. But nothing. Around the third home game we lost five–two to Reggina, remember? and that's when it started. PAS-TO-REL-LO VAF-FAN-CU-LO!'

'And you've no idea why they do that?'

'No.' Pastorello leans forward over his desk. 'But you know,' he says, 'the odd thing is, from the day I said I wanted to sell, from that day everybody started begging me to stay: "*Presidente*, you're the only one who can save us," they said – and at the same time the *vaffanculo*s stopped. There hasn't been a single one since I threatened to go.'

Pastorello clearly feels that this turn of events is at once a deep mystery of human nature and a great vindication for himself. Whereas it seems fairly obvious that while the fans intensely dislike him for his apparent aloofness and his readiness to turn players into profits, they nevertheless know that this kind of modern market football is here to stay and that Pastorello is sharper at it than most.

'Talk to me,' I invite him, 'about how you see the money side of the game. Why did you sell off all of our best players at the end of last year?'

Rearranging the expensive ornaments on his desk, the man launches into a rapid and lucid explanation. 'The Bosman ruling was a disaster for small clubs like ourselves,' he begins. 'From that point on, no contract could hold if a player wanted to break it. They became free agents. The richer teams, who are not interested in developing talent, were now in a better position to prey on our youngsters. The only way a club like Verona can now make money on a player they've discovered and trained is to get a fee for breach of contract. So contracts never run to the end of their term because then the player would be free to leave as and how he likes. In any event, as soon as a player feels he is worth more than he's presently being paid, it becomes impossible to hold him.'

'Give me some figures with a player I know.'

'Cristian Brocchi,' Pastorello says promptly (our midfield dynamo of last season). 'I paid the boy 350,000 million lire a year [£110,000]. Inter offered him 1,500,000,000. [£450,000].'

'*Esagerato!*' I'm indignant. 'It was the team that made Brocchi, not Brocchi the team.'

Pastorello nods. 'How can I keep someone who has been offered four times as much elsewhere, and at least three times as much as he is worth? The more successful a provincial team is, the more likely that it will have to break up at the end of the year. The seven sisters – you know, Juventus, Inter, etc. – each have an annual budget deficit of between thirty and one hundred and fifty billion lire a year [one to five million pounds]. They make it up with their private fortunes. I can't compete.'

I ask him if there isn't a conflict of interest with his sons being the agents for many of his own players. After all, he has family members taking a commission when he buys or sells the player.

'People who say that are just jealous.' The man always has this smile which might be affable and might be the grin of someone pulling the wool over your eyes. 'It's very useful having my sons involved. We'd never have got Giuseppe Colucci if my son hadn't been his agent. He just wouldn't have come here. And of course when you're dealing with a member of your own family they don't insist on being paid forty million under the table every time you do a deal with them.'

'Are you saying that there are illegal payments every time players change teams?'

'Oh not at all!' he laughs, spreading his arms. As at that lunch before the game in Lecce, I find myself liking Pastorello more than I meant to. He leans across the table, then confides, 'I wept when we got the winner against Napoli.'

'Signor Pastorello,' I tell him, leaning forward myself now. 'We *all* wept.' And then I ask, 'But this emotion never leads you to open your wallet a little wider.'

'No.' The answer is abrupt.

'So why did you stay on last summer? You had the club up for sale. Why didn't you go?'

'It's a challenge, isn't it? I can't resist it. I'd like to hang on here, what, at least five years and to have the Veronese say: there, Pastorello took the team from B to A and kept it there all this time.'

Rising to go – for I've seen him look at his watch – I remark that I myself have been in Verona twenty years and have always been treated as if I were in transit: sooner or later, like every other foreigner, I would do the honest thing: go away and leave them alone again.

'Oh the Veronese!' Pastorello exclaims. He seems to appreciate this shared resentment of the town we have chosen to live in. All the same, he wants to show me that he has got further in local affections than I have. Along the corridor, he opens a door and invites me to look at a large poster on the wall: it shows himself wearing a warrior's breastplate and yellow-plumed helmet on the great stone terraces of the Arena, the Roman amphitheatre. His beaming face and carefully clipped white beard look ludicrous in this costume. Presumably it was borrowed from a production of *Aïda*.

'They took that during the celebrations when Verona won Serie B the year before last.'

'The victorious gladiator!'

'That's right.'

But didn't the gladiators fight for money? I'm thinking as I drive home across town. Win one day, die the next? 'Die, Pastorello!' says a voice on The Wall that evening before the match. And now in the stadium at five to three on 11 February, my son is rocking back and forward on his seat and moaning and saying, 'I'll die, I'll die if they start their monkey grunts.'

The players have taken their positions. Tossed in the air, the confetti of torn programmes turns the *curva* white. The singing swells. We have to win. We have to win. The game kicks off. A long pass forward. A move on the right. Interrupted. Then Bari's Nigerian striker, Enynnaya, touches the ball. As at the flick of a switch, the monkey grunts begin. 'Oo! Oo! Oo!' But immediately afterwards a storm of whistles smothers the grunts. It lasts for about thirty seconds, then dies away as the fans concentrate on the game. Verona are attacking, nervously. The players seem scared of the ball. This match is just too important. Again Bari intercept, again there is the long ball forward to the red-shirted Enynnaya. At once the grunts begin, at once the whistles rise to drown them out.

This is new: the grunts, then the whistles. Oddly, they seem to be the same whistles that shortly before were drowning out the exhortations to avoid racist sentiments. To understand what's going on we shall have to stop a moment and look at that new regulation on racist chants more carefully. For one invariable and distinguishing feature of all Italian regulations is that they are complicated. Often hellishly so. If the racist chants are 'uncontested', the regulation says, the club will be responsible and the stadium banned. But if the chants are contested and 'covered' by 'normal' fans, then there is no penalty.

So how are we to judge whether a racist chant is covered or not? After all, somebody has to hear it before he can react to cover it. Enynnaya carries the ball a few yards. The die-hards begin their *oo oo*s. The rest of the *curva* begins to whistle. The *oo*s are drowned, but of course we know they are there; otherwise why would people be whistling so much? Is this what covered means?

As soon as the fans have discovered this new game, it happens every time the Nigerian touches the ball. *Oo oo*, whistle whistle. And since all the noise comes from the heart of the *curva*, not the rest of the stadium, I begin to suspect a sly complicity between the two groups: they are having their cake and eating it: the grunts *and* the whistles. It's pure theatre. Which is just as well, for the game so far is dire.

Then exactly on the half hour, entirely against the run of play, Bari get a penalty. It's mad. Gillet, their keeper, kicks upfield. The ball runs long. Gonnella is chasing back behind it, Ferron is hurrying to the edge of his area to meet it. The defender slows to leave the ball to the keeper, but suddenly both realise that it isn't quite going to make it into the box before the arrival of Bari's Osmanovski, the very man who won a penalty from us back in October. Ferron steps over his line. He can't use his hands now. The ball has bounced high. The keeper raises a clumsy left leg. He connects, but the ball strikes Gonnella in the chest and, with the terrible precision of catastrophe, bounces neatly over Ferron directly towards the goal. Osmanovski, needless to say, is haring after it. Ferron turns and grabs the striker's legs . . .

So you spend all week training hard, hour after hour, preparing for every eventuality, and then you go and make a mistake that most schoolboys know how to avoid. And this in the absolute crunch game of the season after three losses in a row. Ferron looks up. The referee is pointing at the spot. He pulls the red card from his pocket. Off! Which means Doardo again. Please spare us from Doardo! And some other player will have to be taken off to let even this least reliable of reserve keepers on. Who? Perotti is calling in Gilardino. There's a huge yell of protest from the *curva*. We absolutely *have* to win and the man takes off a striker! Doardo is putting his gloves on. Could he save the day? I imagine Puliero's inevitable response if he does. '*Miracolo! Miracolo di Doardo!*' The huge blond Andersson lumbers up, places the ball on the spot, gives the keeper one shrewd glance and crashes the ball into the net.

The one burning question that I chose not to ask Pastorello the afternoon before the game was, 'Will you fire Perotti if we lose?' Two members of the staff had indiscreetly told me that *il presidente* was already in touch with possible replacements. But I knew it was pointless asking.

'Perotti's finished,' Pietro agreed at half-time. 'Why on earth is he playing Cassetti in a game like this? The team is lightweight. Why has he left Oddo on the bench? Why did he take off Gilardino? And where's Mutu? What did we buy him for if he never plays?'

To Pietro's left, his swarthy friend says, 'Perotti *porta iella.*' *Iella* is something that goes beyond even the jinx. It's unspeakable bad luck. Meantime, my son is refusing to speak. He refuses the offer of a Coke from the vendor working his way along the terraces. Despite the cold afternoon, he refuses the offer of a packet of biscuits. 'They're awful,' he mutters. 'Awful.'

'Bring on *lo zingaro,*' the pessimist in front of us keeps repeating. He's beating two gloved hands together in a gesture that has nothing to do with keeping warm. 'Bring on *lo zingaro, dio povero!*'

Lo zingaro is 'the gypsy'. Mutu.

Time drags terribly at the interval. I try to think of Perotti. I think of his mild manners, his taciturn character, his modest man's defensiveness. 'Fire him!' I whisper to myself. 'Fire him, fire him, fire him!' He's ruining the team, he's ruining my book! What can he be saying to the players? What can he say that he hasn't had all week to say? The man has to go. Now!

As it turned out, it was Pastorello, not the coach, who did all the talking in the dressing room at this critical moment in the season. 'I went to give the players a big shock,' he explained to the *Arena*'s journalist after the game. This in itself must have been a pretty disturbing hint for Perotti. The coach's later comment was, 'Bari scored in the thirty-first minute. At that point I knew I would be coach until the ninety-fifth.' He added, 'I was also wondering what I could do to get the team out of the mess they were in.'

What he did was to take out the midfield player, Italiano, and bring on *lo zingaro*. Rumour has it that the coach loathes the boy, but no doubt he felt it was a card worth playing. Or perhaps the plan was to make it Mutu's fault as much as anyone else's. Nobody could say he hadn't fielded our star striker.

The players had gone off to whistles. They reappeared to gloomily determined chants of *Verona alè*. Duty chants. Not five minutes had passed when a through ball put Bari striker Bellavista alone in front of Doardo and only about ten yards out. He struck hard, sure of scoring. Doardo threw himself wildly. 'I just managed to get a hand to it,' he would later tell the newspaper. The video shows that the shot struck him casually on the knee to balloon away only an inch or so over the bar. Fate. A few moments later Mutu took a cross in Bari's area, fought off a storm of shoves and kicks from the defender behind, sent Gillet the wrong way and scored. It was a masterpiece. *Reeeeteeee!*

And at that moment the *curva* discovered that to yell Mutu, Moo-too, sounds almost exactly like yelling *oo oo*. The chant didn't even need to be covered by whistles. The fans were still at it – Moo-too! Moo-too! – in a triumph of mockery when five minutes later the Romanian jumped for a high cross beside Gillet. The keeper fumbled the ball, which kindly dropped right on to the feet of the hitherto invisible Camoranesi. He tapped it into the goal. We were ahead.

How everything speeds up in the euphoria that follows! The black Enynnaya was substituted in a tumult of grunts and whistles. Mutu was celebrated again as he miraculously sneaked in Verona's third. Moo-too! Moo-too! And in the dying moments of the game the Egyptian player, Said, dribbled past the whole Hellas defence to get one back for Bari and become the first Arab ever to score in Italy's Serie A. Three–two. Five goals. Every scorer a foreigner. 'Moo-too!' the crowd insisted. The gypsy boy took his bow under the *curva*. What a day for racial tolerance! What a break for Attilio Perotti!

18A GIORNATA

Bologna – Roma 1–2
Brescia – Udinese 3–1
Fiorentina – Parma 0–1
Inter – Reggina 1–1
Juventus – Napoli 3–0
Lazio – Atalanta 0–0
Lecce – Perugia 2–2
Verona – Bari 3–2
Vicenza – Milan 2–0

CLASSIFICA

Roma	42
Juventus	36
Lazio	34
Atalanta	30
Milan	27
Parma	26
Perugia	26
Fiorentina	25
Udinese	25
Inter	25
Bologna	24
Lecce	22
Brescia	20
Vicenza	19
Verona	18
Napoli	17
Reggina	14
Bari	12

Paranoia

A typical snippet of news in the magazine *Rigore* (from 9/3/2001) goes like this:

Passports – Summons for Recoba Delayed

It was ready a week ago! The summons for Recoba and Inter for false acquisition of an Italian passport was all set to be delivered. Then, in response to orders from above, everything was postponed till Monday. Why? Because on Sunday Inter were playing Roma and the powers-that-be didn't want to give the impression they were destabilising the Milan team before their clash with the league leaders. They were afraid Juventus [in second place] would accuse them of favouring Rome.

If it seems far-fetched to imagine that the judiciary would pay such careful attention to the football calendar, what about this, from 26/1/2001.

Perugia – Why Gaucci is furious with La Signora

['La Signora' is one of the nicknames for Juventus]
Luciano Gaucci [president of AC Perugia] believes that his two players Baiocco and Liverani were sent off in the game against Brescia so that they would not be available for the

following week's match against Juventus. It all began with a misunderstanding. During Perugia's game at Brescia, Moggi [the chief executive at Juventus] called the TV journalist at the match to ask how it was going. Informed that two Perugia players had been sent off, Moggi joked: 'Only two? We'd asked for more . . .' When a press agency carried this comment, Gaucci was enraged and in a fit of anger accused referee Boriello of having favoured Juventus.

There is no people more ready to imagine a conspiracy than the Italians. No people could be more constantly on their guard against the stab in the back, more willing to blame an unhappy turn of events on a diabolical plot against them. Why?

You haven't been long in this country before you notice how people have a vocation for arranging themselves in groups and factions: families, clubs, unions, whatever. And the characteristic of all these groups, whether they have official status or not, is that one isn't so much a publicly enrolled member – that will get you nowhere – as an initiate in an exclusive society whose actual powers and range of influence are never clarified or declared. How powerful exactly is Gianni Agnelli? Could the professor I am attached to at the university swing a national selection commission to make me a full professor? How much clout does Pastorello have in the Football Federation? Nothing is clear.

Of course, none of this is peculiar to Italy. In any country there is a gap between formal boundaries and reality. But the peculiarity of Italy lies in the exact balance between rival versions of the world, the equal intensity of people's emotional commitment to private loyalties and moral commitment to public justice. Everyone wants their team to win at all costs and everyone earnestly wishes the world to be fair. It's not an easy state of mind of administrate.

'Anybody with false papers should be expelled from the country at once!' Pastorello leans across his desk to tell me. He's furious. 'It's a fraud! It's criminal!'

But the Federation has decided that before the sports world can proceed to sanction the offenders 'penal law must first take its course'. Which means we are talking about a decision in five or ten years' time. At which point it will be meaningless to say: Verona wouldn't have gone down if Inter, or Udine or Vicenza, had been docked ten points. Procrastination, it turns out, offers the easiest compromise between intense commitment to fair rules and an equal determination to fight one's corner to the bitter end. The rules are always about to be reformed, in Italy. Things are about to be clarified, we promise, after the forthcoming event, which is of paramount importance to us. The cruel fight goes on.

Over lunch with Saverio Guette, the Hellas marketing man remarked, 'Martin Laursen always plays with total determination, even though he knows he is leaving us next year. This is part of his Danish Protestant upbringing. His whole personal integrity is at stake in his public behaviour on the field. Whereas your Italian, once he knows he is going elsewhere, is already thinking of new alliances, new masters, other prerogatives.'

'Oddo *vaffanculo!*' announces a voice on The Wall. 'You never make any fucking effort. You don't give a shit about the team.'

It's widely believed that Massimo Oddo already has an arrangement to play with AC Milan next year. He has completely lost the zest of the earlier games of the season. He picks up a pass on the wing and kicks it carelessly upfield. Caught on the break, he trots rather than races back. So suspect is his behaviour becoming that for the game against Udine he is replaced by the incompetent but willing Cassetti, who, since no one else wants him, is very much Verona's property.

Yet however paranoid some fans are about betrayals and suspect refereeing, this never prompts them to abandon the game. Rather, it intensifies their engagement, it makes them all the more eager to win *against the odds*. The more people are against us, the more players let us down, the sweeter the victory if we do scrape through.

Conspiracies or no, then, the Zanzibar has organised its bus as usual for the away game at Udine. It's 18 February, bright and cold. Since the Loma Band don't have a bus this week, some of their boys are travelling with us. As we're waiting to leave, Forza forbids them to taunt a couple of black girls approaching along the street. 'At least not here in town,' he complains. 'The police are just waiting for any excuse.' Already three hundred Verona fans have been banned from attending games this year. During the trip Forza tries to teach everybody how to sing the triumphal march from *Aïda* a little slower. 'With more majesty, *Dio boia*,' he insists. 'You should go to the opera sometime. It's slow. It's powerful. And we clap in syncopation. Like this. Got it? OK.'

Then this shaven-headed charismatic figure tries to persuade the boys from the rival group that this division of the *curva* into factions is a disaster. 'We should form an alliance,' he says seductively to two drunken teenagers. And I can almost hear the debates that are going on all over the country between scores and scores of different political parties on the right and on the left. 'We should form an alliance, otherwise we'll be wiped out.'

'The point is,' Forza says, 'you Loma lot claim to be right-wing, OK, but in fact you're behaving the same way the left does, whining, spoiling things. What does Rutelli do? He whines that Berlusconi has built up a TV empire. He complains. And what do you boys do, you tear down the leaflets we put up. You break up our chants. Why do you have to do that? We're on the same side. People on the right build things up,' Forza insists. 'They work together. The left and the *terroni* tear things down and whine.'

As we take our places in the stadium Forza tells us, 'The first chant is the one that carries the most impact. It sets the tone.' I find I'm right next to him, in the heart of the group. It's a bright, beautiful day. The small stadium with its old-fashioned stands is quaint and colourful. Forza's red scalp is gleaming in the sun against the green of the pitch below. He has an impish grin. 'So,' he says, 'what insult can we use for the Udinesi?'

It's a tough question. None of the younger folks seem to know. Down south obviously, the opposition are all *terroni di merda*. In Bologna they are *comunisti di merda*. In Turin they are *gobbi di merda*, hunchbacks. But what can we say of these respectable northerners way out on a limb near the Slovenian border?

'Come on,' Forza challenges us.

'*Slavi di merda*,' someone suggests.

301

The big man shakes his head. 'It has to be something that will drive them completely mad. Something that will get the afternoon off to a roaring start.'

Nobody knows. We've no idea.

'*Terremotati!*' he declares.

It's obvious. A *terremoto* is an earthquake. *Terremotati* are the victims of an earthquake. In 1976 the region of Friuli–Venezia Giulia, of which Udine is the capital, was devastated by a severe earthquake that caused thousands of deaths. So, in stark defiance of the standard contemporary rhetoric of compassion, we are going to insult these people by reminding them that they have been profoundly unlucky, that they have suffered. Perhaps there are people here who lost fathers or mothers in that quake. For a moment I feel I might be back in one of Giovanni Verga's rustic novels where the peasant community is always contemptuous of those who have been born poor or taken ill, or in some way fallen foul of that ultimate conspiracy of all, nature. If the final truth about the world is that it is a struggle for survival, maximum derision is reserved for the loser.

'This'll get them going,' Forza laughs. He raises his red face, the blue wraparound sunglasses. He cups his hands round his strong lips. His voice is huge. The tune is the ever serviceable 'Guantanamera' Now! '*TER-RE-MO-TA-TI!*' he sings and shouts together. '*Voi siete terremotati. Terremota-a-a-ti, voi siete terremotati.*'

Everybody joins in. There are only a couple of hundred of us, but half an hour before kick-off, the stadium had been fairly quiet. Until now. We have barely started a second round of the song before the place explodes with rage. '*Merda siete, e merda resterete!*' Forza rubs his hands. 'That's set the ball rolling,' he laughs. And I realise he's actually done the Udinese fans a favour. They are feeling properly angry. The game will mean more.

And so it did. It meant disaster for Hellas Verona who were certainly the unlucky ones today. This was the match when Leo Colucci finally made his comeback. He had gone out against Udinese in the second game of the season and he came back against them in the nineteenth. This lean dark southerner is not one of football's great talents, but his determination is total. *Meridionale* or no, the *brigate* love him. He's a constant presence, a volcano of energy. He wins ball after ball in midfield. He harries the classier Udinese players. He completely alters the psychology of the team. Oh if only we had had Leo all season, everybody is saying. Then just before half-time Udinese's international star Fiore catches Doardo half-asleep (for Ferron is suspended of course) and it's one–nil. Meantime Marco Cassetti has been stretchered off, writhing with pain in a way that made it clear we will not see him again this season. And so Oddo was back on the pitch again, playing miserably. *Iella*. It was *iella*. Then the Loma leaders arrived, obliging Forza to stand aside and sulk.

The match finished two–one. For Udinese of course. The police stopped our coach on the return trip. We were forced to pull into a service station. Some of the wilder boys opened the windows to shout insults. Again Forza intervened. Again he explained that the police were looking for any excuse to ban people from the stadium. 'Don't get yourself banned for nothing.' He himself had been banned twice, he confided to me. Once for insulting a policeman to his face. Another time for hitting a policeman, though the man had been in plain clothes and Forza had no way of knowing he was a policeman. 'I just gave him a slap. He could have been anybody.' 'What did you say to the guy the other time, the time they banned you for insults?' 'Only *pezzo di merda*, something like that. Nothing really. They can ban you without any trial or anything. You have no way of proving you are innocent. Then for a whole year, every time I watched the game on TV, I'd be in tears, honestly, not because Verona were losing or anything, but I'm constantly thinking, I could be there, with the *butei*.' Then he added, 'Perhaps I'm getting old, but I feel like a father to them.' Forza must be all of thirty.

The police stood outside. We were trapped in the coach. Twenty minutes went by. They had radioed reinforcements. Two further vans appeared, perhaps fifteen men in all. Meantime, Forza had succeeded in getting everybody to sit down and keep calm. They had stopped us for no reason at all it seemed. Nobody was even particularly drunk. They were just waiting for something to happen. The frustration at being trapped there would cause someone to do something unreasonable. That was the logic of it. 'Then they can beat us.' 'Keep your nerve,' Forza warned. 'Sit down. Don't shout. No gestures.'

It was like one of those movie scenes where the heroes have to restrain their legitimate anger, hide their true identity and wait patiently for the powerful enemy to lose interest. And it occurred to me that rather than a straightforward encounter between those who enforce the rules and those who have a habit of breaking them, this was just a stand-off between two factions with greater or lesser powers. It lasted forty minutes. We behaved. The police finally gave up. The moment their blue cars roared away, everybody broke out in a huge chorus of '*Senza divisa, chi siete senza divisa?*' Without your uniforms, who are you without your uniforms? Nobodies. But the word *divisa* also means 'the insignia that represents a society', or again, as my dictionary says, 'the colours of the insignia'. So it's as if we were singing: you have no real community, no team, no group worthy of allegiance. Only that dumb police uniform. So why are you getting involved?

I9A GIORNATA

Atalanta – Vicenza 1–1
Bari – Juventus 0–1
Inter – Napoli 1–3
Milan – Bologna 3–3
Parma – Brescia 3–0
Perugia – Lazio 0 1
Reggina – Fiorentina 1–1
Roma – Lecce 1–0
Udinese – Verona 2–1

CLASSIFICA

Roma	45
Juventus	39
Lazio	37
Atalanta	31
Parma	29
Milan	28
Udinese	28
Perugia	26
Fiorentina	26
Inter	25
Bologna	25
Lecce	22
Brescia	20
Napoli	20
Vicenza	20
Verona	18
Reggina	15
Bari	12

Latin Lover

Se non fosse per la mona, sempre Hellas Verona.
(If it wasn't for skirt, Verona always first.)
   Camelot@Hellas.it

I first met Martin Laursen back in October at the Povegliano supporters club dinner. Povegliano is a nondescript village in the dreary Veronese plain south of the city, a place where agriculture somehow contrives to be as ugly as heavy industry. In a smoky, low-ceilinged restaurant, three tables were arranged in a horseshoe. Laursen sat in the centre of the central table beside the very young Marco Cassetti. They were there to represent the team and give people a chance to meet the real McCoy.

In the event, the two players were as distant from the supporters as they are at the stadium. With the prettiest girls seated each side of them, they seemed tongue-tied and bored. The hundred or so club members and fans who had come to celebrate tucked into their food, a traditional mixture of pastas, meats and wines. The man beside me spent upwards of half an hour describing a recent holiday to the Red Sea where everyone, he said, was Italian. He was enthusiastic. 'At the airport in Sharm-el-Sheikh all the flights were to Italian towns. All of them!' His list of the destinations sounded very like the Serie A calendar. Turin, Naples, Bergamo. I suggested one might follow Verona's away games using flights from Sharm-el-Sheikh. The irony was not appreciated. Towards the end of the meal, evidently bored, Laursen and Cassetti cut a garishly iced cake – yellow–and–blue may look good in the stadium, but not on your plate – then allowed themselves to be photographed beside the youngsters. The girls only had eyes for the handsome Dane, who wore a white turtle-necked sweater that made his eyes magically blue. He seemed unhappy with the cigarette smoke. Fresh from giving away that penalty down in Bari, Cassetti behaved as though at any moment an irate fan might step forward and insult him. His long black hair fell lank over his face, he stooped. Towards ten-thirty, the players made their excuses and escaped. Everybody knows an athlete needs to be in his bed early.

How long ago that seems now! What an innocent time it was, just one drawn game into the season, when relegation was nothing more than the roar of a waterfall in some distant chasm. Now Cassetti is in a hospital bed – he will not play again this season – and Laursen is at the red-hot centre of controversy.

I met the Danish player for a second time shortly after our last-minute victory against Napoli. If you want to talk to a player, the best time to do it is after his team has won. We had breakfast together in a bar behind the Arena a stone's throw from his apartment. I have always wanted to live in the old centre of town but have never been able to afford to. Money is not a problem for Martin Laursen. We shook hands below the great Roman monument and hurried into the nearest *pasticceria*. The wind was bitter. To my surprise, he was wearing glasses. It seems he wears contact lenses when he plays. He looked like a polite American college boy, shivering in a big ski-jacket. At the counter he helped himself to two pastries and as soon as he was seated announced, 'It was always my dream to come to Italy.'

There it is again, that word dream. The new student magazine at my university is to be called *¿Dreams?* 'The dream becomes reality', announces a headline after another Chievo victory. Will they never be beaten? But Laursen's first months in the *bel paese*, as he now explained, had been a nightmare. And it can't be far from a nightmare that he's going through now as I start this chapter.

He grew up in Faarvang, he says, left home at sixteen for football college at Silkeborg, played for Silkeborg in the Danish Premier League, then woke up one morning to find himself in

Verona. Pastorello had paid two and a half billion lire for him. 'It all happened so quickly. The next day I got injured.'

He had damaged his knee. He needed an operation. He couldn't play or train, he had no friends and above all he couldn't speak a word of Italian. Hellas's management were kind to him, but seemed to have no idea, Laursen thinks, what it means to be alone in a foreign country. 'They invited me to dinner, but I couldn't understand a thing. I felt awful. They had paid so much money for me and I couldn't show them what I could do.' One day he decided to give up football; he had let everybody down. But on the phone his father insisted he stick it out. Even sinking into clinical depression, he was still making big money.

Then at last he was able to train again. The club suggested he work out with Vincenzo Italiano who was also recovering from injury. Spending hours and hours alone with the same person, he began to pick up Italian. Perhaps his friend's name was propitious. Cheered, he decided to go to a language school. He made progress. He met an Italo-Danish girl in a gym and fell in love. 'Everything is so much easier when you can speak the language and you have someone.'

Having missed out on most of the season, he made it back in the team just in time for the last games of Serie B with Verona leading the pack. 'I was the best player on the field,' he says. Next season he would be in Serie A. There was a possible deal for the future with the rich club Parma. A couple of months later he was playing in the Danish national side. The dream had come true.

Martin Laursen really is such an attractive boy, so sensible, so handsome; yet as he speaks, I am bound once again to recognise that a player's personal history and expert reflections are as nothing to the excitement of the game. He talks in detail about his reactions to the critics, his knee problems, his technical shortcomings trapping the ball. He admits that he checks his marks in all the newspapers the day after the game, that sometimes he even catches himself thinking of this or that critic when he makes a mistake on the pitch. 'Perotti is a mediocre coach,' he says. 'We respected Prandelli so much.' He wipes crumbs from his young lips and smiles. 'Now what do you want to know?'

'Have you ever watched a match from the *curva*?'

'No.' He is puzzled.

'Never?'

'Never.'

Martin Laursen has never watched a game from the *curva*. He has never stood in the pack and yelled behind the goal. I put it to this fine player that he perhaps doesn't realise how exciting football is, when you're impotent to do anything, when you can't see the far goal properly, when you're desperate to win. He smiles. 'Some day I must go and watch from the *curva*.' But recently the crowd's racism has been bothering him. 'You know, you think twice before going to wave under the *curva* these days.'

'Will we stay up?'

'I'm very worried,' he admits. Suddenly, the young boy has the solemnity of a politician talking about the dangers of recession. Players never seem to realise how absurd it is that the rest of us take football seriously. 'It's so tense in the dressing room,' he tells me, 'when we're in the relegation zone. It's horrible.'

But if it was tense back then in February, what must it be like now? Immediately after the Udinese game, Laursen amazed press, fans and colleagues alike by giving something more than the usual after-game interview: Hellas Verona, he announced, had played 'scandalously', they hadn't tried. It was unforgivable. 'There are those among my team-mates who seem to want to be playing in Crotone next year, not at San Siro.'

'Oddo!' the boys on The Wall decide. 'It's Oddo Laursen was talking about. He isn't trying.' Three months ago the player was their darling. Now, they hate him. Someone writes to say that Apolloni punched Oddo on the training field for not caring enough. Can this be true? In any event it's clear that there's mutiny in the dressing room.

'Oh Hellas, please don't give up' is the last message I read before setting off for the airport and Rome, the game with Lazio. 'Please, please, keep trying.' We are third from bottom. Napoli have beaten Inter, an extraordinary result. Things are getting hard.

And now I'm sitting on the parapet of the Ponte Duca D'Aosta drinking a beer under a grey sky and whiling away a little time before the game. I've just walked all the way up the Tiber from Trastevere, about an hour and a half's march in soft drizzle, past St Peter's, past the Castel Sant'Angelo, counting the dark cypresses against the ancient red brick. Now the rain has stopped and I've found a decent sandwich in a kiosk and am watching all the Lazio supporters in their pale-blue-and-white scarves flow over the bridge towards the Piazza Foro Italia and the huge structure of the Olympic stadium. I love to watch the home fans streaming to a game. I love the moment, perhaps half a mile from the ground, when the occasional passers-by are transformed into a purposeful crowd: the groups of lads holding their furled flags like swords, the fathers with their twelve-year-old sons. Everybody is hopeful and chattering. Everybody is marching to the stadium, entering the realm of compulsion.

I drink my beer. Spread open on my knees, the Rome paper *Il Messaggero* has nothing to say about the explosive situation in Hellas Verona's dressing room. Instead oceans of space are dedicated to another kind of dysfunctional family. In the small town of Novi Ligure north of Genoa sixteen-year-old Erika survives an attack in which her mother and younger brother are brutally slaughtered. She calls her boyfriend Omar. She explains to the police and her father that the attack was carried out by a gang of Albanians. It would not be the first such killing. Inevitably, the local Northern League organises a rally to protest against the level of illegal immigration.

But the following morning the police announce that they are charging Erika and Omar with murder. Erika's mother wasn't happy with her daughter's boyfriend. Erika was jealous of her younger brother. It's a horrendous scenario: scores of knife wounds on a little boy in the bathtub. But: 'She was an entirely normal, well-behaved girl,' a neighbour says of Erika. 'Omar was a completely normal kid,' says a schoolteacher. It's the refrain we hear after every atrocity. As if normality were a safe state of affairs. As if a normal human being wasn't an extremely dangerous phenomenon. Fatuously, it occurs to me that if only Erika and Omar had been football fans, if only they had yelled insults at the stadium and spat on Juventus supporters from the windows of the Zanzibar bus, perhaps none of this would have happened.

Then a voice said, '*Alè!*'

I looked up from my paper. Since Verona are twinned with fellow-racists Lazio, I was fearlessly wearing my yellow-blue scarf and Hellas hat. A good-looking man in his early thirties asks, 'Do you know where our section is?' He too has a blue-and-yellow scarf, he too had come down to Rome on his own. 'I have no idea,' I said. 'Want to go together?'

Marco – let's call him Marco – walked silently beside me. He looked hesitant, morose, in need somehow.

'Bound to lose today,' I tried. 'So hardly worth worrying about it.'

'*Per carità!*' he said.

'Best we can hope for is that Brescia and Vicenza lose too.'

'Right.' He wasn't interested, but seemed glad of company.

'And Chievo.'

'Fuck Chievo.'

We crossed the Lungotevere from east to west and passed the huge monolith raised to MUSSOLINI DUX. Beyond it, on each side of the pedestrian plaza that leads to the stadium, great white stones announce the successes of Fascism: 'XXIII March, 1919, Mussolini founds the Italian combat groups.' 'IX May, The Duce proclaims the foundation of the Empire.' No doubt if any such monuments were left in Verona, public television would have made sure to film them as proof of the city's right-wing vocation. Here they are just one more exhibit in the great Roman museum of imperial gestures: the pillars, obelisks, memorial arches and mausoleums that give the city its dusty grandeur. Rome is the one town in Italy where you feel the arrogance of empire weighing down on you. Everything is on a grander scale. No chance for Hellas, I repeated to myself. Don't hope.

At the end of the first half it was two–nil. No need to say who to. Marco had hung on beside me but said very little. There was a fierce tension about the man. He was well-dressed, had a pleasant, open face, but seemed angry. We were all angry of course. With Perotti; with the players. But he seemed angry with himself. He wasn't shouting. Despite our inevitable defeat, the spirit of the fans had been festive at first. We were enjoying being in this fantastically dramatic stadium, enjoying the warm welcome of the Lazio supporters, who roared out, '*Vi salverete*' – you won't go down – to console us after they had scored. Some of them even had Hellas flags. Then news came through that the bulk of the Loma Band had been stopped on the *autostrada* by the police and turned back, apparently because the boys were drunk. To protest at this cruelty, the remaining leaders insisted that we all sit down, remove the banners from the railings and stop singing.

'*Merda, merda, merda*,' Marco said.

As soon as we stopped singing, Hellas started performing. Moments into the second half, Camoranesi scored with a furious volley from the very corner of the box. Immediately, Lazio got another. But unexpectedly Verona seemed to be taking over the game. Perotti must have at last convinced the players that they could do it. Or at least that they now had nothing to lose. Two remarks of his during the week had impressed me. 'This is the most difficult moment of my life,' he had announced simply and solemnly in the aftermath of Laursen's accusations, 'both as a coach and as a man.' Of the team's performance at Udine, he added, 'It isn't enough to play well, like good schoolboys who've learned a lesson. When you shoot for goal you have to put your soul in the ball.'

Your soul!

In any event, Verona were attacking. The referee was the famous, the infamous Collina, shaven-headed, fierce-featured emblem of total authority. To be true to his iron-grip image, something he clearly works hard at, regularly stabbing his index finger at the players' chests and roaring at them to shut up, he suddenly and quite unexpectedly sent off the mild-mannered Martino Melis.

Melis had been given a yellow card in the first half of the match for a foul from behind. Fair enough. Now Lazio had a free kick in midfield. They had not, as far as I could see, asked for the

Veronese players to observe distance. They were taking it quickly. Melis was walking away from the ball. Collina blew his whistle and turned away to see where the kick would go. Melis, who had also half-turned, raised a leg. The ball struck him. Collina, who hadn't seen how casual the whole thing was, immediately showed him a second yellow card for failing to observe distance, and sent him off. It was the most capricious expulsion I've ever seen.

And at that Marco snapped out of his gloom. His whole attitude changed. He was beside himself, jumping to his feet, kicking the steps, yelling abuse. 'They're scared of us!' he shrieked. This was improbable. All the same, down to ten men, Verona scored at once. The young Gilardino this time. Three—two.

The fans were now fiercely torn between the need to protest about the police's harassment of the Loma Band, with silence, and the desire to support the team. People kept jumping up and sitting down. Because it was carnival time, many wore synthetic blue and yellow wigs and there were moments that resembled something in a Spielberg toyshop. Lazio scored another. Apparently it was over. But Perotti brought on the big striker Michele Cossato, the only home-bred Veronese in the squad. Since this combative man hardly ever gets a game, he ran on to the pitch furious and snarling like a dog. In less than ten minutes, at thirty-one years old, he had scored his first goal in Serie A, a wonderful header from a long curling cross. Then five minutes from time, Oddo, having played atrociously in defence, struck a free kick that went sizzling over the defensive wall. Marchigiani just pushed it round the post. Oh we were so close to equalising! In the final seconds, Lazio got a bizarre fifth with a lucky sequence of rebounds among defenders and attackers.

Throughout all this excitement, Marco had been quite wild, exactly the opposite of his behaviour in the first half. Now, when the police prevented us from going down the stairs to leave the stadium, he grew even wilder. What possible reason could there be for keeping us? he demanded. We were twinned with Lazio. There was no danger of any fighting. A fat, squat policeman, a caricature of Latin arrogance, with huge moustache and squat, fat cigar between his lips shook his head and refused to let us go. He got his men to form a cordon at the top of the stairs. Marco protested. He had a train to catch. He wanted to get home before midnight. The police put on their riot helmets and pulled out their truncheons. Two or three had tear-gas launchers. The fans sung. Some of them joked with the policemen; a tall, gaunt boy kept leaning down to re-light the fat cop's cigar for him, ironically patting his smart uniform, brushing some ash off his chest. But despite this good humour, they kept us there an hour. When finally we got to the gates we were met by a mob of cheering Lazio boys, mainly in their early teens, eager only to swap scarves. 'I've missed my fucking train,' Marco groaned. I said, 'My flight's not till nine, why don't we sit in a bar for an hour or so.'

So I heard his story. Married with two children, Marco had half-planned to use the excuse of the away game in Rome to start an affair. He had met a woman at a conference recently. In any event, he'd booked into a hotel last night and asked her out to dinner. It seemed she too had a boyfriend, but had sold the man some excuse. They had had a very pleasant and intimate meal. They walked for a bit around Piazza di Spagna and so on. 'But when it was time to invite her up to the hotel room, I didn't somehow.'

As a result he had spent half the night watching porn on the hotel's many channels, then all of this morning simply furious with himself, imagining the wonderful sex he could have had, if only he'd made a move. He was sure she was on for it. He couldn't understand why he hadn't been more decisive. 'Never used to have these problems. When I saw you on the bridge I was feeling like a complete fool.'

But now he felt great.

'Why?'

'Don't know. The game. I thought they played pretty well in the second half, don't you? I mean, you can't expect to win at the Olimpico. *Che bastardo, Collina!* But just being there. Camoranesi's goal. What a great stadium! When it ended, I just wanted to get home as soon as possible. Feel really glad now that I didn't do

anything. You know the mess you get into if you start something
with a woman.'

We finished our beer and I headed out to the airport where,
since this was the only Rome–Verona flight of the evening, I inevitably
came across Puliero and the whole of the team at the departure gate.
Apolloni was talking to Pastorello's wife, a small overdressed woman
with leather pants and stiletto heels. No doubt she uses fixtures in
Rome to get in a little high-class shopping. Foschi was grim. His
complexion looks worse every time I see him. Perotti, as usual, had
disappeared to Genoa. 'I can't deal with the bloke,' Seric said in
loud Australian. 'He takes me off at the end of the first half, and
only when the game's over he says, "Because I thought you'd hurt
your ankle." Doesn't even have the courage to tell me he thinks I
was playing badly. If he thinks I've hurt my bloody ankle, he can
bloody well ask me.'

'Great goal from Camoranesi.'

'Didn't see it,' Seric said. 'I spent the second half in the
shower.'

If only these players knew, I thought, what a service they were
performing for people like Marco, for all of us, for whole armies of
married men, not to mention all the adolescents who are spared the
business of killing their parents, then perhaps it would all be easier
for them to bear.

'At least Napoli lost,' I told Puliero. 'And Vicenza and Reggina.'

'Chievo won again,' Puliero said gravely. 'Who's going to listen
to me next year with Chievo in A and us in B?'

On the plane I sat alone and spoke to no one.

20A GIORNATA

Atalanta – Bari 0–0
Bologna – Napoli 2–1
Fiorentina – Brescia 2–2
Inter – Udinese 2–1
Juventus – Milan 3–0
Lazio – Verona 5–3
Lecce – Reggina 2–1
Parma – Perugia 5–0
Vicenza – Roma 0–2

CLASSIFICA

Roma	48
Juventus	42
Lazio	40
Atalanta	32
Parma	32
Bologna	28
Inter	28
Milan	28
Udinese	28
Fiorentina	27
Perugia	26
Lecce	25
Brescia	21
Napoli	20
Vicenza	20
Verona	18
Reggina	15
Bari	13

Protests

*In case they haven't taken a look at the league table,
or maybe they can't read, someone should remind those
shitty mercenaries and their puppet coach that we are
third from bottom!*
Lo Scaligero

Why do Italian players protest so much? No that's not quite right.
Why do players who play in Italy protest so much? For foreigners
soon adapt. In an article in *Rigore*, Claudio Ranieri, Italian coach
of Chelsea, makes the interesting remark that although his team
sometimes only has one English national on the pitch, nevertheless
they play like an English team: the fans, the atmosphere, the whole
dynamic of the country demands that they play like Englishmen.

Fabrizio Ravanelli, who has himself played in England but
returned to Italy a year ago, confesses that he should have known
better than to protest so much when, in Lazio's Champions' Cup
game at Leeds, he was brought down in the box. He was awarded
a penalty, but nevertheless insisted that the referee send the Leeds
defender off. The referee wouldn't. Ravanelli waved his arms and
shouted. The English crowd went wild and whistled every time he
touched the ball for the rest of the match. Afterwards he confessed
ruefully, 'I'd forgotten the English don't like you to protest about
these things; but normally of course the Mister tells me it's part of
my job to protest to the referee.'

In the Liverpool–Roma match for entry to the UEFA cup
quarter finals, the Italian team had their captain, Damiano Tommasi,

sent off for protesting after the Spanish referee appeared to give Roma a penalty, then changed his mind and gave a corner instead. Tommasi, a Veronese, is famous for being Italy's most politically correct player. Involved in a variety of charities, he speaks endlessly of the need to clean up football. He was prominent at the Pope's famous peace game. He never, it seems, uses foul language on the pitch. Yet here he was getting himself sent off for prolonged and vociferous protest. Why do they do it?

Once again, it has to do, I suspect, with the society's uneasy relationship with the rules it sets itself. An article in the *Arena* announces: '*Cartelle pazze*: to pay is to consent!' The *cartelle pazze* or 'crazy tax demands' are a new invention of the cash-hungry bureaucracy. Using heaven knows what computerised methods, the tax office sends out hundreds of thousands of demands, telling you your declaration of three or four years ago was wrong and that you have a few hundred thousand lire to pay. Then the public radio service warns you that many of these demands may be wrong. But then of course they may not be. Perhaps the government's calculation is that since most people lie about their income anyway, they will be glad to have got away with a relatively small fine.

The anecdote the article recounts is as follows. A man receives a demand. By the time the post brings him the bad news, the deadline for payment is no more than a few days away. So he pays at once. Then his accountant tells him that actually his declaration was OK. He goes to the tax office to reclaim the money but is told that the act of payment is officially considered an admission of guilt, and hence there is now no redress. The first thing one must do before paying any tax demand, is protest, whether or not you are in the wrong.

Perhaps really this is nothing more than a development of the Biblical invitation: ask and it shall be given. The same article also discusses a fascinating aspect of pension law. For some years an elderly woman didn't realise she had a right to a state pension. Eventually she went to the pension office, but was told that, not having made a request for the pension at the appropriate time, she has no retrospective right to have it. If in doubt, make a request!

Make demands! Protest constantly. The laws are ambiguous and fragile. The referee may be inclined to favour a big team, but your protest might remind him of his respect for the regulations. The rule itself isn't so much sacred as a weapon in the power game. One person protests that it must be applied. One person protests that it would be inappropriate to apply it. Hellas Verona's next three games, against Atalanta, Inter and Vicenza, were all characterised by the most vigorous protests, all decided by refereeing decisions taken after agonising moments of hesitation.

It is 1 March. My son has written one hour to make my mobile phone sound off the triumphal march of *Aïda* when someone calls: *Gialloblù, gialloblù-ù-ù*! it trills. The *Arena* has announced that on Good Friday in the *duomo* the Via Crucis will for the first time be read in local dialect. Is this a reaction to Santoro's criticism of our bishop's attending a mass in Latin? The weather has turned cold again after a brief false spring and Hellas, third from bottom, once again *have* to win at home. This time the opponent is Atalanta.

Even before the game starts, someone is protesting: the so-called *popolo di Seattle* are in Trieste. Overstretched, the police protest that our game – 'one of the most dangerous encounters of the season' – be postponed. The fans protest that if it's played on Monday afternoon there won't be a crowd and we'll lose home advantage. It is part of a plot against Hellas. Time for Pastorello to show what his political connections are really worth: what's the point of kissing the Pope's hand and constantly being photographed with celebrities of the sports world if one of the most important games of the season has to be played on a week day? In the event the Football League refuse to move the game. 'A thousand thanks to El Pastor,' someone writes to The Wall, 'he may be a shit as a man, but at least he has the right fucking connections.'

The morning of the game it rained heavily, then suddenly a warm sun appeared, drew up the moisture from the ground and faded into a white disc in thick haze. 'The Bentegodi is now the worst pitch in Serie A,' the *Arena* protests. 'A bog.'

In the stadium, yet another form of protest awaited us. I didn't understand it at first. We sat down as usual and I could sense something was wrong, but what? Finally Pietro, the ever-faithful keeper of seats, explains, 'No banners.' Of course. The whole Curva Sud is dark and grey. The parapet in particular, usually a patchwork of colourful emblems and flags, is just one long stretch of grey concrete. Finally someone hands us a leaflet:

TIRED OF BEING GUINEA PIGS

UNDER CONSTANT PRESSURE, VERONA'S CURVA SUD IS TIRED OF BEING USED FOR TARGET PRACTICE.

NONE OF US HAS EVER EXPLOITED VERONA'S COLOURS FOR ECONOMIC OR POLITICAL ENDS, BUT THERE ARE THOSE WHO USE US FOR THEIR OWN ENDS:

The leaflet goes on to list the culprits:

THE CLUB: WHO ATTACK US TO HIDE THEIR OWN INABILITY TO CONSTRUCT A COMPETI- TIVE TEAM.

THE POLICE: WHO WITH THEIR THREATS AND UNFOUNDED ACCUSATIONS ARE RUIN- ING INNOCENT PEOPLE'S LIVES TO FURTHER THEIR OWN PERSONAL CAREERS.

OUR MAYOR: WHO CLAIMS SHE HAS BEEN THREATENED BY US AND, LIKE A MAGISTRATE DEALING WITH SERIOUS MAFIA CRIMES, GOES AROUND THE TOWN WITH AN ARMED, ANTI- TERRORIST POLICE ESCORT.

THE CITY'S CHIEF PUBLIC PROSECUTOR [PAPALIA] WHO HAS OPENED A CRIMINAL INVESTIGATION INTO THE FAMOUS 'OO-OOS'.

THE MASS MEDIA: WHO ARE USING THE ENTIRE CITY FOR THEIR OWN FILTHY SECRET AGENDA.

THE SO-CALLED 'REAL FANS': ALWAYS
READY TO SPIT POISON ON THE *CURVA* IN
THE BENTEGODI, BUT NEVER THERE TO SUP-
PORT THE TEAM IN OTHER TOWNS.

AND LAST OF ALL THERE IS THE TREAT-
MENT THE FANS WERE GIVEN LAST SUNDAY
ON THEIR WAY TO ROME.

FOR ALL THESE REASONS, TODAY THE
CURVA WILL HANG OUT NO FLAGS OR BAN-
NERS OR COLOURS OF ANY SORT BUT WILL
BE LEFT GREY, GREY AS THE HEARTS OF
THOSE WHO LIVE AND SUFFER FOR HELLAS.

As ever when I read the *curva*'s announcements, I feel a mixture
of admiration and dismay for the rhetoric they use. There are echoes
of Garibaldi, echoes of D'Annunzio. But it wasn't quite true that
no banners would be hung. For just before the game began, an
immensely long slogan – black letters on white – was unrolled and
suspended on the central parapet:

SOLO CONTRO TUTTI
Alone against the world.

'Do Atalanta have a black player?' I asked Pietro. He shook his
head. 'Thank God for that.'

The players line up for the start. Today their shirts pointlessly
announce the club's opposition to torture in the world's police
states. Michele muttered, 'More police state than this!' And then
he said, 'The only torture here is going to be the result.' My son
is growing more and more silent as the year progresses, more and
more morose. I worry for him. Atalanta are fourth from top, they
are having a wonderful season. What's more, in the January transfer
market they bought Morfeo, our hero of last year. He's back. On
the wrong side.

But Verona begin brilliantly. It's really months since we saw them play so well. Camoranesi is on form, a tiny Indios figure dribbling the ball wherever he chooses. Mutu is behaving himself and looking bright. Even the gloomy Salvetti seems to have woken up. And just ten minutes into the first half it's Emiliano Salvetti – the man who, on the return from Lecce, seemed to me one of the saddest youngsters I'd ever met – who crashes in a goal in the mêlée that follows a corner.

It was a few moments after that that the crowd's quarrel with Doni began. Cristiano Doni is Veronese, a tall talented midfielder largely responsible for Atalanta's success this year. But he is also formally under investigation for match-fixing after members of his extended family betted against the odds on a result unfavourable to Atalanta and got the score exactly right. Doni and various others should surely have been suspended. But as ever the Federcalcio's way is to let enquiries go on *ad infinitum*. Doni's still playing. And being a rash man, in the frustration at finding his team unexpectedly outplayed by lowly Verona, he commits a couple of bad fouls and collects a yellow card. So the *curva* begin to taunt him about his betting problems: '*Calcio scommesse, voi fate calcio scommesse!*' 'Football fixers.'

Inevitably the game grows tense. Then just moments before half-time, Morfeo performs one of the small miracles for which we worshipped him so much last year. Picking up a loose ball outside the box, he back-heels at once to send Doni, arriving in full flight, clear through the defence. The big man streaks into the area and hits the ball straight into the top corner of the net. It's a wonderful goal. Even in your misery you can't help but admire. Then, to the fans' shocked surprise, Doni runs to face the *curva* and makes the gesture of holding a finger to his lips, as if saying shush to a rowdy child.

What on earth possessed the boy to launch such a challenge? For the whole of the following week The Wall would be filled with shrieks of indignation: 'It seems impossible', writes Il Bandito 'that a Veronese born and bred should have made that gesture to the mythical yellow-blue *curva*.' No sooner was Doni on the pitch for the second half than the monkey treatment began. As if to demonstrate that in the end grunting has nothing to do with blacks or racism, the *curva* was giving the works to a local boy.

I often wonder if this deafening and very specific racket distracts the players. Is Laursen thinking, Good, they're giving Doni the grunts? Is Doni thinking, Now I'm going to play even better and silence them again? The minutes slip by. Verona are in deeper and deeper trouble. They've lost the sparkle of the first half. We have to win. When you always lose away, you have to win at home. Perotti grows desperate, brings out defenders, throws in strikers. But already we're into the last ten minutes. Atalanta respond by taking off Doni and bringing on another defender. They're settling for a draw. The odious scorer goes off to a gale of whistles but again has the temerity to make a gesture of derision to the crowd and, instead of retiring to the dressing room, goes to sit by the coach on the bench to watch out the last few minutes. '*Doni Doni faccia da cul*,' the *curva* are singing. Arse-face. They won't let him be.

It was after this game with Atalanta, standing under the shower at home, that I first asked myself: who was it, more than a century ago, who decided that ninety minutes was the right length of time for a game of football? Who was it who understood that the players would be able to hold up for about eighty, or even eighty-five minutes, but that very few would have the stamina for the full ninety? It's in the last few minutes that everything starts to happen. However much they've trained, the boys are exhausted, they begin to make mistakes. And it's in the very last minutes, as the result is about to crystallise, that the crowd's frenzy reaches its climax. '*Su, su, su!*' everybody is shouting. Up up up! Meaning upfield. Attack! But we might just as well have been willing the team up the league table point by desperate point.

Monday's *Arena* always lists the scoring opportunities minute by minute:

Cross in the 80th, Cossato brought down as he goes up to head. No penalty, the ref says.

   Corner at the 84th, Bonazzoli heads across the goal, Laursen and Gonnella both slide together at the far post, but the ball escapes by a whisker.

Cross from Salvetti in the 86th, Cossato heads just over the bar.

Three chances in six minutes. Atalanta had stopped playing. They were all in their area, panting, hands on their thighs, praying for the end. Magically, the crowd were putting energy in the home team's legs.

'Cross from Melis in the 88th, again Cossato heads, this time just wide of the post.'

The *curva* is a storm. Anxiety is exploding. The opponent is on the ropes, but we have to find the knockout punch. Then in the ninetieth minute, as the *Arena* reports, Melis crosses from the left. At the far side of the area Camoranesi takes the ball high on his chest. Or did he control it with his arm? In any event he dribbles round his man and from the top of the six-yard box sends the ball back across the area to the left. Salvetti is there. 'Not Salvetti,' Pietro always groans. He crashes in the most perfect of shots. His second goal of the day.

The referee points to the centre. Goal. But the Atalanta players won't accept it. They're protesting. The coach, Vavassori, a big bluff man, is protesting. He's on his feet. He's on the pitch. Handball! they're shrieking. Camoranesi has slunk away. The referee consults the linesman. The linesman indicates that from his position Camoranesi was covered by a defender. He didn't see how he took the cross. A knot of players has formed. People are pushing and shoving. And now Doni is on the pitch again. Substituted, he's nevertheless come back on to protest! The Atalanta players obviously believe they might convince the referee to change his mind, the way so many of us have convinced a ticket inspector not to fine us, a policeman to ignore an illegal overtake, a teacher to improve an exam result. The *curva* go back to their monkey grunts. *Doni Doni, faccia da cul.* It's pandemonium. The seconds tick by. Then the referee is holding up a red card. It's for Doni. He's sent off a player who was already off! The man will have to miss the next game. The fans are in a delirium of pleasure. Got you! Arsehole! At the other end the Atalanta fans are fighting the police. A tear-gas canister has been fired. The police are throwing Atalanta's banners down from the parapet.

Somehow the referee gets play going again. Three minutes of injury time are given. Morfeo is at his most violent and provocative. He's chasing Mutu. What must it be like to live through these moments on the pitch, trembling with tiredness, deafened by the crowd, exhilarated by unexpected triumph? Out of his mind with excitement, the Romanian gives our ex-darling a hefty shove. Morfeo leaps backwards as if he's been shot. He rolls around pretending he's received an elbow in the face. Video will show there was no such contact. The crowd know it. The two players had been facing the *curva*. It was just a shoulder-shove. But the referee goes directly for the red card. Mutu's off. And it's here that one has to ask oneself whether Atalanta's protest wasn't worth something after all, for surely the referee is partly acting in an attempt to show he is being fair. He is sending one of our lot off as well. In fact our key man. Mutu too will miss the next match. The game ends with the rules dissolving into anarchy and the players collapsing with cramps. Ninety-three minutes. Perfect. Whoever it was decided how long a game should last, they got it just right. Hellas are back in business. Doni has been punished. Salvetti is a hero. We've even learned to hate Morfeo. I never want to see him again.

2IA GIORNATA

Bari – Fiorentina 2–1
Brescia – Lazio 0–1
Milan – Parma 2–2
Napoli – Lecce 1–1
Perugia – Vicenza 1–0
Reggina – Bologna 2–1
Roma – Inter 3–2
Udinese – Juventus 0–2
Verona – Atalanta 2–1

CLASSIFICA

Roma	51
Juventus	45
Lazio	43
Parma	33
Atalanta	32
Milan	29
Perugia	29
Bologna	28
Inter	28
Udinese	28
Fiorentina	27
Lecce	26
Brescia	21
Napoli	21
Verona	21
Vicenza	20
Reggina	18
Bari	16

San Siro

*We really must sing like mad on Sunday, we must
give them such determination that when they run they
plough up the pitch, I want those miserable peasants
in overalls to have to work hours and hours to put clods
back where they belong!!!*
Offab, boi@chimolla

If only the political battle could be resolved in ninety minutes! On 10 March the President of the Republic, Carlo Azeglio Ciampi, finally tells us when election day will be: 13 May.

That's sixty-four days away. And the election, of course, is only the beginning of the battle. Centre-left deputy Massimo Mauro, erstwhile footballer and winner of two league championships along-side Platini and Maradona, announces that he won't be standing again. 'It takes too long to get a result in politics,' he explains. 'When you go on to the pitch you know you'll come off ninety minutes later, for better or worse, with a final score. When you go into government you work for months and months only to find there's no parliamentary time for the law you have drawn up.'

To add to the general blurring of boundaries, *Rigore* fields an article on the growing tendency to describe the election campaign in football terms. The advantage of this, the paper decides, is that football metaphors simplify things and de-dramatise (favourite Italian word) a potentially contentious situation. I'm standing in the big piazza outside the Curva Sud as I read this reflection. It's 11 March. This afternoon we'll be playing Inter away. The wind is tugging at the paper. And honestly, I can't believe it. How could anyone who regularly goes to the stadium imagine that the use of football terminology could *de-dramatise* an already comatose election campaign? What on earth could be more dramatic than those last ten minutes against Atalanta, against Napoli? When have I ever seen collective passions more violently aroused? How could contemporary, management-driven politics possibly be as dramatic as this? 'I will never forget', Massimo Mauro says, 'my debut in Serie A. Catanzaro–Milan Nineteen eighty. Nor will I ever forget my first day as a deputy in a packed parliament. But the latter was a different feeling, it wasn't so intense.'

And don't tell me, I say to myself out loud, that football vocabulary *simplifies* things! My wife, who is an extremely intelligent woman, doesn't even begin to understand the complications of the offside trap. 'You can count me out as a translator for this book,' she tells me. 'All this weird terminology is beyond me.' 'There's one team in form,' says Roberto Formigoni, member of Forza Italia, governor of the Region of Lombardy, whose plans for giving financial assistance to private schools have just been vetoed by central government in Rome, 'and that team is the Lega Nord. But we're obliged to play away [in Rome] with a referee who always favours home teams and is likely at any moment to give them a penalty or stretch out injury time for as long as they need.'

What's simple about that?

Explaining, at a press conference in Peking, why the government didn't manage to pass its electoral reform during the five years of the present parliament, Giuliano Amato remarks: 'The opposition [i.e. Berlusconi] was time-wasting before we were even into the second half. They used ruthless *catenaccio* tactics of a variety not even Milan [Berlusconi's team] ever used.'

My wife wouldn't even begin to understand this, I tell myself, never mind the poor Chinese journalists. No, politicians don't use football terminology because it's simple, and least of all because it tones things down. They use it because for the most part politicians are men and football is the most exciting thing they've ever been involved in. Standing outside the Bentegodi, I'm already nervous.

Will Verona at last get a point away? Inter have been playing miserably of late. In the end, they only have seven points more than us.

I'm waiting for the charismatic Forza to travel by car with him to Milan, San Siro. And the reason I'm waiting for Forza, rather than travelling in the special train, which is even now pulling out of Verona Porta Nuova with the bulk of the fans, once again has to do with protests and rules. The Brigate Gialloblù have long had a *gemellaggio* with Inter, a friendship, a twinning. But the Loma Band, or Butei della Curva, as they call themselves, want to break it. They would have broken it when Inter came to the Bentegodi, but there are strict 'rules of honour' which state that a *gemellaggio* can only be broken away from home, when there are less of you than of them.

In any event, Forza and the old group from the Zanzibar are against breaking the *gemellaggio* because they have friends at Inter. So, in protest at the Loma Band's decision, they are refusing to travel by train and have arranged a fleet of cars. I've been invited to join them. In the general fizz of factionalism that reigns in this country, whether at the university, the stadium or in politics, it is always wise to make sure that you do actually belong to one group. Otherwise you are a pariah. For myself, I seem physiologically attracted to losing factions: the literature brigade in a university that is fast becoming a marketing school, the Zanzibar faculty in a *curva* that is going Loma.

Of all Italian stadiums, San Siro is the one that most amazes. Or is it just that I'd had so much to drink by the time I arrived? Perhaps ten cars departed from the Curva Sud. Five of us were packed into a small Opel. Forza is driving, his girlfriend, the charmingly tough, sly-mouthed Raffaella, sits beside him. In the back are Marta, recovering from a hangover, and Mauro, a wiry, self-confident loudmouth who starts telling me about his experiences at Oxford. He went to attend a language school, but then stayed and joined the university. 'Love England. Love the English.' He even rowed, he says, in the bumps. Can this be true? I don't press him. He seems nice enough.

The cars are supposed to stay together, but at the first service station our group gets stuck at the bar for more than an hour. All kinds of people keep appearing. Old friends, old enemies. This is the way with service stations on the road to a game, not unlike Rome airport for the players. Suddenly I find myself standing beside Aiooogalapagos, he of the Più-mati. Doardo, he tells me proudly, comes from his home village of Colognola ai Colli. This calls for another round of drinks. In no time at all I'm on my third. It's extraordinary, I'm thinking, how the Italians sell beer in *autostrada* service stations. And extraordinary too that the red-faced Forza isn't drinking any. 'Driving,' he explains. He stands there patiently with his Coke while the two girls get tipsy.

'Why do the Loma lot want to break the *gemellaggio*?' I ask.

'Because nobody obeys anybody any more,' Forza says. 'Inter's leaders couldn't stop some of their troops from attacking us. There was even a stabbing. All the same, I think it should be saved.'

I've often thought that the progress of individualism is at once harder to chart and more dramatic in a society traditionally split into fragments. Sometimes you mistake for individualism what is only factionalism. But when the tightly knit faction itself breaks down, then you're splitting the atom. It's explosive. In the more faceless Anglo-American institutions nobody cares what you do.

'It's getting harder to keep a *curva* together,' Forza goes on. 'The old days are gone. Since you can't fight the other fans, people fight each other.'

Nodding, I tell him about a game last week in Serie D where two players from the same team started fighting because one was blaming the other for having made the mistake that allowed the opposing team to score. The referee sent both of them off and the team was thrashed.

'Bet it was down south,' Forza said.

It was.

'There you are.'

'Why did your lot lose control of the *curva*? Why don't you take it back?'

Forza is pragmatic. 'Well, theoretically we could. But we just don't have the balls any more. We don't want it enough.'

To hear him, it might be Cioran analysing the difference between the satiated decadence of western Europe and the raw aggression of the emerging Slavs.

'It's a question of how brutal you're willing to be, you know? If deep down you don't really want trouble, then you're lost, it's time to step aside.'

And so it was that afternoon. In the two or three minutes that I was in the loo on entering the stadium, Forza and Mauro ran into some Loma boys on the terraces. Somebody felt that Mauro looked at him in a way not entirely respectful. The boys attacked. A dozen against two. Forza went down but was then left untouched. He's respected. He has a past. But Mauro, who has the manner of the braggart, with thin blusterer's moustaches, was seriously kicked and punched. When I found them again he had a tooth chipped and cheeks cut and swollen. He sat on the steps, head swaying, unable to stand for fear of fainting. Curiously, the two girls travelling with us, who had stood to one side, assured me that this final acknowledgment of the shift of power had been expected for a long time. Meantime Forza didn't seem overly unhappy with the result. How many things there are, I thought, that I still don't understand.

And how many different ways there are of building a stadium! While the huge Delle Alpi and oneiric Olimpico open outwards like generous saucers, turning your face up to the tallest skies, San Siro is severely vertical and closed. Eight or a dozen fat towers with spiralling walkways support massive, dungeon-dark walls. It's sort of futuristic re-think on a very grand scale of a form that is decidedly medieval, a fort or bastion, at once tall and square, as if the Bastille had been transformed into a leisure centre.

Inside, stacked one above another like boxes at the opera, the terraces slope very steeply downwards to plunge right to the touch-line. There is no athletics track. Above the head, the sun and stars are forgotten. Eighty thousand people thus face each other at the closest possible quarters. It's an unparalleled scenario for mounting the thundering chant. And no sooner were we packed into our tiny segment than the Inter fans took advantage of it to break the *gemellaggio* before we could: *Verona, Verona, vaffanculo.* The chant was different today, formal somehow, like the tearing-up of an old contract. Later, a few hundred Inter supporters tried to get across the terraces and attack us. But again the gesture seemed more a ritual than a real attempt at violence. The police were well-informed and prepared. They had their gear and they were there in force. There was no getting past them.

'Pretty unimpressive,' Forza complained. Despite the fact that he hadn't wanted the break-up, he seemed disappointed by how tame it all turned out to be.

As for the game, it might be summed up in a small sub-title at the bottom of a full page dedicated to the match in tomorrow's *Gazzetta*: 'Ferron's Protest: "There was no penalty."' Having filled columns of print with flattery for a team whose supporters make up a large proportion of the paper's customers, the little article, set apart in a box that is not for the consumption of Interisti, admits that Ferron is right. At the very end of a first half in which Bonazzoli missed an open goal and Adailton struck the post, Ferron rushed out to dive at a through ball. Vieri came charging towards him and, although Ferron was already stretched on the ground before the big striker arrived, he deliberately ran into the man and fell over. The referee was uncertain, but the linesman raised his flag and thus decided the game.

'At least Chievo aren't winning,' Pam said. I had found this pillar of the Più-mati at the very top of the guest section. She was standing erect and grim in a pink jacket, arms folded, gaze set, like Napoleon at Waterloo. The news had just come up: Chievo 0 – Ravenna 0. But incredibly, as we soon discovered, all Chievo's rivals had lost. The dam boys had extended their lead. 'It can't be happening,' Pam shook her head. 'It can't be.'

On returning home that evening, I opened the Più-mati's site, Solohellas.net, but then discovered that the familiar link from that to the official Hellas site had been cut. A window appeared on the screen: 'Cutting this link is my way of beginning the protest against an inept management that has thrown away years of hard work.'

Beside this sombre statement was a photograph of a hearse with the Hellas badge on the door.

But down in the basement where we keep our TV, my son just can't get over Vieri's dive. He's watched it a dozen times on the video. 'He dived. He dived! And Morfeo last week, pretending he'd been hit when he hadn't. How can they look at themselves in the mirror? Why don't the guys who give out the suspensions do anything about it? They could easily say, OK, Vieri dived, out for a game.'

My son is right. They could do that. They could clean up football.

'Why don't they, Dad?'

While I've never had any trouble talking to my son about God and death, and even sex, these matters are more perplexing.

'Because in the end, Mick, people must want things as they are.' Really, this is the only conclusion I can come to. The game is how we want it. Otherwise this obvious cheating would be punished. People don't want their sportsmen to be men of moral stature. They don't want the rules to be absolute. They want protest and drama. They want a scenario that they can argue over till doomsday. 'We lost,' Michele says, 'but we didn't deserve to lose.' There is a dour satisfaction in his voice.

Asked about the end of the *gemellaggio* between Verona and Inter fans, Rino Foschi says grimly, 'Ridiculous. The serious thing is the game. There was no penalty.'

22A GIORNATA

Atalanta – Milan 1–1
Bologna – Lazio 2–0
Inter – Verona 2–0
Juventus – Reggina 1–0
Lecce – Udinese 2–1
Parma – Bari 4–0
Perugia – Fiorentina 2–2
Roma – Brescia 3–1
Vicenza – Napoli 2–0

CLASSIFICA

Roma	54
Juventus	48
Lazio	43
Parma	36
Atalanta	33
Bologna	31
Inter	31
Milan	30
Perugia	30
Lecce	29
Udinese	28
Fiorentina	28
Vicenza	23
Brescia	21
Napoli	21
Verona	21
Reggina	18
Bari	16

Qwerty

*Ever and only Hellas Verona, everything else . . .
nomads outside the city gates.*
Ivan, Vicenz@cittàsecondaria

My friend Roberto and I are concerned about a mutual friend,
Alessandro, a man in his fifties. His affair with a plain young
Neapolitan girl, barely twenty-two, of no special intellect or personality, has being going on for almost three years. Every week,
twice or three times, he risks all kinds of trouble with wife and
family to see the girl for no more than ninety minutes. Exasperated,
Roberto, an AC Milan supporter, tells me, 'I said to him, Sandro,
I said, I have the video of Milan beating Ajax to win the European
Cup. Fantastic game, historic moment. Orgasm for the *rossoneri*. You
know. I've seen it, what, a dozen times. But in the end, enough is
enough, Alessandro. Enough! How many times can you watch Van
Basten slotting it in? People start to find you weird. Get on with
something else!'

How many times? Football and erotic experience have this in
common: there's an inevitable sameness about each game, each
encounter, yet a seemingly inexhaustible yearning to repeat. Both
generate around them a mad abundance of mental material: conversation, boasting, dreams, writing, nostalgia, photographs. If the
most common kind of website is pornographic, football can't be far
behind. In a German hotel on a Saturday midnight, alternate TV
channels will be showing girls or goals. What else is there? The
same limited series of poses, of actions, are endlessly contemplated.

And lying on your bed, zapping back and forth between one and the other, you can't help asking yourself: how different are we then, one from the other? Every sexual embrace is the same embrace perhaps, every goal is the same goal. It's a needless superabundance.

Then Sky Sport interviews Maradona and with some relief you tell yourself: no, Maradona was unique. On CNN they're showing old footage of Marilyn Monroe. Monroe was quite unique, you're obliged to reflect. You're relieved. Paul Gascoigne is definitely an unrepeatable phenomenon, you finally acknowledge, going back to Sky Sport. Would we ever want to repeat it? So the mind toggles back and forth between a vision where we are all an expression of the same unchanging human spirit, nothing to choose between us, nothing to choose (take note, Perotti) between Bonazzoli and Gilardino, Mutu and Adailton; or a vision where we are every one of us quite individual and irreplaceable. 'What will we do without Laursen next year?' someone writes on The Wall. 'Stay with us, Martin, or I'll kill myself.'

Between these two forms of aberration lies what makes all our gloating and repetition possible: the particular time, the special place, the combination or collision of historical circumstances – blonde hair, an awkward bounce, a sudden downpour and, above all, the surrounding community, the other people you come across. Monroe doesn't exist without Kennedy and Joe DiMaggio. Who would Gascoigne be without Tottenham and England and Jimmy Five-bellies? It's the freshly shuffled pack that makes each new card game possible, the weather, or a bout of flu. And so, although this book is nothing more than the repetitive account of thirty-four games of football, let me insist that the twenty-third game, the derby between Verona and Vicenza, most often repeated of all Verona's games, was, despite the poor-quality football, nevertheless quite special. For one young man in particular it marked a crisis point in his life.

It was Friday 16 March. I had watched Hellas training under heavy rain. Again! Having dried off back at the office, I was surfing through a different kind of liquid, a deluge of insults between Vicenza and Verona fans on The Wall. As ever, what strikes you about these messages is the sense of a shared identity in a centuries-old antagonism. 'Dear Vicentino,' reads one message, 'the only thing you have to be proud of is the hate you feel for us . . . without us you wouldn't exist.'

How reassuring it all is! The teams and their fans, the towns and their stadiums, their women, monuments and restaurants are all interminably compared and contrasted. The Vicentini are happy to sign themselves *Lane*, Wools, in remembrance of their industrial past. The Veronese never forget to condemn them as *magnagati*, cat-eaters, in remembrance of their previous poverty. 'We have the finer architectural tradition.' 'We have a bigger centre and better entertainments.' And all the while the validity of furiously opposed visions of each other is allowed to hang on the result of Sunday's game. The game will decide which town is superior. 'Ready to lose the nth derby, arseholes?' writes a Vicentino. 'Poor dreamers, for you SERIEEEEE BBBBBBBBBBB HELLAS = NAZI.'

Then right in the middle of the most animated back and forth, a sad and unexpected truth emerges. Not everybody involved in this culture war will be able to come to the game. A new contributor, who signs himself Qwerty, confesses that his girlfriend 'doesn't let him come to the stadium'. She has other ways of spending Sunday. Football and erotic experience may have much in common, but they rarely mix. Qwerty is facing a major conflict of allegiance. 'Dear Aiooogalapagos, Pam, Penn,' he writes, 'since it seems there's just a chance that I'll make it to the game, tell me where the Più-mati hang out so I can meet you . . .'

'OK,' Aiooo replies. 'Looking down at the field from the top of the *curva*, move left from the main entrance. *Welcome to paradise*.'

But paradise is notoriously hard to get to. Other fans from both sides of the Verona–Vicenza divide break off their insults to help this man on the road to salvation:

'Qwerty, don't tell me you're going to miss the derby!!! I left a girlfriend because she wouldn't let me go and see Verona–Monza, in Serie B . . . *Dio can*, show her who's boss!'

'But Qwerty, how can you let yourself be sodomised like this? It's Verona–Vicenza, for God's sake. Shit, it's just two or three hours, you're not going to be away all day. *Dio bono*, I've been married four years and was engaged for ten before that and I've seen all the games at the Bentegodi, all of them!'

Qwerty is humbled: 'Dear Bandito, dear Icio, dear Pam, I'm sure you're right . . . but, well, hmm . . . in any event, you never know, the long work of slow and gradual persuasion continues and I haven't as yet despaired of achieving positive results (at least she lets me hear Puliero on the radio these days . . .)'

Bandito, as his pseudonym suggests, goes more for the *fait accompli* than the patient negotiation: 'Listen, Qwerty, on Sunday, you get on your Vespa and head off to the stadium without a word to anybody. You go home at five, and without making any comment you take the lady to AT LEAST THREE SHOPPING CENTRES . . . You'll see: next year you'll be with us in the *curva* every Sunday, away games included.'

But that's a high price to pay: 'Bandito, shit, not one but three, THREE, shopping centres! I hate the places. Still, I promise I'm doing everything I can to be there. Meantime, I'd like some advice from the Hellas girls, Pam, Cinzia: what about, if, in return for being able to go to the game, I offer, in this order:

To shave every day (or almost)

To buy a new shirt or two to replace the worn-out rags I have

To take her to the lake more often . . .

Do you think that will be enough?

The girls don't respond. The man signing himself Icio is unimpressed:

'Qwerty, that's pathetic. All you have to do is look your lady in the eye and tell her that she's a very special gal, that without her you'd die, that you'd scale K2 for her, that no other woman, repeat, NO OTHER WOMAN is as good as her, that nowadays no other girl, however luscious, so much as turns your head, so absolutely and completely are you pleasured, satisfied and indeed overwhelmed by her vivacious beauty . . . that for her you would throw yourself from any bridge, parapet or in general high place and that, above all and finally, for her and only

for her on Sunday you are going to the stadium to watch THE
DERBY!'

Will Icio's method work? Does Qwerty have the panache to
pull it off? On Friday evening, just before everyone knocks off
from their work computers, the discussion is still going on:

'So, Qwerty, are we going to see you Sunday or not?' It's
Aiooogalapagos.

'Dunno, Aiooo. Hope so. Tonight, I launch the decisive offensive. In any event, looking down at the pitch, I go to my left from
the top of the stairs. OK? Presumably I'll recognise you.'

'No problem. We're under our banner.'

So Sunday afternoon, looking down at the pitch, from my
position on the east of the *curva*, I also turn left to where the
Più-mati have hung their banner. Is Qwerty there? How many
of the thousands of young men milling on the terraces have had
to struggle to be at the Bentegodi today? How many will return
home to anger and resentment? And how many not present at the
stadium today are resentful and angry because this time they were
the ones to back down? Didn't I myself have to tell my wife I was
going to write a book about football before my presence at all these
games could be agreed?

Since we've arrived very early today, I pop back down the
stairway to get myself an espresso in the bar. In the throng of men
pushing back and forth in the broad corridor I feel wonderfully at
home. People you hardly know salute you. People you've never
seen exchange a comment on the game. It's the intimacy of
strangers, an experience that makes the web and the stadium so
similar. Chatting to a supporter with a stud in his tongue, reading
an anonymous message on The Wall, you at once feel an intense
complicity, a complicity often directed against those who are most
important to you in your life, those who would rather you didn't
come to football games. Is one of these boys Matteo, I wonder,
shoving my way to the till? I scan the faces. About a month ago
someone started e-mailing me match reports after every game. He
has heard I am writing a book. Later he revealed that the season had
become so important to him because he was going through a painful

break-up with his girlfriend. He signs himself Matteo, though I have
no idea if that's his real name. I have never met him. No doubt he
is somewhere down there in the heart of the *curva* where Qwerty
yearns to be. In any event, here is his account – received the same
evening – of this most crucial of all derbies.

So, I left home just before two nourishing within me the
firm conviction that one way or another, however tough
it might be, I would be bringing home the three points.
The pressure rose of course during the long wait, the long
back and forth of the players warming up for the game –
and the nice thing at this point is to enjoy yourself with
your friends trying to see which eleven are going to start
the game. Beppe Colucci is there but not Italiano. That
was a surprise. Fucking Perotti. Camoranesi comes in and
someone next to me starts waving an Argentinian flag.

In the event, Camo is the one who gives us the biggest
buzz in the first half. He runs, pushes, blocks, searches out
Bona way up front. Giant Bona shoots, Sterchele punches
it away as best he can. Verona step on the gas, maximum
acceleration, we're looking great, Laursen is everywhere. At
one point he gets four headers in a row, beating Vicenza's
strikers in the air every time. NO WAY THROUGH.
Vicenza are losing hope. But we still haven't scored. Captain
Leo heads over the bar, Mutu shoots past the post. IT'S
NOT ENOUGH.

Half-time. The two *curve* glower at each other, insult
each other. We have a banner that says: 'Watch out for
spongiform cat disease.' And then another with a Whiskas
advertisement.

Second half begins as a bit of a mess. We can't keep up the
pressure. Then Camoranesi invents a long through ball, as
ever for Bonazzoli. Bona hasn't been playing well recently,
certainly he hasn't looked that good today, but he's got grit
and to spare. Left-back Cardone makes to block him. Bona
leans on him a bit, but if you ask me it's mainly the defender

who falls over on his own, looking for a foul. Fool! The referee doesn't blow. Sterchele gets a foot to the shot but the ball goes straight back to Bona and he shoots into the bottom corner. GOAL!

Mad run to celebrate under the triumphant *curva*. General delirium, inevitable yellow card for leaving the field of play. Doesn't matter. Calm down. Hold on. Fortunately the red-and-whites are mediocre. It's us on the attack again. Mutu goes down (oh that knee! Stretchered off, we'll hear the worst during the week), Italiano takes his place, then Cossato comes in for Bona looking more than ever like a growling dog.

Five minutes' injury time and at last the suffering is over. I'm clapping, I'm happy, I'm shouting, we're that bit nearer to saving ourselves. Napoli have drawn, Brescia have lost, Lady Luck is beginning to smile on us at last. In my mind I'm flicking through the calendar, I'm thinking about the two tough games ahead, Rome away, Juve at home. There's all week to wait. Tension. League tables, calculations. If we beat Brescia away, if we get a result with Fiorentina and Lecce at home, and then down in Naples we could always snatch a . . . The fan in stand-by mode. Not the best feeling in the world. All the same, two points up on the fourth from bottom, I can sleep a little more soundly now.

So, last night, to celebrate I opened a bottle of excellent Marzemino, the wine Mozart's Don Giovanni celebrates. May the celestial gods come to our aid. But for the moment, with Horace, 'Nunc est bibendum'. Ciao, Tim!

Poor Matteo, every time Verona win he feels better about leaving his girlfriend; every time they lose, it's more of a catastrophe. But what about Qwerty? Monday morning, nine a.m. on the nail, he sends his first message to The Wall:

'Morning all . . . ciao Pam, ciao Aiooo, great Monday, what else can one say?'

Pam is furious: 'Qwerty, I shouldn't even speak to you after the way you let us down yesterday . . . still, I imagine that your punishment (nice afternoon with the radio?) was exemplary. Ever and only Hellas, everything else . . . your girlfriend!'

So they didn't meet. But that doesn't mean Qwerty wasn't there.

'Pam . . . if I'm not much mistaken I was actually watching the game about five metres from you . . . oh yes . . . after long negotiation, permission granted and Qwerty all present and incorrect. Don't believe me? Want me to describe the girl I reckon was you?'

It's the worst thing he could have said.

'Qwerty, aside from the fact that, no, I don't believe you, even if you were at the game, you're a shit!!! You didn't come and speak to us. Why not? Choose from the four following options:

You are ashamed of us.

You are ashamed of yourself.

You weren't there.

You don't exist.'

For my own money, the explanation is that Qwerty only got his permission by convincing his girlfriend that it would be an interesting experience for her too. Once in the stadium he feared she might grow suspicious if he tried to introduce her to the blonde and attractive Pam, always prominent at the heart of the Più-mati. Or perhaps having read the fierce messages of McDan and Cris@do-I-bother-anyone, he was afraid they might be beyond the pale and shock his precious partner. While I love to see girls at the stadium, my feeling is that it's always a mistake to take a girlfriend you care about unless she would have gone without you. At the game, the fan wants to be Mr Hyde, not the respectable Dr Jekyll, and this can be hard for a non-footballing partner to take. No doubt Qwerty spent the whole game being too respectable, wishing he could cross those five metres to the Più-mati and roar.

23A GIORNATA

Fiorentina – Bologna 1–1
Lecce – Inter 1–2
Milan – Bari 4–0
Udinese – Parma 1–3
Verona – Vicenza 1–0
Napoli – Perugia 0–0
Lazio – Juventus 4–1
Reggina Roma 0–0
Brescia – Atalanta 0–3

CLASSIFICA

Roma	55
Juventus	48
Lazio	46
Parma	39
Atalanta	36
Inter	34
Milan	33
Bologna	32
Perugia	31
Fiorentina	29
Lecce	29
Udinese	28
Verona	24
Vicenza	23
Napoli	22
Brescia	21
Reggina	19
Bari	16

CD Rom

Watch out, Roma! On Sunday we're going to steal the Coliseum . . .
Il Bandito

In early April I sat on a thesis commission in Milan where four or five graduating students presented theses on the CD Rom as a new medium for narrative. The students, for the most part pretty young women, are excited about CD Roms. Perhaps they imagine that the essential nature of storytelling has changed, and with it the balance of power between themselves and the older generation. 'The simultaneous deployment of text, picture and sound together with the interactive nature of the medium make it at once more involving and more intense than traditional forms of text–bound expression.' So reads a typical conclusion.

I am sceptical, but a little nervous too. And as the tedious afternoon drifts by, it dawns on me: Tim, you should have presented this book as a CD Rom! Football is a game after all, why not make one's approach to it a form of play? I sit there, fiddling with my pencil, listening to the eager student, my mind suddenly thronged with all the ways I could have engaged people had I gone for the CD Rom: pictures of the *curva* seething with banners, highlights from the games, endless links between cities, teams, sports, politics. Just to think of the rich back and forth of all those connections is quite intoxicating. And there would be sound too: the witty slogans, the *curva* in full song, the wild roar when the ball balloons the net. I can already see the reader opening the hypertext map, skimming through a list of games, the names of the players, who was on the bench at Delle Alpi, cam-shots in the Zanzibar bus. Damn. I've made a great bollocks of it all. This book should be a CD Rom!

One of the characteristics of the Italian thesis commission is that if the student presenting his or her work is not your student, you are free to ignore the presentation, to read a book perhaps, write a letter, mark exams. Some professors even chat to each other. *Sotto voce* of course. In this regard, being a professor on a thesis commission is altogether less demanding than, say, being a linesman in the Stadio Olimpico.

Linesmen!

Sitting in the theatrical professorial gown that establishes my role, I feel my body temperature rise. Linesmen! If I had written this story on CD Rom, I tell myself, a click on the entry 'Linesmen' would have taken the reader straight to 1 April, April Fools' Day, straight to the magnificent Olimpico, and the fifty-fifth minute . . .

While the girl defending her thesis with microphone and mineral water speaks of 'the new parameters that will have to be developed if we are to offer adequate criticism of hyperfiction', I rapidly jot down all the links that would take us to last week's game in Rome.

Tickets: I remember opening my wallet on the Thursday or Friday and experiencing a quiet surge of contentment on finding that stiff pink-and-red ticket snuggled there among the dwindling bank-notes: 'AS Roma vs Verona, Stadio Olimpico, Settore Ospiti.' Yes, just possessing a ticket – this will have to be said somewhere, whether in book or CD – makes the world a better place and myself a calmer person. There it is. Safe in my wallet. It can't be taken away from me. I'm sure all fans feel this: the immense reassurance of the ticket bought!

'Police' might be another important link. I am writing rapidly now as the student expounds on the CD Rom's use of 'cognitive space and symbolic metaphor'. Or again, 'Supporters' clubs'. On Saturday evening, 31 March, just as my train was pulling into Roma Termini, I received an SMS on my *telefonino*. 'Il Lupi Scaligeri request the honour of a drink with Il Parroco [my nickname has not only stuck but travelled] on the evening before this historic encounter.'

Il lupo, the wolf, is the Roman animal *par excellence*, the beast that suckled Romulus and Remus, twin sons of Mars. The Lupi Scaligeri are a small (very small!) group of Roman citizens who support Hellas Verona. 'I don't believe it,' the passenger beside me shook his head when I explained. We had fallen into a conversation. 'Why would they do that?' You can see his point. It would be like someone born and bred near Stamford Bridge supporting Burnley.

'Why do you do it?' I demanded towards midnight. I was getting excited, what with the beer and the ticket in my pocket. 'You grew up here,' I said belligerently, 'you still live here. In Rome. Support Roma, for God's sake! Or at least Lazio. Why not?'

The Lupi's answers were unsatisfactory. 'My aunt is Veronese,' says a small barrel-chested man. 'We went on a school journey to Verona in my teens,' says another. And one very quiet fellow could offer no explanation at all. It then emerged that he works as a parliamentary reporter for the tiny and attractively subversive Radio Radicale; and even later it came out that he is a signed-up member of the stuffy and now almost extinct Partito Repubblicano. This lucid, intelligent man, I realised, as he talked about Radio Radicale and Il Partito Repubblicano, has constructed his whole identity around the support of minuscule but embattled minorities and manifestly lost causes. What other connection could there be between the notoriously right-wing Brigate Gialloblù and the infamously left-wing Radicali, or for that matter the austere and obsolete Repubblicani?

'*Ragazzi*,' I finally put it to this bizarre fragment of footballing fandom, 'supporting Hellas in the eternal city of Rome is a pathology. You guys have big personality problems. In the powerful centre of empire, you hunger for provincial martyrdom. You're sick!' And all the Lupi Scaligeri nodded eagerly and laughed and raised their glasses and together we cried, '*Forza Hellas! Forza gialloblù!*'

The *presidente* of the thesis commission raised her eyes and looked from one side to the other along the row of distracted professors. 'So,' she was saying, 'if none of my colleagues has any further questions, *la signorina* may retire while we discuss her presentation.'

This passing invitation to those not directly involved in a thesis to make some comment upon it is the merest formality, not unlike the clergyman's 'If any man can show just cause or impediment . . .' No one ever intervenes. Why should we? We don't want to upset the tutor involved. We don't want to pester a student who is about to be given her degree. Above all, we don't want to be in this room a moment longer than is necessary. But today, after what was now the third or fourth eulogy to the CD Rom as the future of narrative, and perhaps precisely because I had become so distracted with the notes I was making, I suddenly found myself intervening:

'Er, *Signorina*, you have mentioned that the CD Rom brings the user or consumer closer to reality because it involves the simultaneous use of various media.'

'That's right.'

My colleagues were open-mouthed.

'You have also suggested the superiority of the non-linear and interactive nature of the medium to the tedious and obsolete linear succession of the pages in a book, pages that the reader is obliged to take or leave, as they come.'

'That's right.'

'I was just wondering' – I toyed with my notes – 'whether perhaps it wasn't precisely this linearity, this succumbing to the sequence of events that brings written narrative so close to our experience of life, and thus makes it so seductive. In the end, we all find ourselves involved in stories whose ends we cannot know and over which we have little control. We turn the pages in an agony of expectation, wanting to know how things will turn out.'

The student, a good-looking girl, turned to her thesis tutor with the expression of one who has been betrayed. This question hadn't been expected. She was unprepared, the way Doardo seemed so unprepared that day against Bari when Ferron was sent off and the boy suddenly found himself facing a penalty beneath the Curva Sud. Doardo just dived to the right and hoped. The girl, whose tutor could help her no more than Perotti on his bench can help his players, fell back on a defensive *non-sequitur*.

'Obviously, we can't say that the CD Rom is already superior to the traditional narrative. I mean, it's in an embryonic stage, we don't know how the form will develop or what it will lead to. All we can do is wait and see.'

'Precisely,' I said. 'The development of the CD Rom is a linear narrative. It unfolds page after page.'

Rete! Gol!

When the girl retired, my colleagues evidently thought that I had been aggressive and unkind. Why had I done that? I'd never been so unpleasant before. How could they have known that I had been thinking of the football season, of the terrible fact, as I prepare this book, that I cannot know whether Perotti will be fired or not, or whether Verona will be relegated or not, I can only wait and see.

If I did the book as a CD Rom, I thought as I hurried away from the university, it would lose the pathos of the sequence. The games come one by one. And then certain people I know would only click on the matches we won and never on the defeats, the way my son now only videos the highlights of Verona's victories, and refuses to bother with the games we lose. 'Dad, what's the point of five minutes of Bonazzoli not putting the ball in the net?' So I could hardly expect, on 1 April, that he would be recording our performance at the Olimpico. What chance had we got against Roma, the league leaders?

Again I walked up the Tiber. It had rained only the day before, but this afternoon the light was so bright that the fierce dark of the umbrella pines seemed scissored out of the midday sky, while the Renaissance brickwork and the white stone of the baroque stood out against each other in harsh and beautiful contrast. What a rich scene this is: the hills with their churches and fortresses, the quiet pull of the river, the loud political posters, the vendors selling red-and-yellow hats, scarves, flags, pennants, the swelling crowd drawn with simmering excitement to the great magnet of the stadium. My ticket in my wallet, I was in a reverie of quiet pleasure when all of a sudden a beer bottle struck the pavement beside me. Then another and another. I was under fire.

This happened round the north side of the stadium. I had been approaching the *settore ospiti*. Came the blast of a siren. That meant the buses of the Verona fans were approaching. In seconds the innocuous crowd around me had been replaced by a group of a hundred or so Romanisti with scarves tied round their faces and caps pulled down over their eyes.

The police had sounded their sirens, alerting the Roman welcoming party, but they hadn't radioed ahead to warn their colleagues to have the big gates into the guest sector opened. Two buses arrived. A group of perhaps forty policemen formed a cordon to defend them. I was no more than two or three yards away, heading for the gate, when the shower of bottles came from behind.

I was wearing no colours. I have no desire to find out what it is like to be stabbed in the buttocks. But as a result I could not run towards the police and the gate. The men were gripping their truncheons. They wouldn't understand I was a Hellas fan. Yet I was so close to the gate that I couldn't run back to the Romanisti. They would know I wasn't one of them. I decided to stand still.

It lasted two minutes. The police held their line behind their big riot shields. The gates swung open. The buses, repeatedly hit by cans and bottles, rolled forward to safety. It was over. Luckily, I hadn't been hit. I hadn't even been afraid. That was strange. Then, just as I imagined that we were back to normality – for the Rome fans had begun to disperse – the police ran past me and charged them from behind. They didn't arrest anyone. They caught two or three and gave them a good beating, and that was that. A routine Sunday afternoon.

When I think back on this incident – the arrival of the buses, the bottles and beatings – it all seems quite inexplicable. I can't believe that the police sound their sirens *on purpose* to generate trouble. Yet that is the effect. I can't believe that they planned to wait until the Rome fans were dispersing and vulnerable before attacking them. But that's what they did. And if the Rome fans really wanted to attack the bus, to do serious damage, why didn't they gather at some other place, the *autostrada* tollbooth, for example, not the ceremonious gate to the Olimpico.

No, this is one of those incidents that cannot be explained by assessing the conscious intentions of those involved. You have to look at the end result, the social function. And the result was that the group identities of the Veronese, the Romans and the police were all powerfully reinforced, while adrenaline ran in rivers. Never have I felt more *gialloblù* than when I got into the stadium that day. Never have I shouted louder, right in the core of the Loma Band. I sang myself hoarse. I remember a chorus of '*giochiamo con voi*' that lasted at least ten minutes. And when Verona scored – yes, we scored – I was pleased to find myself in a chaos of jumping falling surging bodies. It was the most exciting moment of the season. The whole vast Olimpico, sixty thousand Romanisti with their red-and-yellow scarves, silenced by the tiny figure of Mauro Camoranesi, obliged, in their misery, to listen to five hundred Veronese roaring their scorn.

And then came the business with the linesman.

Verona scored after twenty-five minutes. They held on easily till half-time. Nor did they show any sign of collapsing at the beginning of the second. But a huge tension was building up in the stadium. Juventus were beating Brescia in Turin. If things remained as they were, Roma's seven-point lead at the top would be cut to just four. The crowd howled at every decision against their team. The scene was set.

There is offside and offside. There is the ball launched forward by the midfield while three strikers break for goal on the edge of a ragged line of four opposing defenders. Anybody can be forgiven for getting this wrong. But when the defence advances and a striker is left behind, static, alone, and then receives the ball over the heads of the tall centre-backs, then there is no excuse. So it was. Evidently offside, Totti receives the ball, passes across the face of the goal to the advancing Batistuta who shoots, poorly, against Apolloni, whose interception goes into his own net. The spell was broken. Ten minutes later the big team were three–one up. The Lupi Scaligeri were drowned by an ocean of red-and-yellow.

Returning home late that night it was to find the Hellas website steaming with indignation and paranoia.

'Offside, Totti??? What on earth are we talking about . . . I'm telling you, the linesman checked very carefully on his new Rolex and saw perfectly well that it was not the right moment to raise his flag . . .'

It's a reference to a scandal of a couple of years ago when Roma's president, Franco Sensi, was found to have given Rolex watches to all the Serie A referees.

More ominously, there was this: 'Here we are complaining about Totti, but what do you think we're going to get next week with i Gobbi [Juventus]? Reflect, folks, reflect. Davids will hack like a butcher, completely unpunished, Inzaghi will at last find an "understanding ear" – butei, I'm afraid the big yellow–blue heart won't be enough against those old thieves.'

It's uncanny, coming back to my notes now more than a month after the event, to think that this man, tapping on his keyboard after another disappointing Sunday afternoon, could have got it so exactly right. It was as if he had already clicked on a link and seen next week's game before it happened.

24ª GIORNATA

Bari – Lecce 3–2
Atalanta – Napoli 1–1
Juventus – Brescia 1–1
Milan – Lazio 1–0
Parma – Bologna 0–0
Perugia – Inter 2–3
Reggina – Udinese 1–1
Roma – Verona 3–1
Vicenza – Fiorentina 1–1

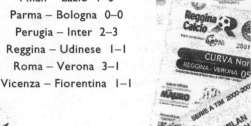

CLASSIFICA

Roma	58
Juventus	49
Lazio	46
Parma	40
Atalanta	37
Inter	37
Milan	36
Bologna	33
Perugia	31
Fiorentina	30
Lecce	29
Udinese	29
Verona	24
Vicenza	24
Napoli	23
Brescia	22
Reggina	20
Bari	19

Caporetto

Blah blah blah, 'NEVER AGAIN SERIE B' . . .
Blah blah blah, 'NO TEAM OF MINE HAS EVER
BEEN RELEGATED' . . . Blah blah blah, 'ALL
WE HAVE TO DO IS WIN AGAINST OUR
DIRECT RIVALS' . . . Blah blah blah . . . DIE,
PASTORELLO!
    Cinzia, solohell@scontrotutti

It's 25 April. This morning, three weeks after the trip to Rome, two weeks after the game with Juve, an e-mail popped up on my screen bearing the legend 'Re. Caporetto'. It's a familiar and unhappy name. In October 1917, after two and a half years of trench warfare on the frozen peaks of the Alps, the Italian army was overwhelmed at Caporetto, north-west of Trieste. In a matter of days, and despite the most courageous rearguard action, vast areas of the *patria* and six hundred thousand troops were lost. So when I see that e-mail appear, I know exactly what it is about. And I know that I have no desire to open it. I'm still in the denial phase.

Now it's Wednesday and I'm travelling in Germany with my laptop and my mobile phone. A brief reading tour. At a presentation last night a nice young woman asked me why my novels deal with such sad subjects. In response I fielded the idea that one of the vocations of fiction is to find some pleasurable way of talking about those terrible things we feel we need to talk about, because they're so important to us, yet at the same time shy away from, because they're so painful. 'The novel seeks to cast a spell', I romantically suggested, 'that makes it possible to enjoy the contemplation, at least while we are reading the book, of all those things that are painful to us.'

Then, retiring to my room after the obligatory celebratory dinner with booksellers, I found an SMS on my phone, from Andy, one of the Lupi Scaligeri. 'I thought we'd touched bottom Sunday', the message says, 'but last night [Monday evening] Hellas surely plumbed new depths.' New depths, I wondered. Was that possible? 'I'm in Germany,' I tap out my response. 'Haven't seen the papers. What's up?' The reply comes back. 'Perotti to stay.'

Perotti. The only scrap of silver lining, I had thought, Sunday afternoon, slouching out of the stadium with a funereal crowd, will be Perotti's inevitable resignation. How could anyone stay after a performance like that? 'Pastorello on tranquillisers,' the *Arena* had announced before the game. And afterwards? Would psycho drugs be enough? I myself was awake into the early hours. And now Wednesday morning, in Cologne, while all of Italy celebrates the day the country was finally rid of German occupation – for 25 April is Liberation Day – I find this message 'Caporetto' in my e-mail. Caporetto, the unacceptable defeat, the final humiliation. How, I wonder, staring at my laptop, how could any writer cast the spell that will make all this misery a pleasure?

Sometimes, in the midst of the flood, the mind grabs at the strange coincidence, clutches at an incongruous piece of flotsam in the waves, and so rides down safely over the rapids. Concentrating on the uncanny, you are spared from considering the rest. I can but try.

Before the game with Juventus I had a long talk with Gigi Apolloni. On the trip to Lecce and again at the airport returning from the Rome game, I had found our centre-back severe and off-putting. His close-set eyes and protruding brow under dark copper hair give him an air of angry gloom. Yet he smiled warmly when we met in the foyer of the Hellas offices. He had his five-year-old daughter with him, another intensely coloured red-head. 'My wife's in hospital,' he explained. 'Food poisoning.' A smaller child was with a babysitter but he had no one to look after Irene. The little girl held out her hand.

I immediately offered to cancel the meeting. 'Not at all.' He was earnest. It was as if I had an important job to do and he was determined not to let me down. We went into the conference room and sat at a large polished table beneath a giant TV screen. This is where the team watch the videos of their defeats.

'Sit down and be patient, Irene,' he said.

Having three children myself, I knew that this wasn't going to work and went back to reception to find the little girl some paper and pens. Then what I wanted to ask this most experienced of our players, a man who has played for Italy and in European cup finals, was how the team, individually and together, dealt with extremes of stress protracted over such a long period of time, what did the players do when the press were heaping scorn on them, the fans whistling, their market value falling? How do you pass from the cauldron of the stadium to the breakfast table the following morning?

Apolloni joined his hands together on the table, sat up straight in his club blazer and began to make a series of the most general remarks: the players grew up with this, they are used to a ferocious selection process. He paused. 'Anyhow, the fortune of a football player is to have a partner who understands the state you're in after a bad game, because the danger is that you might take it out on her, or on the kids. So in a way,' he goes on, 'it was maybe easier when I wasn't married at all and went out a lot with the other players.' He stops, perhaps wondering if he has contradicted himself. 'Now I don't go out very much.' He adds, 'Of course, you always have to remember, however bad things get, that you're lucky and that this is probably the best job anyone could ever have, playing football all day.'

At once I fear that, like Martin Laursen, Luigi Apolloni won't tell me anything I hadn't already imagined. 'Shush Irene,' he snaps. The man has a fine soft voice and a rich Roman accent, but he was being very abrupt with his little daughter. 'Be quiet and sit still, I have to talk to this gentleman.'

He begins to tell me the things he thinks I should know. A player is always learning even after a lifetime in the game. Every goal conceded is a lesson to be studied with humility. On the other hand, the racism in the stadium shouldn't really be taken too seriously because it's just part of a tradition of stadium insults. '*Irene, basta!*' He hesitates, pondering a moment. 'Group spirit is desperately important.' He wanted to insist on this point. Was he trying to tell me that Verona don't have any?

'Sometimes you're pretty violent,' I tell him.

As we speak, Irene has finished a picture of a little girl pushing a pram and tosses aside the paper.

'Football's incredibly tense. Sometimes you lose your head. Italians are very tense people. The game is more stressful in Italy.'

As with so many conversations, it's as if I had arrived in the country yesterday, or as if the difference between Brits and Italians was so great that it could never be overcome or even truly measured: like the difference between men and women, perhaps. But now Apolloni is telling me of a famous occasion when he elbowed a striker in the face causing some damage. 'I was ashamed. I mean, I really wished I hadn't done it. But you get nervous, you know, you're working each other up all the time, and if he's sharper than you on the day and you feel he's going to score you get tense. Things are bound to happen.'

'Does the coach or the club ever encourage the players to be violent or to cheat?'

'It's in your character,' Apolloni casts about. 'It's how you were brought up and what you saw at home.' Then, unprompted, he says something that any Englishman living in Italy would be shot for saying. 'Basically, you know, the further south you go, the trickier people get and the more likely to cheat. It's a Latin thing.'

'Morfeo is tricky.'

'Domenico really winds you up. And Adrian [Mutu] was an asshole, if you'll excuse my language, to fall for it and get himself sent off at the end of that game with Atalanta. With respect,' he adds.

He starts to talk about Mutu. 'He's married recently, of course, that should calm him down. Though he's very young to marry, isn't he? Twenty-two.' Again this big man knits his handsome brow. 'Adrian comes from a culture, you know, the Eastern Orthodox, where marriage is very, very serious. You don't bail out of it easily. So it's a big risk marrying at twenty-two.'

It's as if Apolloni could already foresee some awful personal crisis in Mutu's life that will undoubtedly damage the team's performance.

'Irene, please, it's not polite and I have to talk to this gentleman.'

The girl was climbing over him.

'Let's call it a day.'

'Not at all.' But now he says that he doesn't know how to deal with kids. He's shaking his head at the girl as if she were an impossible conundrum. 'I often wonder, why isn't there a book or something that tells you how to bring up your children?'

'There are millions of books.'

'But they don't tell you *exactly* what to do, do they, I mean, when it actually comes to it, when you're in some situation, you don't feel you've been told how to behave.'

One of the Più-mati recently claimed, on the net, that he had seen Apolloni go up to Perotti in training and demand of him rather abruptly, 'So Mister, why don't you tell us *exactly* what we're supposed to do?'

'I mean,' Gigi was saying now, 'I'm always so worried she's going to hurt herself, I don't know, on the stairs, in the lift.'

'Why's that?'

He sighs and explains that it all started with his brother. 'I had this younger brother, you know, who was accident-prone. You turned your back and he had fallen out of a tree. You started some game and the next thing you know he had broken his leg. We were always in the casualty ward. I was constantly nervous that he would be killed.' He paused. '*C'è sempre l'incidente in agguato.*' There's always an accident/incident lying in wait.

Only later, driving home, did I realise that these few casual remarks had been the core of the interview. They were the only thing Apolloni had really told me. Our big central defender is a man whose whole life is dedicated to accident-prevention and damage-limitation. And the most terrible damage of all is when the other side scores.

Stopping at a traffic light, I recalled something I translated, years ago, about the sacred texts of ancient India. The greatest moral value, it said somewhere in this translation, was intense 'wakefulness'. The accident is always someone's fault. You must be hyperconscious, hypercautious. You mustn't blink. It was the distinguishing feature of the gods that they never blinked. Watch, watch, watch and pray. How exhausting! No wonder Apolloni's whole face is alive with nervous tension. 'I'm getting older,' he told me, just before we parted. 'I don't know if they'll want me for another season.'

How could I not remember all this when the following Sunday the accident happened, and happened above all thanks, no thanks, to Gigi Apolloni? Here is something uncanny to take us through the game with Juventus.

It was the forty-eighth minute of the first half. The fourth man had indicated two minutes of injury time, but for some reason Juve's keeper, Van der Saar, was being allowed to kick the ball upfield in the forty-eighth. Verona had just taken a corner. The ball sailed across the centre-line towards the Curva Sud. Laursen was not there to clear it. He had gone up for the corner. There was only Apolloni to watch over the tall, strong and immensely tricky Pippo Inzaghi. The ball bounced long. Could Apolloni have got a foot to it at this point and whacked it clear? Maybe. But his attention wavered. He blinked perhaps. In a flash Inzaghi had sprung between the defender and the ball. Apolloni saw the disaster now and began to push and grab. Inzaghi wouldn't go down. Strong as an ox, he fought his way into the area. Apolloni had his arm round him. At that point Inzaghi decided it was time to fall. Penalty. Yellow card. One–nil.

And so, despite a gutsy second half, the game ended. It's an unhappy tale. But we're still far from Caporetto. Losing one–nil on a penalty to Juve wouldn't even be humiliating for Manchester United or Bayern Munich. Nor is our position in the league table irretrievable. Before going to Rome we were sixth from bottom. Before the game with Juve we were joint-fifth. Now we are joint-fourth and so back in the relegation zone. But we have two relatively easy fixtures to get ourselves back in the running: Brescia (third to bottom) away, then Reggina (second to bottom) at home.

So the *brigate* were in pretty good spirits, cheerfully tipsy and optimistic, as we boarded the train to Brescia on 14 April. Tomorrow was Easter Sunday. We would rise again. Suddenly, pushing along a corridor, I found myself face to face with Albe, the man who made up so many songs on the bus to Bari. 'Tim Parks!' he said. He knew who I was now. 'Where have you been?' I asked. I hadn't seen him since the game against Vicenza. I hadn't seen Glass-eye at all. 'Oh personal difficulties on my part,' Albe chuckled, but he went on to explain that others had been given a stadium ban. He began to list various names. Cain's was among them and many others I had met and lost sight of. It was for throwing seats in Turin; though they hadn't, Albe insisted indignantly, thrown them *at* anyone.

The Brescian landscape is distinctive. The town sits at the northern extreme of the Po plain beneath a barrier of steep and menacingly dark hills. Little more than four sheds round a pitch, the small, quaint stadium is hugely overshadowed by these hills, which, like Tolkien's Mordor, seem always to be capped by a pall of black cloud. This afternoon the effect was made even more disturbing by a sharp spring sunshine that had the pitch glowing emerald-green while just beyond, sky and mountains seemed about to topple forwards. Far from rising again, we were about to be smothered in a great mass of gloom.

We were delayed more than an hour by the police. Having rushed up the staircase and out on to the stands just as Collina blew his whistle, I found myself at a railing with a policeman on one side, intent on the game, and the young Alcohol – tall, chubby and gormless – on the other. For exactly two seconds, he stopped moaning to say hello to me. Then he began again. 'Why why why? *Deficiente!* Idiot. Perotti's a fool. Oh please. Please! But why does he always play this formation. Why can't Mazzola stop the ball. Why is he playing. Useless. You're useless. Where's Italiano? Why does he change the team every fucking game? Oh Christ, pass, pass, *Dio boia*, pass!'

Immediately I arrived, Ferron saved brilliantly from Hubner who had broken through the defence and was running straight at him. Then the same again, an exact action-replay. Meantime, Alcohol's litany went on and on. 'But this is hopeless, hopeless, hopeless!' Inevitably, about twenty minutes in, Baggio scored from a sweet free kick just outside the box. Upon which, I abandoned Alcohol and moved to the other side of the guest section. It was too much like babysitting a dying dog.

The second half might as well not have happened. Perhaps bored by the sheer dullness of the game, Collina, who had refereed impeccably until ten minutes from time, suddenly sent Camoranesi off for what looked like no more than the usual shoulder to shoulder on the ball. Then, fatally, Laursen was given a yellow card for brushing with Baggio, around whose pony-tail and slightly camp kudos the referee was determined to preserve a demilitarised zone. Since Laursen has already collected three yellow cards in previous games that means he will now be suspended.

Meantime, and these were the only exciting moments, Ferron continued to save instinctively, brilliantly, from the lanky Hubner who for the fourth, fifth and then, amazingly, sixth time found himself alone in front of Verona's goal. But he couldn't score, and as a result Verona, only one down, were forced to keep trying to equalise, though without ever getting near the goal. In the final seconds, Collina sent off Gonnella for swearing at him and the match was really over. Not only had Hellas lost the game, most deservedly, but three key players – Camoranesi, Laursen and Gonnella – were out for next week. It was another self-destruct job.

Hellas were now third from bottom. Voices on The Wall announced that at the Tuesday training session we must launch a *contestazione* – a protest. Like so many things in Italy – a government crisis, a half-day metro strike – there is something highly ritualistic about the *contestazione*. It's a sort of formal declaration of rupture between fans and players, who have to be reminded that we pay to see them. They must honour the team colours.

I went along. It was raining. Only fifty or so people had gathered at the gates to the training ground. On the other side of the road was the stadium and the railings behind which the players parked their cars: Mercedes, BMWs, Alfa Romeos, a Porsche.

The players had changed into their shorts, but then we saw them sneak out of the dressing room and into some conference place. We waited, some with umbrellas, some without. At least three distinct generations of fans were present: the older men, grumbling among themselves; the young boys, fierce and callow, and in the middle, most respected of all, the leaders of the so-called *brigate storiche*, the now aging boys of the *Primo Febbraio* group who had followed the team around Europe in their glory years.

A small shaven-headed, bull-necked man dressed in overalls carried on a conversation by walking up to the group he was addressing, talking to them intensely, belligerently, then walking away, then turning round and shouting at them again. Then he laughed and embraced a tall, stout, Dickensian figure, under whose office jacket and tie, just slightly askew, you could see the powerful body and manic energy of the fan of twenty years ago. '*Oddo è venduto*,' this man said. Paid by the other side.

Beppe, the Solohellas webmaster, arrived. I had never seen him in his insurance-office clothes. Glasses made him vaguely owlish. 'Who would insure against relegation now?' I asked. 'You could buy Maradona with a premium like that,' he laughed. He shook his head and nodded towards the stadium. 'Down south they wouldn't have the courage to stick those cars under our noses. They'd have more respect.'

The players were late. The small crowd moved over to the stadium and the gate they would appear from. 'They're scared.' The drizzle sifted down. Finally a couple of players appeared. In ones and twos they crossed the yard to the gate, then the road to the training ground. Heads were bowed, features anxious. As they passed us at the gate, the words *scandalo* and *vergogna* were frequently muttered, but no one said anything out loud until at last Perotti arrived. Once again I was struck by the man's immense unease. Was it significant that none of the staff – the doctor, the deputy trainer – had chosen to walk out with him? He hurried past the fans, two of whom half stepped forward to block his way.

'*Vergogna!*' Just one voice was raised. Perotti accelerated. Our chance was gone.

Then for the first time in my life I heard the Veronese expressing serious respect for southerners. 'If this was Naples, we would have spat on them!' 'We're too civil, *Dio boia!*' '*Butei*, we should have been yelling!' 'If this was Calabria we'd have insulted their mothers, *Dio boia*, slashed their car tyres.'

'But would that really help?' I asked Beppe.

'You bet,' he told me. 'They'd show a bit more respect for the colours if they knew they were going to be spat on, if they knew our women wouldn't look at them.'

But even this wasn't quite Caporetto. Hellas had lost honourably against Roma and Juve. They had lost miserably against Baggio's Brescia. But one–nil away still wasn't Caporetto. OK we were third from bottom, but now we had Reggina, the second to bottom club, at home. It was 22 April.

Another way you can try to turn misery into some kind of second-rate pleasure is through analogy. At its most extravagant, this is the territory of Blackadder: 'The worst capuccino since Pavarotti's diarrhoeic dog shat in the cat's milk.' More usually, the unhappy mind seeks out some obvious resemblance and reposes there, glad to be distracted from the ugly event itself by this parallel. At five to three the *brigate* unfolded the week's big banner across the parapet of the *curva*.

MERCENARI INFAMI, TUTTI I VOSTRI MILIARDI NON VALGONO LA NOSTRA FEDE.

Disgraceful mercenaries, all your billions are not worth our loyalty.

So later that afternoon I tried to detach my mind from the catastrophe being played out before me by thinking about mercenaries. Wasn't there an analogy with the situation in medieval times, when the city states of Italy used to debate whether it was better to rely on one's own homebred soldiers, or whether riches amassed could usefully be spent bringing in paid troops from elsewhere? As I recall, it was Machiavelli who had the last word. 'With mercenaries,' he writes in *Il Principe*, 'victories are slow, tardy and unconvincing, whereas defeats, when they come, are unexpected and overwhelming.'

This defeat was both. Twenty minutes into the first half, a figure in Reggina's claret-and-white streaked down the left wing. Oddo, who should have been there, was nowhere to be seen. From the other side of the field another dark shirt was converging. Does anyone actually know the names of Reggina's no-name team? Only the Pulieros of this world. The cross came high. Ferron moved out, as he should, to pluck it from the striker's head. But there must have been some wind higher up. It had rained hard; now there was bright sunshine and an Alpine smell in the air. Driving to the stadium, you could see it had snowed on the peaks. A smell of Caporetto, perhaps, of avalanche and abyss. The ball ballooned, spinning bizarrely backwards. Too late, Ferron realised that it was doomed to fall plumb out of the blue sky and right into his goal. He dived back and scooped. The linesman's flag was already up. One–nil!

By half time it was two–nil. After months of giving him the benefit of the doubt, the *curva* had resumed their old chant: '*Pas-tor-el-lo vaf-fan-cu-lo!*'

All the same, Reggina had had a defender sent off. Surely now Verona would make headway. For about five minutes we hoped. No headway was made. The players seemed to have no idea how to get the ball from the halfway line to the opponents' goal. What does Perotti do with these people all week? All around me, a strange feeling of resignation had set in, quite different from the anger of the Juve game. Pietro propped his strong chin on an open hand and watched stony-faced as the minutes ticked by. He's getting ready to withdraw, I thought. He's preparing not to care.

Suddenly there was a brusque movement in the *curva*. Twenty minutes from time a large number of fans were sucked down into the central stairs to reappear moments later low on the west side of the *curva*, as near as they could get to the bench. They began to jeer. '*Perotti, Perotti vaffanculo!*' Whenever Verona made a mistake the whistling was fierce. Somebody decided it was time for Oddo to get the monkey grunts. Oddo has let us down seriously. Oo, oo, oo!

The team went to pieces. Substituted, Bonazzoli appeared to be telling Perotti to go to hell. Adailton was sent off for an incident off the ball. Another suspension. The crowd began to applaud every move Reggina made. The *brigate* pressed against the railings behind Perotti. It was menacing. A squad of riot police in full gear appeared below us on the east side of the *curva* and marched behind the goal to the west side. They had a military step. In the VIP section, Pastorello got to his feet and headed for the exit. He was thus spared the scene when, with just seconds left, Reggina grabbed a third on the break. The *brigate* cheered. The final whistle blew. 'Come under the *curva*!' the fans invited the players. But they had disappeared. 'If this were Naples, they'd have to leave the stadium in a helicopter,' Pietro said grimly.

'That's it,' Michele announced in the car. 'I'm not coming to the last games.' I drove in silence. Unusually, we didn't turn on the radio to pick up the other results, though we already knew Chievo had won again. Chievo were coming up. We were going down. We were still third from bottom, but five points away from safety now. Is it time to detach myself, I wondered? The season was beginning to take on the trajectory of a love affair that had never been easy and was now turning decidedly sour. Time to cut losses perhaps. 'I'm not coming again,' Michele repeated. I didn't try to persuade him. Back home I threw myself into some harmless task, gardening, fixing a broken shutter. It wasn't until the following evening on my author tour in Munich that I conjured up the necessary mental energy to check The Wall. Once again, someone had found exactly the analogy that both expressed the dismay and made it easier to bear: 'Supporting Verona yesterday was like being in love with a whore.'

Two days after it arrived – in Berlin now – I clicked open the message headed 'Caporetto'. It was from a Hellas fan, Alvise, who lives and works in London. 'Tim, we're no longer the first team in Verona. I never thought I'd live to see such shame. Were we really that bad? Is there no hope?'

Brusquely I tapped out: 'None.'

25A GIORNATA

Lazio – Parma 2–1
Bologna – Perugia 3–2
Brescia – Reggina 4–0
Lecce – Atalanta 0–2
Napoli – Milan 0–0
Udinese – Bari 2–0
Verona – Juventus 0–1
Inter – Vicenza 1–1
Fiorentina – Roma 3–1

26A GIORNATA

Atalanta – Parma 0–1
Bari – Napoli 0–1
Brescia – Verona 1–0
Fiorentina – Lecce 2–0
Juventus – Inter 3–1
Milan Udinese 3–0
Reggina – Lazio 0–2
Roma – Perugia 2–2
Vicenza – Bologna 4–2

27A GIORNATA

Napoli – Brescia 1–1
Inter – Fiorentina 4–2
Bologna – Bari 4–2
Lazio – Vicenza 2–1
Lecce – Milan 3–3
Perugia – Atalanta 2–2
Udinese – Roma 1–3
Verona – Reggina 0–3
Parma – Juventus 0–0

CLASSIFICA

Roma   62
Juventus   56
Lazio   55
Parma   44
Atalanta   41
Milan   41
Inter   41
Bologna   39
Fiorentina 36
Perugia   33
Udinese   32
Lecce   30
Brescia   29
Vicenza   28
Napoli   28
Verona   24
Reggina   23
Bari   19

Credere, Obbedire, Combattere

I don't want them to wear me. Help! Please!
A shirt of Hellas Verona
Mercen@ries!

In Afghanistan, the Taliban continue to destroy the great statues of Buddhism. In the smoky bar where I go to read *La Gazzetta dello Sport* a row of bottles has appeared on the shelves behind the counter. '*Cappuccino e brioche, per favore*,' I tell the barman. But for a moment I can't believe my eyes. '*Credere, obbedire, combattere!*' the bottle directly opposite me is shouting. On a white label against shiny black glass Il Duce raises a solid arm. 'Believe, Fight, Win.' The imperatives of Fascism.

Waiting for my cappuccino to appear, I look more carefully. 'DUX' the bottle to the right announces. Mussolini's torso rises gigantically from the tiny figures of a crowd in silhouette. '*Ein Volk, ein Land, ein Führer*' claims the next bottle in line. Adolf himself is inviting me to join in the Nazi salute across the polished marble of the bar top.

I choose a croissant with a custard filling. I am fascinated by these powerful images so unexpectedly presented to me with my morning coffee. The verticality of the wine bottle, its statuesque cylindrical form, allows these old icons to take on a new if contained strength. 'Führerwein' declares the next bottle, featuring that famous greatcoat, the peaked cap.

But I'm taken aback too. Isn't it illegal in Italy to display the emblems of Fascism in a public place? Weren't these provocative images supposed to be imprisoned in history books or properly condemned in TV documentaries?

'It's a company from Friuli,' the barman laughs, sensing in my interest a possible sale. 'This one's a cabernet.' He picks up a bottle showing a little boy in uniform. 'Balilla' the label declares. Balilla was a patriotic hero whose name was used for Fascism's youth brigades. 'That's the one most people choose,' he says, when I ask for a bottle of *Credere, obbedire, combattere*. What better motto for Hellas? 'It's a merlot. They find Hitler a bit hard to stomach,' he admits. 'Pity because the wine's good.' He brightens up. 'Most of the youngsters go for Che.'

'Che? Che Guevara?' I hadn't noticed him, but there he is, on the far left of the line.

'Che's a cabernet again,' the barman explains, drying a glass, 'but lighter and fresher than Balilla. Question of vintage. There's a Che bubbly too if you're interested.'

I stare at the bottle. The Communist revolutionary has his beret of old, the proud face for ever upturned in that gesture of defiance and hope.

'Where's Lenin?'

'Suppose they haven't got round to him yet.'

I like the barman. He has a long bony face, a sort of triangle opening upwards, and then a thick tangle of curly hair.

'There's nothing political about it then?'

He looks at me surprised. 'Oh no, not at all.'

It's what the *brigate* always say about their monkey grunts.

I sit down with my coffee and my rather expensive bottle and take a good long look at Benito Mussolini. In ancient times we bowed down to idols. They underpinned a mythology. The mind couldn't escape them. Then when they had lost their power and the world seemed empty, it occurred to someone we might invent new icons and new mythologies to enthral the masses and have them rise up on the politicians' behalf. That particular folly was an Italian first; the problem being that once you had created the images you had to produce the story they gestured to: war. And when at last that was over, we locked these new images away. People were scared of them. But now it seems they are seeping out again, free to circulate in bars and on dinner tables. They are free because they no longer mean anything. Che's red label and Hitler's black are equivalent now: grand gestures, strong lines, cut loose from any context: the way in a big museum you might find yourself equally interested in a Renaissance Madonna in one room and Shiva in the next.

Il Duce safely bottled beside me, I open the papers. This is a major scandal, the atheist West laments of Islam's destruction of these ancient statues. Various world celebrities are expressing their dismay. We're jealous of the Taliban, it occurs to me. For us sacred images are merely art, an aesthetic aura that inspires no fundamentalism. But incredibly, the Taliban take those statues seriously. For them the symbol is potent, it can possess the mind. The only comparable concern I can think of is the left's preoccupation that Berlusconi's TV stations are winning the elections for him.

'Below we publish a list', the *Arena* announces, 'of the party symbols that the voter will have to choose between on election day.' There are more than a dozen of them: the oak tree, the olive tree, the daisy, the carnation, the national flag, the hammer and sickle, the sunflower, the raised sword, the tricolour flame, the red cross, the ivy leaf. But no one seems to be fundamentally attached to any of these icons. The paper lists all those candidates who in a frenzy of last-minute opportunism have pinned a new badge to their chests. More interestingly, the *Gazzetta* has an in-depth interview with Christian Vieri: 'I'll leave Inter at the end of the season if the team doesn't make it to the Champions' League,' he says. 'A player of my calibre should be in the Champions' League.' What does he care about the mythical blue-and-black shirt of Internazionale? Nothing. It means no more than a bottle of cabernet with a Nazi salute.

I salute the barman and leave. It's 29 April. This afternoon we play Milan at San Siro. Does anyone take images seriously now? I wonder, wrapping up il Duce in the boot as I park the car at the station. But my thoughts are interrupted by a song. '*In Italia, Hellas, in Europa, Hellas, e ovunque Hellas, per sempre gialloblù.*' For ever yellow-blue. And I realise I have the answer before my eyes.

On the plaza outside the station the familiar faces are gathering: Forza, Fondo, Mauro, Albe, Busso. Even though it's warm they're wearing their blue-and-yellow scarves, they have their banners. The fans are the Taliban among us. At least on Sunday afternoons. It's fantastic how much they care.

Not that the fans' banner is quite the same as the pagan's idol. I'm sitting on the stone border of a flowerbed, beer in hand, watching the kids sing arm in arm. What's the story here? Perhaps it starts with a sort of generalised nostalgia for the icon. The first nightmare we have any record of was that of a Mesopotamian queen who woke in panic after dreaming that the sacred images had been stolen from the temple. I once met a fan who complained he'd dreamed that the Curva Sud had been bulldozed to the ground. 'Thought doesn't aspire to emancipation,' wrote the Colombian Gomez Davila. 'but to bow to the appropriate yoke.'

But it's so hard to believe in sacred images now. From time to time the TV shows a cardinal holding a picture of the Virgin, while the faithful queue up to kiss it. This is hard for the thinking man. Or an idiot is arrested for daubing satanist symbols and swastikas in a cemetery in Soave. That is harder still. To remain transfixed by a Celtic cross requires a very special form of delirium.

The fans, on the other hand, have invented a new, if more precarious, form of enslavement. We can carry the Hellas banner because it means no more than *ourselves*. Nothing beyond is gestured to. Nothing means more than us, our shared emotions, our antique company. We cheer and laugh. We have no saints. The players, who are really only eager to make money, are merely a necessary disturbance, as opportunist politicians are no doubt a disturbance for the voter who wants to enslave his mind to some ideal.

'Out of respect for the colours, you mustn't play in blue-and-yellow again till you have shown some balls.'

Being in Germany, I couldn't go to the altogether larger *contestazione* that followed our disastrous game against Reggina, but this, apparently, is what one of the leaders of Primo Febbraio told Perotti when he came out of the dressing room. The big man was forthright. 'The next match, you don't play in blue-and-yellow.

OK? You're not fit to.' And they didn't. When finally we arrived at San Siro, five minutes after kick-off, it was to see Hellas on the field in all-white.

Of course, whatever your attitude to scarves and banners, one image the mind, or at least the male mind, can always fasten to is that of the female form. When I returned from Germany on Saturday morning, the day before the game, it was to learn that another disaster had befallen Hellas. The previous evening, Alberto Gilardino, only eighteen, his driving licence just a few weeks old, plunged his Golf into a canal. Actually it wasn't his Golf. He was planning to buy the car from one of two sisters whom, together with a mutual friend, he was driving back to their home in Treviso. Treviso is 150 kilometres from Verona. The girls were aged twenty-two and twenty-seven. It was 9.15 in the evening. Dazzled by oncoming headlights, he veered off the road and plunged into the canal. The car sank rapidly, but with his lightning reactions our star striker had managed to open his door and, despite injuries, he pulled his friends to safety. He is now in hospital with a compressed vertebra. Out for the duration.

The following morning, The Wall was aflame with anger and insults. 'Miserable mercenary brat out with his Treviso sluts only two days before a big game! When was he planning to get some sleep? We've lost four in a row, for Christ's sake!'

The two sisters are called Silvia and Cosetta Puppinato. In very short order someone has tracked them down on the web. '*Butei*, go to this address and check out the *poppe* [tits] of the Puppinato!'

It was a site that had something to do with night-clubs. Almost immediately the tone of the messages changed. 'Great knockers!' 'What a pair of melons! Someone better tell Gili, she'll eat him alive.' 'What an arse, *Dio boia*!' 'You can understand why he was distracted, *butei*. You have to forgive him.' One of Hellas Girls grew angry. 'Little boys, haven't you seen a pair of tits before? If you want to carry on this conversation, move over to a porno site.' Then came the familiar refrain: '*Ancor prima della mona, sempre Hellas Verona*.' Before the skirt, the shirt.

'I've got a girlfriend,' Mirko said. It was the fan from Trento whom I'd met way back in November on the train to Turin. As before he was polite and friendly. We were still stuck at Verona train station an hour after our train was due to leave for Milan. Apparently the station in Vicenza had been closed to defuse a massive English bomb from the Second World War, a relic curiously associated with the wine bottle in the boot of my car. As a result, the special train we were due to use wasn't available, and we would be put on a regular *interregionale* that would get us to Milan perilously late. 'Want to drive?' I asked Mirko. 'It's only an hour and half in the car.' 'Not for the game with Milan.' He shook his head. 'We need police protection.' I remembered hearing the same story from Aiooogalapagos about Brescia. 'I'd never go to the Brescia game,' Aiooo told me. 'Too dangerous.' In the event I had found it tame, just the usual business of people hurling themselves against fences, spitting, shouting and tossing a stone or two.

'So you're happy now?' I said.

'Yes.' Mirko is a pleasant young man, with a strong chin and cautious eyes.

'And she lets you go to away games?'

'She doesn't like it, but she says: have a nice pilgrimage.'

'Great.'

'Problem is my mother doesn't like her.'

'Why not?'

The girl had some kind of asthmatic condition. She had to use inhalers and so on. Needed medical treatment. Mirko's mother, who is extremely religious, feels it's wrong for him to bond with a woman who won't be a healthy wife and mother. At thirty-one Mirko still lives at home. He travels fifteen miles home from work at lunchtime to eat the pasta she prepares.

I put it to him that it might be time to tell Mamma that his love life is none of her business.

'I can't.' The haunted look in Mirko's eyes intensified. 'I can't do that.'

Looking over the crowd, drinking, laughing, barracking the surly policemen who always travel with us, I wondered how many among us were basically phobic young men who came to football to demonstrate to themselves that they weren't entirely without courage, even if they did find it impossible to confront their mothers. I quoted Mirko a song I'd found on a fan website:

> *Come farò a spiegare alla mia mamma*
> *questo occhio nero,*
> *sono caduto a terra,*
> *lei mi dice non è vero.*

> How can I explain this black eye to mum?
> I fell over, That's not true, she says, son.
> And these footprints on my arse,
> That was a carabiniere showing his class.

Mirko laughed. 'I've never been involved in a fight.' His tone was: how could I ever have imagined that he would be involved in a fight?

One person who is definitely not phobic is Forza. At quarter past two we finally piled off the train at Milano Centrale, where I enjoyed one of the most rewarding experiences of my footballing year so far. Week after week I creep through this busy station, bound by timetables, weighed down with students' theses, plagued by train delays, ticket-office queues, overcrowded carriages. And instead here I am suddenly under the huge arch of one of Fascism's finest architectural achievements, standing in a solid group of Veronese yelling '*Milan Milan vaffanculo*' and generally intimidating the railway staff and the Japanese tourists. The acoustics are excellent. The boys raised their fists. And in that magical way that happens in crowds, I found myself next to Forza, his big shaven head glowing with pink pleasure. 'I love the game against Milan,' he said. 'I love the feeling of walking into San Siro and all around there are fifty thousand people who hate you. They hate you. They *hate* you. It's fantastic.'

Forza was right. '*Butei*, this isn't one of our best crowds,' shouted the chorus leader as the police at last marched us into the stadium plaza. 'But we must show pride. Banners high now, *butei, facciamo bella figura.*' Let's cut a fine figure!

Just at this moment, as we engaged in the classic Italian gesture of self-presentation, chanting our chants, holding high our banners, becoming, in short, the icon of ourselves, a solid yellow-blue phalanx, compact and combative, at precisely this marvellous moment, the Milan fans waiting on the higher ramparts of the stadium fired three red rockets into our group. They really do hate us. There was confusion. The police began to yell as if it were our fault. Forza was hit on the nose by one of a shower of coins tossed from the stands above. A deep scratch bled copiously. By the time we had got into the stadium everyone was feeling properly wired-up and as the field of play came into view, it was to see that Hellas, in all-white, were attacking. They had won themselves a corner. I felt great.

Verona have never beaten Milan at San Siro. Did they have any chance today? Just a couple of weeks ago, in a pre-election speech, Prime Minister Giuliano Amato concluded that, thanks to his government's performance, 'Italy is in fact higher in the European league tables than AC Milan is in Serie A.' The subtext being: if Berlusconi can't even get his super-expensive team any higher up the championship than that, what chance has he got of running the government successfully?

Judging by the banner dominating Milan's *curva*, the fans are also critical of their president's achievements. 'NOT PROMISES FOR THE ELECTORATE,' they have written in letters more than a metre high, 'BUT CONCRETE INVESTMENTS FOR CUPS AND CHAMPIONSHIPS.'

Eliminated from Europe, out of the running for the *scudetto*, it hasn't been a good year for AC Milan. After half an hour's play this afternoon they looked quite incapable of scoring against us. But as I've mentioned before, opinion polls suggest that every time Milan win, Berlusconi's prospects for becoming Prime Minister improve. With the general election only two weeks off, this must be a crucial point of the season for him. So sure enough, fifteen minutes from time the referee broke the deadlock by awarding Bierhoff a dubious penalty. He had charged into the six-yard box with his leg at head height. Dangerous play? Trying to get to the ball first, Ferron knocked him over. Penalty. Goal.

'*Di questa partita*,' the *brigate* began to shout, '*non ce ne frega un cazzo*.' We don't give a toss about this game. We never cared. It's a noble lie. As the chant died away a brilliant pattern of passes put Super-Mike Cossato alone in front of Milan's goal. Keeper Sebastiano Rossi was on his knees by the far post. All the striker had to do was to drive the ball home. He hit wide. The day ended in dismay. Reggina had beaten Napoli. We're now second from bottom with only six games to go. Chievo have won again. 'Hellas, you're dead,' gloats a politically correct Chievo fan, writing to our Wall. 'You and all your racist supporters. Ignorant pigs. Roast in hell!'

28A GIORNATA

Vicenza – Parma 0–1
Reggina – Napoli 3–1
Atalanta – Bologna 2–2
Bari – Perugia 3–4
Brescia – Inter 1–0
Fiorentina – Udinese 2–1
Juventus – Lecce 1–1
Milan – Verona 1–0
Roma – Lazio 2–2

CLASSIFICA

Roma	63
Juventus	57
Lazio	56
Parma	47
Milan	44
Atalanta	42
Inter	41
Bologna	40
Fiorentina	39
Perugia	36
Brescia	32
Udinese	32
Lecce	31
Vicenza	28
Napoli	28
Reggina	26
Verona	24
Bari	19

Elections

*Ciao everyone. Verona aren't in B yet. Support them
to the end. Penn, who are you voting for tomorrow?
Berlusconi or Rutelli? I'm voting for the Polenta Party.
Polenta for everyone.*

    Dany

For those who have grown out of religion but haven't yet learned
to enslave their minds to something spectacular and harmless like
football, political causes have become the only respectable object of
those emotions we once associated with the sacred. So a very large
number of people are growing extremely heated about the Italian
general election, even people who would appear to have nothing
to do with them. *The Economist* tells us very sternly that we mustn't
vote for Berlusconi because he is corrupt. Margaret Thatcher tells us
that we must vote for Berlusconi because he is an innovator. More
understandably in the fray, Umberto Eco warns that the elections
will be a 'moral referendum', with the evil and the ignorant voting
for Berlusconi and the good and the intelligent voting for Rutelli.

    Of course none of these people imagine that their attachment
to their party is that of the fan to the colours. Politics is a respectable
subject to grow heated over (far more than sport or religion)
precisely because it is presumed to be an area for reasoning and
logic. Isn't that an odd formulation? All the same, the crassness of
the arguments offered and the evident emotional engagement of
those offering them makes it clear that we are deep in the realm
of fandom here. How can *The Economist* imagine that the alleged

corruption of a candidate is a problem for Italians who regularly vote for politicians under investigation, who daily face situations where to side-step the law seems the only sane form of behaviour, who for decades go on giving all their passions to a *campionato* that they know is riddled with cheating? The passport scandal is a classic example. Any number of teams have broken the rules but that doesn't do anything to change our allegiances, or our excitement. There is nothing more galvanising than the thrill of disgust. And how can an intelligent man like Umberto Eco imagine that, with the majority of Italians saying they will support Berlusconi, his last-minute cry of moral referendum will be seen as anything but an indirect insult to those whose opinions he doesn't share. '*Ignoranti*,' the Veronese shout at more or less any opposing group of fans who come to the Bentegodi. We have no desire to enlighten them.

Anyhow, within the messy goal-mouth scramble that the last days of the election campaign have become, it's a real pleasure to find someone who has kept his mind absolutely focused. Checking up one morning on a favourite fan website – tifonet.it/rovereto – I found the familiar homepage revolutionised. On one side was the symbol of Berlusconi's party, the Italian tricolour with the FORZA ITALIA logo. Oh dear, I thought, another man who has to tell us how he's voting. But no! That logo now says FORZA HELLAS! Similarly, on the other side of the screen, the symbol of the extreme-left party, Rifondazione comunista, has been altered to PARTITO SCALIGERO – RIFONDAZIONE. To complete the montage, the hammer and sickle at the centre of the symbol have been replaced with the ladder, emblem of the Scaligeri. Both powerful images have been appropriated to our cause. Meantime, the banner running left to right across the top of the screen announces (and I can almost hear the fans chanting): *Di queste elezioni, non ce ne frega un cazzo* . . . We don't give a toss.

Good. But then what do we give a toss about? Sunday's game against Fiorentina of course. 'Every game is a last-ditch now,' says Perotti. 'Every match must be played like a Champions' League final.' Wondering what the coach was doing to prepare the team for this level of tension, I go to check out the team in training the day before the match. The players are standing in a circle passing the ball around while two in the middle have to dash back and forth to intercept it. Laursen plunges this way and that. He has the energy and awkwardness of a young horse. Apolloni is laughing, joking. Leo Colucci intercepts a ball with his hands and pretends he hasn't. What me? Despite the team's precarious position, they are having a great time. Why not? The players are not going to die when we go down. Football is a sport. They are healthy young men on a spring morning. Never have I felt so strongly the gap between the hopes and fears of the supporters and the pleasures of the players' routine.

Then the deputy mayor arrives. Luca Bajona is a member of Alleanza Nazionale, the party to the right of Berlusconi which commentators so eagerly refer to as neo-Fascist, just as Rifondazione comunista, to the left of the present government, is eagerly referred to as neo-Stalinist. How the media hankers after the conflicts of the 1930s. How Bajona yearns for the excitement of the *curva*. He used to stand together with the *brigate*. 'Now I have to watch the games from the stands above the halfway line. A question of institutional image,' he explains sadly. He's disgusted with the team. He's disgusted with the attempts of the international press to discredit Berlusconi. As the ball goes back and forth among the players, our conversation bounces quite naturally from politics to football and back. Rutelli is a puppet figure, there to be manipulated by others if he wins, discarded if he loses. Berlusconi, on the other hand, is his own man. Of course Verona are going down, he says. Of course Berlusconi will win the election. Then he adds: still, if we beat Fiorentina, you never know.

My son forgets that he'd said he wouldn't watch the last few games. We take our seats beside Pietro. The stadium is distressingly empty. Only the *curva* is crowded. The day is hot and humid and, as the players come out, I am suddenly aware that since I started following the team away, facing the uncomfortable journeys, joining in the shouts in stations and subways, being ill-treated by police and stadium officials, the home games are losing their excitement for me. The experience isn't strong enough. I would like at least to be standing in the heart of the *curva*, not stuck out here above the corner flag with my polite friends of old. However much I love them.

Let's be brief about this game, and the one that followed it, against Lecce. Of the match with Fiorentina, let's take just three images, two of the game, one of the stadium as the final whistle blew. The first is the sight of Nuno Gomes, gathering the ball on the break. He's clearly offside, but the linesman doesn't raise his flag. The *curva* explodes with anger, then falls silent. Doardo – for Ferron is suspended – runs to the edge of the box to meet him. What chance does our incompetent reserve keeper have? None. The Portuguese striker passes him with enviable ease. He looks up at the empty goal and strokes the ball right at the middle. But he hasn't noticed Massimo Oddo. Hated by the fans, booed and whistled and grunted at, Oddo has sprinted fifty yards to connect with the ball just as it should surely have gone in the net. It's a moment of redemption. In Doardo's favour it has to be said that at least he didn't pull Gomes down as I suspect Ferron would.

But it's the second picture that will never fade in my mind, that will still be etched there when Nuno Gomes and Oddo have long been forgotten. We're fifteen minutes from time. Verona have snatched a goal from a corner, but are struggling as Fiorentina fight to equalise. In desperate defence Vincenzo Italiano is involved in a collision. He goes off. He stays off for a couple of minutes. We all know he has a serious knee problem. It's kept him out half the season. Is he going to be substituted? No, he's standing by the touch-line, a slim Sicilian of medium height, eager earnest face, arm raised to catch the referee's attention. Eventually the referee turns and waves him on. Unpromisingly, he hobbles on to the pitch. As he does so, there's a loose pass in Fiorentina's midfield. Italiano lifts his head. He begins to run, to race. Quite alone, he intercepts the ball just before the halfway line. All the Florence players are pushing forward; there is nobody behind. Injury forgotten, Italiano is sprinting madly now, twenty yards to pick up the ball, and now thirty in a mad gallop towards the enemy goal and the Curva Sud where everyone is on their feet. 'Run!' they're screaming. 'Run!'

Italiano is not known for his speed. There are two defenders beside him. He's five metres outside the box. One more second and they will slide the ball from him. Italiano strikes it on the run. The trajectory is high but dipping. He's hit it hard. The excellent Toldo, Italy's national keeper, leaps, gets a hand to it, but can only push it against the post and in. Two–nil. The whole incident has lasted about twenty seconds. It's a dream goal, a Roy of the Rovers goal. Italiano, sent off for exulting against Inter, goes crazy. He waves to the *curva*, does a dance, returns to the bench to hug the doctor who took the decision to send him back on the pitch. As soon as the game resumes, he collapses. His knee has given way. He's substituted.

Two minutes from time Fiorentina pulled one back. The fourth man gave an incredible six minutes' injury time. Unheard-of. But still it wasn't enough. Verona held on. Exactly as the final whistle blew, the darkening sky exploded in the most violent of thunderstorms. The players celebrated under sheets of rain to the applause of the gods. It was a moment to remember.

'Wasn't it?'

'You bet you,' Italiano told me a couple of weeks later, after the Lecce game. He's a straightforward boy in his early twenties. Verona bought him when he was just seventeen and he's at home in the city now. In the bar he's brought me to, he knows all the staff and half the customers. 'Never felt any anti-southern feeling here,' he says sincerely. The only thing that worries him is when he's out of the team for a while, or when we lose badly, as against Reggina. 'People stop me in the street and say, why are you playing so badly, what's wrong with you. That pisses me off.'

'Talk me through the game with Lecce.'

'What can I say?' He's drinking a fruit juice. 'After beating Fiorentina, we had to win to pull them down into the relegation zone. They only needed a draw to stay clear of trouble. We attacked for ninety minutes in scorching heat. They played *catenaccio*.' He pauses. 'When I think of their goal, when I see that ball going in the net, I get the shivers, honestly.'

That was 12 May. It was election weekend and the games had been moved forward to Saturday. The vote was on Sunday. That morning an editorial in the paper announced: 'Everybody knew that these elections would be played more with the studs than the ball.' In the Bentegodi – for we had the rare luxury of two home games in a row – the few brave souls who'd made the long trip from Lecce arranged three long banners one above the other:

THE STADIUM IS AN ARENA

OUT WITH THE PLAYERS

IN WITH THE GLADIATORS

'It was so hot,' Italiano said, shaking his head, sipping his orange juice. 'Really punishing. I can't understand the criticism in the press. I don't think they understand football. We went at it tooth and nail. I don't think we could have done any more.'

'In that kind of sun it's exhausting just sitting in stands.'

'So we take the game to them for almost ninety minutes and then that goal with their first shot.'

Five minutes from the end, Lecce pushed forward and shot at random through a crowded box from thirty yards. The ball struck Laursen and deflected into the net.

'I thought I would die.'

'But then the linesman gave offside. Frankly, I think he felt sorry for us. He took pity. There was nothing wrong with the goal. He just couldn't believe how unlucky we were.'

Italiano laughs. 'Could be. It was a terrible moment anyhow. And can you believe they complained afterwards and said we'd stolen the game? Did you read the interviews? If I'd come off the pitch after ninety minutes in my own goal-mouth I'd think, well, nil–nil was pretty lucky, and instead they have the courage to go and whine, when a draw was fine for them, it was all they'd come for anyway, but disastrous for us.'

'A draw would be the worst possible result,' the paper says of the elections. 'The country needs a government that can govern.' Not, in short, a replica of the Football Federation. And in the event, we got one. On Friday evening AC Milan beat Inter by an incredible six–nil and by Monday evening it was clear that

Berlusconi had scored an equally historic victory in the elections.

For the record, it should be said that Verona voted solidly for the moderate right. The Lega Nord was way down and the racist Forza Nuova who hand out their leaflets at the Bentegodi polled just 1.5 per cent. So much for the endless drivel the international press writes about my town's extremism. Now it's down to Napoli next week for what really will be the final showdown for Hellas. Napoli are equal second-to-bottom with us. This is a game we can win. On the net, someone writes: 'Great, thank God the election's over, now we can concentrate on football again. Everybody down to *terronia* next week and remember: only our hatred will bring us victory!'

29A GIORNATA

Bologna – Udinese 1–1
Lecce – Brescia 0–3
Inter – Atalanta 3–0
Lazio – Bari 2–0
Parma – Napoli 4–0
Perugia – Milan 2–1
Verona – Fiorentina 2–1
Vicenza – Reggina 2–1
Juventus – Roma 2–2

30A GIORNATA

Fiorentina – Juventus 1–3
Inter – Milan 0–6
Bari – Vicenza 2–2
Brescia – Bologna 0–0
Napoli – Lazio 2–4
Reggina = Parma 1=0
Roma – Atalanta 1–0
Udinese – Perugia 3–3
Verona – Lecce 0–0

CLASSIFICA

Roma	67
Lazio	62
Juventus	61
Parma	50
Milan	47
Inter	44
Atalanta	42
Bologna	42
Perugia	40
Fiorentina	39
Brescia	36
Udinese	34
Vicenza	32
Lecce	32
Reggina	29
Napoli	28
Verona	28
Bari	20

Napoli

Every day I thank God I'm not a Neapolitan.
Zeno-for-Hellas.it

There are thirty-four cantos in Dante's *Inferno* and thirty-four games in Italy's Serie A. At one point I thought of writing a book of thirty-four chapters with an allusion to the corresponding circles of torment in every one. The easy analogy is always seductive. How else would Joyce have got the Aegean so fatuously mixed up with Dublin? But I decided against it. What sense would it make trying to stay in Serie A if it were the *inferno*? All the same, when it came to the thirty-first game, down in Naples, I couldn't help remembering that parallel. I looked up Canto 31 and found this quotation: '*e fu tal ora ch'i' avrei voluto ir per altra strada.*' 'and it was then that I wished I had gone by another road.' This at least was appropriate.

The road we went was the iron road, the railway. At the training session on the Thursday before the game, I ran into Stefano who always travels with Forza's group. It was Stefano who gave me the nickname 'il Parroco' that night returning from Bari. He agreed that Bonazzoli and Mutu, our only two serious strikers, were entirely alienated from the rest of the group. Our chances of winning were minimal. 'We don't travel for the result,' he said in sharp contrast to the voices all around me. He's a wry, soft-spoken, contained young man, never without a pair of small square dark glasses, never quite clean-shaven. 'The rendezvous is at ten-thirty Saturday evening,' he said, 'for the eleven o'clock night train. We're organising things for the booze and the food.'

At Verona station the ticket offices close at ten-thirty, the automatic distributors were broken. There was no way of buying a ticket. 'Who needs a ticket, *butei*? Who needs a ticket? El Pastor will pay! He hasn't paid a lira for new players so he can't be short of cash.'

Stefano, Antonio, the phocomelia case and others of Forza's group arrived pushing a supermarket trolley stacked with salamis, roast chicken, Parma ham, French bread, beer and a 25-litre canister of Lambrusco. To everybody's dismay, there were only about a hundred of us. To my surprise, I knew almost everyone. 'You were at Milan, you were at Vicenza, you were at Bergamo.' 'But where's Albe?' 'Can't make it.' 'And Fondo. Where's Fondo?' 'Working.'

'Working?'

It turns out that Fondo works with handicapped children. Sometimes he has to take them on trips on Sunday. I couldn't believe it. 'Fondo, looking after people!' Fondo who always needed looking after on these trips. 'Oh Fondo's good at his job. He's conscientious. Just that the moment he finishes work he gets blind drunk.'

'And where's Brillo?' I asked. It occurred to me that this was the season's last long trip, and most probably the last trip when the result still mattered. Brillo was the boy who had shrieked at the policemen from the train window leaving Vicenza. I'd got to know him together with this boy Scopa on the terraces at Rome. Scopa was travelling in khaki shorts and a long loose T-shirt. He has a wry sense of humour. 'Brillo's with his *nonna*.' He looked at me with mock offence. 'You think Brillo's a wild boy, don't you, Englishman?' 'He looked pretty wild to me.' In Rome he had been bare-chested and drunk. 'Brillo's *nonna* is ninety-two. She can't be left alone and his parents are away for the weekend.' 'Poor guy, he must be pissed off.' 'Not at all, Brillo loves his *nonna*.' Then he said, 'Ciao *nonna*! And saluted a woman in her early sixties dressed entirely in *gialloblù*. This strange, half-witted soul always travels with the *brigate* when there's a train laid on. She speaks to no one, watches the game, accepts another defeat and returns. The boys pull her leg. 'What you doing tonight, *nonna*? Want to share a compartment?' Like the church community I grew up in, the *brigate* are always ready to accept the oddballs, those desperate for a spiritual home. They're a catholic bunch in the end. The old lady smiles vacantly.

'Your phone, Marco!' says Stefano. 'No, it's yours.' A constant electronic buzz hangs around the group. People pull out their phones, inspect them and put them away again. 'Some *figa* no doubt.' Meaning skirt. 'The only skirt ever calls me is my mum,' Stefano grumbles.

The order came to move. The police led us through the subway to the platform. Then, climbing on the train among the others in the garish dark, I experienced a strong pulse of emotion. Contrary to all expectations, you have become part of this group, I realised. Or at least you are accepted by them. I shook my head. I don't know why, but I sensed this acceptance more completely and convincingly tonight than on any other trip. As if to confirm the feeling, even the heads of the Loma Band wandered up and chatted to me in the mill of the train corridor. I had never spoken to them before. 'We're not really *cattivi*,' the chorus leader I'd been following for months told me. Let's call him Spada. 'We shouldn't be called the Loma Band at all, just that we used to meet in Loma's restaurant before it closed. We're just *brigate* like all the others,' Spada said.

Another of the leaders joined us, tall, lumbering, powerful. But he too apparently felt the need for earnest self-examination. 'Trouble with the *brigate*', he said, 'is that we've lost our style. You know. You get people being stupid on their own and getting the public to hate us for nothing. When we do something we should do it together.'

There was no danger of not being together for the duration of this trip. The railways had segregated two carriages at the end of the train for us. The communicating door to the rest of the train was locked. We settled down with beer and wine and food and the evening began to take on the feel of a slightly extravagant but never outrageous picnic. Singing caught on from one compartment to the next, wine was poured into beer cans, boys rushed out into the corridor to yell improper remarks at girls on provincial stations. Yet I recall not a single act of vandalism directed at the property of

Italian State Railways. At most people put their feet up on the seats. Nobody was coked tonight. A tall, bragging clown of a boy, Nato (from Innominato – the unnamed), got into a fight at the station in Bologna and punched a man in the face. The man was kissing his girlfriend goodbye. 'Go for it, go for it,' Nato encouraged. 'Get your hands down her bra. Go on. Get a finger up.' The couple were amused at first, then the man lost his temper and made the mistake of going to shout at the Veronese. 'Leave off!' the boys called from the window. It was too late. Nato punched him and the young lover went down. A posse had to be sent out to drag him back before any serious trouble began. The picnic atmosphere resumed. The old woman drifted aimlessly up and down the corridor in her tattered yellow-blue. She had her things in a small pink backpack like a schoolgirl. 'Ciao, *nonna*, want a beer?'

'Oh, *butei*, the ticket inspector's coming.'

'Don't believe it.'

The inspector had unlocked the door from the main part of the train and was working his way down the compartments. Nobody had imagined he would have the balls. I was in a compartment with one of Forza's group at this point, a huge man, Boio, who together with his girlfriend had pulled the seats down into beds and was trying to get some sleep. When the inspector opened the door, Boio lifted a yellow-blue cap from his face, half-opened his eyes, said, 'Don't take offence inspector, but the sad truth is we've decided not to pay.' The man nodded. 'I have to ask of course,' he said politely. 'We understand,' Boio said. 'It's your job. Don't take offence.' 'The train was going to go anyway,' he added to me. 'All they've done is added a couple of carriages. I can't see why we should pay.' And from all along the corridor as the man did his futile rounds, people were shouting, 'Oh, Pastorello will pay.' And other boys said, 'I have a ticket, inspector, but I'm not showing it to you, on principle.' Or more realistically, 'Inspector, you should have made us pay before getting on, it's pointless asking us now.'

When I think of all the trouble I've had with inspectors over the years, surly, nit-picking men telling me I've forgotten to stamp my ticket, or that I haven't taken the route indicated, or my Intercity supplement needs to be upgraded for Eurostar, or my Carta Verde isn't good for the Wednesday afternoon train, it is hard not to feel attracted towards this different approach.

Then suddenly it was six in the morning – I had actually slept, I have learned how to sleep in impossible, crowded, noisy conditions with people singing and laughing. We were being turfed off the train in Rome. We had to change. People headed down the platform, hoping for a coffee, but the police were there to block us. 'You can't leave the platform.' And we weren't allowed to take pictures either. 'Who are you?' a young policeman asked me. I had just taken a snap of the scene. Seeing the flash, he was seriously hostile. He held me by the wrist, a rather studious-looking boy whom I felt I could easily have dealt with, were he not so secure in his black uniform. 'Oh, *maresciallo*, this man's taking pictures. We'll have to confiscate that.' 'Why? It's just a picture.' 'You're not supposed to take pictures of the police.' 'Who says? Nobody's behaved badly.' 'Give me that camera.' He was determined to have it. All at once I found I was applying the technique Obi-Wan Kenobi teaches in *Star Wars*. 'This isn't a problem,' I said. I looked him in the eyes. 'There's no problem with my taking photos. You don't need my camera. It's just a stupid disposable. Look. Let me keep it.' He seemed puzzled and his grip on my wrist relaxed. He let me keep it. Some weeks ago I met a photographer from Padova who is suing the police for destroying the film in his Nikon when he was taking pictures of after-game disturbances.

One speciality of the police is giving contradictory orders. You can't stand there. You must stand there. You can't go now. You must go now. They discuss our movements intently on their radios. Apparently it is difficult to get different sections of the police to agree on a line of action. 'Want some fried mozzarella?' Scopa offers. He has some very sticky paper in his hands. 'Not for breakfast, thanks.' Suddenly four policemen are running up the platform to prevent us from coming into contact with Roma supporters gathering in an area three or four platforms off for their away game with Bari. Around the coffee machine, the boys laugh and clap: '*Hop hop hop!*' they shout. It's what gym teachers call out when they're getting kids to do exercises. In their heavy uniforms, the police officers are already sweating. They grip their truncheons tighter. Now someone's seen a red-and-yellow flag. '*Roma merda!*' they begin to chant. Nonna beams vaguely. 'I saw you at Vicenza,' I tell her. Right in the middle of the trouble actually. 'I've been following Verona for forty years,' she says.

We were supposed to get on the quarter past eight train that stops at Napoli Campi Flegrei not three hundred metres from the San Paolo stadium. But now suddenly there was a change of plan. *Coincidenza!* Quite unexpectedly we had to get on the quarter past seven local to Napoli Centrale. The advantage no doubt was that the train was waiting there beside us. The local police could wash their hands of us at once. But the guard was already blowing his whistle. The doors were closing. And no segregated carriages had been provided. All of a sudden the notorious Brigate Gialloblù were being hurried on to a packed train where they were actually going to mix with normal people. And not only normal people but even *extra-comunitari*. It was a startling development.

Literally pushed through the doors by the police, we filed along the crowded gangways of an open carriage, working our way up the train. 'Got your passports, have you, gentlemen?' asks Scopa of a group of Senegalese, 'your *permessi di soggiorno*? If not, we know someone who can forge them for you. You can trust us.' His voice was kind and convincing. 'No, we're fine,' they smiled. 'We forged passports for Cafu and Veron, you know. No kidding. If you need any help.' 'No, really we're all in order.' They spoke in rudimentary Italian. Deadpan, Scopa mimicked them. '*Bravi. Bravissimi.* I'm happy for you.'

Looking vaguely Australian in his short baggy trousers and broad brimmed hat, Scopa was now trapped by a door that kept opening and closing. A bulky blonde *Signora* appeared, extravagantly perfumed and stylish on this miserable early-morning train. 'Are Madame's papers in order?' Scopa asked politely. 'Need any help with your *permesso di soggiorno*?' She pushed past him angrily. 'No sense of humour down south.' He shook his head.

So much for the terrifying *brigate*.

It was a warm, leaden morning. Bare scorched hills rose shape-lessly from the deep cutting of the line. The train stopped, started, rattled through tunnels. By a miracle I found a seat at a window opposite a pretty young girl. She was smoking in an absorbed kind of way, an exercise book on her lap, face turned determinedly to the window. Beside me was one of the Loma leaders, Spada, and opposite him one of the younger *butei* with long black hair bursting out of his *brigate* cap. Seeing the girl, Scopa stops in the corridor. He flourishes a cigarette. 'Got a light, *signorina*?'

The girl has a floral pink plastic handbag on the floor by her feet. She reaches down, rummages and finds a pink lighter. Scopa takes it and runs the slim cylinder back and forth under his nostrils. He shakes his head. 'Perfumed,' he says. 'It's too much!' The girl giggles.

Suddenly everybody needs a cigarette, everyone is asking for a light, everybody has smelled the girl's perfumed lighter. 'Chanel. Fantastic. So delicate!' Scopa begins his twenty questions. Who, where, when? It seems she's called Gabriella. 'That's a beautiful name. Isn't that a beautiful name, *butei*? Gabriella. Can we call you Gabi?' She's Roman. She's nineteen. She studies pedagogy, which means she goes to teacher-training college. As if embarrassed by her childish handwriting, Gabriella puts the exercise book away in her bag.

Scopa starts getting serious. 'Could you fancy a guy like me, Gabi? What do you think? I'm *carino*, aren't I? Well, just a little bit. Do you think I'm *carino*? Could you go with a guy like me?'

Nato appears. There are people who, when travelling in groups on trains, feel the need to work their way endlessly back and forth along the carriages, checking up on all their friends. He has a beer in one hand, a leg of chicken in the other, a flag round his shoulders.

'What have we here?' He looks at the girl. 'Hey hey hey hey hey! Is she going to give it to us boys?' He looks at the others. 'Is she?' Then to the girl: 'What's the point of having it, if you don't use it. Open your legs, kid!'

'Leave her alone,' Spada says, annoyed. 'Don't be so invasive, for God's sake.'

He actually used the word invasive! This crude behaviour in front of a nice young lady isn't the *brigate* style he dreams of, the style that has people on The Wall writing: 'Honour to the *butei* who went to Naples, honour to the yellow-blue army.'

'Out with those tits, show us those tits,' shouts Nato. He starts a little chorus frequently sung at the expense of women policemen in the stadium. '*Fuori le tette.*' Sitting by the window as all the boys join in, I'm getting nervous. I'm wondering how I'll react if something really unpleasant starts to happen. The girl is now surrounded by a crowd of wild boys. I begin to feel vaguely responsible. But Nato has already lost interest. He's wandering off. It's only seven-thirty in the morning after a pretty rough night.

'Could you fancy me?' Scopa repeats.

'I'm sure you're very nice. But it's not the right moment.'

'Oh, so we already have a boyfriend, do we?'

'Yes.'

Gabriella is small and very girlish with a denim skirt pulled down to slim, even bony knees, pale, thin calves, white socks and grey gym shoes. Up top she has a pretty blue cardigan open over an impressive and very deliberately exhibited cleavage. Her features are small and neat under a ruffled helmet of black hair, the kind of style one associates with the 1960s. A glint comes into Scopa's eyes. 'No, don't tell. Don't tell me you're going down to Naples to see this boyfriend.'

'Yes.'

'Oh no!' everybody groans. '*Butei*, she has a *terrone* for a boyfriend!'

'Leave off,' Spada mutters.

'Aren't there enough handsome boys in Rome without going out with a *terrone*?'

'I fell in love with him,' she says. 'He's very *dolce*.'

'Do you have sex?' Scopa asks. 'Sorry if I seem rather inquisitive.'

'Oh God,' Spada says. He gets up in disgust and leaves his seat. Immediately it's taken by one of the others in the group, an older man, in his mid-thirties perhaps, who leans forward and smiles meaningfully.

'Ciao, Gabi! You're a beautiful girl.'

'Do you?' Scopa insists. 'I mean, I'd just like to know where I stand. It's important to know if a relationship has been consummated.'

She grimaces, but answers cheerfully, 'Of course.'

Everybody sighs. 'And is he a Naples fan? Don't tell us you're going to the game?'

'No, he hates football.'

'And of course you support Roma.'

'Juventus,' she says.

Now there's an even louder groan. Everybody is joining in, perhaps a dozen boys, kneeling on their seats in various parts of the carriage.

'A Juventina with a *terrone* for a boyfriend!' Could anything be worse?

'Will you think of us when you're making love this afternoon. Will you think of me?' Scopa asks.

Gabriella giggles.

'No really, let me give you my phone number. I know you're planning to leave him today. You're planning to leave him, aren't you? How can you stay with him now you've met us? Will you call me?'

'Maybe,' Gabriella says sweetly. Scopa is a handsome boy.

Thirty-Five-Year-Old starts to croon. It's an old song. 'I don't mind you seeing others now, but please don't tell them it was just sex between us.'

Gabriella giggles. She offers everyone her cigarettes. The perfumed lighter does the rounds.

'I'm the one you're interested in, aren't I?' the older man says.

The girl has a lovely way of raising one black eyebrow in a pained but at the same time affectionate expression. Our 35-year-old has a rather wasted, morning-after look about him, but a merry sparkle in his eye. 'You've stolen my heart,' he announces.

The girl explodes with laughter.

'Really. Tell her it's true.' He turns to me. 'Tell her it's true, Englishman.'

'I don't doubt it,' I assure her. 'Gabriella, you're looking at a seriously passionate man.' And to him: 'The fact is, she's never come into contact with the charm and wit of the north before.'

The journey drags on. Gabriella is chain-smoking. A fat fan appears and very grossly bares his beer belly at her, wobbling it up and down. 'Oh please,' she protests. He disappears. Boys are constantly offering her greasy roast chicken and fried mozzarella and salami and ham. At eight in the morning. When she refuses, they beg her to flash her tits. Or just one tit. 'Oh please, just one. You see we've come down with our demands. We've halved our request. We're willing to compromise.' This might be Umberto Bossi discussing how many ministers the Northern League is going to get in Berlusconi's new government. 'Just one.' Then Nato walks by again. 'Has she given it away yet? What's the point of having it if you don't open your legs, girl.' He disappears down the train.

'Come on, one little nipple,' Scopa says. 'One dark little nipple.'

'No way.'

'Show us a bra strap then.'

This, to my surprise, she is willing to do. She reaches inside the blue cardigan and pulls out a silky grey strap. The boys all groan. But now they've seen there's a second light–blue strap. 'What's that?'

'My slip.'

'Her slip, *butei*, her slip!'

'Oh, I'm head over heels in love!' shouts Thirty-Five-Year-Old. He stands up, grabs his knapsack from the luggage rack and produces a Hellas flag. 'Take it,' he says. 'I want to give you this gift.'

'I couldn't.'

'Take it.'

Gabriella accepts and folds the thing in her lap.

'You don't know', I tell her earnestly, 'what it means for him to give you that.'

'A piece of my heart,' he says. 'My yellow–blue innards.'

'I'll always cherish it,' Gabriella says with head cocked on one side. She has pretty incisors.

'I want you to spread it on the bed when you make love this afternoon.'

She hesitates. 'I will.'

'And when you come you must shout, "HELLAAAAAAS!" Like that. HELLLLAAAAAAS!' And all the boys begin to shout, as if in orgasm: HELLLLAAAAAAASSSSSS!!!!

'Go on, say it.'

'Hellas,' Gabriella says, matter of fact.

'But wouldn't that be sacrilege,' someone objects, 'a Roman Juventina with a *terrone* on the Hellas flag.'

'Hmm, not in this case,' Thirty-Five-Year-Old disagrees. 'Accepting the Hellas flag, Gabriella has become an honorary *buteleta*.'

'A what?' It's a Veronese word.

'A Hellas girl,' I explain. 'One of the group.'

'Thank you,' she smiles.

Then very unwisely, the boy beside her pulls two sheets of paper from his bag and says, 'What about these?' He thrusts them in her hand. It's pornography downloaded from the web. One page of obscene cartoons and jokes, one page of women masturbating, couples fucking. Immediately Gabriella pushes it away. 'Don't be disgusting.' There's a brief silence. Then she relents. 'Say something in dialect,' she says. 'See if I understand.'

Now the boy is embarrassed. Though he speaks dialect all the time, he can't think what to say. At the very same moment, a squat lad with shaven head and bright black eyes appears and sits on his friend's lap so that he's leaning right over the girl and immediately he starts talking to her in the fiercest dialect. His friend with the pornography translates. '*Mi fai un sesso tremendo*,' the skinhead says. You're giving me a hell of a hard-on. '*O per favore!* Come on, I'm in love with you. Come on. It's a once in a lifetime opportunity. Your boyfriend'll never know. We can go in the toilet.'

Gabriella giggles. She seems fascinated by his dialect. The charade goes on and on. Now there is another boy sitting on Thirty-Five-Year-Old's lap. It's quite a crush. Six of us in a space for four. 'Won't you give us your bra. You could slip it off without us seeing your tits. Give us your bra. Please, a token of this meeting. Otherwise it'll be as if we'd never met. Won't you show us a nipple?'

'If she did,' I whisper to Thirty-Five-Year-Old, 'the boys wouldn't know what to do.'

'Dead right,' he laughs. 'Everybody would be shocked.' Then sagely he adds, 'It's just a joke, so as not to think of the game.'

At once, there I am, back in the hotel in Lecce with Agnolin explaining that any scurrilous conversation I've heard is purely therapeutic.

'Please can I touch your cardigan.' It's Scopa. She lets him. A chorus of demands begins

'Could you just let us see what material your panties are made of?'

'Would you let me touch your earlobe with my little finger?'

'Could I kiss your cheek, please?'

'Verona,' someone explains to her. 'Romeo and Juliet. Home of romance. Have you ever been?'

She hasn't.

'Oh, you must come to Verona. It's the most beautiful city in Italy. You wouldn't believe it. And so clean after the south.'

There's a moment's civic pride.

'I'd love to,' she says.

'Perhaps we're being too subtle,' Scopa reflects for the benefit of his friends. And to Gabriella: 'I mean, we haven't touched you or pinched you, have we? I hope you weren't getting worried. We haven't done anything we shouldn't, have we? Not like those southern men who just whip it out and come all over you, don't they.'

She's shaking her head. But she seems nervous now, checking the names of all the stations. It seems she has to get out a stop or two before Naples.

'I bet if you'd known you were going to find us lot on the train, you'd have got on a different carriage wouldn't you?'

'Not at all,' she smiles wanly. 'It's fun.'

Her handbag trills. It's her boyfriend calling her mobile. She's relieved. Thirty-Five-Year-Old tears six inches off the end of a

French loaf and jams it on to the top of his plastic flagpole. It's obscene. Meantime, while she speaks on the phone, all the boys have started singing a popular song: '*Che fretta c'era, maledetta primavera, lo sappiamo io e te.*' What hurry was there, bloody springtime, you and I know.

'Hope you've got sponge panties on, otherwise your boyfriend'll know.'

She shuts her eyes. She refuses a beer, a leg of chicken, a sandwich, a *brigate* cap. Then at last it's her station. She jumps to her feet.

'Please, please take this in remembrance of us.'

One of the boys with a hedgehog head of hair has put a piece of chicken skin in a small transparent plastic bag. Flustered, Gabriella accepts it. She stumbles over extended legs out of the train. Everybody rushes to the other side of the carriage, falling over the passengers there to pull down the window. They want to see the boyfriend. He isn't there. Gabriella waves, clutching her flag and her handbag and disappears down the stairs. Someone yells a generic '*Napoli Napoli vaffanculo*' and then it's all over.

'So,' I put it to Scopa, 'so, imagine you have to choose: you can either have a night with Gabriella, and Verona lose, or no Gabriella and Verona win. What do you go for?'

Scopa shakes his head at the stupidity of this question. 'Verona have to win today,' he says. 'We have to. There are plenty of Gabriellas, but only one Hellas Verona.'

'Abandon all hope . . .'

Yesterday I consulted the Tarot cards and alas they didn't have anything good to say about tomorrow's game. Napoli are going to beat us two–nil . . . FORZA HELLAS!!! *ALONE AGAINST FATE!!!!*
Piotre

However few of us there are, they are always there waiting for us. However hot the weather, they are always dressed the same way: the black boots, the black bulky trousers, the belt with the holster and gun, the heavy black jacket, bursting with pockets, the blue riot helmet with Perspex visa. And however calm we are, however relaxed, or sometimes despondent, they always have their truncheons in their hands, tightly gripped. Perspiring abundantly in the suffocating heat of Napoli Centrale, one holds a tear-gas launcher on his arm. Another raises his video camera to follow every move we make. Walking down the platform, the *brigate* are singing, '*Pizza quà, pizza là, Napoli va a cagà!*' Pizza here, pizza there. Napoli piss off.

We're taken to a side-entrance to be frisked. 'No flagpoles.'

'What?'

'You heard. No flagpoles.'

'But we brought them on purpose. It's a choreography for the team.'

'Crap. You've only come here to cause trouble.'

'That's not true. We're here for the team.'

'Crap.'

Thus the head of the police to Spada. We're obliged to strip our flags from our poles and chuck the latter in a pile in a filthy corner.

'They're potential weapons.'

'No, they're not. We had them made specially thin so they couldn't hurt anyone. Look!'

Spada takes a pole and bends it. It folds like polythene.

'No poles, you've only come to cause trouble.'

There are about thirty policemen. My bag is opened. I have a bottle of mineral water. The policeman pulls it out, removes the plastic top and thrusts it back in my hand.

'But I need the water!' It's ten in the morning. It's a hot day.

'You can carry it open. A bottle-top is a potential weapon.'

Spada is despairing over his flagpoles. Somebody starts up a chant, '*Teròn, teròn, teròn è uno solo, si chiama San Gennaro ed è un vero teròn.*' There's only one *terrone*, San Gennaro, Napoli's patron saint. Perhaps one has to have lived in Italy some time to appreciate how offensive this is. Some of the boys tell the culprit to leave off.

'What you could do,' I suggest to the policeman, 'is take the flagpoles to the game in the police van and give them to us when we're already in the stadium and can't hurt anyone. Then we give them back when we leave.'

The policeman hesitates. Spada insists, 'What can possibly go wrong with that? We had them specially made to *fare bella figura* at the stadium.'

'OK.'

So we go back to the pile in the corner, get the flagpoles and start loading them up in the police trucks. The policemen still frisking the last few *butei* are confused by this change of plan.

Then, exactly as we pile into the two buses waiting in the filthy little piazza at the station's back entrance, a group of thirty or so young men appear from behind parked cars hurling cobblestones. Two windows smash. Someone goes down in the corridor struck from behind. Then about five rockets are fired. They are big red fireworks, perhaps flares, aimed to pass through the broken windows. They miss, sizzling away over the bus. The *butei* rush to the door to get out and face their assailants. The police block them. They are banging with their truncheons on the driver's cabin. 'Drive! Go!' The bus accelerates away from the scene. The police make no attempt to follow the vandals. Nor do they use their tear-gas. 'Why not?' The boys are incensed. They've been frisked, then immediately attacked. 'Oh if only I had my plastic bottle-top to throw,' someone mocks. 'That'd scare them.'

But there is always one friendly policeman. This seems to be a law of group dynamics. I remember a very chatty, ordinary man on the edge of the scuffles in Vicenza; a matey wit with a riot shield on the tube in Milan. Today it's the officer with the tear-gas launcher. He sits down by the smashed window, weapon pointing out at the street in case of further trouble. He shows us how it works, where the canister is loaded, how you fire. 'Go on, go on, shoot, shoot!' the *butei* laugh. 'Those guys over there. Go on.' The policeman grins and points, doesn't shoot. 'We don't go after the hooligans in Naples', he says, referring to the incident of a few minutes before, 'because we're afraid they might have guns.'

It was at this point that the day began to take on a seriously Dantesque quality. Naples is not a big town. From the station to the stadium can't be more than five or six kilometres. But the packed bus contrives to take half an hour, setting out on a stretch of *autostrada*. Instead of the Naples I know I see a group of commercial tower blocks a couple of miles away on our left. After twenty minutes they are still there, still a couple of miles away on our left, but now we are seeing them from the other side. We're making a huge circle. On each side of the bus, police vans have their lights flashing. Below the elevated road are the squalid suburbs, the abandoned factories, the seedy tenements. In a street of broken asphalt a dozen dogs are fighting over scattered garbage. 'This is the south,' the man beside me is muttering. 'What shit!' It is one of the lovely ambiguities of the *brigate* that though they infallibly leave behind a litter of beer cans and greasy paper, they are nevertheless very sensitive to urban decline. One suspects that at home they have a wastepaper basket in every room and always clean up the bathroom after themselves.

'Where's the bathroom?' somebody demands.

Having taken us right round the city, we are unloaded and pushed through a rusty gate into a desolate yard. I look up to find the stadium but it isn't there. There are crumbling brick walls and what looks like a ruined warehouse. Weeds are flourishing in the gravel.

'Where's the bathroom?'

'There is no bathroom. You can piss in the grass.'

'I need a shit.' The policeman shrugs his shoulders. Their boss promises that soon a mobile kiosk of some kind will materialise to sell us food and drink. We haven't had access to any kind of bar or shop since ten yesterday evening. The kiosk doesn't materialise. The grass has been abundantly pissed in by others before us. We are going to be in this yard under a sultry sky and thirty-degree heat for at least three hours. People mill. They try to arrange a game of football with newspapers wrapped tight in a flag. It doesn't work. We can't get involved. Everybody's tense. Verona are surely going down if they don't win this one. They stretch on the ground. After a while people begin to accuse each other of farting. 'Oh disgusting.' '*Dio boia.*' 'Oh gross, *Dio can.*' But then we discover that the smell is coming from a drain a few yards from where we're sitting. Everybody jumps up. 'What filth, what shit the south!' We're like a group of sinners arriving in hell and finding it doesn't have adequate sanitary services. Perhaps hell, it occurs to me, will be the ultimate away game, an interminable wait for a match that never begins in the circle of some infernal stadium, tormented by devils in the shape of policemen and opposing fans.

Finally we're piled back into the bus, unloaded at the stadium and rushed into the gates past a hostile crowd, the police shrieking and shoving us from behind as if trying to get a group of paedophiles past an enraged lynching party. In the stadium we are allotted a low corner-segment, safely segregated and hung round with nets to prevent any projectiles from going in or out. The famous San Paolo is a huge, old-fashioned, grey cement bowl. To greet us is a banner: 'VERONESE MAIALE: L'AFTA IL TUO VERO RIVALE.' Veronese Pig – foot-and-mouth the match for you. There's still an hour to wait.

After a few brave choruses, it's unusually quiet. Forza sits on his own and stares. Stefano sits on his own, his head in his hands. This is the crunch game. An unusual number of people find they need a shit. There's only one toilet with a door that doesn't lock, a flush that doesn't work and no paper. As always, people ask me if I have tissues. I do. When eventually I get to use the place myself it's filthy. A policeman comes to check on me while I'm performing. Is he worried I'm vandalising the place? Or is it more likely that I'm committing suicide?

At least the pitch is in good condition. At last the players come out. The Neapolitans perform the ritual hanging of a blue-and-yellow manikin from the parapet of their *curva*. The *brigate* give them the ironic slow handclap. The game begins.

Verona are at full strength today. So no excuses. Seric seems to be back for good now, deservedly so. He's feisty in defence, confident when he pushes forward. Italiano is there too. Would that Perotti had settled on his strongest team some time ago. In any event, Verona attack. For a while they look better than Napoli, who are muddled and frequently whistled by their own fans. On the break Bonazzoli beats their keeper to a bouncing ball, and tips it over his head. It lands on the top of the crossbar. At a corner Apolloni is left on his own to head for goal. He heads wide. At another corner Laursen heads on target. Excellent save from Fontana. In the forty-second minute, with their first real shot of the game, Napoli score. Verona try to hit back, but they are losing their nerve. Things are going wrong too often. For the whole second half they push forward, but ever more raggedly. Apolloni again finds himself alone with a cross to head in. Again he heads wide. I remember the boy who consulted his tarot. Hellas, alone against fate. In the eighty-second minute Laursen makes a careless back pass to Ferron, the young striker Mauri slips in and scores. Two–nil, as predicted.

'My world is falling apart,' the boy beside me starts to curse rhythmically. He has his face in his hands. 'Let it be over now. Let it be over. I don't want to hear anybody talking about hope. I don't want to hear anyone saying that it's not mathematical yet, that they still believe we can make it. Let's go into Serie B. It's where we belong. Let's not even try to get into Serie A again. It's too painful. It's too painful. Pastorello is a shit. The players are shits. They didn't try. I'm not going to get a season ticket next year. I'm giving up football. Let's stay in Serie B for ever. It's stupid expecting Verona to play in Serie A. All we do is go to games and suffer and suffer and suffer and suffer to no end. There's no hope, that's the truth. We've got to get used to there being no hope.'

'Abandon all hope, you who enter here.' What distinguishes the suffering in hell from the suffering in purgatory, my commentary says, is that in hell we have suffering without hope, suffering that doesn't purge, that doesn't ennoble, that has no end. 'Let it end.' The boy keeps shaking his head. He's crying. He's seriously upset. 'Let it be Serie B and that's that.'

An hour later, accelerating away from the stadium, our bus is hit by a shower of stones. In the piazza outside the station, three or four middle-aged women yell hysterically from high balconies. Wearing a thin night-dress, one is leaning dangerously over the railing, long grey hair falling forward. Forza is furious when some of the boys yell back. 'Where's your dignity? The *brigate* don't talk to old women frothing in their slums.' This time the police make sure we pay before getting on the train. A turnstile is formed with two policemen holding each end of a truncheon. Each person must pay before that makeshift barrier lifts.

They've put us on the regular night train to Munich. Passengers already on board bang on windows and shout insults at us as we march up the platform, gallantly singing '*Hellas la mia unica fede*'. We have two segregated carriages at the front of the train. Under unnecessary police guard, a vendor pushes his trolley to the connecting door to sell us Cokes and sandwiches. Already people are joking again. A resigned irony reigns. Serie B. 'Tomorrow, the black armband, *butei*.' Hats come over eyes. Try to sleep.

A couple of hours later, only five minutes after leaving Roma Termini, the train comes to a standstill. The lights go off. Outside is a shadowy slum, a snip of neon. Four of us are stretched from side to side across the seats. The air is stale, the night warm. '*Attenzione*,' the PA eventually announces. '*Attenzione*. *Il capotreno* wishes to inform the passengers that this *convoglio* will be stationary *per un tempo indeterminato* due to the breakdown of the locomotive.'

No! We're stuck. Fucking trains! Fucking inefficient southerners! Hell. The minutes tick by. The lights don't go on. Oh where, I wonder, is that poet Virgil to lead us out of here, where is the man who's terza rima took him so nimbly from circle to circle, stadium to stadium. '*Dio boia*, I have to be at work by eight,' Stefano mutters. There's a chorus of me-toos. Eventually we pull into Verona at 5 a.m.

'*Ciao ragazzi*.' We say our goodbyes. Verona are surely in Serie B. So this will be the last meaningful trip together this season. 'Ciao *butei*.' Then Scopa shouts, 'Oh but the wonderful thing about going to Naples is how good you feel when you get back to Verona! Back home! How good, *Dio can*!' Driving round the circular road, I pass the big police station by the river. A long queue of perhaps a hundred blacks and Asians has already formed outside. For them it will be another day in their long struggle for the *permesso di soggiorno*, the work permit, the right to call Verona, as Scopa does, home. The drama of the immigrant's life, it occurs to me, is so urgent that he has no time for the intense but oddly unreal catastrophes of association football.

31A GIORNATA

Parma – Inter 3–1
Milan – Fiorentina 1–2
Atalanta – Reggina 1–1
Bari – Roma 1–4
Bologna – Juventus 1–4
Lazio – Udinese 3–1
Napoli – Verona 2–0
Perugia – Brescia 2–2
Vicenza – Lecce 0–0

CLASSIFICA

Roma	70
Lazio	65
Juventus	64
Parma	53
Milan	47
Inter	44
Atalanta	43
Fiorentina	42
Bologna	42
Perugia	41
Brescia	37
Udinese	34
Vicenza	33
Lecce	33
Napoli	31
Reggina	30
Verona	28
Bari	20

Commedia dell'Arte

*Veronese, you're one of those people who can't
distinguish football from real life.*
solonapoli.eb@sta

'The Italian comedians learn nothing by heart; they need but to
glance at the subject of a play before going upon the stage. It is this
ability to perform at a moment's notice which makes a good Italian
actor so difficult to replace. Anyone can learn a part and recite it,
but something else is required for Italian comedy.'

Such was the opinion of Evaristo Gherardi, seventeenth-century
star of the *commedia dell'arte*, a form of drama where the actors wore
masks and played characters, or more precisely roles, that remained
the same whatever the story; instead of learning a script, they
improvised and might well change the plot in mid-stream if a better
idea occurred to them. Gherardi played Harlequin. He goes on:

'For a good Italian actor is a man of infinite resourcefulness;
he matches his words and actions so perfectly with those of
his colleagues that he enters instantly into whatever acting and
movements are required of him in such a manner as to give the
impression that all that they do has been prearranged.'

Well, how much *was* prearranged?

'These plays are never withdrawn on account of illness among
the actors or because of newly recruited talent.' So remarked the
enthusiastic Count Carlo Gozzi. 'An impromptu parley before going
on the stage, as regards both the plot and the way in which it is to
be played, is sufficient to ensure a smooth performance. It often

happens that in special circumstances, or because of the relative importance and skill of certain actors, a change in the distribution of the roles is made on the spur of the moment just as the curtain is rising. Yet the comedy is borne along to a gay and sprightly conclusion. It is apparent that these actors penetrate to the very core of their subjects with so many varieties of dialogue that, with each performance, the interpretation seems to be quite new, yet inevitable and permanent.'

Doesn't this begin to sound a little like football? Never withdrawn on account of illness. An impromptu parley before going on the pitch . . . to ensure a smooth performance. A change in the distribution of roles because of the relative importance and skill of certain players. But still there's the thorny question of exactly *how far* the plot has or hasn't been prearranged. On 29 May, 2001, the president of Napoli, Giorgio Corbelli, protested that the penultimate game of the season, between Parma and Verona, was going to be prearranged, to Napoli's detriment. What we were going to see was twenty-two actors playing their parts. The result had already been decided in Verona's favour.

But weren't Hellas Verona supposed to be dead and done with? Indeed they were. But one of the consequences of the melodrama of Italian life is that every defeat and every victory is interpreted in a much-exaggerated fashion. If, around Christmas, a club is six or nine points clear at the top, the championship is considered over. Then everybody can be amazed when, with a couple of draws and a defeat, it is all suddenly open again. People are easily depressed and elated. Being so is an attribute of the roles they play. And I, too, over the years, must have become a little more Italian, because when I saw Verona five points away from safety with only three games to go, I was convinced that it was over. How can we catch up Vicenza, five points away, not to mention first having to pass Reggina two points ahead and Naples three? The paper calculates that we must win all of the last three games to have any chance. Three victories in a row. We haven't won two games together all season. No team has ever come back from second-to-bottom only three games from the end. On the train back from Naples,

I told Stefano, 'If Perotti says he still believes we can do it, I'll kill him.'

In Tuesday's ritual post-match interview, Perotti declared, 'I still believe we can do it.' Furious, I phoned Saverio Guette. 'They've ruined my bloody book,' I protested. 'They're clowns.' The marketing man sighed. 'Chievo are only one point away from Serie A,' he said. 'They're going to overtake us.'

So now there was the game with Bologna. It was Sunday 27 May. Because many towns were having the second round of voting in mayoral elections, all games were played in the evening, which was a relief, because Italy is hot now. Just as humours shift rapidly from hope to despair and back, so the weather turns a sudden corner in spring and it is blistering. Thirty-two degrees. Even at eight-thirty in the evening the stadium was suffocating. Pietro and company were cheerful and resigned. The girls to our left were yawning. 'Too much sun.' The men were analysing a season that was already over. It was Pastorello's fault. He should have fired Perotti way back. He should have spent more money. 'Let's just watch the game and enjoy,' Pietro said. 'If we can.' After three minutes, Bologna scored. We were mathematically in B.

Then I realised that although I thought I had already abandoned hope before the game, actually I hadn't. Not quite. I had pretended to despair, precisely to keep alive the tiniest hidden hope, flickering deep, deep in my breast. Now it was extinguished. It's over, I thought. You can relax. Write the last few elegiac pages tomorrow.

A minute later Verona had equalised. Then on the half-hour came a startling pattern of rapid passes such as the team hasn't put together all season, ending with the perfect through ball to Adailton, 'the only Brazilian who can't play football', as the fans like to say. Much-whistled, playing awfully up to this point, Adailton looked up as Pagliuca came out, and curved the ball round him so sweetly that it seemed, as Evaristo Gherardi might have said, inevitable, prearranged.' Two–one. A little less prearranged was the own goal a Bologna defender deflected into his net just before half-time. But it was greeted with equal enthusiasm. Likewise the penalty conceded to the Brazilian striker just two minutes into the second half. Four–one. Needless to say, the boys then did everything they could to throw away even this lead. Again Apolloni was sent off. His fourth expulsion this season. Fifteen minutes from time it was five–two, then five–three, then five–four. But the team hung on, and when it was finally over the whole crowd was trembling with excitement. For from the other stadiums came the perfect set of results. All our rivals defeated. Suddenly Hellas were only two points off the cut, with two games to go. And all along terraces everyone is whispering, 'Parma. Surely Parma will let us win next week. They'll give us the game. Then all we have to do is beat Perugia at home. We can do it!'

Why do people think this? Only a week ago the Italian tote suspended betting on half the games in Serie B. With some teams already promoted or relegated and others still desperate for points, there was the suspicion that the games might not be entirely 'transparent'. You could put a bet on Rovaniemi–Jokerit in the Finnish league, but not on Empoli–Torino, nor Chievo–Piacenza.

The following week suspicion switched to Serie A. In the last minutes of the tie Lecce–Parma the Cameroon player Patrick Mboma scored the winning goal for Parma. But did he mean to? A cross comes drifting over. Mboma rises to it, but without conviction. The ball strikes his head and goes into the net. Seeing what has happened, he clutches his hair in dismay. Far from rushing to take the salute of his fans, he bangs an angry fist against the post. Lecce really needed that point to stay out of relegation trouble. Parma were already safely in Champions' League territory.

And if Parma were willing to do Lecce a favour, then they should be all the more willing to do one for us. Everyone knows that Pastorello worked at Parma for many years. Isn't Bonazzoli on loan from Parma? Likewise Seric. Isn't Laursen going to play for Parma next year? Don't Parma have various old players of ours? Haven't they already secured a place in the Champions' League? They don't need a result. Above all, didn't Pastorello buy Hellas Verona with money borrowed from the Tanzi family who own Parma?

The Tanzi family is fabulously rich. They control Parmalat, a huge food-processing company with various subsidiaries and various interests in football. 'The rules of the game have been subverted by a dangerous conflict of interests,' say the left-wing losers in the elections. How can a man who owns half the country's TV get elected? How can two teams who have financial interests in common play each other at a crucial moment in the season? demands Napoli's Corbelli. On The Wall someone comments:

GRUPPO PARMALAT 1 – PARMALAT S.P.A. 2
PARMA CALCIO S.P.A. 5 – HELLAS VERONA S.P.A. 6

Over the next few days, interviewed by the press, all the Parma players swear they're going to do their best, just to show they're not corrupt. 'Pastorello, make that phone-call!' the fans start writing to the website. 'Call him. Call him!' And they mean Stefano Tanzi of course. 'If we are buying the match,' writes my Caporetto friend in London, 'please do send me the bank details so I can make my contribution.'

Meantime an extraordinary tam-tam is beginning. 'Everybody to Parma.' 'Parma or death!' 'Parma AND death!' On Tuesday morning, Parma football club, after consulting with the police, provide only 1,800 tickets. After all, Verona haven't had more than a few hundred fans at away games recently. The tickets are sold in three hours. 'To Parma, tickets or no tickets!' 'Hellas Army on the move!' '10,000 Brigate Gialloblù! We'll blow the ball in the net!'

But, alas, there's more than a week to wait. The national team are playing and Serie A takes a week off. On the intervening Sunday, Chievo clinch the point they need for promotion in front of a big crowd that must already include thousands of defectors from Hellas. Needless to say, Monday's *Arena* bears the headline: 'The Dream Becomes Reality'. But it's more like a nightmare in the Hellas camp. 'People here are suffering, suffering, suffering!' Guette says grimly. 'Everybody's *chievando*' – Chievoing – comes an ironic voice over the net (*Chiave* means 'key', *chiavare*, to fuck). 'The Mayor is *chievando*, the football league are *chievando*, the left are *chievando*, traitors all over the world, *chievando*!'

The only advantage, as it turns out, is that the horrible truth of Chievo's promotion may have a positive effect on the game with Parma. Hellas must make a last effort. Hellas supporters must come out of the woodwork. It's now or never. Anything but a win is mathematical relegation and with it a handing of the baton to Chievo. Perhaps for ever. Seven thousand on the move, announces the *Arena* the day before the game.

Sunday morning the scene outside the Zanzibar is extraordinary. There have never been so many people. Where have they been all season? Albe, who works in a restaurant, turns up with a huge cake in whose icing he has somehow had imprinted a photograph of the team. Fondo is there. Scopa, Stefano. And amazingly, Glass-eye. 'Where have you been?' He embraces me as if we had climbed off the bus from Bari yesterday evening. 'My season,' he summarises: 'Bari, police-station. Vicenza, police-station. Torino, police-station!' Then at work I break my leg. Out injured, like Colucci.' 'Why weren't you banned?' 'Grace of God.' He's in excellent spirits.

Then another familiar face appears. The handsome man who loaded us on the bus that first night and told us all to leave the headrests white. Banned after the Juventus game, he has just served his time. Came back last week for the Bologna game. Mantice, he's called. Bellows. He's tall, strong-featured, full of energy. At once you sense that here is a figure of charisma on a level above all the others, a man who is friendly, excitable, seductive, dangerous. 'Today we're going to win,' he announces. 'But no racist chants. If we start any racist stuff, Parma will fight to the death.' Is he talking to Glass-eye? Has Glass-eye understood? He does seem remarkably clear-headed today. But turning to me, he sniggers. 'If we win, crowd trouble. If we lose, crowd trouble. And if we draw?' 'Crowd trouble,' I chime.

Piled on the buses, the convoy begins to roll. A further army are setting off on Vespas. It's only sixty or seventy miles. Flags are streaming. 'Couldn't sleep,' a voice behind me is saying. 'Had this nightmare where the ball just won't go in the net.' 'Don't worry, it's fixed. Two–one to us.' Then someone says that Pastorello actually phoned a friend of his to say that it was fixed as long as there were no racist chants. 'Oh bullshit! Pastorello would never be so stupid as to phone anyone.' '*Butei*, it's not fixed. They'd never fix it after all the monkey grunts we gave Thuram back at home.' 'No monkey grunts today, *ragazzi*. Absolutely no excuse for the ref to get mean.' Someone hands me the paper and points at an article. The *New York Times* is sending a photographer to the game to capture the racism of Hellas fans. The *New York Times*! In provincial Verona the name seems magical. 'Not a single oo, *butei*! We'll send him home empty-handed.'

An hour early we pull into the stadium compound. Parma is a team built entirely on the Tanzis' money with no footballing tradition, no real public. The stadium only holds 22,000. The crush to get in the gates is as suffocating and dangerous as anything I've seen. As we spill inside the organisers are simply obliged to concede segment after segment to make way for this tidal wave of Veronese. In the event, we take over a whole *curva*. It's a fantastic gathering of the clans. Perhaps the last. A fortress of yellow-blue. A solid wall of sound. I haven't seen anything like this before. 'Brought shivers down my spine,' says Leo Colucci afterwards. But now the whistle's blown, the game is off.

If you knew a game was fixed, you would hardly want to watch it, would you? But the suspicion that it *might* be fixed only makes it all the more fascinating. Right behind the goal, in the thick of the crowd, I anxiously scan the back and forth of play for some sign that something unusual is going on. But how can you tell? Verona attack. Parma are elegantly calm, but inconclusive. Behind the fence a black photographer walks up and down taking pictures of us. It's the man from the *Times*. Naturally, they have sent a black. Meantime Parma are playing every black in their squad. 'Five of them,' says the boy next to me. 'Five! I didn't know they *had* five blacks.' It's a red rag to a bull. But there are no grunts today. Nor any insults to their players. And on the half-hour we're awarded a penalty in what looked a fairly innocuous situation. Goal.

So it *is* fixed. I feel relief and concern. At half-time everyone is festive. We're going to do it. It's OK. The results from the other stadiums look good. If things go well we'll catch up with fourth-from-bottom. Then next week, if we can only beat Perugia . . . Twenty minutes into the second half, Parma equalised.

There are no words for what follows. I'm so depressed. And ashamed too. You were happy it was fixed, Tim. You were happy that the game was set up. And now you're appalled that it isn't set up. And appalled that you should wish it was. Appalled that, once again, for the seventeenth, repeat *seventeenth*, time this season, you have made a long journey to see Verona fail to win away.

The minutes ticked by. The crowds tried to sing. Behind me a pretty young girl with freckles stood anxiously beside her bellowing boyfriend. Directly in front, a huge fat bare-chested man with paunch and pony-tail began the monkey grunts. Ominously one or two others joined in. Immediately Mantice yelled through the megaphone to stop. 'VE-RO-NA.' I made an effort to join in. At least the players are giving it everything, I thought. The attacks were incessant now. In Parma's goal, Buffon saves. And again. If it was fixed, surely he wouldn't? Laursen goes down in the box. I'm barely ten yards away. I can see this is a penalty. Why doesn't the ref give it, if the game's fixed? It's not fixed and we're not going to win. Then Ferron saves. Twice. Why would Parma try to score, if it was fixed? Oh what's wrong with these people! The fans are chanting constantly, admirably. But my voice falters. I feel sick. I need to sit down. I'm going to faint. In the last ten minutes Verona have three, four, five opportunities. Adailton misses from point-blank range. Perhaps it *is* fixed, but all the same somebody still has to stick the ball in the net. And we can't even do that. We're useless.

Once again, the lumbering Cossato is wheeled on. Our only Veronese. He's only there because Bonazzoli is out. Gilardino is out. I always feel Perotti has lost hope when he wheels on Cossato. And I remember that Cossato used to play for Chievo, till they passed him on to us last year, just as he turned thirty. That passage, I tell myself, of a striker past his best from the smaller team to the larger marked the transfer of power from Hellas to Chievo. They thought the man wasn't good enough for Serie B. Inexplicably, we took him in A, and what has he done? Nothing. Just that one goal against Lazio when it was already too late to matter.

Cossato charges madly into the fray and immediately misses a good chance. It's too much. I have to crouch down for a moment. We're finished. I'm really not well. It's mathematical. At the eighty-seventh another cross comes curling low into the box. Cossato launches himself in a wild dive. He makes contact and crashes the ball past Buffon. Goal. Deprived of exhibitions of racism, the guy from the *NYT* must have taken splendid pictures of thousands and thousands of yellow-blue bodies falling over each other. Among whom myself shouting, shamelessly, 'Cossato, Super-Mike, I love you!'

Honi soit qui mal y pense. Shortly after the game, Napoli's angry chairman offers a different version. 'Thinking ill is a sin,' Corbelli tells the TV cameras, 'but all too often one gets it right.' He promises he is going to demand an enquiry into the relations between Parma and Verona and the exact nature of the ownership of Hellas. Over the web comes the inevitable answer: '*Corbelli vaffanculo. Hellas, campione d'Italia.*' On the coach back someone swears to me he saw Buffon wink as he retrieved the ball from the back of the net. I don't believe it. Your Italian Harlequin is too professional for that kind of silliness. A week later, over a cappuccino, Martin Laursen earnestly assures me that the game wasn't fixed. 'It was a real, hard game, Tim.' 'Would they have told you if it was?' I ask.

32A GIORNATA

Brescia – Vicenza 2–1
Fiorentina – Atalanta 1–1
Inter – Lazio 1–1
Juventus – Perugia 1–0
Lecce – Parma 1–2
Reggina – Bari 1–0
Roma – Milan 1–1
Udinese – Napoli 0–0
Verona – Bologna 5–4

33A GIORNATA

Atalanta – Udinese 0–1
Bari – Inter 1–2
Bologna – Lecce 2–2
Lazio – Fiorentina 3–0
Milan – Brescia 1–1
Napoli – Roma 2–2
Parma – Verona 1–2
Perugia – Reggina 1–1
Vicenza – Juventus 0–3

CLASSIFICA

Roma	72
Juventus	70
Lazio	69
Parma	56
Milan	49
Inter	48
Atalanta	44
Fiorentina	43
Bologna	43
Perugia	42
Brescia	41
Udinese	38
Lecce	34
Reggina	34
Verona	34
Vicenza	33
Napoli	33
Bari	20

Il Giorno del Giudizio

*In the week preceding Verona–Perugia, Perugia will
be training on the beach, in the morning under the
sunshades, in the afternoon strolling along Viale Dante,
in the evening eating maccaroni and drinking Martinis
till late.*

Ps. Free drinks for me afterwards in Piazza Bra.
San Francesco (Perugia)

I come downstairs sevenish on the Sunday morning, feeling pretty
rough, can't sleep, turn on the radio. 'Beep beep beep.' The news.
An ominous silence, then· '*Oggi è il giorno del giudizio.*' It's a solemn
voice. Judgment Day! God, what's happened? Palestine in flames?
Only after about thirty seconds do I realise that today's main headline
has gone to football. It's Judgment Day for Serie A. 'Two points clear
of Juventus,' the voice goes on, 'Roma must win against Parma to be
sure of the *scudetto*. One point behind Juve, Lazio are still hoping in a
miracle.' And they begin to interview the big stars, the heavyweight
coaches. I turn it off. Who cares about what's going on at the top?
The can of worms at the bottom is so much more interesting. An
hour or so later, we head off as a family for our Sunday morning
cappuccino. It's a ritual. Entering the bar, Michele rushes to grab
the *Gazzetta*. The main banner headline reads '*IL GIORNO DEL
GIUDIZIO*'. Uncanny!

But what kind of judgment is it going to be? Fast and fair as
Saint Peter at the pearly gates? As far as the relegation scenario
is concerned, the *Gazzetta* offers a bewildering series of tables,

415

percentages and hypotheses. It's almost as bad as the election results. Four teams must go down. Only Bari are mathematically out. Vicenza and Napoli are on 33 points. Lecce, Reggina and Verona are on 34. Of these five, three will be lost, two will be saved. 'Given the rule of one point for a draw and three for a win, there are 243 possible combinations of results between the five interested teams,' announces the *Gazzetta*, 'with correspondingly numerous consequences.' The paper goes on to list them. All 243. Spooning the foam off our coffees, Michele and I gaze and gaze at the names and the figures, while the women folk shake their heads.

Essentially:

Napoli (33 points) are away to Fiorentina. In normal circumstances they would lose and go down.

Vicenza (33 points) are away to Udinese. In normal circumstances they would lose and go down.

Reggina (34 points) have Milan at home. In normal circumstances they would lose, but perhaps stay up if all the others lose.

Lecce (34 points) have Lazio at home. In normal circumstances they would lose, but again could stay up just the same.

Verona (34 points) are at home to Perugia. In normal circumstances they would draw or win and stay up.

'Fantastic,' Michele concludes. 'Easy.'

'Look at the betting odds, Mick.'

He looks. In each game the bookmakers are favouring the weaker side. Reggina will beat Milan, they predict; Lecce will beat Lazio. These aren't normal circumstances.

'May the best team win!' announces my wife.

'The hell with the best team,' Michele tells her. 'It's got to be Hellas.'

The day is furiously hot and sticky. Everybody's in the ground unnecessarily early. 'Trembling,' Pietro says cheerfully as I take my place beside him. 'Trembling.'

Then all around us people start to remember that last year Perugia, miserable Perugia, took the *scudetto* away from Juve by beating them on the last game of the season under torrential rain. 'Strange team,' says the pessimist in the row in front, 'strange tradition. I mean, they had nothing to gain by beating Juve. They were already safe. And everything to lose. Imagine having the power of Juve against you when something's being debated in the Football Federation. Most teams would just have let them score. Like Parma with us.'

'What's going to happen in the other games?' I ask Pietro.

'They'll all win,' he says. 'Reggina, Lecce, Napoli, Vicenza.'

'But that's scandalous,' Michele bursts out. 'They can't *all* beat teams like Lazio and Milan.'

'Something'll go wrong somewhere,' I hazard. 'Someone will screw up the gift penalty, or someone on the other side will score by accident. Like Mboma.'

'No.' It's the pessimist in front of me. 'They'll let them win. You'll see.'

'Our only hope', Pietro concludes, 'is if Roma don't score early against Parma. Or if Parma should actually take the lead. In that case, with the half-chance that Roma might actually lose and Juve maybe only draw, then Lazio will want to be winning at Lecce so as to catch up with the leaders for a play-off for the *scudetto*. Otherwise Lazio'll give up and Lecce are safe.'

It's bewildering. The combinations, the psychology. Apparently nobody can just go out on the field and play their game. Only the ingenuous English could ever imagine or even desire such a thing. What a huge amount of mental energy, I tell myself, is going to be required in the ninety minutes ahead. The whole length of the *bel paese* will be frenetically tangled together in a back and forth of results as now this team now that slips into B, crawls back into A.

The referee looks at his watch. It's particularly important that the battles across the country be synchronised so that nobody has the advantage of knowing the final result from elsewhere while they're still playing. The normal Saturday *anticipi* and Sunday *posticipo* have been cancelled. The whole of Serie A, all eighteen teams, are playing simultaneously. There! The whistle blows, the Day of Judgment. At least after ninety minutes, it'll be over. I'm already exhausted.

Perotti has made one of his bizarre decisions, preferring the aging wardrobe Mazzola to the peppier Italiano. The front page of this morning's *Arena* carried two small colour photos. One of Roma's coach Fabio Capello, one of Perotti. Capello was leaning forward, shaking his fist, jaws tense in a craggy face, a fierce frizz of hair, huge mouth wide open in a bellow of incitement. Attilio Perotti was leaning against the trainer's bench looking vacantly into the sky, as if the world had ended some time ago and he couldn't understand why he was still down here. 'We never listen to a word he says,' Laursen told me just a couple of days ago. 'He's hopeless.'

All the same, Verona go on the attack. In Perugia's goal Mazzantini makes a reflex save. After just ninety seconds the scoreboard begins to flash. Vicenza are already a goal up at Udine. They've overtaken us. Serie B. The crowd groans. Mazzantini saves again. After ten minutes Vicenza are two–nil up. Again Mazzantini saves. After twenty minutes it's Udinese 0, Vicenza 3. 'It's an outrage,' Michele is screaming. 'It's impossible. Vicenza can't score three at Udine. They're hopeless. It's fixed.'

Ten yards outside a crowded Perugia box, Anthony Seric looks up, shoots. It's a futile piece of presumption. Seric is left-back. He's feisty and fast, but he's never scored. And Marco Mazzantini is on form today. A big burly caveman with straggly shoulder-length hair and a barrel chest, he has the unexpected agility of the giant. Seric shoots from thirty yards. Why do professional players waste promising situations like this? Why didn't he look for a head and cross? Still, there's something odd about this shot. It's not that it takes a deflection, but, already low, it seems to be dipping and bobbing. Sure of himself, Mazzantini goes to gather it. As if radio-controlled, the ball drops very suddenly and passes through his legs.

This was the turning point of the game. The thought that he would be accused of fixing the game by letting in the easiest of shots must have driven Mazzantini mad. Precisely because of the suspicions and paranoia that surround these end-of-season matches, it was now suddenly imperative for the keeper that Verona shouldn't win. He was beside himself and he transmitted this fury to the whole of his team. At once the pitch was a battlefield. Again Apolloni was sent off. His fifth expulsion this year. A record in Serie A. With him went Liverani, one of Perugia's stars. The atmosphere was electric.

Then, on the stroke of half-time, the scoreboard announced that Lazio had gone one up against Lecce. Now Verona and Vicenza were both safe, the others doomed. No sooner had the crowd's roar died down than the pessimist in front turns to say, 'Bari, Napoli, Lecce, Reggina. There wouldn't be a single club south of Rome in Serie A. They'll never let that happen. You watch.'

The interval drags by. What can one do during an interval but savour one's anxiety? At last the teams reappear. Ten against ten. But the referee has to wait for a man on the touch-line with a radio to tell him that all the other games are ready to kick off. Reggio Calabria, Lecce, Florence, Rome, Udine. We must stay synchronised. The ref waits. One of the games must be late resuming. The man on the touch-line has the radio at his ear. It's hilarious to watch the ostentatious mechanics of fairness when nobody believes for a moment that all these games are being fairly contested. The crowd wait. The referee is impassive. The players are wilting in the sunshine. Serie B or A in forty-five minutes. Hell never ends, I tell myself, but the football season finally does. This is it. Why won't the referee blow? Blow, damn you! The players are sitting down. It isn't football weather. The crowd are baying. Finally, he blows.

Barely three minutes have passed before Napoli score away at Fiorentina. They're just a point behind us. '*Ecco!*' the pessimist says. One of the advantages of being a pessimist is that you find a kind of warped consolation when things go as badly as you predicted. Almost simultaneously, Lecce equalise against Lazio. '*Ecco!*' 'That's because Roma are beating Parma,' comments Pietro. 'Lazio have given up.' So Lecce are now only two points behind us. The whole thing's so confusing, I'm as disorientated as Verona's miserable defence when, only a couple of minutes later, Perugia send in a cross from the left and, all alone on the far post, a red-shirted striker is there to stretch a leg and score. One–all. Serie B.

Mazzantini, now standing directly beneath the Curva Sud, goes wild with delight. His blunder is no longer determining. Now he can concentrate on making sure nobody believes the game was fixed. And he does. For the next half an hour the whole game is going to be atrociously focused on this one man and his extraordinary antics, which are not unrelated to the now-intense antagonism developing between himself and the crowd behind. These are things that TV will never capture.

For Verona are now back in the only situation they really know how to play in: trying to climb out of a deep deep hole. As at Parma, the appropriate substitutions are made, the attacks begin, uninspired but effective: down the wing, cross, header, Mazzantini saves. Down the wing, cross, header, Mazzantini saves. As entertainment it's nothing but pure nerves. Anxiety, anxiety, anxiety. The *curva* are chanting every chant they know. It's a way of keeping the pain in the back of the mind. You sing so as not to think. '*Tu sei il Verona, il mio Verona*,' – this to the tune of 'You are my sunshine', – '*mi fai feli-ce! Se segni un gol!*' You make me happy when you score.

Mazzantini starts to waste time. It's the goalkeeper's prerogative. When the ball goes out he insists on walking to get it, ignoring the ball that the ball-boy tosses to him. The *curva* go wild. They begin to bait him. They're giving him the monkey grunts. He makes an irritated gesture with his arm as if brushing aside a fly. '*Mazzantini faccia da cul.*' He wastes even more time. He sets up the ball for a kick, retreats, decides it isn't in quite the right place, sets it up again. The referee waves for him to speed up, but doesn't show a yellow card. Mazzantini is enjoying it. He's enjoying wasting this precious Serie A time. He made a stupid mistake in the first half, a mistake he knows will be shown again and again on TV, especially if Verona stay up because of it. They won't show all his spectacular saves. It's very important for Mazzantini, personally, that Verona go down. The man's diabolical, a devil demanding our soul from Saint Peter at the gate. The goal is the gate. He won't let us through.

Another cross comes over. It has to be said that Verona are good at getting into a crossing position, even if they apparently know of no other way of approaching the goal. It must be the tenth or twentieth cross. I'm not impressed. Cossato dives for it. How many has he missed? This time he gets there. This time he sends the keeper the wrong way. Mazzantini is already in the air.

You've gone the wrong way! But with an incredible contortion of the hips, this terrible man gets a leg to it. Or is it a tail? Saved. I can't bear it. It's too much. I'm actually watching through a crack between my fingers when Salvetti pops up among four defenders to pick up the loose ball and belt it in. Serie A.

Serie A. In the celebrations that follow even the pessimist seems to have been silenced. To confirm our success Milan at last break the ice at Reggina. The southern team are now three points adrift. Fiorentina equalise against Napoli. Likewise three points behind. Perhaps these games aren't fixed, after all. We've done it.

Not if Mazzantini can help it. There are fifteen minutes left. Now he takes a goal kick in less than two seconds. Now he starts advancing out of his area with the ball. Now he starts running up the field to try to score himself when Perugia win a corner. It's obscene. Why is he so determined to bury us? Meantime, Lecce have scored again against Lazio. They're winning. They've caught us up. A team who haven't won in their last eleven games are beating Lazio. Who cares? We stay up with Lecce. All the others down. Everyone to Piazza Bra after the game. The ritual plunge in the fountain. Endless beers. What an end to my book. Impossible salvation.

Amid the noise someone's shaking my shoulder from behind. It's Massimo. He who shouts 'mongolo'. He has a radio. 'Reggina have equalised,' he says. Who cares? Who cares so long as they don't win? Two minutes later, always precious seconds ahead of the scoreboard, he shakes my shoulder again. 'Reggina have gone ahead.' Reggina are beating Milan. It's impossible! To complete the scandal, just as the final whistle blows at the Bentegodi, the news comes through that Edmundo has scored for Naples at Fiorentina. All five bottom teams have won. The bookies were right. In exemplary Christian fashion, none of the big teams were willing to bury the small ones. This is Italy. Blessed are the weak, when nothing's at stake for the strong. After all, they might return the favour some day. Video will show how improbable those last-minute winners were. Forget the Parma–Verona fix. Watch Milan letting Reggina score two in four minutes. Watch the Fiorentina defence stand still as Edmundo runs round them all.

And the consequences? Despite their wins, Napoli and Vicenza on 36 points are down. But what about Lecce, Reggina and Verona on 37? Which one must leave the limelight and the cash? Is it Judgment Day, or isn't it? A strange silence has settled over the torrid circle of the Bentegodi. The team are not coming to the *curva* to celebrate. It's as if Saint Peter were mumbling in his beard. He won't tell you whether you're in or you're out. Somehow this is even worse than the knowing the worst. Football, I'm thinking amid the general confusion, has never felt more like a punishment.

34A GIORNATA

Brescia – Bari 3–1
Fiorentina – Napoli 1–2
Inter – Bologna 2–1
Juventus – Atalanta 2–1
Lecce – Lazio 2–1
Reggina – Milan 2–1
Roma – Parma 3–1
Udinese Vicenza 2–3
Verona – Perugia 2–1

CLASSIFICA FINALE

Roma	75
Juventus	73
Lazio	69
Parma	56
Inter	51
Milan	49
Atalanta	44
Brescia	44
Fiorentina	43
Bologna	43
Perugia	42
Udinese	38
Lecce	37
Reggina	37
Verona	37
Vicenza	36
Napoli	36
Bari	20

Complications

This week is never-ending . . . Come on, let's play,
I'm fed up of being so tense!!!!!
   Offab (Verona, Italia), boi@chimoll@

I said that the Italians have a flare for making life complicated. What I didn't say is that the more tense a situation is, the more is at stake, so the more complicated it will be. It's a rising scale. On 30 May when Parliament was convened, its opening was immediately postponed. So complicated are the electoral rules between the majority and proportional systems that some seats in the lower house hadn't yet been assigned. It was hard to work out who they belonged to. Needless to say, then, the rules governing that most traumatic of all dramas, relegation, are not simple. Here, more than anywhere else, life must appear to be fair. That is, complicated . . .

Take that moment in the second half when Vicenza were winning against Udinese, Napoli losing against Fiorentina, Lecce had equalised against Lazio, Reggina were still nil–nil with Milan, and Perugia had just crashed their miserable goal into Verona's unhappy net. At that point Vicenza had 36 points while Lecce, Reggina and Verona all had 35 and Napoli 34. Obviously Napoli go down with Bari way below. But why were Verona bound to go down too? Why was there such gloom on the terraces? The rule is that however many teams have the same points, there can only be one play-off. God knows why. In England they seem happy to play off between three or even four teams. In Italy no.

So the first thing you do is to calculate how many points each of the tied teams has scored in the matches they played between each other, that is, in this case and to be perfectly clear, in six matches: Lecce–Reggina, Lecce–Verona, Reggina–Verona, home and away. Since Verona have scored the least in this little league table (only two points), they automatically go down, leaving Lecce and Reggina to play together to decide the last place, this regardless of the fact that Lecce have scored more points than Reggina.

Isn't this odd?

But of course the afternoon didn't finish with that scenario. On the contrary, all the teams won. Which means we have Lecce, Reggina and Verona all on 37 points, Vicenza on 36 and Napoli on 36. This is a quite different scenario. Vicenza and Napoli go down with Bari (our thanks to Bari here for offering at least one fixed point in all this discussion). Now, instead of two of the three tied teams having to go down, only one must take the plunge. Which? You look again at the points scored in games between the teams in question. Now you select the team that scored the most points, Lecce, and they are automatically safe while the other two have to play off, even though, in that little count, Reggina have three more points than Verona. So the silence and shock that settled over the Bentegodi towards five p.m. on the hot afternoon of 17 June was first the silence of thousands of minds rapidly making all kinds of complicated calculations, then the paralysing shock of realising that, far from being over, this exhausting season is going to run on for two more games in blistering June heat, one here in Verona and one a thousand kilometres away among the infernal Calabrians in Reggio.

Italy, then, is a place where things tend to drag on because everything is complicated and fair. A court case goes through first level, appeal and counter-appeal, after which it frequently gets sent back to the beginning again. The deadline for paying your taxes is frequently extended. In the hope that more people will pay. Yet, paradoxically, Italy is also a place where everybody does the same thing at the same time. They eat at the same time, visit their grandmothers, dead or alive, at the same time and above all they go on holiday at the same time, or at least in well-defined waves. The first of which leaves immediately after the schools have closed. So on June the 18th I'm driving the family down to the sea in Pescara – the beach, the sunshades, the cold drinks and pizzette – knowing that on the Thursday the 21st I'm going to have to be watching Verona play Reggina (there is absolutely no question of my dropping out now. The more painful the whole thing is, the more hooked I've become).

But where will that game be?

In order to be fair, and to increase TV revenues, the play-off involves two games, home and away. Yet everybody knows that the team that has the second game at home has a distinct advantage. Especially if the whole thing goes to extra time. When the most basic circumstances of life – in this case the impossibility of playing in two places simultaneously – mean that a certain unfairness is inevitable, then the only fair thing is to draw lots. On Monday morning, in the presence of Pastorello and Lillo Foti, president of Reggina, the sequence will be decided.

From the car, I phone Francesco Grigolino, the photographer whose pictures of our agonising last-minute come-backs most regularly fill the sports pages of the *Arena*.

'Is it decided yet?'

'No, but you can be sure the first leg will be in Verona.'

'Why?'

Francesco sighs. How could an Englishman ever understand? 'Because they don't want us to win, do they? They need another southern team in A. We've already got Chievo. Hellas is racist. The first game will be in Verona. And there's supposed to be a big rock concert in the Bentegodi on Friday. Vasco Rossi. They're already putting up the stage, which means we'll have to play on a neutral ground. No home advantage.'

I put the phone down, fascinated and disconcerted. How pessimism and paranoia go hand in hand. 'Bet the first leg'll be in Reggio,' I tell my wife. An hour later the phone trills: 'First leg in Verona. Or more likely Florence if the stadium's not available.'

I spend three days pretending to relax on the beach, throwing my children about in the sea, swimming beyond the breakwaters with my wife. At the same time I'm frenetically buying all the papers and sneaking back to my mother-in-law's house to plug my laptop into the net and find what The Wall is saying: 'I implore you, President Pastorello, on my knees I beg you, I beg you, not to let them move this match to Florence. Without the *curva*, we're lost.'

A fierce battle is raging between the club, the organisers of the rock concert and the town council which owns the Bentegodi. Vasco Rossi is Italy's biggest popstar. The stadium has been sold out. A huge lights show was planned requiring at least forty-eight hours' preparation.

'Forza Vasco,' writes a Chievo fan. 'Hellas and all their Fascist bastards in B.'

'I swear to God', replies a certain Offab, 'that if we have to play in Florence, on Friday I'll come to the concert with a crowbar.'

Yet this is nothing compared with the war likely to wage round the game itself. Reading Monday's and Tuesday's papers, any notion that football is a sport falls away. The nearer you get to relegation, the closer you are to Leopardi's vision of the ballgame as war. The night before Lecce's game with Lazio, it now emerges, local fans kept the Lazio players awake all night, smashing windows in their hotel, breaking through a half-hearted police cordon into the lobby. When Milan went one up in Reggio, their acting chairman, Adriano Galliani, was threatened, some say with a knife, others insist with a gun. In any event he left the ground in a hurry and did not see the local team equalise and win. The touch-lines were thronged with threatening young men. Worse still, just across the water from Reggio, a Messina fan was hit by a so-called paper bomb, thrown by a Catania fan. He is presently in coma. Football is about to have its first fatality in years.

'If it had been anyone but Reggina,' Puliero tells me on the phone, 'I'd be optimistic. Any other team but Reggina.'

In the lazy hours after lunch, I turn on public radio and hear an official announcer say: 'After all, we mustn't cancel the south from Serie A.' Then Lillo Foti is saying the same thing: 'Our team must stay up so that the south can be represented.'

'Well then, let's just have one team from every bloody region,' rages Michele.

Consummate politician that he is, Pastorello reaches a compromise with Vasco Rossi and his band. The stage can be set up in front of the Curva Nord, the visitors' area. The few fans from Reggio will be put somewhere else. So on Thursday I leave the sparkling Adriatic behind me and board the train for the five hundred kilometres back to Verona. In the paper an article tells me that Serie A as a whole is about 500 million pounds in debt, 'as a result of an over-heated spirit of competition,' comments *Corriere della Sera*'s leader writer.

The game is at eight p.m. The train arrives at six. I wait out the break in the Bar Bentegodi where a particularly ugly thug whom I have never seen before is drinking heavily. 'Where are they hiding those five thousand filthy *terroni*?' he demands. His pretty girlfriend hangs uncertainly on his arm. 'Wait till I get my hands on them.'

Standing right beside him, I remark, 'Bet there won't be more than a thousand.'

At once he picks up my accent, but is too drunk to place it. '*De che rassa sito?*' he demands in dialect. What race are you? It's the urgent question that underlies the game, the season, everything. '*De che rassa sito?*' he repeats, belligerent.

'Do I look Calabrian?' I ask.

His girlfriend pulls him away. Already, shamefully, I'm hoping Reggina will not be fielding any blacks. Despite the ban on bottled drinks, I pick up two bottles of beer from the fridge.

As the game kicks off, the evening is scorching, the sun still fierce and blindingly low. The *sud* is milling with flags, booming with noise. The ritual insults are exchanged with the Reggina fans, who apparently pulled the emergency cord on their train and tried to load their pockets with stones from between the sleepers. Someone has a banner, 'DIO NON SALVI LA REGGINA.' God, don't save the Queen.

The game? I lived through it in such a state of nervousness it would be folly to imagine I could offer reasonable comment. So here, instead, is part of a long letter from my faithful correspondent

Matteo, he who is combining relegation battle with girlfriend break-up. Watching from the heart of the *curva*, Matteo picks up the game deep into the second half. It's still nil–nil. Once again, the encounter is characterised by the brilliance and antics of the opposition's keeper, this time the charismatic if inconsistent Massimo Taibi.

When Seric is stretchered off I sense it's the beginning of the end. I look for comfort from the friends around me. But Piero just keeps shaking his head and saying, 'Third substitution. Now we can't bring on Cossato,' while Ernie is smoking one cigarette after another in silence. Reggina have done exactly what they came to do. After a thousand narrow escapes in the first half, they've finally put the game to sleep. Taibi turns from his goal towards the *curva* and looks at us mockingly. Everybody's shouting, '*Figlio di puttana!*' He deserves it. Standing there enormous, it seems he wants to take up the whole goal with those awful hands that pushed away such great shots from Mutu and Oddo. Teodorani takes Seric's place. With his long neck and clumsy way of running he looks more like an insurance agent than a player. And now Reggina are even attacking. The floodlights come up to full power. It's night. They make the field look longer, endless, especially if you just have to score at all costs. Now we've got a corner. Mutu to take it. The cross is sharp and hard. I see Laursen's blond head climb up and up and up, right to the third floor. And still up. The impact is superb. He crashes the ball down. Taibi doesn't even have the time to wonder where it's going . . . Goal!!!

The minutes blink by on the big display board. Huddled in the East Stand the Reggina fans have gone silent. Their drum is silent. Bang it now! Bang your fucking drum now, you bastards! Ferron snatches a possible equaliser from Dionigi's feet. I smoke two, three, four cigarettes in a row. I can hardly breathe. The players are exhausted with the heat and the tension. Ferron saves again. The referee gives four minutes' injury time. Four fucking minutes. But Reggina are finished. The game's over.

Afterwards, Ernie says, 'One–nil. That's OK, it'll have to do.' I'm thinking, it's OK about Federica too. It's the right thing, splitting up. Only with her there won't be a return match, no more suffering, anxiety, pain. Piero is trying to work out how much it would cost to fly down to Reggio. At least three hundred thou. I haven't got the cash. I have to be at work Monday. We go and drink at the Bar Bentegodi till the others have to go off to their women and I feel completely superfluous. It takes three beers to put me vaguely back in tune with the world, with the songs in the bar. '*Campion, Campion, campion è uno solo.*' Then suddenly the place begins to fill with tear-gas, the police are on the rampage and I run off down Via Palladio back home where Dad's already drunk and sticks a Heineken in my fist and a couple of cigarettes and it's off to bed at three thinking tomorrow in the office will be awful.

Matteo, having opted out of military service, works for the local archives of the Ministry for Cultural Heritage.

Reggio

*If by ill chance there were to be any refereeing 'errors'
in this game . . . if, that is, we were to plunge into
Serie B . . . well then fuck it we've got to cause
havoc . . . but real havoc this time. We've got to let
people know we exist. Don't let the team or the referee
leave the stadium in one piece. Block the station and
the airport. They'll be talking about us for months!*
  Fucking Furious Reggina Fan,
  There'll-be-trouble@we'll.smash.everything

Matteo's improbably named friend, Ernie, was wrong about the
prices of charter flights down to Reggio. It cost me half a million
lire to get on the one plane that was making the journey: the team's.
Of course, I'd sworn I wouldn't travel with the players again. Can
you imagine how depressing the return flight will be if we lose:
Serie **B**eaten, **B**ereaved, **B**ankrupt. But it's the nature of life that
when you swear you won't do something again, very soon you find
yourself doing it. In any event, it was easier this time. The team
were accompanied by twenty or so journalists, including the local
TV who were to produce an hour-long documentary on the trip.
So there are more people to talk to and it's easier to keep a low
profile. All around me the chatter is intense. The team's startling
resurrection over these last four matches is allowing us to think of
the season as epic, rather than merely depressing.

  You yourself thought it was all over a month ago, I reflect,
as I take my seat on the plane. Opposite me are two big beefy

boys with shaven heads and smart grey suits. Like a journalist writing an obituary before the electrocardiogram is quite flat, you had even started a dismal last chapter. And instead, here we are in late June with a perfectly poised play-off: after thirteen defeats in seventeen away games, Hellas go to Reggio Calabria to administer the one-goal lead for ninety minutes. 'Impossible,' Adailton smiled wanly in the airport lounge. 'We've never gone ninety minutes away from home without conceding a goal.' Then it's north versus south, it's what happens on the field versus what would be convenient for football politics nationwide; above all it's sport wound to a tension far beyond that which galvanises any cup final. Here we're fighting for the right to exist. It's fang-and-claw Darwinism. At the end there will be weeping and gnashing of teeth on one side, wild rejoicing on the other.

Rino Foschi walks up and down the aisle, all nerves, manner tense and blustering as ever. His arms swing unnecessarily, grabbing the backs of the seats, as if the plane were a boat in high seas. He stops briefly over me. 'So, a prick and an arsehole check into a big suite in a luxury hotel, only they haven't found the light switch yet. What does the arsehole say to the prick?' He laughs. 'Stick this in your book, come on. What does the arsehole say to the prick?'

'No idea, Rino.'

'Come on, Englishman. Stick this in your book.' He leans to somebody in the seat behind. 'What does the arsehole say to the prick? Prick and arsehole in a huge room. Haven't found the light switch.'

Nobody can guess.

'How big is this place?' Rino says.

'Fair enough. And so?'

Foschi leans right over me. I love the man. I love the way he makes his distraction strategies so obvious. '"How big is this place?" the arsehole asks? And the prick says, "Oh, big enough for at least four people." And so what does the arsehole say?'

'No idea. Tell me.'

'Only if you'll put it in your book.'

'Rino, I promise I'll put your joke in my book.'

'The arsehole says, "Then why in God's name are you pushing so hard."'

Foschi stumbles away roaring with laughter. The two shaven-headed boys opposite are smiling discreetly. Both of them wear threatening shades. Who are these people?

Halfway through the flight, Pastorello also makes a trip up and down the aisle, but in a more dignified fashion. He's playing *padrone*, cordially shaking hands with all his entourage. 'You make me travel too much,' I tell him.

Last of all, Agnolin does the tour, inspects the troops. His face is that of the seriously worried man, the politician flying into a war zone perhaps. 'Who would have expected there'd be this coda to the season.' I offer him some small-talk. 'Let's hope it's not in vain,' he says grimly. Evidently he fears it will be. I'm reminded of an article in *Rigore* by the gaoled terrorist Adriano Soffri. 'In prison, the football game at recreation is our one moment of emotional release. How it makes me laugh when I read in the paper about the big-name players suffering, the fans suffering. They should come to prison to find out what suffering is.' Yet the pain on Agnolin's face is real enough. He's imprisoned in a tortuous psychological space. Serie A, or Serie B.

I try to chat to the men in the seat in front. 'What's your name?' I ask one. He smiles strangely. 'Oh, you know me, you've seen me plenty of times on the Zanzibar bus.' I look at him. I feel I have seen him before. But he's not one of the fans who stand in the *curva*. Why didn't he tell me his name? And who are those two beefy boys who talk to nobody but each other, who are so discreet and elegant? 'Who are these guys?' I demand of the man behind me. It's Francesco, the photographer. He leans forward:

'Seems Galliani, after he was threatened, you know, at the game last Sunday, phoned Pastorello and told him not to go down to Reggio without at least two bodyguards.'

'But if he was really threatened with a gun, why didn't he make some public statement about it?'

The fat journalist next to Francesco sniggers. He's a TV man. 'Galliani is Milan, isn't he? Milan is Berlusconi. New Prime Minister doesn't want trouble with one of the cities where he hopes to build up support. Another reason for Milan losing . . .'

Can this be true? The fat journalist assures me that on the Monday morning he did everything to find out what really happened down there to Galliani. No one would say.

The plane lands towards nine p.m. and a half hour later we're in Reggio. It's Saturday evening. How fitting that the story should end here, in this one town in Serie A that we haven't visited so far, playing the one team who seem most responsible for our risking relegation: that victory thrown away in the last seconds in neutral Catania; the three–nil humiliation at the Bentegodi, worst home result of the season. Pulling into their hotel, the players are met by a band of jeering locals.

I escape to a sea-front restaurant with a few of the journalists and a man they all refer to, behind his back, as the Unnameable, because convinced he brings bad luck. Whenever there's a group in Italy there is always one person who's supposed to bring bad luck. On the way we're joined by a commentator for public TV. Small, dry and dapper, this man has no other conversation than to remind us from time to time that he is a commentator for public TV, a cut above us provincials that is. Dullest of conversationalists, he eats far more than his slim, dried-up figure would appear to need. The waiter, facetiously elegant in his white jacket, puts on the usual show of southern hospitality. A cool breeze is blowing in off the Strait of Messina. The lights are pricking out in Sicily on the further shore.

'There is a wide variety of hors d'oeuvres,' announces the waiter. 'Let me bring you a selection.' His step has a flounce that makes the jacket even more theatrical. 'There is a wide variety of main dishes,' he says. 'Let me bring you a selection.' His moustaches smile fondly as the bill piles up. The other guys are obviously on expenses. But even the fat journalist can't keep up with the man from public TV who astounds the waiter by actually asking for seconds of one of the hors d'oeuvres. I'm already way over capacity, gasping.

Meantime, the conversation is a fierce battle as to whether

Pastorello is a genius or an idiot. The Unnameable thinks he's a genius. Another journalist thinks he's an idiot. There's no middle ground. But we all hate Chievo. By the time it comes to the ice-cream that follows the main course *and* the main dessert, I just have to say no. The dinner seems to be dragging out as unnecessarily as the football season. It's as if I were being forced to fight against cramps through the last minutes of extra time. Then someone points across the restaurant – 'Look guys!' – and there, dragging out the evening with us, is tomorrow's referee, Stefano Braschi. It's one-thirty in the morning.

'What's his record with Verona?' I ask. 'No, I can't eat this ice-cream,' I tell the waiter.

'Never kind to us,' the fat journalist says, 'or to Reggina for that matter. But known not to be a pushover for home crowds.'

'That's a relief. No, I'm sorry, I can't.'

The waiter is still hovering. 'Oh, you must try it. It's a local speciality.' The man never stops smiling.

'To refuse a dish brings bad luck,' the Unnameable says with a self-regarding smile.

The fat journalist nods solemnly. 'It is bad luck not to accept food. Especially down south.'

'Fuck fucking bad luck,' I shout. And to the waiter: 'If you bring it, I won't eat it. Not even if it means Verona losing ten–nil.'

The others are taken aback. The tension must be getting to me. The waiter brings the ice-cream all the same. Briefly reminding us he's from public TV, the small, dapper fellow generously eats it for me. By the door as we're leaving, I find Braschi right beside me. He's an imperious figure, head held high, Roman nose, strong chest, the perfect, cinematic referee. An elderly man gets up from a table and comes over to speak to us. There's a whine in his voice. He knows Braschi is within earshot. 'You've got to let us win tomorrow. Here in Reggio, our football team is all we've got. You have so much up north. You have work and opportunity. You have Chievo. We have nothing. Let us at least keep our team in Serie A.' Brusquely, I reply, 'I'll be sure to tell the players they have to lose for your sake.'

Towards three in the morning there's a dull explosion. Then the racket begins, chants, klaxons. It goes on for an hour and a half. The following morning a man from the *Gazzetta dello Sport* tells me he went down into the street and saw the police in obvious connivance grinning and even chatting with local fans determined to give Hellas a bad night. 'The noise stopped', he claimed, 'when the man from the Verona Digos went down.' The Digos is Italy's most expert plain-clothes police branch. It seems the club has actually brought along not only a couple of bodyguards, but its own policemen. I remember that strange moment in the plane when the vaguely familiar face said: 'You've seen me many times on the Zanzibar bus.' The fans always say there are plain-clothes policemen among them. Nothing could be more emblematic of the divisions in Italy than a northern team's need to bring its own policemen to a southern game. On the other hand, the fact that the lower-rank southern policemen responded to a senior officer from the north suggests there is a oneness at some level.

'Why didn't you take a hotel maybe fifty kilometres out of town?' I ask Foschi in the foyer after breakfast. He explodes. 'It would have been exactly the same. Exactly. You don't understand anything. What's a little lost sleep to a twenty-two-year-old? Nothing. Nothing. It'll only wire them up. They need to be wired.'

Clearly the guy who's most wired of all is Foschi.

Pastorello and Massimiliano, the press boy, have gone out to mass. Pointless to ask them what their prayers might be. I take a walk along the waterfront. Only a stone's throw from the hotel, this must be one of the most beautiful waterfronts in the world, yet the players can't come out to enjoy it, in case some idiot should throw a stone. They won't see the giant palms, the generous medlar trees, the waves and sails and the sparkle across the water along the Sicilian shore. They will be imprisoned in the hotel all day till the evening's six-o'clock kick-off.

Turning in from the sea, though, it's a different story. The town climbs steeply into the makeshift and ugly, buildings piled haphazard on the barren rock. It's Sunday. Everything's closed.

The whole town is waiting for the game. The last game at last.

'*Bastardi! Merda!*' Getting back to the hotel, it's to find that five or six players have poked their noses outside the porch. Two police cars are parked in the road and on the opposite pavement a crowd are shouting insults. '*Figli di puttana!* Go home!' The players watch calmly, savouring the atmosphere. A couple of them have even brought out seats so they can take it easy while they're insulted. 'This is Italy,' announces the handsome, phlegmatic Mazzola.

Then I'm told that the building immediately behind the protestors is the city's Museo Nazionale. I cross the road, skirt the demonstrators, pay my entrance fee. The museum houses the beautiful warrior bronzes of Riace, larger-than-life Greek sculptures salvaged from the sea thirty years ago. On the upper floors, rather less distinguished, is an anonymous eighteenth-century painting showing Cain slaying Abel, and a couple of those tedious scenes of cannon-fire over Napoleonic charges that you find in all museums. '*Bastardi. Merda!!*' The voices rise from the street below. Cain brings down his club on Abel. The muskets rattle. The Greek warriors strike defiant poses. Looking out of the window, I see Perotti has appeared. Arms folded, gaze vacant, there is nothing Napoleonic about him.

'*Bastardi, merda,*' the crowd are shouting as I climb the stairs of the stadium. An hour before kick-off, the stands are already full, except, that is, for the small section reserved for 'guests'. The Verona boys are just arriving. Less than a hundred I'd say, a poor showing, but then the journey is sixteen hours by train. The crowd greet them with monkey grunts, then a thunderous chant that's new to me: '*Uccidere, uccidere!!*' Kill. Kill.

It's a quaint little stadium, housing perhaps twenty-five or thirty thousand. From the stairs, you can look out to the idyllic sea. 'Kill, Kill!' Since Reggina play in claret, there's a disturbingly dark red look to the sea of bodies. 'Kill, kill!' The Brigate Gialloblù make their inevitable gestures in response. I can just make out Fondo and a couple of the others. They hang up their old banners. Then Pastorello appears with Foschi, Agnolin and the bodyguards. Immediately, the crowd responds with a shriek. '*Fuori!*' they begin.

Out! *'Fuori, fuori!'* Then, *'Ladro!'* Thief. Even the people in the
VIP section are screaming and making gestures. Corrado Ferlaino,
Vice-president of Napoli, has come along with his wife to support
Reggina. They too are shouting, *'Fuori. Fuori. Ladro!'* Betraying
no emotion, Pastorello takes his seat. My respect for him rises
enormously. The bodyguards are stationed one at each end of his
row of seats.

This time I'm not with the club representatives. And I can't
join the *brigate*, because then I might never make it to the plane
afterwards. So together with a boy called Stefano, who looks after
the Hellas website, I've been given a place among the Reggina
fans. Our seats aren't together. Stefano is frightened. The closer it
gets to kick-off, the clearer it becomes that things are going to get
hot if people realise we're not one of them. 'You're a scout from
England,' Stefano says. 'We don't speak a word of Italian.' But
I know it won't wash. I know that it will be impossible for the
person next to me not to sense that I want Verona to win. These
are feelings you can't hide. Eventually, we fight our way to the
press section and persuade someone to let us climb the railing. At
exactly six o'clock Braschi blows his whistle. In a couple of hours,
or a little longer if we go to extra time, if we go to penalties, this
game, this season, will be over. I will finally be free to think of
something else.

Actually, it's not nail-biting at all. Sitting in the front row
of the press section, head pushed between two railings, I watch
Verona perform admirably. Apart from the inexplicable selection,
again, of Mazzola, Perotti seems to have got it right. He's packed
five in midfield, with four at the back and just one up front. It's
Gilardino, now recovered from his accident in the canal. The result
is that Verona are making all the running. Overwhelmed by nerves,
Reggina keep giving away the ball. What a mystery this Verona
team is, I'm thinking. How strange that these talented boys, who
now seem to have nerves of steel, should have to be here at a
miserable play-off, and this in a year when the quality of football
in Serie A has been at its worst for a decade.

'The first place you're relegated is inside your head,' the

experienced Ferron had said to one of the journalists before the game, 'then only after that on the field. And in their heads these boys have never gone down.' After about forty really rather pleasant minutes, I'm beginning to believe Ferron was right. This team are not going to go down. Until, in one of those terrible lapses that have characterised the season, Reggina are given a little space and striker Zanchetta is allowed to shoot. From outside the box he finds exactly the dream diagonal that will beat the wise Ferron and bounce in off the post. One in a million, I'm shaking my head. One in a million! The crowd have hardly stopped baying when Reggina score again. This time there's an unforgivable defensive mix-up, a lucky rebound. The stadium explodes. Two–nil. Reggina in A. All round Pastorello people are giving the man the so-called 'ombrello'. Ferlaino's wife included. Stick that up your arse! She stands up and clenches her fist. 'God plays in claret,' someone's shrieking.

At half-time I try to console myself with the thought that at least this way there will be no crowd trouble at the end. People will be nice to us and tell us not to be too upset. In their compound, the *brigate* are trying to chant, but it sounds feeble. Puliero comes to speak to me. Even in the radio box, he's having to keep his voice down. He was hit on the head by a plastic water bottle. 'Pessimistic.' He shakes his head. 'It's tough now.'

The second half is one of emotional paralysis. We've come all this way, through time, through space, for nothing. Prepare for defeat. Prepare to be quiet and respect people's unhappiness on the plane home. Yet . . . there is the away-goals rule. Never have I felt more grateful for the away-goals rule. If we were to score now, I remember, unlikely as that may seem, at two–all on aggregate the away goal will count double. We can still do it.

After the game I heard from so many people what they were doing during these impossible minutes. Matteo is at his friend Ernie's house, watching on pay TV, smoking endless cigarettes. Driving back from a brief holiday with wife and kid, Pietro keeps turning the radio on and off, on and off. It's bad luck to listen to a whole game on the radio. The Più-mati are gathered round Beppe's television. The gloom is deep. Cris-do-I-bother-anyone can't bear it: on holiday, he's left the hotel TV lounge and has gone to the beach to stare at the sea. My son Michele, meanwhile, is at his grandmother's in Pescara lying on his bed, not afraid to hear every last sad detail on the radio. He doesn't believe in bad luck. But he has lost hope. Absent fans in London, in New York even, are sending me SMS messages. 'You must tell us at once if we score.' The president of Chievo – I have it on good authority – is rubbing his hands with glee, thinking of all the extra ticket sales he will get when the middle-class fans at last abandon Hellas to join the boys from the dam.

'Serie B, Serie B!' The crowd are merciless. Perotti has taken off Mazzola, brought on Cossato. Now out goes the turkey-necked Teodorani, for Melis. It's all attack, defence forgotten. As the tension rises, Braschi is being as fair as he can. He's not whistling everything, but enough to keep things under control. And the extraordinary thing about football, I tell myself in a little surge of optimism, is that while it may be surrounded by the trappings of mortal combat, and while all kinds of money and politics are inevitably involved, still, on the field there are rules, and talent counts, and likewise the lucky bounce, the unexpected rebound. Go for it, Hellas. I'm shouting the words in my head. I mustn't say anything aloud. Go for it till the final whistle.

But the best chances are falling to Reggina now. Three times they miss the clearest of opportunities on the break. Still, the heat is overwhelming and slowly they fall back. They sense they've done enough. Pack the box. Waste time. As in Naples, the ball-boys disappear. It takes for ever to restart after every interruption. As soon as a Verona player retrieves the ball, a ball-boy miraculously reappears and throws another ball on to the pitch. Now that has to be removed. And every time Verona move up the wings, plastic bottles rain down on the players from the stands. A linesman is struck and falls. He needs medication. More time is lost. There are places where it's difficult to dribble the ball for all the bottles on the pitch. Cossato gallops and elbows about, but he's too slow. He misses a header. As the noise-level rises beyond anything I've experienced before, scores of young men begin to appear on the touch-lines. Who are they? Why are they there? They don't seem to be fans.

The men have now formed a solid wall right along the near touch-line. Braschi walks over to complain to a Reggina official. The men stay put, numerous, threatening. Taibi takes ages to set up a goal kick. Ten minutes to go. I sit perfectly still. The men each side of me are clearly not journalists, but Reggina fans. They've realised what side I'm on, for I keep muttering 'Obscene!' I can't help it. The bottles rain. A second and even third ball is tossed on to the pitch. 'Scandalous!' Five minutes. Four. Then, as Reggina's defenders clear their lines and move up for the offside trap, something happens. Giuseppe Colucci gathers the loose ball, lifts his head, sees the mistake. Scooping with his foot, he sends the most perfect lob over the advancing Reggina players to Cossato. Just onside, he already has Taibi charging out to him. With unexpected aplomb, Super-Mike doesn't even let the ball bounce. He taps it up in the air over the keeper's approaching hands, rushes round him and fights off two defenders to head home for perhaps the classiest strike of his career. 2–1. Verona winning on away goals.

Absolute silence. After the constant roar of the last forty minutes, there's something surreal about it. Cossato doesn't exult. He can't believe it. He turns to the referee to check that the goal has been allowed. It has. He's bewildered. Then, tiny, insignificant, tinkling, come the distant shouts of the *brigate*. There's Fondo, shrieking, pumping his arms up and down in a gesture of derision. On the field, a mischievous Gilardino lifts his finger to his lips to shush the Reggina *curva*. They howl in pain. There's a huge surge of rage. There are people lurching forwards against the fences. Pastorello jumps to his feet and heads for the dressing rooms with staff and bodyguards. The noise swells. A noise of agony. Of death throes. Discreetly, I also abandon my seat to watch the last minutes among people who haven't had a chance to see I'm not one of them.

The game restarts. It's one heart-attack after another. Fights, fouls, punches. Gilardino goes down. Someone stamps on him. Stamps again. Yellow cards, red. As always when in front, Verona lose their heads. Reggina create more chances in two or three minutes than in the previous ninety. Ferron produces two top-class saves, one from the closest possible range. I swear to God here and now that on the day Fabrizio Ferron is one of the finest goalkeepers of all time. I swear to God I shall never say an unkind word about him again. For five terrible minutes it seemed there was only Fabrizio Ferron between Verona and Serie B. Until at last Braschi blows the end. As the Verona players dash for the tunnel, those ambiguous figures on the touch-line converge.

Sport merges into war now. There's no clear boundary, though only later can one piece together what actually happened. Anonymous as possible, I make my way back to our two coaches. Ominously, the police haven't formed a cordon round them. A boy is standing on a car, a scarf wrapped round his head pirate fashion, brandishing a sabre. Bodies are rushing back and forth. Then I find the photographer, Francesco, crouched in the gutter, sobbing, shaking. He speaks of being hit by bottles, his camera banged against the wall. 'This isn't football,' he's weeping. I find the coach driver and get him to open the bus.

'They were going to kill me. They were going to kill me. Just because I photographed the goal.'

'It's nothing,' the obese driver reassures him in his southern drawl.

'They destroyed my camera, they would have killed me.'

'You should worry,' the driver goes on. 'My wife is a depressive. What's a couple of punches beside a depressive wife? What's Serie A or Serie B when your wife spends all day in her room crying?'

Francesco is trembling uncontrollably. The coaches are undefended. I slip back into the crowd. 'Pastorello has been punched,' someone says. They didn't let him take his bodyguards into the dressing rooms. They got him in the corridor. He went down. He passed out. For two hours the team refuse to leave the changing rooms. They've all been kicked and punched. Not by the fans but by those men crowding the touch-line, stadium officials apparently. Crowds of Reggina fans are milling round the players' exit, but still no police cordon has formed. The players are refusing to give the ritual after-game interviews. The Unnameable wanders around nervously. 'Pastorello is a genius,' he says. 'He saved the team.' In the street Reggina fans are in tears. Then they rush forward to try and get at Braschi as he's driven away in a black Mercedes. '*Assassino!*'

At last Foschi emerges, waving his arms, yelling, beside himself. 'I've resigned. That's it. Agnolin can run this club, since he knows so much fucking better than I do how to deal with people. I was laid out, I was down and they were kicking me. Write that in your fucking newspapers if you dare.'

Foschi is distraught. Agnolin is deadly pale. It seems the *professore* is insisting that the club shouldn't try to pursue the matter in the courts. It will do no good. Sport is one thing and courts are another. 'Foti himself – Reggina's owner – was kicking the Verona players as they went into the tunnel,' Salvetti tells me as he climbs on to the players' bus. There are police around us now. 'I saw him clear as day, kicking people down the stairs.' I move off with the journalists. 'They were trying to force the dressing room door with a crowbar,' Saverio Guette confirms. 'We were all pushing against it, blocking them.' The meek warehouse man has a seriously swollen ear. There are bruises and scratches.

For reasons I don't understand, we aren't flying back from Reggio. We have to go to the small airport of Lamezia Terme, eighty kilometres away. As our coach moves off, we're told to pull all the blinds down and crouch in case of stones. None come. But about ten minutes out on the *autostrada* the coach loses power. It slows down. The obese driver shrugs and pulls up in a small parking bay with the night-time traffic racing by.

'Sabotage!' someone whispers. 'We'll be attacked.' The bodyguards rush to the door. They insist on getting off first. No film-caster could ask for better than these two young men. They play the part so well. But it's just an ordinary breakdown. Recovering from his ordeal, Pastorello gets off and now at last everyone's shaking hands and hugging and congratulating each other in the dark with the headlights racing by. 'Thousands and thousands of kilometres with the *brigate* and never a breakdown,' I tell the president. He smiles. 'We did it!' The fat journalist is dancing in the dark among the smells of piss and the used condoms. 'We did it!'

Then in the general excitement an ancient taboo is broken. The players' coach is brought back and we are loaded on. I get to travel on the players' bus. Not a bad moment for it. They're euphoric. Italiano is mocking Gilardino for letting himself be thumped so much in the tunnel. 'When you're attacked,' he explains, 'you either run away, or you hit back. You don't stand still and take it.' He himself floored two of them, he boasts. The coach races through the dark as the events of the evening are turned into myth. For years the collective imagination will go back to this moment. Everybody has his mobile in his hand. They are calling and being called, there's an endless trilling and talking to each other and passing around of phones. It's as if this bus were now the communications centre of the world. 'We're in Piazza Bra,' Stefano phones to tell me. 'People are bathing in the fountains. When should we come to the airport?'

At Lamezia, at midnight, they're trying to close the bar. But I haven't had anything to drink for ten hot hours. 'I'll buy,' Laursen tells me.' 'Not to worry, Martin, I'm going to pick up six beers for a few people.' 'But I just won a hundred million,' he laughs. A hundred million was their bonus for staying in Serie A. 'OK, you buy.'

I take a beer to Perotti. He's wandering about all alone. Nobody wants to talk to him in victory, just as no one wanted to listen to him in defeat. 'Thanks.' He accepts the beer. I feel a little sorry for him, a little guilty for believing he was absolutely the wrong man for the job.

'So, another away defeat, Attilio . . .'

'But . . .'

Then he realises I'm joking. 'We had a *pizzico di fortuna*,' he says. 'It was what we needed.'

'And did you really never give up hope, not even after Napoli?'

He shrugs. In the end he's a nice man, a genuinely modest man, who knows what he knows, which is no doubt a great deal more than I do. 'After Napoli? I kept doing my sums, you know. I thought, well, we might still do it. So we've got to try.'

On the plane I sit beside Puliero who is already beginning to withdraw from the general triumphalism. 'They're exaggerating this talk about the assault,' he comments wryly. 'No one's seriously hurt. They're turning the game into a magnificent victory, when actually it was the narrowest of escapes.' Behind us, beer in hand, Anthony Seric is making a pass at a pretty air hostess. He winks at me. 'Seize the day!'

At Villafranca, Verona's airport, two officials try to whisk us away on a bus. It's three in the morning. But the players are having nothing of it. They cross the tarmac to embrace those who have loved and loathed them all year. The police are trying to hold back a huge crowd. They can't do it. The supporters surge through, Stefano is there and Scopa and Glass-eye and so many other familiar faces. The deputy mayor. Pam. Penn. Paruca. They push past the customs and passports barriers, into the baggage collection lounge. It's a huge ritual mixing. It's the community. '*Hellas, la mia unica fede!*' they're singing. Cossato is raised on their shoulders. He's lost his shirt, he's lost his shorts. Even Pastorello is raised aloft. It seems impossible to me after all those angry banners that the fans should forgive the man so much. And vice versa. But it's happening. '*Pastorello, portaci in Europa,*' they're singing. Take us into Europe. A girl shrills, 'Martino Melis, rape me. I'm healthy!' Finally the players are lined up, bare-chested now, for cameras and TV. They stand arms linked, sixteen or seventeen men, surprised to be friends, amazed to be heroes. Cossato, who fought so hard to find a niche in the team, is now the centre of the group, the saviour of the *patria*. With a fantastic sense of release they all belt out, '*Reggina, Reggina, VAFFANCULO!!!*'

It's four-thirty when I drive home. The immigrants are already forming their queue outside the police station. We're still in Serie A, I tell myself. I know I haven't taken it in yet. I race through the lights, out of town. The season starts again in just two months. So many players to buy and sell. Seems I'm the only car on the road. A new trainer to find. I drive up the hill towards our village.

Just two months to disintoxicate myself. Two months and it all starts over again, this sick sick football business. But what a weekend, it's been! What a year! Bari to Reggio. So sick and so exciting. Squealing to a stop, I fling open the door of my filthy Citroën Visa and step out at last under the cool stars.

On 25 August 2001, the black Colombian player
Johnnier Estainer Montano made his debut for
Hellas Verona at the Bentegodi.
He was warmly welcomed by the Curva Sud.

Also available in Vintage

Tim Parks

MIMI'S GHOST

The brilliant sequel to Cara Massimina

'Tarantino meets Peter Mayle'
Independent on Sunday

Morris can't get over Mimi. But then he should have
thought of that before he murdered her and married her
sister. Now Mimi's back, as a ghost, and she seems to be
suggesting the way to redemption for Morris. He must help
the poor immigrants of Verona; but if anybody should get in
his charitable way then so much the worse for them...

'*Cara Massimina* was a triumph of the darkly-comic-
thriller-and-something-more-besides genre. This is an even
greater one'
Daily Telegraph

'Parks writes with a brutal, snapping wit, reinventing the
crime novel as a capricious campy romp...A piece of con-
clusive reasoning that leaves the reader collapsing into
squeamish giggles'
Sunday Times

VINTAGE

BY TIM PARKS
ALSO AVAILABLE IN VINTAGE